GLOBALISATION AND RESISTANCE

In comparing existing research on Eastern and Central Europe, Central Asia and Latin America, it is clear that legal developments in East and South Asian societies are somewhat under-researched. This volume fills a gap in studies of the effects of globalisation and the role of law in processes of globalisation. What the book contributes to the debate is an 'area study', that is interdisciplinary research pertaining to a particular geographical or cultural region. The region discussed here presents an ideal testing ground for legal pluralism, for economic, cultural, and political influences on the role of law in development. The 'developmental states' of Asia are regarded as refuting both Latin American dependency theory and classical modernisation theory. They seem to follow quite distinct political, economic and legal developments. However, especially after the Asian Crisis, their approaches have come under intense pressure. The book examines the resulting reform efforts and the tensions they generate in areas such as constitutional and administrative law, commercial law and human rights.

Oñati International Series in Law and Society

A SERIES PUBLISHED FOR THE OÑATI INSTITUTE
FOR THE SOCIOLOGY OF LAW

Titles in this Series

Social Dynamics of Crime and Control: New Theories for a World in Transition edited by Susannah Karstedt and Kai Bussmann

Criminal Policy in Transition edited by Andrew Rutherford and Penny Green

Making Law for Families edited by Mavis Maclean

Poverty and the Law edited by Peter Robson and Asbjørn Kjønstad

Adapting Legal Cultures edited by Johannes Feest and David Nelken

Rethinking Law Society and Governance: Foucault's Bequest edited by Gary Wickham and George Pavlich

Rules and Networks edited by Richard Appelbaum, Bill Felstiner and Volkmar Gessner

Women in the World's Legal Professions edited by Ulrike Schultz and Gisela Shaw

Healing the Wounds edited by Marie-Claire Foblets and Trutz von Trotha

Imaginary Boundaries of Justice edited by Ronnie Lippens

Family Law and Family Values edited by Mavis Maclean

Contemporary Issues in the Semiotics of Law edited by Anne Wagner, Tracey Summerfield, and Farid Benavides Vanegas

The Geography of Law: Landscapes, Identity and Regulation edited by Bill Taylor

Precarious Work, Women and the New Economy: The Challenge to Legal Norms edited by Judy Fudge and Rosemary Owens

Theory and Method in Socio-Legal Research edited by Reza Banakar and Max Travers

Luhmann on Law and Politics edited by Michael King and Chris Thornhill

Juvenile Law Violators, Human Rights and the Development of New Juvenile Justice Systems edited by Eric L Jensen and Jørgen Jepsen

The Language Question in Europe and Diverse Societies: Political, Legal and Social Perspectives edited by Dario Castiglione and Chris Longman

Globalisation and Resistance

Law Reform in Asia since the Crisis

Edited by

Christoph Antons

and

Volkmar Gessner

Oñati International Series in Law and Society

A SERIES PUBLISHED FOR THE OÑATI INSTITUTE
FOR THE SOCIOLOGY OF LAW

•HART•
PUBLISHING

OXFORD AND PORTLAND, OREGON
2007

Published in North America (US and Canada)

by Hart Publishing
c/o International Specialized Book Services
920 NE 58th Avenue, Suite 300
Portland, OR 97213-3786
USA
Tel: +1 503 287 3093 or toll-free: (1) 800 944 6190
Fax: +1 503 280 8832
Email: orders@isbs.com
Website: www.isbs.com

Hart Publishing, 16c Worcester Place, Oxford, OX1 2JW
Telephone: +44 (0)1865 517530 Fax: +44 (0) 1865 510710
Email: mail@hartpub.co.uk
Website: http://www.hartpub.co.uk

British Library Cataloguing in Publication Data
Data Available

ISBN-13: 978-1-84113- 680-6 (hardback)
ISBN-13: 978-1-84113-681-3 (paperback)

Typeset by Columns Design Ltd, Reading
Printed and bound in Great Britain by
Biddles Ltd, Kings Lynn, Norfolk

Preface

With the exception of one chapter (Chen), this book results from a workshop on 'Globalisation and Law in Asia: From the Asian Crisis to September 11, 2001' held on 10-11 April 2003 at the International Institute for the Sociology of Law in Oñati, Spain. The papers were subsequently updated and thoroughly revised and take into account developments until the end of 2005.

The editors would like to thank the following: the Oñati International Institute for the Sociology of Law for organizing and supporting the workshop; the ARC Key Centre for Asia-Pacific Social Transformation Studies (CAPSTRANS) and the Centre for Comparative Law and Development Studies in Asia and the Pacific at the University of Wollongong for financial assistance during the editorial process; Bill Felstiner and the editorial board for including the book in the Oñati Series on the Sociology of Law; Malen Gordoa Mendizabal for her assistance in organising the Oñati workshop; Elaine Newby in Wollongong for many hours of proof reading and correcting the chapters; and two anonymous reviewers for their comments and suggestions.

Christoph Antons and Volkmar Gessner
Wollongong and Bremen, January 2006

Contents

List of Contributors

Antons, Christoph, Professor of Comparative Law and Director, Centre for Comparative Law and Development Studies in Asia and the Pacific, University of Wollongong, Australia; Queen Elizabeth II Fellow of the Australian Research Council (ARC); Adjunct Research Fellow at the Max Planck Institute for Intellectual Property, Competition and Tax Law in Munich, Germany. E-mail: cantons@uow.edu.au.

von Benda-Beckmann, Franz, Head of the Project Group 'Legal Pluralism' at the Max Planck Institute for Social Anthropology in Halle, Germany; Honorary Professor at the Universities of Leipzig and Halle, Germany. E-mail: fbenda@eth.mpg.de.

von Benda-Beckmann, Keebet, Head of the Project Group 'Legal Pluralism' at the Max Planck Institute for Social Anthropology in Halle, Germany; Honorary Professor at the Universities of Leipzig and Halle, Germany; Chair in Anthropology of Law at Erasmus University in Rotterdam, the Netherlands. E-mail: kbenda@eth.mpg.de.

Carruthers, Bruce G, Chair and Professor, Department of Sociology, Northwestern University, Chicago, USA. E-mail: b-carruthers@ northwestern. edu.

Chen, Jianfu, Professor of Chinese Law and Legal Globalisation, School of Law, La Trobe University, Melbourne, Australia. E-mail: j.chen@latrobe.edu.au.

Gessner, Volkmar, Professor of Sociology of Law and Comparative Law at the Law Faculty, University of Bremen, Germany; Head of Department in *Sonderforschungsbereich* 597 'Transformation of the State'. E-mail: Gessner@uni-bremen.de.

Halliday, Terence C, Senior Research Fellow, American Bar Foundation, Chicago, USA. E-mail: halliday@abfn.org.

Harding, Andrew, Professor of Asia-Pacific Legal Relations, University of Victoria, Canada. E-mail: harding@law.uvic.ca.

Mendelsohn, Oliver, School of Law, La Trobe University, Melbourne, Australia. E-mail: o.mendelsohn@latrobe.edu.au.

Ohnesorge, John K M, Assistant Professor of Law, Law School, University of Wisconsin, Madison, USA. E-mail: jkohnesorge@wisc.edu.

1

Introduction

CHRISTOPH ANTONS AND VOLKMAR GESSNER

I LAW AND DEVELOPMENT DISCOURSES

LAW AND DEVELOPMENT research and practice, previously criticised by legal sociologists and political activists, has reached a remarkable level during the last decade. In contrast to the original movements (in particular the Ford Foundation sponsored initiatives in Latin America), the basic policy goal of law and development—the 'rule of law'—has already drawn subtle debate. A formal definition of the concept of the 'rule of law' underestimates implementation problems; a substantive definition requires judgment about what is a 'good society'; and a functional definition may also suffer from difficulties in selecting objective and universally applicable functional goals. The current debate goes beyond the legal transplants literature which is unanimously blamed for neglecting legal cultural variables and which lacks empirical insights into the actual preconditions of law reform and its social consequences. The importance of a solid empirical base is mostly emphasised—the exception being comparative law, where technical and doctrinal approaches still prevail. This interest in empirical realities often leads to the discovery of informal mechanisms, which are sometimes more effective and efficient for economic, institutional, and political development. Interdisciplinary law and development research agendas encompass statutory law, courts, legislative bodies, legal professions (including the judiciary), legal education, and public opinion about law and legal institutions.

Independently from law and development debates (in the narrow sense) are other social-scientific approaches involved in studies of social and political transformations around the globe (transformations partly due to globalisation processes). Of particular interest within the context of this book is research in economic sociology, institutional analysis and institutional economics. Institutions—according to these disciplines—'matter' and are particularly decisive for economic performance: for example, commercial dispute resolution, contract enforcement, ownership rights, financial transparency, terms and modes of sale, purchase, finance, etc. Institutions vary: they may or may not create trust and legal certainty, hinder or facilitate transactions, be formal or informal, unstable or path-dependent. Increased knowledge of the nature of institutions has been gained recently, in particular in the context of transformations in Southern and Eastern Europe and Central Asia. Although difficult to assess, the research intends to measure the quality of institutions and often prescribes specific institutional reforms.

This impressive level of reflection about legal and institutional development is not confined to academic discourses but may also be discovered in publications of international organisations and donor-support institutions. The World Bank (2005) offers a website on 'Legal Institutions of the Market Economy' which not only covers all these aspects but also advocates complex approaches to law reform and recommends more investigation to address a number of difficult and unanswered questions. Its authors confess that it is at this stage virtually impossible to sort out the complex and contingent relationships between the different components of real-world institutions. It warns against simply using easily observable characteristics of formal institutions (such as the 'law in the books'). Neglecting informal institutions may, according to the World Bank, not only limit the domain of study, it may also seriously skew the findings. Instead of promoting a sort of 'rule of law' optimism that one might expect from the World Bank, many pages are devoted to reporting experiences with reform strategies: 'What Works, What Hasn't'. And if one reads the case studies, it seems that most of them have not worked.

Given this background, it is not easy to produce another book in the same area of study and claim originality. Where is the niche our contributions could fill? The literature offers sophisticated theory and quite a large quantity of empirical evidence. Our only excuse for publishing this book is that in comparing existing research on Eastern and Central Europe, Central Asia and Latin America, it seems that legal developments of Eastern and Southern Asian societies are somewhat under-researched. What the book contributes to the debate is a sort of 'area study', interdisciplinary research pertaining to a particular geographical or cultural region. The region here discussed presents an ideal testing ground for legal pluralism, for economic, cultural, and political influences on the role of law in development. Just a few short years ago one of the experts who now contributes to this volume, noted: 'The truth is that we really have no idea what to say about the legal systems of South East Asia' (Harding, 2002: 49). In addition to global doctrine, we need local knowledge (see also Hendley, 2004).

In geographical terms, this book examines developments in the countries of East Asia (Japan, Korea, Taiwan, China), Southeast Asia (with a particular focus on Indonesia, Thailand and Malaysia) and India as the only country in this volume from South Asia. The book follows an earlier edited volume on 'Law and Development in East and Southeast Asia' (Antons, 2003a), in which a similar geographical focus was chosen and that was the result of a workshop at the International Institute for Asian Studies in Leiden in 1998. The departure point for the discussion at the time was the argument that Asia had found a different path to modernity and to economic development from that taken by the West (see, for the example of Japan in particular, Eisenstadt, 1996) and that the study of Asian society, its modernisation and development strategies, including those in the legal field, required a different mixture of analytical tools. In development theory, the 'developmental states' of Asia were regarded as refuting both Latin American dependency theory and classical modernisation theory. The new regional approach created the 'flying geese' picture, with Japan as the developed economy of the region and an historical role model as leader, followed by the 'newly industrialising countries' of South Korea, Taiwan, Hong Kong and Singapore, and countries such as Indonesia, Thailand and Malaysia that were sometimes referred to as 'second tier Southeast Asian newly industrialising countries' (Rasiah, 2003: 19).

While economists were debating the role of the state and the effectiveness of its interference in the economy, lawyers and political scientists became interested in the question of what consequences the 'state-led approach' to development would have for law. There were attempts to find methodological approaches to the study of law in 'Asian developmental states' (Antons, 1995 and 1997) as well as books analysing the different notions of the rule of law and their impact in Asia (Jayasuriya, 1999; Peerenboom, 2002 and 2004). The focus of the earlier mentioned volume on 'Law and Development in East and Southeast Asia' was on commercial law and its use in the context of economic development in Asia. The present book is thematically broader and follows from a workshop at the Oñati International Institute for the Sociology of Law in 2003 on 'Globalisation and Law in Asia: From the Asian Crisis to September 11, 2001'. The contributions in this book are not confined to state policies and state law as a mirror of development strategies, but also look at developments at the grassroots level, at the way individual and institutional actors react to law reform measures that are partly home-grown and partly imposed from outside. This tension between 'international', 'transnational' and 'global' forces, and the resistance, transformation or adaptation and implementation at the local level is at the heart of the book. The tensions are delineated for categories of law concerning the political decision-making process, human rights, administrative decentralisation and commercial law. The time frame is the period following the Asian Crisis with its sometimes conflicting goals of democratic reform, improvement of human rights, transparency of business regulation and national stability. To this already complicated set of goals and interests, anti-terrorism policies have added a further dimension.

The notion of globalisation is a contested one, both as a political force and as a concept in the social sciences (Held and McGrew, 2002). Anti-globalisation protests at World Trade Organization (WTO) or G8 summits demonstrate the opposition to its political strength. As a social science concept, it emphasises the constraints of time and space brought about by massive technological change in communication and transport. The new technologies open up opportunities for international business and for political opposition and social forces at the grassroots level to easily cross borders and challenge the regulatory powers of the nation state. Globalisation sceptics, on the other hand, point out that there are more nation states at the end of the twentieth century than ever before in history and that the nation state is far from losing its grip on the developments. In this interpretation then, globalisation is ultimately nothing else than an attempt by hegemonic nation states such as the United States to assert their influence.

In any case, the developments of the last few years in Asia and elsewhere show that the nation state will not simply wither away, but that local elites and communities affected by globalising influences are resisting. In the countries that are examined in this volume globalising forces have been aided by the policy preferences of the international institutions and the Washington Consensus, with its stress on privatisation and deregulation, as well as transparency and the elimination of corruption.

However, there is also a geopolitical and strategic dimension to international trade that is often neglected. It leads to preferential trade relations and stands sometimes at the beginning of regional trade groupings such as, for example, in the case of the Association of South East Asian Nations (ASEAN). Such geopolitical considerations helped enable 'Asian developmental states' devise their particular policy mix (for a summary of these arguments, see Stubbs, 2005; see also Stubbs, 1994). Those policies have come under pressure since the end of the Cold War. The question now is whether the new security crisis following the attacks of September 11, 2001, and the subsequent 'war on terror' may again strengthen the bargaining powers and strategic positions of those governments that are regarded as strategic allies in the region during this current security crisis. While it seems too early to come to conclusions in this regard, some of the contributions in this book include glimpses at this issue in their analysis.

II ASIAN STUDIES IN THE SOCIAL SCIENCES

Outside the area of law, 'Asia' has been defined and studied in many different ways by social scientists. Theorising about Asia's political economy was particularly popular in economics departments and in the social and political sciences during the 'Asian economic miracle' years of the 1980s and early 1990s. The framework for comparative studies varied, but often the focus was on a sub-region of Asia, for example, East Asia, Southeast Asia or South Asia (see, for example, Robison et al, 1987; Hewison et al, 1993; Lee, 1993). It also became increasingly common to analyse parts of Asia in terms of intra-regional trade, where either such grand concepts as 'the Asia Pacific region' or the 'Pacific Rim' were used (for example, Dobbs-Higginson, 1993; Abegglen, 1994; Jones et al, 1993; Simone and Thompson Feraru, 1995; Islam and Chowdhury, 1997; Appelbaum and Henderson, 1992; Linder, 1986) or regional and multi-regional trade groups such as ASEAN or Asia-Pacific Economic Cooperation (APEC) were the focus (Tan, 1996; Tay et al, 2001; Davidson, 2002). At the same time, Asian political leaders such as the Malaysian Prime Minister Mahathir Mohamad and Japanese Liberal Democratic Party politician Shintaro Ishihara appealed to feelings of pan-Asian unity and solidarity by stressing common cultural traits such as family values as well as common political and economic goals (Mahathir and Ishihara, 1995; Ishihara, 1991). Sometimes their claims were based on cultural and religious communalities stemming from moral virtues based on, for example, Confucianism or Islam. At other times, the construct of 'Asian values' was used to distinguish the region from the West (Ghai, 2000). A peculiar version of this in Japan is the debate about the essence of being Japanese (*Nihonjinron*) (Mouer and Sugimoto, 1986).

It is therefore not surprising that there has been a sceptical reaction among social scientists to such claims, and attempts at deconstructing such regional concepts followed (see the contributions in Dirlik, 1993). Many social science and history books begin with a careful explanation of the concept of 'Asia' or of a particular sub-region of Asia (Cauquelin et al, 2000; Reischauer and Fairbank 1958 and 1960). After all, the term 'Asia' is a socially constructed concept and has been used by various writers in multiple ways in accordance with their respective aims and viewpoints (Jenkins, 1996). It can be used to refer to internal cultural commonalities as well as to stress differences vis-à-vis other continents, such as Europe. In a similar way, Eriksen (2001: 44) has pointed out that the concept of culture(s) may refer to something universally shared or serving as a marker of difference between groups. In this volume, the concept of 'Asia' is not used to point to internal characteristics of Asian culture in general or of legal culture in Asia in particular, but merely as a geographical reference.

That is not to say, however, that commonalities created by the length and depth of the historical and cross-cultural interaction within the region should be ignored.

After World War II, area studies and regional Asian studies with their focus on politics, society and the economy were important to overcome the limitations of the mainly linguistic studies of India, China and Japan that had dominated European university curricula in particular for so long and that had limited the study of 'modern Asia'. As the example of Vietnam (as a Southeast Asian society which also belongs to the sphere of Northeast Asian Confucian culture) shows, the borders of Asian studies disciplines were often deliberately chosen and based as much on historical and political as on cultural circumstances. They have recently been joined by even grander concepts such as the 'Asian Pacific', 'Asia Pacific' or 'Pacific Asia' and 'Asia Pacific Studies'. These terms are often used to point to relations with the United States as East Asia's most important trading partner, and to a lesser extent to other trans-Pacific linkages emerging within APEC. Within Asia, the focus was for some time on a number of countries that seemed to follow the lead of Japan in industrialisation strategies, some of which were studied in the World Bank's 'East Asian Miracle' report of 1993. Interestingly, however, this report did not include China. For those interested in the political economy of the region as more broadly understood, the 'Asian Pacific' concept was always problematic, as it most certainly included the ASEAN countries but also Myanmar, a country that actually faces the Indian rather than the Pacific Ocean. With the rise of India as a major foreign direct investment (FDI) destination in the 1990s, the interest of observers shifted further west and the Indian Ocean came into view again. The collapse of the Soviet Union has also renewed interest in Central Asia, while the discussion around terrorism and Islam has reminded observers in the West of the historic links between the Near and Middle East and the southern and eastern parts of Asia.

III LAW IN ASIA

In legal terms the East, Southeast and South Asian regions represent a bewildering variety of laws, both traditional and modern (Antons, 2003b: 13-14). Chinese law, Hindu law, Islamic law and a multitude of customary laws were present prior to the arrival of the European powers (Hooker, 1986). The European, and somewhat later the American and Japanese, colonial powers subsequently introduced the idea of the nation state and laws from Britain, France, Germany, the Netherlands, Portugal, Spain, Japan and the United States (Hooker, 1975 and 1988; Hahm, 1996). Those countries that avoided colonisation studied laws from a variety of countries as models for their law reforms (Chen, 1995: 23; Takayanagi, 1976).

While this seems to make the finding of commonalities almost impossible, the countries share, to a varying degree, values based on religion, historical influences and experiences such as colonialism, and similar strategies in pursuing industrialisation and modernisation. Neither the political and economic strategies nor the religious values are really peculiar to the region. In fact, with economic globalisation, many of the 'rough edges' that differentiate one culture from another are disappearing. Nevertheless, what defines a region is the length and depth of the interaction of its members over prolonged periods in history (what the historian Braudel has called the '*longue durée*': see Held and McGrew, 2002: 6; for an application of Braudel's concept to the Indian Ocean, see Chaudhuri, 1985). This interaction was intense in Asia with the sea trade depending on the monsoon winds and bringing traders from the Arab Peninsula and the East Coast of Africa to the port cities of India and Southeast Asia, where they met traders from the southern parts of China. In trading ports, such as Malacca, they had to wait for the return of the monsoon to sail home, thus creating a sizeable foreign presence long before the arrival of the first European ships in this part of the world. When the Portuguese finally arrived, as the first Europeans in the region, they were at first relatively weak and after a while were to some extent integrated into the Asian trade (Chaudhuri, 1985; Andaya,1992: 355). But the never completely successful attempts by the Portuguese and Dutch to monopolise the spice trade finally marked the beginnings of colonisation that would ultimately require territorial control. Thus over many centuries, Indian, Arab, Chinese and European influences were diffused across the region.

IV A BRIEF INTRODUCTION TO THE CONTRIBUTIONS TO THIS VOLUME

In the first part of this volume, 'Asian Capitalism(s) and Law Reform: Globalisation and Resistance', Volkmar Gessner, Franz and Keebet von Benda-Beckmann, Christoph Antons and John Ohnesorge set the scene for the more specific chapters by explaining the tensions outlined above, using respectively a sociological, anthropological, historical, and comparative perspective.

In chapter two, 'Legalisation and the Varieties of Capitalism', Volkmar Gessner scrutinises the classical theories regarding the role of law in the process of modernisation and economic development. This examination includes modernisation theory, transaction cost analysis and the new institutionalism of Douglass North, and Max Weber's theory of economic development and legal rationality. Gessner points to a frequent misinterpretation of Weber's theory and explains that, contrary to popular understanding, both Weber and the institutional economists recognise the role of informal norms and institutions as important and equivalent to legal coercion, but regard them as either inefficient or obsolete in a modern economy. Informal and non-legal institutions may, however, be perfectly rational in their respective settings. Gessner provides the examples of social bonding, the *lex mercatoria* and mega law firms. Chinese business relationships involving *guanxi* and the autonomous normative community of diamond traders are examples of social bonding. Here, the views of Bernstein (1996) and Macaulay (1963) can be contrasted. Whereas Macaulay sees formal contract law as largely symbolic, according to Bernstein it plays a role in ending the relationship after autonomous norms have failed to preserve it. Public international law is equally guided by relational practices.

Another example of substantive rationality without formality is the *lex mercatoria*, whose vagueness accommodates the culture of global business transactions better than municipal law or private international law. In a final example, Gessner points to the changing role of the legal profession in the common law world in particular, where it has acquired a key role in the establishment of global political, economic and financial structures. Between 50 and 70 US and British law firms are involved in this restructuring of the global economy, which involves the drafting of contracts largely independent of state law, the creation of new forms of corporation, the avoidance of state control for financial transactions, the discovery of tax havens and the exploitation of gaps in local or international trade law. Gessner concludes that economic sociologists and economists understand the embeddedness of institutions better than lawyers. Whereas Western laws regulate the actions of people, Asia's societies emphasise regulation through roles. Cognitive rather than normative expectations are necessary in these dynamic and complex societies, but they may be supplanted by the transmission of legalisation from Western countries.

Franz and Keebet von Benda-Beckmann in the third chapter, 'Transnationalisation of Law, Globalisation and Legal Pluralism: a Legal Anthropological Perspective' focus on legal processes of adapting and capturing globalising law. This focus sees local populations as actors instead of mere subjects of globalising forces. They may at times be quite resilient and capable of reversing flows of influences. The chapter begins with a definition of the often interchangeably used terms 'transnational', 'transnationalised' and 'globalised' law. While much of 'transnational' law is specifically enacted to flow across national borders, 'transnationalised' law also includes other forms of legal transplants or models originally created within the context of a different nation state. Finally, 'globalised' law is transnational law with a greater spatial dimension. The chapter paints a picture of transnational flows of laws with varying degrees of permanency and often overlapping geographical spread. Importantly, the flow is not just one from North to South, or from West to East, but also within regions and reversed, such as in the spread of customary and religious laws to Western, industrialised countries via migration from the developing world. Transnational forces have effects not only at the national level, but also at sub-national levels, for example through the influence of transnational agencies on law-making at the provincial or district level. There is also a contrary flow with new varieties of legal pluralism, such as when religious or customary laws are being transnationalised as a result of the internet and the influence of media, non-governmental organisations (NGOs) and internationally connected social movements. The authors conclude with a recommendation that the common division between 'macro' and 'micro' studies be abandoned. They believe that Moore's concept of 'semi-autonomous social fields' can be equally well applied to transnational or global social fields.

In chapter four, 'Law Reform in the "Developmental States" of East and Southeast Asia: From the Asian Crisis to September 11, 2001 and Beyond', Christoph Antons writes from an historical perspective. In formerly colonised countries such as Indonesia, migration for work in the colonial economy was encouraged by the colonial powers and the various population groups were legally distinguished according to their respective roles. This officially-sanctioned legal pluralism continued after independence, when the various communities saw their respective interests best served by a greater recognition of 'their' laws. At the same time, developmentalist governments had little time for a systematic approach to the legal system and emphasised commercial law development instead. 'Traditional values' were officially sanctioned because of their important role in providing a 'back-up system' in social security in countries that were unable to implement Western welfare models. Such 'traditional values' were also strengthened to discourage extensive use of Western-derived legal models and to keep litigation rates low.

Approaches to law in the Asian developmental states were building on a long tradition, especially in Confucianist countries, but also in the feudal traditions of Southeast Asia that emphasised personified understandings of virtuous governance. This resulted in a lack of differentiation between public and private law, with the administration of penalties by private institutions, such as the family on the one hand, and the use of criminal law by the state to enforce private obligations on the other hand. The administration of public law in general, and of criminal law in particular, has been authoritarian and only somewhat restrained by international human rights monitoring. However, the historical roots of this authoritarianism are not just of an indigenous nature, but are often to be found in the instrumental understanding of law introduced by the colonial powers.

Asian governments showed a preference for 'administrative guidance' and administrative decrees implemented by bureaucrats with great discretionary powers.

With economic success as the primary justification for a restrictive political system, many Asian governments came under pressure in the wake of the Asian Crisis of 1997 and 1998. The result were uneven attempts at political liberalisation (see in particular Harding, this volume), administrative decentralisation (see Franz and Keebet von Benda-Beckmann, this volume), the establishment of human rights commissions and the strengthening of various areas of commercial law, such as bankruptcy legislation (see Halliday and Carruthers, this volume). However, the institutions to support the reforms have often been lacking and various measures have encountered resistance from the political and business elites of the countries concerned. Parts of the region, in particular in Southeast Asia, have also been affected by the 'war on terror' with its shift in emphasis to security concerns. While the new policies have not led to a fundamental change in the law reform debate in East and Southeast Asia, they have somewhat diverted attention from the economic issues.

In chapter five, 'Politics, Ideology and Legal System Reform in Northeast Asia', John Ohnesorge draws upon examples mainly from Japan, South Korea and Taiwan. Beyond the common criticism of law and institutional reform, Ohnesorge perceives also a tendency to judicialisation, where courts are seen as being at the centre of governance processes. This trend was strengthened by the Asian Crisis, but was already well under way in the early 1990s. The goal of the chapter is to explore the alignment of foreign and domestic interests in the reform of shareholder derivative litigation and in administrative law reform. The two reform agendas are related as they aim to curtail the power of bureaucrats and corporate management in favour of individual shareholders and civil society respectively by creating and enhancing private rights. Ohnesorge sees these reforms as supported by 'Neoliberal' constituencies on the one hand and by 'Populist/Progressive' (P/P) interests on the other hand. Of course, these are ideal type positions, which may sometimes conflict and at other times be aligned with each other.

All countries surveyed in the chapter have introduced measures to make derivative litigation more attractive to plaintiff shareholders. These reforms have been welcomed by both Neoliberal and P/P constituencies and supported by foreign interests. The reform went furthest in Korea, which was most dependent on IMF assistance after the Asian Crisis. In the field of administrative law, the reforms have brought a legalisation of the state / civil society interface. They have focused on 'rule of law' benchmarks and information disclosure laws. With the Asian Crisis and Japan's recession, 'administrative guidance' has come under pressure, particularly in Japan, which had experienced spectacular failures of administrative risk-taking in the health, nuclear energy and banking regulation sectors. Again, in matters relating to the creation of a level playing field for business or the establishment of democratic government mechanisms, Neoliberal and P/P views are often aligned against those of the 'developmental' state.

Since many of the reforms are usually seen as 'Americanisation' of the Northeast Asian legal systems, Ohnesorge adds an American caveat. Shareholder derivative litigation in the United States is not without its problems and critics. Transplanted into the context of Northeast Asia, it could change industrial relations or long-term planning in technology development. The US 'due process revolution' in administrative law has also led to a politicisation of the American judiciary and its advantages in achieving effective administration are by no means clear.

In Ohnesorge's assessment of the success of the reforms thus far, it seems that derivative litigation has been mainly attractive to shareholder activists and public interest lawyers, but that restrictive civil discovery rules have prevented a wider impact. Ultimately, therefore, P/P interests are advanced better by these developments than the Neoliberal agenda of maximising shareholder value. Both civil society groups and business have made use of the reformed administrative law environment, with the latter achieving more mixed results than the former.

In the final part of his chapter Ohnesorge turns to two events that have implications for legal policies in both Asia and the United States: the crisis of American corporate governance following the Enron collapse and the attacks of September 11, 2001, with their effects on politics in the United States and elsewhere. After Enron, those recommending US-style corporate governance had to become somewhat more cautious, particularly as a transfer of US concepts in this field would also require the embeddedness into an institutional and cultural framework of what Ohnesorge calls the 'gatekeeper' professions of accountants, lawyers, securities analysts, investments banks, etc. However, rather than leading to critical questioning of US-style corporate governance, Enron will strengthen US influence in Northeast Asia in this regard. This is because the tighter post-Enron regulatory structure will be replicated in foreign systems that wish to facilitate access to US capital markets, while at the same time investment by US institutional shareholders will challenge the existing norms in Asia. Finally, the Enron crisis also strengthens the agenda of minority shareholder advocates.

September 11 and the 'war on terror' have somewhat reduced the importance of commercial law reform and the pressure on strategic allies to comply with US demands on trade. The Bush administration has adopted a pro-management agenda at home that will be more compatible with the views of Northeast Asia's traditional business elite. In the field of administrative law, the Homeland Security Act has brought new exceptions to information disclosure requirements and pluralist assumptions about disclosure requirements in areas such as energy policy. The author concludes that September 11 may well slow down the Neoliberal legal reform agenda, which on the whole has benefited P/P interests in Asia more than Neoliberal constituencies.

In the second part of the book, Andrew Harding, Oliver Mendelsohn and Jianfu Chen examine the political sphere of interaction between the nation state and its citizens, as reflected in the recent agenda of constitutional reform, human rights and strengthening of the rule of law. Prior to the Asian Crisis, many governments in the region displayed an authoritarian political style and showed little interest in constitutional reform. As long as authoritarianism was combined with economic success, political opposition and demands for reform were muted. However, in those economies affected by the Asian Crisis lack of success resulted either in political change or, at least, an intensified debate about constitutional checks and balances, and an improvement in human rights standards. This debate too has recently become influenced by the 'war on terror', which has renewed an emphasis on emergency powers and security acts or brought about criminal law amendments.

In chapter six, 'Southeast Asia, 1997-2003: Two Case Studies on the Politics of Law and Development', Andrew Harding presents case studies of Thailand and Malaysia. They demonstrate two very different approaches, and lead to apparently different conclusions. While much of the debate following the Asian Crisis was about fixing regulatory problems related to the economy, Thailand placed political reform ahead of economic reform. However, as in other areas discussed in this book (decentralisation, bankruptcy), the Crisis merely accelerated a reform process that had started in 1991, when the Thais rejected the military government of General Suchinda Kraprakorn and constitutional amendments were adopted and a drafting assembly for a new constitution set up in the process. Perhaps ironically, it was the military that ensured the swift passing of a new Constitution in 1997 by the National Assembly at a time when many wanted to give preference to the Crisis. While reform of essential business laws followed, in the Thai approach the constitutional reforms are essential to solve the problems of corruption, military rule, government formation, and the abuse of power, as well as meet the needs for increased accountability, transparency, greater human rights and the rule of law. The balance of power between the various parts of the legislature was readjusted to ensure that members were competent and not easily corrupted. Equally, a number of 'watchdog' bodies such as the National Counter-Corruption Commission were created. The new Constitution included a catalogue of human rights and rights of the accused as well as rights to participation in decision making processes, those related to environmental concerns in particular. While public law reform in Thailand must be regarded as significant, Harding also points to the appointment of family members of the former Prime Minister to high military and other key positions, and to the former government's virulent anti-drug campaigns and controversial response to the separatist insurgency in the Muslim South. These developments indicated new tensions between government policies and the constitutional apparatus. They finally triggered Thailand's seventeenth military coup since 1932 in September 2006. The 1997 Constitution has been abrogated and drafting of a new constitution is currently underway.

In contrast to the developments in Thailand, Malaysia's government continued to give preference to economic stability over political reforms. In Malaysia, the Asian Crisis led to a political rift between then Prime Minister Mahathir Mohamad and Deputy Prime Minister and Finance Minister Anwar Ibrahim. The men were at odds over the most appropriate reaction to the Crisis. Mahathir prevailed and Anwar was subsequently jailed on corruption charges. The government used the Internal Security Act to suppress public dissent over the affair and the lack of reform, but the ruling *Barisan Nasional* (BN) coalition survived a temporary voter backlash to re-establish public support under the new Prime Minister Abdullah Badawi during the 2004 elections. Nevertheless, the turbulent period following the Asian Crisis has not failed to leave a legacy. The ethnic preference rules prescribing 30 per cent ownership by ethnic Malays and natives of Sabah and Sarawak (*bumiputera*) in investment projects have been relaxed, particularly in areas where attracting foreign investment is regarded as crucial, such as the Multimedia Super-Corridor on the outskirts of Kuala Lumpur. Cyberlaws and similar laws have been drafted to respond to a globalising economy, a National Human Rights Commission has been created, and some concerns regarding judicial independence have been addressed. However, Malaysia has largely failed to respond to the call for good governance, while the security concerns after September 11, 2001, have again lent justification to the use of the Internal Security Act and to authoritarian government. Harding concludes that the Asian Crisis has revealed a crisis of governance and a culmination of problems that had been increasing for years. There is thus no guarantee that the state-led developmental approaches of countries like Malaysia will remain unchallenged, but equally it seems unlikely that 'globalisation law' will prevail without concessions to local knowledge, circumstances, politics and value systems. The two case studies show that different results can be expected in the process, leading to some degree of convergence and divergence at the same time.

Oliver Mendelsohn's chapter on 'Law, Terror and the Indian Legal Order' (chapter seven) shows how skilfully the previous coalition government led by the Hindu nationalist Bharatiya Janata Party (BJP) exploited the political opportunities presented to it by the anti-terrorism policies after September 11, 2001. The chapter begins by outlining the liberal aspects of the Indian Constitution as well as the authoritarian emergency powers available in case of, for example, 'internal disturbances'. A lack of clear separation of powers has resulted in extensive use of preventive detention orders. Mendelsohn explains how India has moved back and forth between various emergencies and liberal periods during which NGOs and public interest litigation have flourished. He praises the Supreme Court of India for its performance that has made it a central pillar of India's constitutional order. The Court has shown activism in cases involving pavement- and slum-dwellers, women and children, bonded labourers, prisoners, detainees in psychiatric institutions, and sex workers, and it has also not avoided the issue of corruption.

However, while India has matured politically, Indian politics have become less tolerant of difference and in particular of religious difference. During the period of BJP rule, Indian Muslims became increasingly identified with Pakistan, and the Hindu nationalist fraction continues to promote *Hindutva*, the ideological view that Indian civilisation and the Indian state are essentially Hindu. Equally, the political discourse on terrorism has tended to focus on Kashmir, in spite of the fact that India has had a long history of various forms of terrorism and insurrectionary movements since Independence. As a result, there has been a series of acts allowing for preventive detention and focusing on the maintenance of internal security. The Prevention of Terrorism Act was opposed in Parliament in 2000 but rushed through as an ordinance in 2002. This was transformed into the Prevention of Terrorism Act (POTA) later in 2002. The Act allowed, among other things, for special courts and extraordinary rules of seizure and evidence. However, given the previous history of India and the developments elsewhere, these security laws were neither a complete departure from previous practice nor uncommon by international standards.

In the 2004 elections the Congress Party returned to power, claiming to represent 'secularism' and promising to repeal POTA. Shortly after being elected the Government made good on its promise. Initially by ordinances that were later converted into Acts, it repealed POTA and introduced substitute legislation. The Unlawful Activities (Prevention) Act 1967 (as amended in 2004) restored many of the established procedures and provisions of the law of evidence and of ordinary criminal law. However, remaining provisions, which may be regarded as problematic relate to the open-ended definition of terrorist acts, the lack of procedure for the listing of organisations 'involved in terrorism' and to the holding of in camera proceedings if the court so desires. Mendelsohn concludes that the re-election of Congress at this time of increasing religious division may be a development of considerable value.

Jianfu Chen in chapter eight, 'Role / Rule of Law in China Reconsidered', expresses scepticism about China's progress towards establishing the rule of law, in spite of substantial progress in implementing WTO-compliant regulation. He reviews the many different understandings of the rule of law. In fact, the Chinese economy has grown rapidly in the absence of the rule of law, and it is resentment of corruption, rather than the need for market reform or the rise of civil society, that leads to current demands for reform. During the early years of reform, under Deng Xiaoping, law was used as a tool for institutionalising and generalising ad hoc policies for economic reform. The shift in 1996 to 'Ruling the Country According to Law' brought another slogan with initially little substance, although the phrase was incorporated in the Constitution during its revision in 1999. In 2002 it was also incorporated in the constitution of the Communist Party, although this constitution also stresses that 'ruling the country according to law' should be combined with 'ruling the country by virtue'. The latter could in fact signify a return to the traditional understanding of the 'rule of man'. Most recent documents are again rich in rhetoric, but provide little substance and no timetable for reform.

Chen warns readers not to confuse the 'rule of law' as an academic topic with the practical reality or official policy. Chinese academic discourse has used the term *fazhi*, which can refer to both the rule of law and the rule by law, since the *Qing* period. Real impetus for change came with economic reform and the introduction of the concept of the 'socialist market economy' in 1992. Academic discourse began to emphasise rights, including private property rights and human rights, judicial independence, equality before the law and the idea of administrative law as providing a control on government and its activities. In comparison to this breakthrough in the academic debate, the phrases and slogans used since 1996 provide little that is new.

The sheer output of laws and regulations, followed by many revisions since 1978, has been impressive, especially within those areas of law that were subject to requirements for WTO membership. There has been some administrative reform, largely to curb corruption, while judicial reform has been piecemeal. The focus of law-making has been on the establishment and regulation of the socialist market economy. Otherwise, lack of judicial exercise of checks and balances leads to privatisation and localisation of public powers, again exacerbating the problem of corruption.

Overall, Chen believes that the academic debate has had some limited effect in civil and administrative law reform. In the near future, economic law reform will continue, but there will be no substantial breakthrough in areas of law affecting political control and party dominance. Examples of the lack of democratic checks and balances include the influence of Party Committees on the revision of the Constitution, and the adoption—without public consultation—of an amendment of the criminal law to cover terrorist activities. The new criminal provisions have meanwhile been used to prosecute a prominent dissident and against separatist activities in the Xinjiang Uighur Autonomous Region. There is a fear that the 'rule of law with Chinese characteristics' will be used to reject the Western understanding of the concept and that its universal notions may be ignored. The author concludes that it would be fair to say that the foundations for the rule of law have been laid in China, but that its actual establishment will be a long process.

In the third part of the book, Franz and Keebet von Benda-Beckmann (chapter nine) examine administrative decentralisation as yet another *mantra* that has been used by international donor agencies, NGOs and grassroots initiatives to bring about 'good governance'. However, government structures in strongly pluralist societies such as Indonesia cannot be compared to the relatively simple federal model that is familiar to Western observers. As the authors point out in their chapter 'Between Global Forces and Local Politics: Decentralisation and Reorganisation of Village Government in Indonesia', there has as yet been little systematic research as to what happens at the local government level once such decentralised structures are introduced. As with many of the other areas of law reform, administrative decentralisation had entered the 'good governance' debate well before the Asian Crisis. However, again as in many other fields of law, the Asian Crisis became a trigger for these efforts to intensify.

The von Benda-Beckmanns have carried out their research in the Indonesian province of West Sumatra. Local *Minangkabau* communities in this part of Indonesia always had to reconcile matrilineal traditions based on pre-Islamic *adat* with Islamic principles based on the *syari'ah*. The chapter shows how some of these issues are now re-emerging in the process of decentralisation, as are other forms of conflicts and power struggles that result from more recent changes to the village government structure during the period of President Suharto. However, the decentralisation legislation empowers the districts and towns rather than the provinces for fear of secessionist movements in resource-rich provinces. In this regard, Indonesia did not adopt the recommendations of foreign donors, who had favoured the provinces as focal points for the process. The central government has also intervened via Presidential Decree to exempt from decentralisation important responsibilities such as the National Land Board. While experiences with decentralisation so far have been mixed, powerful lobbies of local organisations have been formed and these have occasionally achieved a readjustment of the distribution of resources.

In an historical survey of village government in West Sumatra, the authors show how Islamic officials had been incorporated into the matriclan system and how the Dutch had institutionalised the traditional village structure to diminish the influence of Islam. This resulted in a dualistic government structure with the *Adat* Council separated from the local village government (*nagari*). During the twentieth century the village 'intelligentsia' became the third pillar of village government in addition to *adat* lineage heads and religious officials. To these were added various 'functional groups' (such as women or youth) after independence. Centralisation and standardisation of local government during the Suharto years introduced the Javanese village structure of the *desa* into Sumatra. However, the new arrangements allowed for the *Adat* Council to continue and gave it an important role in the distribution of the wealth of the village. Such councils became government controlled in the process and bureaucratic in their functioning.

The chapter follows the process of political and financial decentralisation. While substantial progress has been made in the former, the splitting up of financial and natural resources is a much more thorny issue. The return to the *nagari* policy has also brought a return to the decision-making process of deliberation until consensus is reached (*musyawarah untuk mupakat* in Indonesian or *sakato* in the local *Minang* language). This is a familiar concept to students of Indonesia's political and constitutional history because it was used by Indonesia's first president, President Sukarno, and later by his successor, President Suharto, to justify 'Guided Democracy' and the appointment of 'functional groups' to Parliament. The return to traditional forms of village government will also resurrect traditional forms of social stratification and eligibility for political participation. The latter is of concern, particularly to the younger generation and to migrant communities, whose rights to political participation and to property are not the same in *adat* as those of the original *Minangkabau* clans, and who had benefited to some extent from the standardisation of village government during the Suharto years.

Many of the financial decentralisation issues are currently unresolved. For example, the future of temporary rights of usage granted by the state is in doubt, as is the size of block grants to be received by the villages and the extent of authority to levy additional fees and taxes and to exploit natural resources. Similar tensions to those in the political sphere have emerged over economic issues, in particular over whether the new village government or the *Adat* Council is to control the resources of the village. And here, as elsewhere in the Indonesian reform process, established elites that had benefited from the former project funding provided via Presidential Instructions are likely to see their revenues diminished and to be less than enthusiastic about the new system. The authors conclude that the results of decentralisation and the uptake of the new opportunities by the local population have so far been mixed. Paradoxically, the return to previous territorial boundaries can also be seen as a centralising element at the local level, and the continuation of the role of 'functional groups' and the rejection of party politics are, to some extent, also a continuation of Suharto era policies. Altogether, the village government remains firmly embedded in the state legal system. Rather than shaping the developments, transnational actors such as donor agencies find themselves often co-opted by various local parties struggling for predominance. They provide just one additional factor to the uneasy embrace of state, *adat* and religion as the main moral and regulatory orders.

In the final part of the book, Terence Halliday and Bruce Carruthers examine bankruptcy law reform in Indonesia, Korea and China as an example of the ongoing process of commercial law reform in much of the region. Bankruptcy law reform is an excellent example of the struggle between globalising forces and domestic interests in the commercial law arena. Corporate restructuring, with the possibility it offers to increase the influence of foreign creditors over local companies, often aligns national governments with various factions of the local elite in an effort to 'foil the hegemons'. Halliday and Carruthers' chapter 'Foiling the Financial Hegemons: Limits to the Globalisation of Corporate Insolvency Regimes in Indonesia, Korea and China' analyses the various strategies that are employed in the process.

The chapter begins with the apparent paradox that the Asian Crisis provided the international financial institutions (IFIs) with unprecedented influence in those countries affected by the Crisis, yet the achievements of the corporate insolvency reform process have so far been limited. The three countries chosen for the study had to contend with varying degrees of IFI pressure. It was most intense in Indonesia, only initially intense in Korea, and relatively weak in China, which had been largely insulated from the Crisis. As was the case in the example of decentralisation in the preceding part, bankruptcy reform was not new to Asia at the onset of the Crisis. The reform efforts in the countries under examination were preceded by new or amended bankruptcy legislation elsewhere in developing Asia (India, Singapore), in developing countries generally, or in leading OECD members such as the United States, the United Kingdom, France, Japan and Germany. Nevertheless, the intensity of IFI pressure on East and Southeast Asian loan recipients was unprecedented.

The discussion about the reception of bankruptcy reform in Asia is placed in the context of the larger debate about transplants of law in general and of commercial law in particular. Here, there is an array of different positions ranging from simple assumptions by comparative law scholars about easy transferability to more sophisticated studies requiring an examination of demand for the new law and the context of its adaptation. For Indonesia, these assumptions are tested against the backdrop of a legal system that had been falling into disrespect after many years of rule by authoritarian governments. Much of the international donor community was also divided about the best approach to corporate debt restructuring in the country. The first major reform measure was the creation of a Commercial Court with initially exclusive focus on bankruptcy matters, but the court remained embedded within the old court system and appeals continued to go directly to the Supreme Court. Judges were selected from the general courts and provided with only limited training. Equity considerations vis-à-vis the rest of the judiciary prevented the payment of more attractive salaries to Commercial Court judges. In spite of efforts to monitor cases and to improve the performance of the courts by using outside experts as ad hoc judges, the initial decisions of the Court in bankruptcy cases were highly controversial and much criticised. According to the authors, many of these decisions reflect a coincidence of personal economic interest, nationalist sentiment, social consciousness and plain political expediency.

A further reform mechanism was the Jakarta Initiative Task Force (JITF), a debt restructuring agency which handled US$17.5 billion in foreign currency debt and 7.8 trillion Rupiah in domestic debt by 1999. However, the JITF had little power, and the Memoranda of Understanding (MOUs) it helped to negotiate were merely letters of intent. The final focal point of IFI-influenced reform was the creation of the profession of receivers. Members of the newly-created profession also have to be members of the Receivers Association, which requires oral and written examinations in *Bahasa Indonesia*, thereby excluding the bulk of foreign professionals resident in Jakarta. Appointment of receivers depends on a court decision, which in turn has led—according to some allegations—to the appointment of debtor-friendly receivers. The authors conclude that for Indonesia most of the institutional reforms have been subverted.

In Korea, the IFIs were seeking nothing less than a restructuring of the power balance in the economy away from the technocrat ministries and towards the National Assembly and the President. Law, the judiciary and the legal profession were supposed to play a significant role in this process. Ironically, this enthusiasm for law was shared rather more by the Korean Ministry of Finance and Economy (MOFE) than by the Ministry of Justice, the Supreme Court, legal academics and practitioners. Because of the different approaches, reforms included both in-court, law-based initiatives as well as out-of-court, market-based experiments. Amendments to the bankruptcy procedures introduced in 1998 were designed to reduce judicial discretion and accelerate liquidation. A Management Committee was created to permit private sector experts to sit with judges on the courts. A specialised bankruptcy court was contemplated, but rejected as too expensive. Instead, a bankruptcy division was created within the Seoul District Court.

As for the out-of-court approach, the government brought together Korea's major financial institutions to enter into workout programmes for the largest conglomerates (*chaebols*). The problem for the IFIs with this approach was that it was contrary to their intention to reduce the role of the government, as the government had a controlling interest in many of the banks. Collusion and free riding by foreign banks were further problems. Because of the voluntary nature of this scheme, the government tried to give corporate restructuring a more forceful framework with the Corporate Restructuring Promotion Act of 2001. The Act allows for a restructuring plan to be passed by 75 per cent of the creditors. Lawyers objected to this inequitable solution, and foreign banks—who were mostly minority creditors—felt that they were excluded from the decision-making process.

Unification of the Bankruptcy Law, previously divided among three separate Acts, was another major reform measure included in a memorandum of the government to the IMF in 2000. By that time, Korea's economy had already recovered so that the IMF's influence was reduced to moral suasion. Lawyers in particular were unconvinced of the necessity for this reform. However, government circles sympathetic to the new law, in particular in MOFE, prevailed and it was enacted in 2005. In spite of IMF attempts to reduce MOFE intervention in the economy, the two institutions thus shared many goals. Ultimately, however, it remains to be seen whether the reform measures will last and how effective they will be.

Because of its attractiveness as a destination for foreign direct investment and because of the limited impact of the Asian Crisis, China has been in a much stronger bargaining position vis-à-vis the IFIs and foreign investors. As a consequence, international influence is much more limited. An Asian Development Bank report of 1996 on bankruptcy reform was simply buried without consequences. A subsequent World Bank report in 2001, together with expert advice from the German aid mission in Beijing, was much better received. Yet a draft bankruptcy law has remained under consideration by the Standing Committee of the National People's Congress since 2003. Ideological concerns about preserving China's 'socialist market economy' are difficult to overcome, as are concerns about the lack of social welfare institutions and the potential for political unrest.

In the final part of their chapter, Halliday and Carruthers outline various 'weapons of the weak' that help to explain the limited success of the IFIs in achieving corporate restructuring in the wake of the Asian Crisis. Avoidance of conditional foreign capital and aid is an obvious measure, and it has been successfully demonstrated by Malaysia during the Crisis and, to a lesser extent and for different reasons, by China. A government may further explicitly refuse, or only partially implement, specific recommendations by international agencies. There may also be fragmentation of both powerful external and internal coalitions that allow governments of nation states to disperse and segment their influence. Governments may further invoke cultural exceptionalism, as with the 'democracy/rule of law with Chinese characteristics' mentioned in Chen's chapter. A further strategy is symbolic compliance through legislation, but lack of enforcement, partial implementation or qualification through enabling legislation. Then there is the substitution of 'home-grown' solutions as in the various corporate restructuring proposals of the Korean government. Perhaps most common are delays in both legislating for reforms and implementing them, and these were used by all three countries to slow down the reform process. A similar strategy is to segment the reform measures and to try them out 'step by step' over a longer period, as is often practised in particular by China. Finally, there is the possibility of constructing exclusions and 'escape routes' from the reform process, as in the case of China's excluding state companies from the bankruptcy law. Other examples include retaining the option of ad hoc government intervention by China, and the retention by Korea of its equity interest in major banks.

The reasons for the limited success of the IFIs have to do with the IFI's lawyers' and economists' lack of institutional and cultural knowledge about the particular countries where they operate. The use of precedents from elsewhere often appears as a lack of sensitivity to national interests and sensibilities, and this in turn strengthens national resentment and resistance to reform proposals. What is most difficult with the various strategies outlined above is to tell the difference between intentional foiling of the IFIs and real institutional constraints. The effects of law reforms are difficult to measure and appear only after long lag-times. In spite of its apparently technical nature, bankruptcy law reform reaches deep into the institutional order and power structure of a society. The case studies further show that developing countries do have a choice, and may foil the financial hegemons even in rather extreme circumstances, such as the aftermath of the Asian Crisis. The question remains how long such resistance can and will be sustained.

BIBLIOGRAPHY

ABEGGLEN, JAMES C (1994) *Sea Change: Pacific Asia as the New World Industrial Center* (The Free Press, New York, Toronto).

ANDAYA, LEONARD Y (1992) 'Interactions with the Outside World and Adaptation in Southeast Asian Society, 1500-1800' in Nicholas Tarling (ed) *The Cambridge History of Southeast Asia – Volume One: From Early Times to c. 1800* (Cambridge University Press, Cambridge).

ANTONS, CHRISTOPH (1995) 'Analysing Asian Law: The Need for a General Concept' 13 (1) *Law in Context* 106.

—— (1997) 'Methodological Approaches to the Analysis of Asia-Pacific Legal Systems' in Johannes Feest and Erhard Blankenburg (eds) *Changing Legal Cultures* (International Institute for the Sociology of Law, Oñati).

—— (2003a) *Law and Development in East and Southeast Asia* (RoutledgeCurzon, London).

—— (2003b) 'Legal Culture and History of Law in Asia' in Christopher Heath (ed) *Intellectual Property Law in Asia* (Kluwer Law International, London).

APPELBAUM, RICHARD P and HENDERSON, JEFFREY (1992) *States and Development in the Asian Pacific Rim* (Sage Publications, Newbury Park-London-New Delhi).

Bernstein, Lisa (1996) 'Merchant Law in a Merchant Court: Rethinking the Code's Search for Immanent Business Norms' 144 *University of Pennsylvania Law Review* 1765.

CAUQUELIN, JOSIANE; LIM, PAUL; and MAYER-KÖNIG, BIRGIT (eds) (2000) *Asian Values: Encounter With Diversity* (Curzon, Richmond).

CHAUDHURI, K N (1985) *Trade and Civilisation in the Indian Ocean: An Economic History from the Rise of Islam to 1750* (Cambridge University Press, Cambridge).

CHEN, JIANFU (1995) *From Administrative Authorisation to Private Law – A Comparative Perspective of the Developing Civil Law in the People's Republic of China*, (Martinus Nijhoff Publishers, Dordrecht).

DAVIDSON, PAUL J (2002) *ASEAN: The Evolving Legal Framework for Economic Cooperation* (Times Academic Press, Singapore).

DIRLIK, ARIF (1993) *What is in a Rim? Critical Perspectives on the Pacific Region Idea* (Westview Press, Boulder-Oxford).

DOBBS-HIGGINSON, MICHAEL S (1993) *Asia-Pacific: Its Role in the New World Disorder* (Mandarin, London).

EISENSTADT, S N (1996) *Japanese Civilization: A Comparative View* (University of Chicago Press, Chicago).

ERIKSEN, THOMAS HYLLAND (2001) *Small Places, Large Issues: An Introduction to Social and Cultural Anthropology* (Pluto Press, London and Sterling, VA).

GHAI, YASH (2000) 'Rights, Duties and Responsibilities' in Josiane Cauquelin, Paul Lim and Birgit Mayer-König (eds) *Asian Values: Encounter With Diversity* (Curzon, Richmond, Surrey).

HAHM, PYONG-CHOON (1996) 'Korea's Initial Encounter with the Western Law 1866-1910 AD' in Sang-Hyun Song (ed) *Korean Law in the Global Economy* (Bak Young Sa, Seoul).

HARDING, ANDREW (2002) 'Global Doctrine and Local Knowledge: Law in South East Asia' 51 *International and Comparative Law Quarterly* 35.

HELD, DAVID and MCGREW, ANTHONY (2002) *Globalization/Anti-Globalization* (Polity Press, Cambridge).

HENDLEY, KATHRYN (2004) 'The Rule of Law and Economic Development in a Global Era' in Austin Sarat (ed) *The Blackwell Companion to Law and Society* (Blackwell, Oxford).

HEWISON, KEVIN; ROBISON, RICHARD; and RODAN, GARY (1993) *Southeast Asia in the 1990s: Authoritarianism, Democracy and Capitalism* (Allen & Unwin, Sydney).

HOOKER, M B (1975) *A Concise Legal History of South-East Asia* (Clarendon Press, Oxford).

—— (1986) *Laws of South-East Asia – Volume I: The Pre-Modern Texts* (Butterworth & Co (Asia), Singapore).

—— (ed) (1988) *The Laws of South-East Asia – Volume II: European Laws in South-East Asia. Essays on Portuguese and Spanish Laws, the Netherlands East Indies, English Law, American Law in the Philippines and the 'Europeanization' of Siam's Law* (Butterworths, Singapore).

ISHIHARA, SHINTARO (1991) *The Japan that can say no: Why Japan will be first among equals* (Simon & Schuster, New York).

ISLAM, IYANATUL and CHOWDHURY, ANIS (1997) *Asia-Pacific Economies* (Routledge, London and New York).

JAYASURIYA, KANISHKA (ed) (1999) *Law, Capitalism and Power in Asia* (Routledge, London and New York).

JENKINS, RICHARD (1996) *Social Identity* (Routledge, London and New York).

JOMO, K S (2003) *Southeast Asian Paper Tigers? – From miracle to debacle and beyond* (RoutledgeCurzon, London and New York).

JONES, ERIC; FROST, LIONEL; and WHITE, COLIN (1993) *Coming Full Circle: An Economic History of the Pacific Rim* (Oxford University Press Australia, Melbourne).

LEE, KEUN (1993) *New East Asian Economic Development: Interacting Capitalism and Socialism* (M E Sharpe, Armonk, NY, and London).

LINDER, STAFFAN BURENSTAM (1986) *The Pacific Century: Economic and Political Consequences of Asian-Pacific Dynamism* (Stanford University Press, Stanford).

MACAULAY, STEWART (1963) 'Non-Contractual Relations in Business: A Preliminary Study' 28 *American Sociological Review* 55.

MAHATHIR MOHAMAD and SHINTARO ISHIHARA (1995) *The Voice of Asia: Two Leaders Discuss the Coming Century* (Kodansha International, Tokyo).

MOUER, ROSS and SUGIMOTO, YOSHIO (1986) *Images of Japanese Society* (Kegan Paul International, London).

PEERENBOOM, RANDALL (2002) *China's Long March toward Rule of Law* (Cambridge University Press, Cambridge).

PEERENBOOM, RANDALL (ed) (2004) *Asian Discourses of Rule of Law – Theories and implementation of rule of law in twelve Asian countries, France and the U.S.* (RoutledgeCurzon, London and New York).

RASIAH, RAJAH (2003) 'Manufacturing export growth in Indonesia, Malaysia and Thailand' in K S Jomo (ed) *Southeast Asian Paper Tigers? – From miracle to debacle and beyond* (RoutledgeCurzon, London and New York).

REISCHAUER, EDWIN O and FAIRBANK, JOHN K (1958 and 1960) *East Asia: The Great Tradition* (Houghton Mifflin Company/Charles E Tuttle Company, Boston and Tokyo).

ROBISON, RICHARD; HEWISON, KEVIN; and HIGGOTT, RICHARD (1987) *Southeast Asia in the 1980s: The Politics of Economic Crisis* (Allen & Unwin, Sydney, London, Boston).

SIMONE, VERA and FERARU, ANNE THOMPSON (1995) *The Asian Pacific: Political and Economic Development in a Global Context* (Longman Publishers USA, White Plains, NY).

STUBBS, RICHARD (1994) 'The Political Economy of the Asia-Pacific Region' in Richard Stubbs and Geoffrey R D Underhill (eds) *Political Economy and the Changing Global Order* (Macmillan, Houndsmills and London).

—— (2005) *Rethinking Asia's Economic Miracle* (Palgrave Macmillan, Houndsmills and New York).

TAKAYANAGI, KENZŌ (1976), 'A Century of Innovation: The Development of Japanese Law, 1868-1961' in Hideo Tanaka and Malcolm H D Smith (eds) *The Japanese Legal System* (University of Tokyo Press, Tokyo).

TAN, GERALD (1996) *ASEAN: Economic Development and Cooperation* (Times Academic Press, Singapore).

TAY, SIMON S C; ESTANISLAO, JESUS P and SOESASTRO, HADI (2001) *Reinventing ASEAN* (Institute of Southeast Asian Studies, Singapore).

WORLD BANK (2005) <http://web.worldbank.org/WBSITE/EXTERNAL/TOPICS/EXTLAWJUSTINST/0,contentMDK:20745861~menuPK:1989584~pagePK:210058~piPK:210062~theSitePK:1974062,00.html> last accessed 26 February 2006.

PART 1:

ASIAN CAPITALISM(S) AND LAW REFORM: GLOBALISATION AND RESISTANCE

2

Legalisation and the Varieties of Capitalism

VOLKMAR GESSNER

I INTRODUCTION

IN THE AFTERMATH of the Asian Financial Crisis of 1997, attention has shifted from the supposed benefits of East Asian institutional arrangements to their costs. Asia's recent financial crises:

> ravaged the credibility of a supposedly distinctive East Asian, or Japanese, model of economic growth based on cooperation between conglomerates—Japan's keiretsu, South Korea's chaebol, Indonesia's konglomerat—and astute government officials. (Emmerson, 1998: 47)

Administrative discretion, often leading to administrative guidance and previously the core of the Asian developmental state model (Ginsburg, 2001: 585–6), is discredited. The East Asian state is now seen as captured, corrupt and opaque. A similar change has been observed in commercial relationships. Traditionally the role of written contracts in governance of the relationship was very different from in the West. Within a short period of time modern commercial practices, particularly in international transactions, increasingly tended to resemble Western practices and the rule of law as a condition of cross-border commerce is met by enthusiastic acceptance and law-making by Asian policy-makers (McConnaughay, 2001).

This rapid change of view leaves us somewhat uncomfortable. Shall we give up theoretical assumptions as soon as signs of economic inefficiency appear in public discourses? At least for legal sociologists Asian developmental states and Asian styles of economic exchange were and are a constant challenge to theories within the law and development debate. The Asian evidence seemed to cause concerns about the accuracy of modernisation theory and in particular about Max Weber's assumptions as to the close links between legal rationalisation and the rise of capitalism. We will elaborate on these concerns and will support those positions which take the experience of the economies of Asia as empirical evidence for the 'varieties of capitalism'.

The difference between the rule of law and legalisation is a matter of degree, the latter being the attempt to reduce autonomous regulation and legalise public and private activities as completely as possible. The last two decades were characterised by a strong movement towards legalisation. In the domestic sphere some, such as the post-communist countries, are generally defined as lacking the rule of law while others, such as the Latin American countries, are considered as having a weak court system. In the international realm legal rules are developed for public policy areas, such as trade, environment, labour, money laundering and copyright, as well as for contract enforcement (Wiener, 1999). According to Bonell (1990), countless international conventions, uniform laws, codes, and rules of conduct attempt to regulate the most varied aspects of global dealings by means of uniform rulings. In the area of commercial law the first objective is predictability and stability in international commercial relations by the establishment of universal standards and the reduction of legal risks of global trade. Unification efforts have therefore concentrated on contract law and the resolution of contractual disputes. Development strategies emphasise legal certainty as a prerequisite for a market economy. In the words of one of the Vice-Presidents of the World Bank:

> As developing and transition countries began to move en masse towards market economies, they adopted strategies for the encouragement of local and foreign private investment. There is ample evidence that the establishment of the rule of law attracts private investment, to the extent that it creates a climate of stability and predictability, where business risks may be rationally assessed, property rights protected, and contractual obligations honored. More generally, experience supports the proposition that the rule of law is needed to give credibility to commitments on the part of the governments, and reliability and enforceability to applicable rules. This, in turn, leads to lower transaction costs, greater access to capital, and the maintenance of level playing fields. As a result of this experience, recent literature on economic development has placed greater emphasis on institutional economics, notably on preserving the quality of institutions through the establishment and maintenance of an appropriate and workable legal framework. (Shihata, 1997: 1579)

The World Bank offers loans to finance legal and judicial reform projects and has given grants for the initial studies needed for this purpose. Equally active are USAID and the EU Commission through its PHARE and TEMPUS programmes directed towards Central and Eastern European states. Most law faculties in Western countries have some members, or even entire departments, active in promoting the rule of law in developing countries, in countries in transition from state to market economies or in the global arena where cross-border exchanges lack calculability and certainty.

These activities are criticised for their naïvety, for imperialist attitudes or simply for the self-interest prevalent among the lawyers and academics involved. But they may also be discussed on a more theoretical level, focusing on the assumptions underlying the vast literature, programmes and projects. One approach ('law and development'/'modernisation') claims that modernisation processes lead naturally to legal structures similar to those that can be observed in Western societies, and that global structures will also emerge on the same model. Another prominent theory often alluded to as justification for legalisation is that of 'institutional economics', where rules and institutions are considered mechanisms for effective transaction costs avoidance. A third theory offered frequently as justification is Max Weber's process of legal rationalisation running from traditional irrational forms to formal, bureaucratic forms of legal domination. This chapter first (section II) attempts to develop arguments that these theories do not necessarily support programmes of exporting the European model of law to other social environments. Secondly (section III), it will point to some empirical observations as to how social interactions and in particular economic transactions can be secured by rational means but without formal rational law. Whether legal rationalisation is our 'fate' (Weber) and informal rules and institutions are necessarily out-dated cannot be taken for granted. New social situations outside the realm of the Western nation state might require a reassessment of established theoretical assumptions.

Currently two intermediate positions, between the promotion of the European model of law and the recognition of less orderly forms of autonomous regulation, are articulated in and implemented by new law and development as well as in law and globalisation activities. One position recognises structural differences and advocates a cautious approach when formal law is created in a non-Western or global context (see, for example, Seidman and Seidman, 1996). Another position distinguishes between 'good law', protecting property rights, and 'bad law', regulating the market (see, for example, De Soto, 1986). Such intermediate positions make much sense and are highly influential among those preparing policies of international organisations. From an academic point of view it is more challenging to first discuss some basic theoretical assumptions and then look for empirical evidence. Intermediate positions may, of course, also follow from such an exercise.

This chapter will not deal with another debate which turns on the feasibility of law exports to another legal culture. Alan Watson, a legal historian, suggests that law has always been easily transferred from one legal culture to another and has never been rejected for cultural reasons

(Watson, 1985). Many comparative lawyers agree but legal sociologists tend to disagree strongly. Friedman's statement that Watson's position is ludicrous could be the end of this debate (Friedman, 2001; see also Cotterrell, 2001). Law must be observed in its social context and cannot be treated as a technical device instrumental for a tiny group of lawyers in a society 'receiving' a foreign code, a foreign legal institution, a foreign legal principle. A legal change or legal transformation must be observed in action in order to have any sociological relevance.

II THEORETICAL ANALYSES OF THE EUROPEAN MODEL OF LEGAL REGULATION

A Core Ideas of Theories of Legalisation

The concept of 'modernity' has emerged from a number of dichotomies, such as homogeneity versus differentiation (Herbert Spencer), mechanical versus organic solidarity (Émile Durkheim), community versus society (Ferdinand Tönnies), status versus contract (Henry S Maine). Normative structures vary from religious to secular and from particularistic to universalistic types of regulation (Talcott Parsons). According to Friedman (1994), modern legal cultures can be characterised by a number of features: the continuous adaptation of the law to changing social conditions (rejection of the idea that law is 'natural'); a wide coverage of law in most sectors of society; an instrumental legitimation of law (only law which serves a certain acceptable purpose is legitimate); the institutionalisation of constitutional and political control of regulatory agencies; and their focus on the individual (and not some collective such as 'the people', 'the working class', etc). Due to the globalisation of the economy, modern technology, modern communication, urbanisation and the differentiation of society, legal cultures of the world tend to modernise and to converge. It follows that legal cultures which are as yet not modernised are at a comparative disadvantage: they are internally illegitimate, unable to compete in the world economy and contribute little to the development of global regulatory structures (international cooperation). Although modernisation is considered to be an historical trend it can be accelerated by legal education and legal assistance in legislative measures and court reform. 'Law and development' was a strong movement in the 1960s and grew even stronger after the fall of the Berlin Wall. Domestic legal cultures all over the world are currently in the process of modernisation and legalisation. Modernisation theorists also observe the emergence of a transnational legal culture (Friedman, 1996) based on the model of historical experiences of the nation state.

In current economic debate, institutional economics theory supports the idea of legalisation based on transaction costs analysis. In his critique of classical economic thinking, Ronald Coase in his famous article 'The Problem of Social Cost' (1960) followed the Hobbesian tradition that in a society without a sovereign, all would be chaos. In analysing the effect that changes in law might have on human interactions, Coase assumed that governments have a monopoly on rule-making functions. Another of the classic works on law and economics, and law and transaction costs (Calabresi and Melamed, 1972), regarded the state as the sole source of social order. Transaction cost analysis was then further developed by Douglass North (1990) who explains economic performance as a dependent variable of efficient institutions: 'Transaction costs are only two things: (1) the costs of measuring the dimensions of whatever it is that is being produced or exchanged and (2) the costs of enforcement' (North, 1999: 5). If the measurement of quality, the analysis and comparison of price, the enforcement of contracts and so forth cause transaction costs, economic actors can be, and in reality generally are, supported by institutions which reduce the investment in situations of choice. He posits that rationality, in the sense that economists talk about it, works best when the choices of the players are most limited. Markets therefore have to be structured by rules and institutions. In their empirical study Wallis and North (1986) observed that in the United States state expenditures increased for rule-making and institution-building over a period of a hundred years, but economies in developing countries lack institutional support and we do not have such an institutional structure for the global economy (North, 1999).

A third source of support for legalisation is Max Weber's theory of economic development and legal rationality. A conflict of egoistic wills is an inherent part of capitalism leading potentially to a world of radical uncertainty. But exchange in the market, the generalised use of money, rational capital accounting, rational organisation of labour in production and separation of the enterprise from the household all require calculability. After a lengthy development from traditional, irrational, patrimonial, charismatic forms of domination, it is the legal form of coercion which guarantees predictability of economic behaviour in modern societies. A system of government through rules offers more certainty than any other method for structuring coercion. Rules are created by logical and systematic processes, leading to juridical formalism, which enables the legal system to operate as a technically rational machine would and increases the possibility of predicting the legal consequences of one's action. At the same time, rational bureaucracies, independent courts, legal scholars and the legal profession are working together in order to achieve the goal of a rationally organised society (Trubek, 1972). And calculability is crucial for the capitalist enterprise:

> The modern capitalist enterprise rests primarily on *calculation* and presupposes a legal and administrative system, whose functioning can be rationally predicted, at least in principle, by virtue of its fixed general norms, just like the expected performance of a machine. (Weber, 1968: 1394)

Weber's theory of institutional evolution was formed in the earlier periods of his scholarship and was based on Darwinian assumptions about social learning: formal rational institutions are selected by a struggle for survival. Later he recognised tensions between formal and substantive rationality and conceived formal structures rather as an iron cage where individual or collective activities are hopelessly imprisoned. In order to act socially responsibly one cannot only ask *what* has to be done but also *how* it can be done correctly. Despite his own ambivalent attitude, Weber finally seemed to make peace with this arrangement since formal rationality mostly leaves some (limited) freedom for pursuing purpose rational goals.

B Beyond Legal Centralism

These core ideas of sociological and economic theory of law are generally accepted as justification for the centrality of legal reasoning in Western societies and seem to support legal initiatives in developing countries, in transition societies and in efforts for creating legal structures for global exchanges both in China and—since their recent crisis—in the more developed Asian states. But the picture is incomplete if we overstate the role of law in modernisation theory, institutional economics and in the school based on Weber's work on economy and society. What is often under-appreciated is that all those approaches discuss or even emphasise the role that non-legal systems play in achieving social order and predictability. They either recognise informal orders as complementary or argue that their role is limited due to historical circumstances in specific (Western) societies. None of these theories allows us to generalise a thesis of the centrality of law to non-Western societies, to Third World society or even to future developments in our own (Western) culture. As Douglass North (1999: 11) tells us on the background of his historical expertise and his experience as an advisor for law reform in developing countries: 'what works today is not going to work tomorrow'.

Modernisation theory has produced a vast amount of research on legal and non-legal institutions in developing countries, institutions such as tribal forms of dispute resolution, Islamic banking, Chinese *guanxi* business relations, norms of reciprocity among Latin-American squatters, Taiwanese credit associations, etc. The general message is that non-legal institutions work in the specific traditional context but that tensions arise with the imposition of state structures and the changing expectations of a population affected by Western values and habits. Convergence is assumed to happen, not necessarily because of imports and imposition but because of structural changes. Education, industrialisation and increased mobility lead to a 'rights consciousness', the use of state courts, legislation, constitutionalisation and (claims for) protection of human rights. There is a clear bias towards promoting the Western model of the *Rechtsstaat* or US-style of rule of law, but in analysing non-Western legal cultures modernisation theory is certainly not suffering from legal centralism. Modernisiation theory also recognises 'civil society' aspects of social ordering, that is, regulatory responsibilities assumed by non-state actors in the Western model of the nation state. The emphasis on individualism by most representatives of this approach leads to deregulation rather than to legal centralism as the preferred policy objective. Critical positions within modernisation theory have pointed to co-existing traditional and instrumental, particularistic and universalistic, irrational and rational elements in 'modern' societies as well as to frequent contrary developments in history (National Socialism, Fascism, fundamentalism and communitarianism) which cast serious doubts on the assumption of a linear evolution to modernity (Wehler, 1975).

Institutional economics recognise non-legal institutions as important and—even in developed economies—ubiquitous limits of individual choices.

> Institutions define the structure of human interaction. By 'institutions', I mean three things: (1) the formal rules of the game that are defined in legal terms, (2) the informal norms of behavior that supplement and complement and modify institutions, and (3) the effectiveness of enforcement mechanisms. It is the mixture of the three that determines the effectiveness of institutions in influencing transaction costs. And the effect of institutions on transaction costs is obviously important. (North, 1999: 7)

Informal norms of behaviour are customs and conventions, standards, rules and values. They define and limit preferences of economic actors either generally or within specific groups (minorities, occupations, geographically bounded industries, age groups, etc). They complement formal rules or compete with them or negate them. Within the school of institutional economics there are some who maintain that welfare-maximising actors use informal rather than formal rules (Ellickson, 1991). But the realm of cooperation is limited to close-knit groups. Moving from personal to impersonal markets leads to formalisation and institutionalisation: when shifting from a world of personal exchange to a world of impersonal exchange (to use a game theory analogy), one moves from a world in which it pays the players to cooperate to a world in which it pays the players to defect (North, 1999). Cooperative institutions are replaced by coercive institutions in order to cope with 'free-rider' behaviour. Other forms of coercion being absent, or limited to specific groups or specific situations, legal institutions prove more efficient for limiting choices and reducing uncertainty.

The centrality of law in Weber's theory has to be qualified not so much because of his 'England problem' but for empirical assumptions which hold true neither for developing or transformation countries nor for structures created by the globalising economy. The observation that England, the birthplace of capitalism, seemed to lack the calculable, logically formal, legal system that he identified as necessary for capitalist development, troubled Weber (1964: 719, 724, 1036). His discussion on that issue is often considered ambiguous and contradictory (Trubek, 1972: 747; Treiber, 1989: 376). England is certainly a deviant case for a theory of formal legal rationality but not necessarily for a theory of the centrality of law in modern society. Weber criticised the English common law for its lack of formal rationality and its class bias but he recognised its importance for the English economy. Due to strong links between the capitalist class and English lawyers and the lawyers' crucial role in generating precedents, the English legal system was predictable for social and economic elites (Weber, 1964: 1049; Treiber, 1989: 374; Francis, 1983).

Weber's empirical assumptions leading to his thesis regarding the centrality of law read as follows:

> From a purely theoretical point of view, legal guaranty *by the state* is not indispensable to any basic economic phenomenon. The protection of property, for example, can be provided by the mutual aid system of kinship groups . . . But an economic system, especially of the modern type, could certainly not exist without a legal order with very special features which could not develop except in the frame of a public legal order. Present-day economic life rests on opportunities acquired through contracts. It is true, the private interests in the obligations of contract, and the common interest of all property holders in the mutual protection of property are still considerable, and individuals are still markedly influenced by convention and custom even today. Yet the influence of these factors has declined due to the disintegration of tradition, i.e., of the tradition-determined relationships as well as of the belief in their sacredness . . . Modern economic life by its very nature has destroyed those other associations which used to be the bearers of law and thus of legal guaranties. This has been the result of the development of the market. The universal predominance of the market consociation requires on the one hand a legal system the functioning of which is *calculable* in accordance with rational rules. On the other hand, the constant expansion of the market . . . has favored the monopolization and regulation of all 'legitimate' coercive power by *one* universalist coercive institution through the disintegration of all particularist status-determined and other coercive structures which have been resting mainly on economic monopolies. (Weber, 1968: 336–7)

The assumption is that the 'modern economy' has destroyed conventions and customs in particularistic structures which previously had guaranteed contract enforcement and the protection of property. The enlargement of markets resulted in the replacement of small scale regulation by universalistic coercion. Weber thus clearly recognises informal norms and institutions as equivalent to legal coercion in providing calculability and legal certainty. He only believes that those non-legal norms and non-state institutions have ceased to be relevant in a modern economy.

It is already questionable whether this assumption is correct for modern Western economies. Legal sociology and anthropology have produced numerous examples of particularistic regulatory structures, as well as informal universalistic rules, all around us. But the absence and irrelevance of non-state regulation in general, and within the economy in particular, can definitely not be assumed for developing and transition countries or the global economy. Hence Weber's main thesis on the central role of law proves not to be universally applicable. If calculability is the only problem for economic actors—which is questionable—law in most societies is not the only remedy.

C Regulation and Contract Enforcement

Institutional economics and Weber's approach perceive non-legal institutions as in principle equivalent to legal institutions. Modernisation theory has a clear preference for legal institutions developed historically in Western societies but also recognises emergent 'civil society' structures in modern states. Hence social sciences are not generally supporting a legalist strategy in modernisation, rationalisation or welfare-maximising reforms. New environments such as those in developing or transformation countries or the global economy may sometimes require the continuation of traditional forms or the invention of new models of social and economic institutions.

An important distinction has to be made between the protection of public goods and the protection of contractual expectations. In the first case legal institutions tend to play a more important role than in the second case.

Public goods are traditionally also regulated by non-legal institutions: education and religion as universal institutions seek to protect a society and those within it from criminal behaviour, environmental damage, corruption and exploitation. Particularistic norms and standards are enforced by institutions such as the family, corporations, professional communities, peer groups etc. But the expectations of public goods protection are rising with industrialisation, communication, emancipation and many other factors and cannot be met only by informal social control.

There is some scattered evidence of successful self-regulation in areas such as labour standards, human rights, environment, corruption and pornography on the Internet (Furger, 2001). Product standardisation, which might also be called a public good, is certainly successfully regulated by non-state institutions. But in the main these are areas of public law regulation where self-regulation is often created as a shield from state intervention and weakly monitored. Public law and legal sanctions are preferable where self-regulation suffers from the 'free-rider' problem, where regulatory needs go beyond group interests, where major costs occur in preparing and controlling rules and standards, and where democratic legitimation is required.

The protection of contractual expectations is crucial in the modern contractual society where hierarchical relations are replaced by horizontal relations (Shapiro, 1993). In the world of vertically integrated production units, economic relationships are determined by internal command. Socialism is not the only example of vertical integration. Vertical integration has also been the dominant feature of capitalist corporations where not only workers but also suppliers and primary customers are kept 'in house' in order to coordinate economic decisions and avoid the insecurity of markets. All this has changed, socialism has almost vanished and the Western corporation has moved toward decentralized structures where internal directives are replaced by deals, agreements and contracts. Spin-offs, franchises, independent contractors, joint ventures etc are characteristics of these contractual structures and the new economy with all kinds of 'software' services going in the same direction. There is some evidence of similar developments in public administration, universities and public enterprises.

Correspondingly, contract enforcement and calculability are—as in the periods observed by Max Weber—again crucial for the economy and require institutional support. This support is offered by contract law, lawyers and courts as well as by non-legal institutions, such as *lex mercatoria* rules, arbitration and social bonding. Unlike public good protection, contract enforcement is to a significant degree supported by norms (and sanctions) of cooperation and reciprocity. In big or small business, local or long-distance trade, Western or Asian economies, communitarian regulation and social control through reputation mechanisms are common phenomena. Experimental situations in game theory have shown that in the transition from a world of personal exchange to a world of impersonal exchange one moves from a world of cooperation to a world of sanctions (North, 1999). But it is sociology rather than game theory which determines the actual importance of communitarian bonds and personal exchange.

D Comparing Formal and Informal Institutions

There is no general answer to the question whether formal or informal institutions are preferable. Transaction costs, efficiency, flexibility, legitimacy, fairness and rationality are some of the criteria used for a comparison—and valid measurement always depends on specific features of the institution and its environment.

Formal legal institutions tend to be universal, informal ones particularistic. The most formal and most universalistic institution is a legal code. European codifications, such as the French *Code Napoleon*, the German *Bürgerliches Gesetzbuch*, the Spanish *Código Civil*, have been copied in many parts of the world and are held in high esteem for their rationality. Their universalism has—supported by doctrinal research and legal education—created highly unified legal systems. Currently there are strong tendencies to formulate such a universal civil code for the European Union in order to build on the unifying capacity of the codification idea. Apart from rationality the legal code probably also scores highly in providing internal efficiency for the community of lawyers and judges who operate technically highly sophisticated and calculable tools of entitlements and remedies. More doubtful is the external efficiency of such a code since abstract, universal norms do not necessarily take account of problems of comprehensibility for the general public, of alternative preferences and values within segments of the general public or of other implementation barriers. In regard to many other criteria, such as flexibility, legitimacy, fairness and creativity, legal codes have little to offer and are at a clear disadvantage to the common law system based largely on precedents and ad hoc decisions by judges and juries. To my knowledge the transaction costs incurred by both systems have so far not been systematically studied.

As regards the criteria of transaction costs and efficiency in the comparison of legal norms with non-legal norms, many scholars influenced by the law and economics approach have a clear preference for self-regulation (Cooter, 1996; Furger, 2001). The measurement of efficiency of agreed standards is easier for the actors themselves who can also decide on the investment for monitoring rules and the benefits, or otherwise, drawn from sanctions. They calculate the costs of opportunism and governance and choose the rule structure that minimises costs. Institutional economists, on the other hand, strongly disagree. They point to lower transaction costs when preferred patterns of behaviour are institutionalised instead of being created de novo for every single situation. As North (1999) notes: 'Markets have to be structured'. In impersonal markets these institutions tend to be legal institutions.

Whether impersonal markets discourage the building of business networks or close relationships between firms is also controversial. In classical economics mutually profitable exchanges are coordinated by price mechanisms: transactions are continued if the price is acceptable given the market conditions, and are discontinued if the commodity is traded at a lower price elsewhere. Contract law secures and enforces such discrete transactions. A different approach has been developed by relational contract theory (for an economic analysis Williamson, 1975; 1979; 1981; 1985; for a legal analysis Macneil, 1980). Business exchanges are said to range from markets, where buyers and sellers bear no dependency relation with each other and where the identity of the parties is irrelevant, through relational contracts, that is 'various forms of long-term contracting, reciprocal trading, regulation, franchising, and the like' (Williamson, 1991: 280), to hierarchy (the Coasean firm with its cost-avoiding command structures). Increased insecurity in complex economies—caused by limited information, limited rationality, and by opportunism—leads to increasing transaction costs which make the price mechanism less efficient, and relational and hierarchical models more efficient.

As a consequence of the Coase-Williamson critique of classical economics, the social integration of business relations has become a major focus of research in various disciplines. Marketing and management research discusses innovative arrangements and determinants of long-term orientation in buyer-seller relationships, psychologists discover that trust yields economic benefits, and legal scholars recognise and acknowledge the importance of cooperative behaviour that goes beyond purely contractual obligations.

E Law and Other Forms of Rationality

From the preceding discussions it follows that the emphasis on legal institutions in modernisation theory, institutional economics and Weber's analysis of the relationship between economy and society is misleading insofar as law appears to be the only path to modernity and prosperity. It is true that law is considered to be the key variable in explaining Western developments towards rational government and market security. Law was successful in providing rationality. But if rationality is the ultimate goal, alternatives to law are imaginable—if not in Western societies surrounded by nation state boundaries, then possibly in developing or transition societies or the globalising economy. In discussing potential alternative developments toward rationality one avoids ethnocentric or ideological biases of legal centralism. Some or all of the major elements of legal rationality, such as legitimacy, transparency, calculability, universality or scientific support and control, may in other social environments be achieved by means other than legislation, legal scholarship and formal bureaucracy. Numerous examples of rational non-legal institutions are produced in social science literature, ranging from the Chinese clan corporation (Ruskola, 2000), the Polish civil rights commissioner (Jaster, 1996) and Mexican institutions for resolving economic and labour disputes (Gessner, 1975; 1986), to Taiwanese rotating credit associations (Kaufman Winn, 1994). All kinds of social institution have been created in order to foster legal certainty for cross-border transactions (Gessner and Budak, 1998). Without claiming more than those studies have previously done, section III of this chapter will briefly summarise the existing knowledge about institutions created for the global economy in particular and which provide a high degree of rationality, namely relational contracts in the export business, *lex mercatoria* rules and mega law firms.

III RATIONAL ALTERNATIVES TO LAW IN CONTRACT ENFORCEMENT

A Social Bonding

Traditions and customs of social bonding are commonly contrasted to formal law, and described as major barriers to economic prosperity. Societies and economies 'mature' insofar as they accomplish changes from relational to formal legal orientations. In a recent study (Nichols, 1999) this factor is chosen as the key variable for a 'legal theory of emerging economies'—a problematic choice in view of other observations and discussions which emphasise the rationality behind relational contracting in Asian as well as in Western economies.

Social bonding as an alternative to law is still very common, particularly among Asian business communities (Appelbaum, 1998). The literature on Chinese business practices emphasises the role of closely affiliated networks called *guanxi* (established and maintained by ties generated by a sentiment of mutual obligation) rather than purely instrumental calculation (Yang, 1994). In order to achieve this informal mode of integration, based on mutual dependency and trust, business is often carried out on the basis of family relationships. Chinese business relationships involve what is referred to as *guanxi* logic: a mixture of normative, instrumental and affective elements. *Guanxi* relationships 'balance obligation and sanction, on the one hand, and flexibility and instrumentality, on the other hand' (Chung and Hamilton, 2001: 330). In this sense, *guanxi* pervades Chinese economic activity to a high degree, fostering cooperation and predictability. Inter-firm alliances are based on personal relationships and obligations, rather than more formal connections such as legal and contractual bonds. Outside Asian communities Bernstein's (1992) analysis of the diamond trade is most suggestive of a similar level of social control exerted through non-legal means as dealers and brokers 'opt out of the legal system' by creating a completely autonomous normative community with merchant rules, blacklisting, reputational bonds and—as last resort—arbitration.

The diamond trading merchants may be a rather exceptional 'tribe', due to very particular social, economic and even religious bonds. On the other hand, social bonding and *guanxi* can be taken simply as synonyms for networks of personal relationships common among business people the world over. The markets may not be as impersonal as assumed by our theoretical approaches. A closer look at regulatory mechanisms in business networks and an analysis of the role of law in contracts and dispute resolution seem to be promising research areas. In general, the autonomy of these communities tends to be overestimated, due to persisting state law effects. This was demonstrated by Bernstein (1996) in another study where she observed the arbitration practice of the US National Grain and Feed Association. The arbitration awards never take notice of autonomous norms and usages of this trade and apply contract law strictly and even more formalistically than state courts. She develops an interesting hypothesis in explaining her observations: autonomous norms are used to preserve the relationship whereas legal norms offer solutions for ending the relationship. Macaulay, who has first pointed to non-contractual relations between US businessmen (Macaulay, 1963) and since then emphasised the relational approach, strongly disagrees with Bernstein. He asserts that after a long business relationship ruled by custom, a return to the original paper deal, the contract, may be considered unfair. In addition, given the costs of litigation and all the difficulties of enforcing judgments, contract law will often be largely symbolic (Macaulay, 2000).

Despite this controversy in interpreting empirical observations, social bonding has become a major device for creating stable and reliable business relationships, domestically and internationally. Networks of social relationships penetrate different sectors of economic life (Granovetter, 1985). Where economic transactions are embedded in social bonds, the hazards of opportunism are diminished and the need for elaborate formal governance structures is rendered unnecessary. Bradach and Eccles (1989) demonstrate the frequent instrumental use of trust in economic relations, such as between rail-freight carriers and automobile shippers, sales agents and their customers, general contractors and subcontractors, investments bankers and companies. They point to highly rational considerations in choosing either the advantages of trust mechanisms or hierarchical structures such as franchising or contractual relations such as joint ventures, global coalitions or other forms of legal cooperation. Another much discussed example is the Japanese *keiretsu,* large enterprise groups where business is kept as much as possible within the group and a high degree of give and take is expected (Dore, 1983).

The use of inter-firm relationships based on trust is a much debated subject in international management research. Although those relationships are observed more frequently among domestic partners than among firms of different nations (Gulati, 1995: 95, 105), and as a consequence the relative importance of formal contractual arrangements is greater in international business transactions (Kiedaisch, 1997; 171–84) this relative importance of formal written contracts in global trade does not necessarily indicate a strong influence of traditional contract law doctrines in this area. There seems to have developed a new form of rationality which is not yet theoretically fully explained. The international system was re-interpreted as a 'relational society' (Gottlieb, 1983) and as a 'regime' rather than an as institutional structure (Krasner, 1983). Traditional legal approaches to explain behavioural patterns of nation states, international governmental and non-governmental organisations, as well as business actors, are beginning to be perceived as largely inadequate. The conduct of these actors is far removed from the demands of the formal legal order, and is mainly guided by relational practices. Most conventions under public international law are better characterised by a regime of autochthonous rules, procedures, precedents, and practices that emerge out of a sustained relationship between two or more actors. Regimes are concerned with interactions over time. They discourage the assignment of exclusive weight to formal documents and to the original intentions of the parties. Gottlieb (1983) points to international loan agreements where enforcement is simply out of the question for the banks.

B *Lex Mercatoria*

In the globalising economy, legal rules of nation state origin or—exceptionally—of transnational origin, such as European Union law, are competing with rules created by the community of business actors. This so-called *lex mercatoria*, understood in its widest sense, may be customary, conventional, non-conventional, contractual, codified or uncodified, or it may be derived from the general principles of law or trade usages. The different categories of the principles and rules that constitute the corpus of the *lex mercatoria* are of transnational origin and character, and are applicable to cross-border transactions (Gessner, 1996): see Table 1 (opposite).

The legal standing of the law merchant is controversial. Most approaches conceive of an anational, autonomous system of rules articulated by the international business community to regulate its activities. Other approaches, while also recognising autonomous and non-state sources such as trade associations and arbitration, include international conventions and define the *lex mercatoria* as the harmonisation of international and municipal trade law. But the legal discourse also reveals that: (a) the law merchant rules are partly universal but sometimes very specific and particularistic; (b) the rules are imperfect and incomplete and therefore often require additionally a choice of law clause in an international contract; (c) their identity is vague due to definitional controversies; (d) there are no mandatory rules; (e) the process is highly lacking in transparency, due to the lack of sufficient reasoning in many arbitral awards and the infrequent reporting of (mostly confidential) decisions; (f) the application of this body of rules is rarely tolerated in domestic courts and is exceptional even in arbitration; and (g) its legitimacy is doubtful due to insufficient democratic control and participation (Gessner, Appelbaum and Felstiner, 2001). Social-scientific studies which attempt to give an answer to the question of the problem-solving capacity of the law merchant provide a patchwork of theoretical and empirical insights, and seem generally positive as regards the acceptance and efficiency of this approach (Gessner, 1996; De Ly, 2001; Teubner, 1997). From a sociological (not a legal) perspective *lex mercatoria* rules are complementary to contract law, making use of the freedom of contract granted by state law. They are always subject to state interference, therefore precarious, and far from constituting an autonomous (non-state) legal system. The doctrinal controversy about their legal qualification hides the fact that *lex mercatoria* rules are part of a legal discourse and therefore not a good example of legal pluralism (Gessner, 2002).

Lex mercatoria rules lack some of the elements of legal rationality, in particular the formal elements. On the other hand, because of their recognition of the wills of the parties, they offer a high degree of substantive rationality. Autonomous values, specific needs and the received wisdoms of business communities are influential in shaping this set of rules. Most important are arbitral awards in expressing customs and standards of international trade which may in many instances be very different from municipal standards and rules. The vagueness of some of the principles is often conceived as an advantage in comparison to strict and inflexible municipal law and the doctrinal hurdles of private international law. The culture of global business transactions requires a different rationality from that of domestic exchanges.

Table 1: The normative order of the law merchant

1 Universal norms
- York-Antwerp Rules on liability in ship collisions (International Law Association)
- Warsaw Rules on CIF contracts (International Law Association)
- Guidelines for Documentary Credit (ICC)
- Rules for Contract Adaptation (ICC)
- Uniform Rules for International Commercial Contracts (UNIDROIT)

2 Universally harmonised interpretations of contract clauses
- INCOTERMS (ICC)
- Standard Clauses for International Contracts (eg, choice of law, choice of forum, arbitration, act of God) (ECE)

3 Case Law of arbitration courts
- Procedural law
- Breach of contract
- Contract adaptation

4 Trade norms
- Standard conditions
- Standard clauses for particular branches
- Product norms

5 Codes of conduct
- For multinational enterprises (UN, ECOSOC, OECD, ILO)
- For technology transfer (UNCTAD)
- For investment contracts (ICC)
- Against bribery (UN)

6 Private orders of 'third cultures'
- Insurance business (P & I Clubs)
- Banking sector
- Transport (maritime, air, road, railway)
- Mafia
- Diamond trade

C Mega Law Firms

Law firms do not seem to be a good example for informal institutions. The legal profession has been treated by Max Weber as well as by theories of modernisation and institutional economics as part of formal rational legal systems. Court and bureaucratic procedures require legal representation. Private as well as business relations are legally structured with professional assistance. Attorneys negotiate contracts, draft wills, advise creditors and debtors and protect from illegal state interference. In its traditional role, strictly controlled by professional associations, the legal profession is crucial in the implementation of formal legal rules. By promoting legal uniformity and standardisation it fosters the legitimation of the universal character of state law.

For reasons still not fully understood this traditional role has changed, first in the common law world and currently in the global economy. Because the common law world lacks the well-developed civil service bureaucracy of other nations, lawyers were called on to serve in key administrative posts and became powerful public policy-makers. In this new function they were instrumental for business corporations by undermining the regulatory authority of the state. Gradually, small partnerships were transformed into corporate law firms which then turned into semi-bureaucratic organisations with expert knowledge in all areas of public policy and tailored to the needs of big business (Lipartito, 1990). The globalising economy currently offers similar opportunities for even larger and more powerful corporate law firms which again take advantage of a lack of governmental structures. These lawyers are not—as in their traditional role—an integral part of a system of coordinated legal institutions (legislation, courts, bureaucracy, legal scholarship, legal education, etc) but key players in the process of establishing global political, economic and financial structures (Trubek et al, 1994; Flood 1996).

There is no element of formal rationality, transparency, legitimacy or due process in their activities but these mega law firms comply with many other characteristics of modernity, effectivity and rationality. They are what Weber calls 'purpose rational': they use contracts and rules instrumentally and they provide calculability and certainty for their (business) clients. Mega law firms have participated in international securities practices, counselling in transactions involving Eurodollar financings, sovereign and international institutional borrowings, and international tranches of foreign securities offerings. The firms have accumulated expertise with regard to international financing and specialised transactions initiated by banking clients, and they use this expertise to market their services to foreign clients. The firms' value to their clients stems more from their experience with similar transactions under different national legal regimes than from expertise in local law, especially in cases where local law is ambiguous or non-existent (Silver, 2000). The assistance of a creative law firm which structures and restructures the business environment is needed for most global business strategies. Contracts are drafted which are largely independent of any state law, corporations are created in forms previously unheard of, financial transactions avoid state control, tax havens are discovered and gaps in the trade law system or local regulatory structures are exploited. Ben Heineman, Senior Vice-President, General Counsel and Secretary, at General Electric, sees value in this local knowledge.

> So much of practising law these days outside of the United States is understanding the economic and political system, not just the legal system. I think we should not confine ourselves to a narrow view of the law. You simply can't practice law in a country unless you have people there who understand the history and the culture. If we look around the world, legal arrangements are fine, but most of the countries don't have legal systems that are very durable, that provide much certainty. That is probably one of the greatest challenges we face: How do we structure arrangements in countries where the legal system is, to a great extent, undeveloped? It is for that reason that you have to have people who are skilled in the culture and the history of the society. (Cited in Silver, 2000: 1104)

Due to its specific pragmatism in approaching business and legal issues regardless of the applicable law, this style of 'lawyering' is generally viewed as particularly American. It is creative and highly commercial. In important commercial areas, serving big clients such as banks and transnational corporations, some 50–70 US law firms together with a few English firms are currently 'restructuring' the global economy. There is little that nation states, international organisations or NGOs can do in this highly sophisticated and certainly unprecedented form of 'governance without government'.

IV VARIETIES OF CAPITALISM

Legalisation proves to be a biased, ethnocentric, ahistorical and sociologically uninformed approach. First, it misunderstands those theories which are commonly quoted as major elaborations of the emergence of the rule of law. Neither Max Weber, nor modernisation theory nor institutional economics have overlooked informal regulation and informal contract enforcement mechanisms. And secondly, it is ill-informed about developments outside highly developed and, no doubt, highly legally structured Western nation states. If rationality, calculability, risk avoidance and reliability are used as common criteria for economic efficiency and structural innovation, it is not difficult to find all kinds of institutions in Western and in particular in non-Western societies which have few or no legal properties but which are well adapted to economic needs.

The observation that law can be and frequently is substituted by other forms of coordinating mechanisms may not be shared by Western legal scholars but it is an assumption central to a group of economic sociologists and economists who discuss the embeddedness of institutions (Granovetter, 1985), social systems of production (Hollingsworth and Boyer, 1997) and the varieties of capitalism (Whitley, 1999). Their theories are not based on the neo-classical paradigm that the market is the most efficient institutional arrangement for coordinating economic activity and that state intervention and other forms of collective coordination do more harm than good. In their view, market coordination is considered efficient—but only for instantaneous transactions where the identities of the parties and future strategies are disregarded, a situation far less frequent than is assumed in the economic model. Accordingly, the law enabling market transactions (property rights, contract law, anti-trust, company law, etc) contributes to economic efficiency only in this specific sector of spot market behaviour. The theory explaining the coordination of spot market as well as all other economic activities is necessarily more complex: it considers all structural and cultural elements of social systems of production (institutions, organisations, social values, norms, moral principles, rules and law) which tend to cohere with each other into a fully-fleshed system with its own logic. Horizontal modes of coordination are markets and communities; vertical modes of coordination are firms and the state. In addition—placed between the horizontal and vertical modes—networks and associations contribute to the regulatory system (Hollingsworth and Boyer, 1997: 9, 12). Both horizontal and vertical modes make use of two different incentives (called 'action motives'): economic actions are either guided by self-interest (both at the level of the market and of individual firms) or by obligations (to communities and the state). The authors point to numerous examples of how the varying modes of coordination are implemented in different societies, firmly rejecting the idea that they can easily diffuse across countries or converge towards the Western or US model. Asian states and societies operate on radically different organizational principles. Whereas in the West laws regulate the actions of people, Asia's societies emphasise regulation through roles. Chinese institutions rest on relationships and not jurisdictions, on obedience to roles and not on bureaucratic command structures (Hamilton, 1994).

These studies of institutions and of their configuration in social systems of production have, as Hollingsworth and Boyer (1997: 4) emphasise, the potential to facilitate a great deal of integration among the social sciences. It is obviously akin to discourses on the varieties of legal cultures in the sociology of law where similar terminologies are used but where the elaboration of models for cross-cultural comparisons is lagging. Also, the distinction between self-interested and obligational action motives can easily be translated into Luhmann's distinction between cognitive and normative expectations (Luhmann, 1969), a translation which brings valuable legal-sociological insights into the economic debates summarised above. Expectations can either be maintained in case actors do not comply (normative expectations) or they can be adapted to the new 'unexpected' situation (cognitive expectations). This adaptation is a learning process, mostly accomplished through rational communication (Habermas, 1981).

Social organisation is achieved in all societies by both normative and cognitive expectations (Gessner, 1996), although in varying degrees. In more stable societies social organisation is predominantly achieved by the former, whereas in more dynamic and more complex societies it is predominantly achieved by the latter. Western societies develop an ever-increasing number of cognitive structures (as opposed to formal legal structures) in order to cope with problems of order and change (Willke, 1983). Hence also in legal sociological understanding the over-emphasis on normative expectations reduces the learning capacity at the micro- as well as the macro-level of societies, leading to stagnation, lack of flexibility and lack of innovation. The manner in which legalisation is transmitted from the West to South and East Asia may destroy traditional or modern cognitive structures so necessary in a dynamic and complex global environment.

BIBLIOGRAPHY

APPELBAUM, RICHARD P (1998) 'The Future of Law in a Global Economy' 7 *Social & Legal Studies* 171.

BERNSTEIN, LISA (1992) 'Opting Out of the Legal System: Extralegal Contractual Relations in the Diamond Trade' 21 *Journal of Legal Studies* 115.

—— (1996) 'Merchant Law in a Merchant Court: Rethinking the Code's Search for Immanent Business Norms' 144 *University of Pennsylvania Law Review* 1765.

BONELL MICHAEL JOACHIM (1990) 'International Uniform Law in Practice – or Where the Real Trouble Begins' *American Journal of Comparative Law* 38, 865-88.

BRADACH, L JEFFREY and ECCLES, ROBERT G (1989) 'Price, Authority, and Trust: From Ideal Types to Plural Forms' 15 *Annual Review of Sociology* 97.

CALABRESI, GUIDO and MELAMED, DOUGLAS (1972) 'Property Rules, Liability Rules, Inalienability: One View of the Cathedral' 85 *Harvard Law Review* 1089.

CHUNG, WAI-KEUNG and HAMILTON, GARY G (2001) 'Social Logic as Business Logic: *Guanxi*, Trustworthiness, and the Embeddedness of Chinese Business Practices' in Richard P Appelbaum, William LF Felstiner and Volkmar Gessner (eds) *Rules and Networks: The Legal Culture of Global Business Transactions* (Hart Publishing, Oxford).

COASE, RONALD H (1960) 'The Problem of Social Cost' 3 (1) *Journal of Law & Economics* 15.

COOTER, ROBERT D (1996) 'Decentralized Law for a Complex Economy: The Structural Approach to Adjudicating the New Law Merchant' 144 *University of Pennsylvania Law Review* 1643.

COTTERRELL, ROGER (2001) 'Is there a Logic of Legal Transplants?' in David Nelken and Johannes Feest (eds) *Adapting Legal Cultures* (Hart Publishing, Oxford).

DE LY, FILIP (2001) 'Lex Mercatoria (New Law Merchant): Globalization And International Self-Regulation' in Richard P Appelbaum, William LF Felstiner and Volkmar Gessner (eds) *Rules and Networks: The Legal Culture of Global Business Transactions* (Hart Publishing, Oxford).

DE SOTO, HERNÁN (1986) *El Otro Sendero* (Editorial El Barranco, Lima).

DORE, RONALD (1983) 'Goodwill and the Spirit of Market Capitalism' 34 *The British Journal of Sociology* 459.

ELLICKSON, ROBERT C (1991) *Order without Law – How Neighbors Settle Disputes* (Harvard University Press, Cambridge, Mass).

EMMERSON, DONALD K (1998) 'Americanizing Asia?' *Foreign Affairs*, May-June.

FLOOD, JOHN (1996) 'Mega-Lawyering in the Global Order: The Cultural, Social and Economic Transformation of Global Legal Practice' *International Journal of the Legal Profession,* 3, 169.

FRANCIS, CLINTON W (1983) 'The Structure of Judicial Administration and the Development of Contract Law in Seventeenth-Century England' 83 *Columbia Law Review* 35

FRIEDMAN, LAWRENCE (2001) 'Some Comments on Roger Cotterrell and Legal Transplants' in David Nelken and Johannes Feest (eds) *Adapting Legal Cultures* (Hart Publishing, Oxford).

FRIEDMAN, LAWRENCE M (1994) Is there a Modern Legal Culture? 7 *Ratio Juris* 117.

—— (1996) 'Borders: On the Emerging Sociology of Transnational Law' 32 *Stanford Journal of International Law* 65.

FURGER, FRANCO (2001) 'Global Markets, New Games, New Rules: The Challenge of International Private Governance' in Richard P Appelbaum, William L F Felstiner and Volkmar Gessner (eds) *Rules and Networks: The Legal Culture of Global Business Transactions* (Hart Publishing, Oxford).

GESSNER, VOLKMAR (1975) *Recht und Konflikt – Eine soziologische Studie privatrechtlicher Konflikte in Mexiko* (Mohr, Tübingen).

—— (1986) *Los Conflictos sociales y la administración de justicia en México* (UNAM, México).

—— (1996) 'The Institutional Framework of Cross-Border Interaction' in Volkmar Gessner (ed) *Foreign Courts—Civil Litigation in Foreign Legal Cultures* (Dartmouth Publishing Company, Aldershot).

—— (1996) 'Kognitive Elemente sozialer Ordnung' in Monika Frommel and Volkmar Gessner (eds) *Normenerosion* (Nomos, Baden-Baden).

—— (2002) 'Rechtspluralismus und globale soziale Bewegungen' 23 *Zeitschrift für Rechtssoziologie* 277.

GESSNER, VOLKMAR and BUDAK, ALI CEM (eds) (1998) *Emerging Legal Certainty: Empirical Studies on the Globalization of Law* (Dartmouth/Ashgate, Aldershot).

GESSNER, VOLKMAR; APPELBAUM, RICHARD P; and FELSTINER, WILLIAM L F (2001) 'The Legal Culture of Global Business Transactions' in Richard P Appelbaum, William L F Felstiner and Volkmar Gessner (eds) *Rules and Networks: The Legal Culture of Global Business Transactions* (Hart Publishing, Oxford).

GINSBURG, TOM (2001). 'Dismantling the "Developmental State"? Administrative Procedure Reform in Japan and Korea' 49 *American Journal of Comparative Law* 585.

GOTTLIEB, GIDON (1983) 'Relationism: Legal Theory for a Relational Society' 50 *University of Chicago Law Review* 567.

GRANOVETTER, MARC (1985) 'Economic Action and Social Structure: The Problem of Embeddedness' 91 *American Journal of Sociology* 481.

GULATI, RANJAY (1995) 'Does Familiarity Breed Trust? The Implications of Repeated Ties for Contractual Choice in Alliances' 38 *Academy of Management Journal* 85.

HABERMAS, JÜRGEN (1981) *Theorie des kommunikativen Handelns* (Suhrkamp, Frankfurt).

HAMILTON, GARY G (1994) 'Civilizations and the Organization of Economies' in Neil J Smelser and Richard Swedberg (eds) *The Handbook of Economic Sociology* (Princeton University Press, Princeton, N J) 183.

HOLLINGSWORTH, J ROGERS and BOYER, ROBERT (1997) 'Coordination of Economic Actors and Social Systems of Production' in J Rogers Hollingsworth and Robert Boyer (eds) *Contemporary Capitalism – The Embeddedness of Institutions* (Cambridge University Press, Cambridge).

JASTER, GEORG (1996) 'Experiences of the Civil Rights Commissioner in Poland' in Volkmar Gessner, Armin Höland and Csaba Varga (eds) *European Legal Cultures* (Dartmouth, Aldershot).

KIEDAISCH, INGO (1997) *Internationale Kunden-Lieferanten-Beziehungen* (Gabler, Wiesbaden).

KRASNER, STEPHEN D (ed) (1983) *International Regimes* (Cornell University Press, Ithaca).

LIPARTITO, KENNETH (1990) 'What Have Lawyers Done for American Business? The Case of Baker & Botts of Houston' 64 *Business History Review* 490.

LUHMANN, NIKLAS (1969) 'Normen in soziologischer Perspektive' 20 *Soziale Welt* 28.

MACAULAY, STEWART (1963) 'Non-Contractual Relations in Business: A Preliminary Study' 28 *American Sociological Review* 55.

—— (2000) 'Relational Contracts Floating on a Sea of Custom? Thoughts about the Ideas of Ian Macneil and Lisa Bernstein' in 'Relational

Contract Theory: Unanswered Questions – A Symposium in Honor of Ian R Macneil' 94 *Northwestern University Law Review* 775.
MACNEIL, JAN (1980) *The New Social Contract* (Yale University Press, New Haven).
MCCONNAUGHAY, PHILIP J (2001) 'Rethinking the Role of Law and Contracts in East-West Commercial Relationships' 41 *Virginia Journal of International Law* 427.
NICHOLS, PHILIP M (1999) 'A Legal Theory of Emerging Economies' 39 *Virginia Journal of International Law* 229.
NORTH, DOUGLASS C (1990) *Institutions, Institutional Change and Economic Performance* (Cambridge University Press, Cambridge).
—— (1999) 'Dealing With a Non-Ergodic World: Institutional Economics, Property Rights, and the Global Environment' 10 *Duke Environmental Law and Policy Forum* 1.
RUSKOLA, TEEMU (2000) 'Conceptualizing Corporations And Kinship: Comparative Law And Development Theory in a Chinese Perspective' 52 *Stanford Law Review* 1599.
SEIDMAN, ANN and SEIDMAN, ROBERT B (1996) 'Drafting Legislation for Development: Lessons from a Chinese Project' 44 *American Journal of Comparative Law* 1.
SHAPIRO, MARTIN (1993) 'The Globalization of Law' 1 *Global Legal Studies Journal* 9.
SHIHATA, IBRAHIM F I (1997) 'The Role of Law in Business Development' 20 *Fordham International Law Journal* 1577.
SILVER, CAROL (2000) 'Globalization and the U.S. Market in Legal Services – Shifting Identities' 31 *Law and Policy in International Business* 1093.
TEUBNER, GUNTHER (ed) (1997) *Global Law without a State* (Dartmouth, Aldershot).
TREIBER, HUBERT (1989) 'Zur Rechtssoziologie Max Webers' in H Treiber (ed) *Vollzugskosten des Rechtsstaats* (Nomos, Baden-Baden).
TRUBEK, DAVID M (1972) 'Max Weber on Law and the Rise of Capitalism' *Wisconsin Law Review* 720.
TRUBEK, DAVID M; DEZALAY, YVES; BUCHANAN, RUTH; and DAVIS, JOHN R (1994) 'Global Restructuring and the Law: Studies of the Internationalization of Legal Fields and the Creation of Transnational Arenas' 44 *Case Western Reserve Law Review* 407.
WALLIS, JOHN JOSEPH and NORTH, DOUGLASS C (1986) 'Measuring the Transaction Sector in the American Economy, 1870-1970' in Stanley L Engerman and Robert E Gallman *Long Term Factors in American Economic Growth* (University of Chicago Press, Chicago).
WATSON, ALAN (1985) *The Evolution of Law* (Blackwell, Oxford).
WEBER, MAX (1964) *Wirtschaft und Gesellschaft* (Kiepenheuer & Witsch, Köln).

—— (1968) *Economy and Society: an Outline of Interpretive Sociology,* Guenther Roth and Claus Wittich (eds) (Bedminster Press, New York; University of California Press, Berkeley).

WEHLER, HANS-ULRICH (1975) *Modernisierungstheorie und Geschichte* (Vandenhoeck & Ruprecht, Göttingen).

WIENER, JARROD (1999) *Globalization and the Harmonization of Law* (Pinter, London).

WILLKE, HELMUT (1983) *Entzauberung des Staates* (Centaurus, Königstein/Ts).

WILLIAMSON, OLIVER E (1975) *Markets and Hierarchies: Analysis and Antitrust Implications: a Study in the Economics of Internal Organization* (The Free Press, New York).

—— (1979) 'Transaction-Cost Economies: The Governance of Contractual Relations' 22 *Journal of Law and Economics* 233.

—— (1981) 'The Economics of Organization: The Transaction-Cost Approach' 87 *American Journal of Sociology* 548.

—— (1985) *The Economic Institutions of Capitalism: Firms, Markets, Relational Contracting* (The Free Press, New York).

—— (1991) 'Comparative Economic Organization: The Analysis of Discrete Structural Alternatives' 36 *Administrative Science Quarterly* 269.

WHITLEY, RICHARD (1999) *Divergent Capitalism: The Social Structuring and Change of Business Systems* (Oxford University Press, Oxford).

WINN, JANE KAUFMAN (1994) 'Relational Practices and the Marginalization of Law: Informal Financial Practices of Small Businesses in Taiwan' 28 *Law and Society Review* 193.

YANG, MAYFAIR MEI-HUI (1994) *Gifts, Favors, and Banquets: The Art of Social Relationship in China* (Cornell University Press, Ithaca, NY).

3

Transnationalisation of Law, Globalisation and Legal Pluralism: a Legal Anthropological Perspective[1]

FRANZ VON BENDA-BECKMANN AND KEEBET VON BENDA-BECKMANN

I INTRODUCTION

A GROWING BODY of literature on law and globalisation that has been written by sociologists of law and political scientists has focused on the emergence of international and transnational law. Major fields of study are commerce and finance, that is, the changing position of national law vis-à-vis supra-national legal forms and the three-way relationship of transnational actors, international organisations and the nation state.[2] These studies have drawn attention to the legal dimension of globalisation processes, which in the general globalisation literature has been widely neglected. Law has not been treated as a separate issue, but rather has been subsumed under the more inclusive categories of culture, economics, governance and ideology.[3] These studies have also shed much light on the intricate transnational connections and actors engaged in the transnationalisation of law, the laws made in these new contexts, and the relations of economic and political power in which they act. At a more theoretical level, these studies have triggered sociological and legal-dogmatic analyses of the question of to what extent international law, 'soft

[1] This is a new version of a paper previously presented at the conference 'Globalisation and Law in Asia: from the Asian crisis to September 11, 2001' which was held at the International Institute for the Sociology of Law at Oñati on 10–11 April 2003. We would like to thank Christoph Antons, Volkmar Gessner and Julia Eckert for their constructive and critical comments on the earlier version.

[2] See Nelken and Feest (2001), K von Benda-Beckmann (2001), Röhl and Magen (1996) Gessner (2002), Gessner and Schade (1990), Gessner and Budak (1998), Voigt (2000), Teubner (1996, 1997a, 1997b) and Dezalay and Garth (1995).

[3] For instance in Held et al (1999), Appadurai (1990) and Featherstone and Lash (1995).

law', conventions and standards, or the *lex mercatoria* should be defined as law. This in turn has led many lawyers, political scientists and sociologists, who had been previously critical of the term legal pluralism, to address complex legal configurations in terms of global legal pluralism.[4]

Important as these studies are, some of them have quite serious limitations. First, there is often insufficient clarity about what the terms transnational law, transnationalised and globalised law actually mean. Globalisation of law is often used synonymously with transnationalised law, and transnational and transnationalised law are often treated as the same. We suggest that an initial conceptual clarification is useful for the following discussion. Secondly, debates are often exclusively confined to the transnationalisation of legal forms created and 'sent on their way' by states, international agencies and non-state actors such as law firms and INGOs.[5] Transnationalisation of other legal forms, such as religious, traditional, or customary laws have rarely been addressed.[6] Thirdly, analyses have been largely limited to the question of whether supranational and transnational law and governance organisations affect the sovereignty of nation states, their legislative autonomy and their law. Little attention has been paid to the likelihood of transnationalised law affecting other legal orders within the state, for instance, religious law, customary or traditional law, and the interrelationships between these orders. Discussion of legal pluralism in this body of literature is often confined to the co-existence of international and transnational law with state law. Global legal pluralism thus remains dissociated from the consequences of transnationalisation of law for the existing configurations of legal pluralism within states.[7] Fourthly, in order to understand the social and political significance of transnationalised legal forms, we have to trace them through various socio-political and pluralistic legal fields, in which they are used, appropriated and transformed. In other words, it is suggested herein that more attention should be given to the fate of transnationalised law in social and political fields 'beyond the state' and 'after arrival'.

In this chapter it is suggested that analytical approaches to law developed in the anthropology of law discipline fill some of these lacunae in the

[4] See the contributions in Teubner (1997b). See also Teubner (1996), Robé (1997), Callies (2002) and Gessner (2002).

[5] See Higgott et al (2000) on non-state actors. See also Dezalay and Garth (1995), Gessner (2002) and K von Benda-Beckmann (2001).

[6] Religious law is often touched upon but rarely researched in detail. See, eg, Günther and Randeria (2001) and Gessner (2002). For exceptions see Held et al (1999) and K von Benda-Beckmann (2001). Also see Yasuda (2003).

[7] See in particular Robé (1997), Teubner (1997a) and Callies (2002). Only a few authors have coupled this to propositions of how these different forms of transnationalisation lead to new variants of legal pluralism. See Santos (1987), Santos (1995), K von Benda-Beckmann (2001) and Günther and Randeria (2001). See also Vanderlinden (1989), F von Benda-Beckmann (2002), Merry (1997), Wiber (2005), Gessner (2002) and Randeria (2003).

contemporary discussions on law and globalisation. Although the anthropology of law discipline is sometimes criticised for merely focusing on a 'thick description' in social micro-settings (Gessner, 2002), legal anthropologists have been dealing with the influences of transnationalised law ever since they stopped conceiving their field of study simply as the traditional law of small scale socio-political organisations. They widened their empirical and theoretical perspectives to include the law and legal institutions of the nation state around the 1970s. The methodological groundwork for addressing transnationalised law had been laid long before transnational legal flows were discussed under the headings of globalisation and transnationalisation of law.[8] Since Moore (1970) published her research that combined a focus on the long-term historical processes with shorter-term situational analyses, considerable research has focused on the functioning of colonial and post-colonial state laws and their effects on social, economic and political organisations and existing configurations of legal pluralism.[9] More recent research concerns transnational flows of law, often through transnationally promoted legal reforms of family law and property law. Lately, especially through development programmes, good governance, human rights, and environmental law have become prominent issues of transnationalisation.[10] There is also an increasing interest in the ways in which international development agencies are introducing their own 'project law', thereby affecting the plural legal constellations in the areas in which the projects operate.[11] Moreover, legal anthropological research is not confined to transnationalised state law but also looks at transnationalisation of religious and customary laws. It has been shown that this has not been a one-way traffic that moves from the developed Western nations to post-colonial states but has also gone in the opposite direction.[12] Methodologically, legal anthropological research under conditions of legal pluralism freed itself at a relatively early stage from the

[8] See Günther and Randeria (2001). See Ziegert (2000) for similar comments on developments in the sociology of law. Admittedly, the amount of legal anthropological (and legal sociological) research on transnational and transnational law hitherto has been modest and concerned itself mainly with local level impacts of transnationalised law (see Gessner, 2002). It took some time until a more systematic approach to these phenomena was explicitly initiated: see Merry (1997), F von Benda-Beckmann (1997), K von Benda-Beckmann (1997, 2001), Wiber (1999, 2005) and Weilenmann (2005).

[9] See for instance F von Benda-Beckmann (1979), Snyder (1981), Fitzpatrick (1980), Moore (1986) and Starr and Collier (1989).

[10] See F von Benda-Beckmann (1989). For references on the law and development literature, see K von Benda-Beckmann (1990) and Vel (1992). On the recent expansion of legal exports, see Rose (1998) and Seidman et al (1999).

[11] See Vel (1992), F von Benda-Beckmann (1989), K von Benda-Beckmann (1990, 2001), Randeria (2003) and Weilenmann (2005).

[12] For example, the customary and religious law of their homelands were introduced by migrants to the industrialised Western legal systems, these native countries including, eg, Turkey, Morocco and Indonesia. See, eg, Strijbosch (1984, 1999), Foblets (1990), Foblets et al

conventional 'gap approach' in implementation studies, and addressed the wider significance of law and legal pluralism for the social, economic, cultural and political life of the population that is analysed from an agency-structure perspective. This has included the ways in which new law was taken up by courts and local populations: reinterpreted, resisted or gladly embraced, distinguished from, combined or fused with local legal forms into new hybrid legal forms.[13] A wide range of transformations and local adaptations was studied, long before the focus on local 'hybridisation' or 'creolisation' became fashionable in the globalisation literature.[14] Increasing attention is also given to the spatial and temporal dimensions of law in society.[15] The social phenomena made visible by such perspectives are indispensable, for instance for answering the question of whether globalisation leads to a global homogenisation of law.[16] Such a perspective is also relevant for a proper appreciation of the issues described and analysed in the other contributions of this volume on globalisation and law in Asia.[17] Here we shall first briefly clarify our own conceptual usages when speaking of transnational, transnationalised and globalised law. Then we sketch what we understand by a spatio-temporal perspective, and on that basis discuss the significance of transnationalised law for the law of and in nation states. Finally, the chapter looks at the relation between global and local legal pluralism.

II TRANSNATIONAL AND TRANSNATIONALISED, GLOBAL AND GLOBALISED LAW

Many authors have been struggling to find an adequate terminology for the continuously expanding body of law that emerges in a globalising world. The classical terminology of public international law and state law no longer suffices to capture the new complexity that has developed

(1996), K von Benda-Beckmann (1991) and Santos (1995). For transnationalisation of customary law through indigenous networks, see Merry (1997). The ideas of neighbourhood justice in the USA have been inspired by modes of dispute resolution in developing and socialist countries.

[13] Forms of combined or hybrid law have an old history in the former colonies. For the Dutch East Indies, see F von Benda-Beckmann (1979, 1984), K von Benda-Beckmann (1983, 1984). See Collier (1973) on Zinacantan in Mexico. For Africa, see Holleman (1978) and Chanock (1985).

[14] In globalisation literature authors speak about 'creolisation' (Hannerz, 1992), 'hybridisation' (Nederveen Pieterse, 1995) or 'vernacularised' law (Merry, 1997). These are usually treated as variants of 'glocalisation' (Robertson 1995).

[15] See, eg, Santos (1985, 1987); F von Benda-Beckmann (1999, 2001); F and K Benda-Beckmann (1991).

[16] See, eg, Randeria (2001) and Santos (1987, 1995).

[17] See, eg, the contributing authors who dealt with globalisation in Indonesia (Lindsey, 1999 and Antons, 2003).

through changes in international law. Today we experience a great variety of legal forms 'crossing the borders' of national states and their law-making powers, both as sovereign legislators for their own citizens and as members of the international community. International law has come to include law made by international organisations that only have a loose link to sovereign states, and which also comprise relationships between states and non-state collectivities. Law, or law-like rules and standards are increasingly made and operated in functional business networks or international and multinational organisations and associations.[18] The most famous example is the *lex mercatoria* that regulates international business relationships, which is made and sanctioned by the business community itself.[19] Moreover there is an increasing body of law that is 'supra-national', as in the EU's case, which claims validity for several nation states simultaneously. Law that claims universal validity in all states and for all people, for example international human rights law, is sometimes called 'cosmopolitan' law.[20] Most recent conceptual discussions construct comprehensive typologies of transnationalised law,[21] or focus specifically on the type of law that exists in the space between the law of sovereign states and international law.[22] What emerges from these attempts to design new typologies is that the field of law extending the borders of nation states is expanding. This field of law forms a patchwork of regulations, often only loosely connected, that are no longer fully subordinated to the law-making powers of (associations of) nation states. Yet the prevailing typologies are not entirely satisfactory. This is because the concepts of transnational, transnationalised or global are mostly multi-referential. The following sections discuss the various usages of these concepts. They argue that

[18] For organisational and functional networks, see Teubner (1997a). For law firms and arbitration bodies, see Dezalay and Garth (1996). For (I)NGOs and epistemic communities, see Maher (2002), Wiber (2005) and Higgott et al (2000).

[19] Its social source is not an ethnic group or the life world of globalised personal networks but the proto-law of socialised, organisational and functional networks, which are forming a global, but clearly limited identity (Teubner, 1997a) as independent from the state. In the literature there are lively debates on whether the *lex mercatoria* and soft law should be termed law or not. See the contributions in Teubner (1997b). See also Gessner (2002) and in this volume.

[20] See Santos (1995), Held (1995), Callies (2002) and Gessner (2002). Such supra-national law transcending state boundaries and nationality can also be restricted to specific categories of persons. Islamic law, for instance, claims universal validity for all members of the *umma* and transcends ethnic or national boundaries.

[21] Santos distinguishes seven different types of transnationalised law: transnationalised state law, law of regional integration, *lex mercatoria*, law of people on the move, transnationalised *infra*-state law, cosmopolitan law, and *jus humanitatis* (Santos, 1995). In Günther and Randeria's (2001) scheme, these seven types are reduced to five. The law of people on the move is omitted, and cosmopolitan law and *jus humanitatis* are fused.

[22] Authors speak of soft law, 'third category of law' (Nelken, 2001), or 'third cultures' (Callies, 2002). See the contributions in Teubner (1997b), Gessner and Budak (1998) and Gessner (2002).

instead of trying to come up with a new typology, an analytical framework should comprise the social fields and networks of actors that transcend national borders as well as processes of socio-spatial extension of law.

A Transnational Law

There are at least three distinct usages of the concept 'transnational law'. 'Transnational' may refer to rules and institutions regulating (inter)actions, relationships or wider networks that transcend national boundaries.[23] Such law includes legal regulations of international trade and finance, regulation for cross-border debt collection and foreign investment legislation, cross-boundary migration and its labour and welfare implications, as well as the World Bank regulations that govern projects in indigenous peoples' lands. It also includes the *lex mercatoria.* The transnational substance, however, does not allow inferences as to the creator of such law or its scale of operation. Secondly, transnational, sometimes also called global law, may be used for fields in which law operates, or is claimed to be operating, ignoring or transcending national boundaries and respective nationalities. Here it denotes the law in transnational and supra-national legal fields: examples would be universal human rights and the *lex mercatoria*. Finally, transnational law is used to indicate the connections of the actors creating and maintaining law, the members of functional networks, law firms, international or transnational organisations and epistemic communities that are located in several nation states. Transnational law in this sense, however, does not have to be transnational in substance, as in the first meaning. In these transnational fields and networks of actors, law may be made that is supranational, cosmopolitan in substance, or which provides models for national law. Transnational law, in these three different meanings, may thus refer to the transnational character of substance, of social fields, or of actors. Some types of law, such as the *lex mercatoria*, are transnational in all three definitions, while others may be transnational in one or two definitions only.

[23] According to Jessup, presently a Judge of the International Court of Justice, transnational law comprises all law that regulates actions or events that transcend national frontiers. It includes both civil and criminal aspects and may also involve states, individuals, corporations, and other groups (quoted from Callies, 2002). For Teubner (1997a) the *lex mercatoria* would be global rather than transnational. Callies sees transnational law as a 'third category of law' located somewhere in between the traditional dichotomy between municipal laws and (public) international law, as an autonomous legal system beyond the state.

B Transnationalised Law

Another source of confusion is the different meanings given to 'transnationalised' law and the coterminous use of transnational and transnationalised law. According to most conceptual usages, law becomes transnationalised when it flows across national boundaries and enters other states or transnational or supranational social fields.[24] Most transnational law as per the definitions that are provided in the last section is specifically enacted to cross national borders. But law that was not originally made for regulating transnational, international or supranational relationships, or for transnational export may also become transnationalised. For instance, legislation of one nation state may be 'transplanted' to another state for internal use. Or it may serve as a model for legislation in another state.[25] This kind of transnationalisation includes the legal transfers in the colonial and post-colonial history of Third World states, and it still covers most of the laws transnationalised in the context of development cooperation. Such law may also be created and transnationally propagated with the aim of creating 'transnationally assimilated state legal systems' on a wider geographical or even global scale (Wiener, 1999). Sometimes this is done in the form of model legislation, developed by international organisations or epistemic communities, such as for rights over forestry, land tenure or fisheries (Maher, 2002; Wiber, 2005) or for cross-boundary debt collection and financial and banking relations, as many contributions in this volume show. The current pressures on governments in Asia to adopt good governance programmes, models of democracy, decentralisation, and environmental standards are an example (see F and K von Benda-Beckmann in this volume). Members of epistemic communities facilitate transnationalisation of law through their international professional and scientific connections.[26] Moreover, some religious and customary laws can also be transnationalised through migrants, and religious or indigenous networks.[27]

[24] Other authors also use the term 'transationalised' to indicate a form of law that has been influenced by processes of globalisation. This can be the case for any type of law, whatever its claims to spatial validity, which can be thus affected: state law, customary and religious laws as well as (other) international, supranational or transnational law. This distinct transnationalised law—in the sense of crossing boundaries and in the sense of law influenced by global processes—remains particularly unclear in Santos' and Günther and Randeria's typologies. Heydebrand (2001) has suggested distinguishing between the globalisation of law, the law exported together with other goods and services, and the law under globalisation which is affected by global economic processes.

[25] Most of the national legal systems that are dealt with in this volume are examples of such transplants.

[26] Wiber (2005) has pointed out that the regulation of fisheries in eastern Canada international epistemic communities may have a transnationalising effect even if they only pursue national legislation in their respective countries.

[27] For example, see Santos (1995) for 'law of migrants'. See also Merry (1997).

C Transnationalised and Globalised Law

In the literature, transnationalisation and globalisation are frequently used synonymously.[28] Yet it makes sense to distinguish between globalisation and transnationalisation. Transnationalised laws vary considerably in the geographical scope of validity and actual spatial extension, and globalisation more strongly refers to the spatial expansion or spreading of transnationalised law. The argument of this chapter suggests a distinction between the geographical distance and the spatial coverage of these processes. Geographical distance refers to the extent to which the flows, connections and outcomes span distance.[29] This scale ranges from co-presence to processes or relationships that connect transregional and transcontinental places. The *distance* over which law is transported, however, is to be distinguished from the *extent* of their spatial coverage. One may have wide-ranging transcontinental relationships, and goods and ideas distributed through them, whereby the main actors are situated in micro places, in office buildings or cities (Sassen, 1991). But such transfers of goods and ideas may also extend over much larger spaces such as rural areas and tropical forests. The effects of such spatial coverage should then be measured by the number of people affected and by the extent to which powerful political and economic networks are affected.

These analytical tools provide useful multidimensional points of departure that in particular allow us to see and analyse differences in the features and degree of globalising processes in different periods of history. Globalisation is thus a matter of degree in different dimensions. Globalisation in this sense implies transnational flows and connections but is a wider concept than transnationalisation, one that attempts to spatialise transnational flows and their consequences and impacts.

III FLOWS, PROCESSES AND OUTCOMES: A SPATIO-TEMPORAL PERSPECTIVE

There is a tendency, especially in the writings of international lawyers, to assume that law for which transnational or global validity and obligation

[28] Some authors, eg, Günther and Randeria (2001), prefer to speak of transnationalisation in order to avoid some of the implications the concept of globalisation carries with it, in particular, ideological and teleological assumptions of the inevitability of a world-wide market or cultural homogenisation. Such ideological assumptions are indeed unwarranted, and by now there is a growing consensus that increased communicative and interactive connection of cultures may not be equated with an homogenisation of culture (Featherstone and Lash, 1995).

[29] In the sense Giddens (1984a) talked about time-space distantiation. The interest in globalisation has greatly furthered the spatialisation of social theory: see Featherstone and Lash (1995). Robertson (1990) speaks of 'mapping' the global condition.

have been asserted, indeed does flow and exist throughout the transnational or global space. But the normative proclamation of law for a specific location does not necessarily mean that law actually comes to be present and remain in that location, in the sense of being known, used, re-stated, or in other ways becoming a point of orientation for human action. From the normative projection of law in a geographical or political space for which it claims validity, it is not possible to infer whether and to what extent law actually exists or has significance in this space. A multitude of spatial metaphors are used in analytical and methodological frameworks, such as semi-autonomous social fields (Moore, 1973) rooms and landscapes (Galanter, 1981, 1983) or structural places (Santos, 1987). These metaphors usually refer to social spaces and boundaries. But they are rarely concerned with the actual location and movement of such constructions in physical space.[30] The flows have to be traced as chains of interdependent social practices of actors or networks or actors, which are the channels through which laws are communicated and received transnationally and through which they acquire more or less global spreading.[31] Transnational flows, connections and impacts are grounded in physical-geographical and socio-political space, no matter how momentary, permanent or mobile such grounding is, and how extensive its 'local' or 'global' spreading is.[32]

This holds true for state law, international, supranational and transnational law as well as customary and religious laws. There is, therefore, the law *of* the state and other organisational structures (religious communities, ethnic groups, professional or international organisations), as distinguished from the law *in* states or other socio-spatial fields or territories. But even transnational or global law is grounded. If one looks at the sets of relations and interactions and the forces which generate them in isolation, it may indeed appear as if such law were autonomous or independent from states, that is, beyond the state, as Teubner (1997a: 7) claims for the *lex mercatoria*. However, it is beyond the state only in the sense that state agencies have nothing to do with its emergence and little to do with its

[30] See F and K von Benda-Beckmann (1991) and F von Benda-Beckmann (2001) on 'geography of law'. See also Harvey (1996), Lash and Urry (1994) and Marcus (1992).

[31] McGrew (1998: 327) stressed the need for 'crisper conceptual differentiation between processes occurring on different spatial scales' and distinguished the global, the regional and the international scales. While it is useful to distinguish different scales on which processes of transnationalisation take place, we think that the spatial grounding of social processes, relationships, institutions, cultures, religions, ideologies, law and their outcomes in physical-geographical space occurs, and needs to be looked at, on any scale.

[32] See F and K von Benda-Beckmann (1991) and F von Benda-Beckmann (2001). It also applies to Appadurai's metaphor of scapes, processes of de-territorialisation and re-territorialisation as well as for the transnational fields and networks in which global or transnational law operates (Appadurai, 1990).

operation.[33] But the social fields in which the *lex mercatoria* is generated and maintained are also connected and overlap with other social fields, many of which remain within single states.[34] From the perspective of actors using this law, the transnational law is only a part of a wider, usually plural set of legal conditions in which they operate and that may help shape their transnational interactions. Some of these conditions may be entirely national, or even local. As McCarthy (2005) has shown, for example, the specific constellation of transnational, local and national actors around tropical forests in Kalimantan, Indonesia, has been crucial for the way in which transnational regulations concerning ecology affect the exploitation of timber and mineral resources. Focusing solely on the transnational economic connections and rules would divert due attention from the influence of these connected social fields.[35] The spatial grounding of legal regulations and relations thus reveals the importance of distinguishing legal constructions of space from the actual use of law in actual spaces and places. This distinction is also necessary to understand how the processes of reproduction and change of transnationalised law occur and become part of the total set of legal conditions in a specific place.

The temporal dimension of these processes also needs more attention than is usually allowed for.[36] Flows and circulation of legal forms are not one-time affairs. Connections and relationships, once established, have to be reproduced in further interaction. Also the 'impact' of transnationalised law does not stop at the moment of arrival. Once having become 'sedentary', transnationalised law joins the multitude of social, economic, political and legal factors and processes that shape social organisation and

[33] However, transnational law or legal agreements are sometimes executed via state courts.

[34] Transnational or global social fields are not basically different from Moore's understanding of semi-autonomous social fields as relationship and interaction networks that generate their own rules and sanctioning mechanisms (Moore, 1973). Also, see Teubner (1997a).

[35] Another example can be drawn from international arbitration whereby attempts to adapt its rules to American modes of legal argumentation and rules of evidence can in part be explained by looking at such overlapping social fields in which the dominant actors operate. American lawyers involved in international arbitration also operate in national courts and therefore prefer procedures with which they are familiar. They have a strong interest in feeding these procedures into international arbitration.

[36] In some of the globalisation literature there is a tendency to look at globalisation mainly as a dynamic process of flows, movement and circulation. The outcome of this is generally regarded as something static, often associated with teleological expectations, such as a global free market, cultural homogeneity or a form of cosmopolitan democracy. See Robertson (1990 and 1995), Held et al (1999), Urry (2000) and Giddens (1990). Despite the preference for process over outcome, most authors, including Held et al (1999), consider both as elements of the global condition.

law in these settings.[37] Each change that is an outcome of a certain small-scale process enters the condition and context of new processes (Giddens, 1984b). Moreover, reproductions of transnationalised forms occur simultaneously in different national or international contexts of interaction. They all form a continuous stream feeding into local legal forms, including the already sedentarised transnational legal forms. In short, both flow and outcome must be set in time.

The globalising process thus consists of a great number of chains of interaction in which legal forms are reproduced, changed and hybridised, simultaneously, in different contexts of interaction. The maintenance of such flows is often captured under the heading of 'institutionalisation' (Held et al, 1999: 515). But what is summarised as 'institutionalisation', and at that abstract level looks like one process, is in fact typically a chain of social processes, a complex of continuities and discontinuities with different actors engaged in contributing to the flows, often at an uneven pace. There may be disjunctions between global processes and local reproductions. For example, a few years after Indonesia became independent, the *concordantie beginsel*, the rule that Indonesian law automatically follows changes in Dutch law, was abolished. From then on, the transnationalising flow from the Netherlands to Indonesia was substantially reduced, if not completely discontinued. The transnationalised Dutch colonial law that had become the official law of Indonesia continued to be valid, but over time it underwent many substantial changes that were not induced by Dutch law. Likewise, many socialist countries, including Vietnam, have been cut off from the transnationalising mainstream of socialist law after the collapse of the Soviet Union. But socialist law, or parts of it, continue to be applied. In Vietnam, old socialist law merges with even older forms of transnationalised French law, and with new transnationalised American law (Rose, 1998).

Processes of transnationalisation, through which law flows across transnational frontiers and spreads globally, follow different channels of communication and of interaction. Transnationalised law typically enters a multitude of social fields with different actors, villages, business sectors, and interactions between state agencies, companies and village populations. Some fields are normatively and politically bounded as states and have government agencies as gatekeepers. Other fields are more open, with weak and permeable boundaries, and politically more accessible. Some transnational legal influences only reach the national capital or a limited number of people working in legislative arenas and courts, whilst others

[37] Concepts of localisation, globalisation or hybridisation express well the immediate ways in which external legal forms are dealt with in the socio-political and geographical settings in which they become sedentary, but they do not sufficiently capture the temporal dimensions of these impacts.

reach the majority of the rural population living in villages. Models of a bankruptcy law or foreign investment legislation, as described by Halliday and Carruthers in this volume, may flow through narrow channels involving a small and select group of actors. Ideas of human rights, democracy and decentralisation, on the other hand, may be communicated and negotiated with actors at the central government. However they may simultaneously arrive in regions in different ways that are often unforeseen and unintended by legislators. Much of the globalised human rights and environmental protection discourses, for instance, is carried over by the media, NGOs or internationally connected social movements, increasingly using the Internet, and bypasses the state administration. Development agencies and projects are also important carriers of legal ideas, for example, those relating to resource management, environmental protection and community rights into small-scale settings.[38] These movements do not follow a single direction from west to south and east. They may occur in South-South relationships, or within regions, for instance the ASEAN states. Religious and customary legal forms have also spread to 'the West', especially since the onset of large scale migration in the second half of the twentieth century. Nor can one speak of a one-sided push of Western law only. Governments, groups or individuals from states in Africa and Asia may be 'fetching' law from elsewhere and bringing it back home, as in the case of Turkey and Japan and currently in countries which were formerly part of the Soviet Union.[39]

Analysing globalisation processes therefore forces us to adopt two intertwined historical perspectives: the history of transnational flows and the local histories of which these flows become part. What may be regarded as part of the globalising process in terms of distance and extent of coverage may have ceased locally to be seen as part of such a process. In the long run, transnational connections may become obsolete and a legal system may no longer be regarded as a derivative of another legal system, but as a legal system on its own. From a certain point in time, transnationalised law may no longer be locally perceived as such. This typically occurs if there is a disjunction between global processes and local reproductions. In the perception of local actors, what was once transnationalised or globalised colonial law has become 'local' history.[40]

[38] See for instance Vel (1992), K von Benda-Beckmann (2001) and Randeria (2003).

[39] Previously we have described how Indonesians imported Western ideas of democracy to fight colonial rule in the Dutch East Indies, as well as to influence the existing village constitutions (F and K von Benda-Beckmann, 2005).

[40] A striking example is the village of Hila on Ambon where we undertook research in the 1980s. Between 1683 and 1707, the village head had made four testaments, made up in Dutch and written down by the representative of the Dutch East Indies Company. They combined elements of Dutch law, Ambonese traditional law, and what is generally referred to as Islamic law. Thus, more than 300 years ago, there existed hybrid legal forms as outcomes

IV THE CONSEQUENCES OF TRANSNATIONALISATION: LAW OF STATES AND LAW IN STATES

What happens after its arrival depends on the respective political, economic and legal conditions of the social fields in which this law is received. It also depends on the actors who start using the new law.[41] These social fields already have their own, often plural, legal orders. Transnationalised law therefore increases the available repertoire of legal models and offers new resources to rationalise and justify social, economic and political interaction and policy objectives. Transnational law and legal models may be used to oppress the population, or as 'jurisprudence of insurgency' (Tigar and Levy, 1977) against oppressive governments. While rulers may regard human rights and the rule of law as an imposition from the West, many citizens advocate their adoption and implementation (see Chen in this volume). They do not see it as an imposition at all, but as an opportunity to obtain protection against an oppressive state that rules over them. Several authors in this volume provide vivid illustrations of the various fates of transnationalised legal models in different socio-political fields, and of their intended and unintended consequences in terms of social, economic or political parameters (for instance, economic growth, increase of legal security, environmental protection, justice and fairer distribution of economic resources). In this last section the focus will be specifically on the consequences of transnationalised law on the law *of* states and the law *in* states.

A Influences on the Law of States: the National Level

What happens when transnational law 'knocks at the door' of the nation state is quite variable. Different actors (international organisations, consultants and members of epistemic communities, activists, etc) may induce legislators to enact legislation bringing the national law in line with international law and transnationalised legal models. This may require long interactions and negotiations between governments and transnational and international agents in national or international law and policy-making arenas. As many contributors in this volume show, economic law is an important field where foreign actors actively participate in creating

of early processes of transnationalisation of Islamic and Dutch law. In the course of time, the spatial coverage of these testaments remained very limited. They did not play a role in other villages or in the writings of legal experts. But within the village, they continued to play a significant role in property and office politics and in a number of court cases in the nineteenth and twentieth centuries, until the present time. See F and K von Benda-Beckmann (1994).

[41] See Moore (1973) and Robertson (1990).

economic legislation that accommodates their needs and interests. Bankruptcy and foreign investment law may be enacted following the advice of foreign governments or consultants, and epistemic communities prefabricate legislation concerning natural resource rights.[42] As the von Benda-Beckmanns show in chapter 9 of this volume, constitutional law is another important domain in which legislation changes under transnational influences. Transnational pressures have in a number of countries led to increased recognition of religious and customary laws and the rights of indigenous peoples, and thus to significant changes in the legal construction of spheres of validity and normative hierarchy of state, religious and customary law.[43] While there is often a strong pressure on state governments and legislatures to modify their law and reform their administrative apparatus, if such changes are conditional for further lending or development aid governments and other political and economic interest groups may either reject them or selectively take over some elements, copy them wholesale or vernacularise them (Merry, 1997). As Randeria (2003) has pointed out, India has been remarkably successful in selectively complying with some demands and refraining from other changes to protect its own interest. Randeria (2003) has labelled such states 'cunning states' for using transnational law to clamp down on their own citizens while simultaneously claiming to be unable to comply with other demands of transnational law under a pretext of lack of power and resources. Anders (2002) has shown how Malawi legislators have resisted implementing legislation for structural adjustment programmes in Malawi. Bedner (2000) has analysed the pernicious resistance to court reforms in Indonesia. Moreover, Halliday and Carruthers provide in this volume a comparative analysis of the aptitude of the Indonesian, Korean and Chinese governments and business groups to, as the authors put it, 'foil the hegemons', whereby at times such governments refuse to adapt their law to the wishes of the powerful transnational actors, or in some cases avoid implementing the new legal guidelines in administrative and judicial practices.

B Influences on the Law of States: Sub-national Levels

Discussions of the consequences of transnationalised law usually focus on state law, in particular with legislation at the national level and its

[42] See Maher (2002) and Wiber (1999, 2005). See also the contribution by Halliday and Carruthers in this volume.

[43] Examples include more extensive recognition for the rights of indigenous peoples by implementing ILO *Convention 169* or a wider acceptance of traditional customary law in state legislation, or, in a more restricted context, partial recognition of customary law in development projects (joint resource management schemes, community rights-based development projects) by governmental and non-governmental organisations.

application through the administrative and judicial bureaucracy. Far less attention has been paid to state law at provincial, district or village levels. This may largely be due to the fact that information on such law is often difficult to acquire, but we suspect that it is also due to a set of interlocking assumptions: that national legislation in principle covers the whole state; that sub-national regulations mainly consist of implementing the national level law; and that sub-national legislation is relevant 'only' at micro-levels.

Neglecting sub-national state legislation seriously weakens generalisations about state law for a number of reasons.[44] First, provincial or district legislation often does not correspond to national legislation. This is especially the case when the national legislation mainly consists of framework legislation and leaves further concretisation to lower-level legislatures. Our contribution in this volume on decentralisation in Indonesia and West Sumatra provides an interesting illustration of how the few sections of the national decentralisation law of 1999 on village government were first transformed into a provincial regulation, then into district regulations and finally into village regulations. Lower-level state law may diverge from the legislation of the central state for other reasons as well. For example, transnational agencies may cooperate directly with provincial or district governments and may exert direct transnational influence on legislation at these lower levels, with the resulting legislation not necessarily fully in accord with the national legislation. A second reason why legislation below the national level is so important is that the local population is more directly confronted with regional and local legislation than with national legislation. Finally, what is usually conceived as the territory of a state is also an aggregation of regions, each with partly different legislation. Regional law, in other words, is not only law at small-scale levels of state administration; together, these laws cover the whole territory of the state. Generalisations about the impact of transnationalisation or globalisation of law on 'state law' therefore remain superficial unless the totality of state law is taken into account.

C Law and Legal Pluralism in States

Transnationalised law is not a matter of state law and state agencies only. It also affects customary law or religious law. The indigenous peoples may reinvent their law, or create 'neo-law', referring to ILO Convention 169 (Santos, 1995: 325). In other cases transnational actors may aggressively

[44] Earlier studies of how transnationalised law plays out in small-scale socio-political settings and local law suggest that it is indeed important to study these levels systematically. See also Wiener (1999) and Oomen (2002) on the importance of studying 'low-level governance'.

promote orthodox interpretations of, for example, the *Shariah* law and try to substitute these for more traditional versions, as it were, of popular Islamic law. In other constellations, ideas of the universal human rights discourse are taken up to reinterpret elements of Islamic law. Transnationalised law may also simultaneously affect several different bodies of law dealing with the same issues. For example, while indigenous people (re)invent their law, states may also enact laws that govern the affairs of indigenous peoples. Transnationalised notions of democracy may find their way into changes in the constitution, but they may also stimulate reinterpretations and changes of customary law, as happened in West Sumatra (F and K von Benda-Beckmann, 2005). The same notions may also serve as an oppositional template against which the distinct and different character of one's own constitutional notions are emphasised. Thus some of the opponents of democracy in West Sumatra use 'Western democracy' to emphasise and radicalise their superior Minangkabau notions of democracy (F and K von Benda-Beckmann, 2005).

The different kinds of transnationalised law, therefore, are not just additional elements in constellations of legal pluralism. Each type tends to change the role of each of the component parts of these constellations, increasing the dominance of some, while others may become less important. Gessner (2002: 299) has suggested that legal anthropologists have asserted 'equivalence' (*Gleichrangigkeit*) between state and non-state law. He has suggested that this image comes closer to reality under present conditions of globalisation and the internal and external constraints on the state than in the period when the nation states monopolised law-making. We do not agree that writers using the concept of legal pluralism have indeed asserted this kind of equivalence.[45] However, we agree that the question of what are the influences of transnationalisation of law on local plural legal constellations is an important one. The findings that have come out of anthropological studies, including our own, do not entirely support Gessner's suggestion that the (assumed) end of the states' monopoly on law-making decreases the significance of state law and makes non-state normative orders necessarily less precarious (Gessner 2002: 298). Our own research in Indonesia rather suggests that shifts in the relation between

[45] An image that Gessner (2002) draws from the so-called legal pluralists (quoting Griffiths, 1986). According to this interpretation, 'equivalence' means more or less equal social, economic and political significance of non-state normative orders in comparison to the state's normative order. This is mis-conceived. While such an assumption is regularly imputed to researchers expressing the plurality of normative orders through the concept of legal pluralism (Starr and Collier, 1989 and Tamanaha, 1993), this is in fact rarely the case. The concept of legal pluralism is premised on the assumption that for analytical purposes that is in order to be able to capture the precise difference, non-state normative orders could also usefully be called 'legal'. But this does not imply a statement on the relative significance of the different orders in actual situations. See F von Benda-Beckmann (1997 and 2002).

state and transnational and international law have very differential effects on the existing constellations of legal pluralism. They vary according to the domains of social and economic organisation, such as agriculture, business transactions, marriage, property and inheritance, control over productive resources, dispute settlement or taxation. Although customary law hardly plays a role at all in urban business in Jakarta, it has a prominent role in rural agriculture and natural resources management, especially outside Java. Studies of the regulation and management of natural resources have also shown that the new constellation of legal pluralism may change the configuration of the social field in which the transnational law operates (McCarthy, 2005; Wiber, 2005). Individual actors cannot control these changes. While international law may aim at containing and limiting the influence of religious law in state law, transnational Islamic legal influences today may push for a radicalisation of Islamic laws and press for a wider validity of Islamic law at the expense of both state and traditional law. In many regions we see an increasing role of religious law as a consequence of increased transnational connections in the sphere of religion and religious law, and also to an extent as a reaction against the economic and cultural impacts of globalisation. However, it should be noted that there are also transnational debates about liberal interpretations of Islamic law. Likewise, neo-traditional laws and institutions are acquiring greater significance in many developing states, often as the combined consequence of internal political pressures and external donor involvement whose policies give much attention to community participation and a greater recognition of local customary or traditional laws. The present revival of *adat* (custom) law in Indonesia under the condition of greater political freedom and in the context of decentralisation law is a good example.[46] In short, as Santos (1995: 262) remarked, the process of globalisation is selective, uneven, and fraught with tensions and contradictions.

V IMPACTS ON STATE SOVEREIGNTY

The influences of transnational, international and supra-national law and governance institutions have modified the sovereignty of states as autonomous legislators.[47] Changes in the normative constructions of state sovereignty and the monopoly on legislation shape the relationships and interactions of states both internally and externally. But there is a danger of

[46] See also our chapter on decentralisation in this volume. For Africa, see Oomen (2002). For indigenous peoples' rights, see Santos (1995).

[47] Some have remarked that state sovereignty and the power of state law are increasingly challenged from the outside. The call for legal restriction of the legal powers of individual nation states through international law and agencies in the name of the common interests of mankind (Brunnée, 1989) or cosmopolitan democracy (Held, 1995) becomes stronger.

false comparisons here if we do not distinguish between legal constructions of sovereign state power and the actual degree of autonomy of state governments.[48] In the past, as in the present, the normative constructions did not correspond to actual degrees of political autonomy.[49] During early post-colonial times, transnational pressures on Third World governments were strong, but mainly from the former colonial 'mother' states. Third World states are now confronted with many bilateral development agencies from many different nations and a host of multilateral donor institutions (see Rose, 1998). Moreover, the analysis of changes in sovereignty and the autonomy of the state apparatus shows a different picture depending on whether one looks at external or internal sovereignty (Beitz, 1991). Externally, in relation to transnational and international actors, both official legal sovereignty and the state's autonomy may be curtailed. However, these same pressures are internally often quite forcefully handed down and imposed on citizens. The external pressure from the international community and NGOs on states to accept their directives is a major drive and justification for severely curtailing lower-level regulatory powers, especially in the field of natural resources. Internal state sovereignty in such cases resembles a bottomless pit. The authority to pass legislation is claimed and exerted by states in areas where previously they dared not interfere, even if their sovereignty was far less restricted by international and transnational law. This is particularly clear in the domains of environmental protection, rights to land, water and subsoil resources. Populations are being resettled, often without due compensation, in the name of technical progress, wildlife protection and biodiversity and shifting subsistence agriculture is curtailed. States often intervene, even if under the slogan of privatisation, in domains that formerly had been largely left to non-state legal orders (see F and K von Benda-Beckmann, 1999). It appears that governments increase and expand their regulatory powers in the exercise of their internal sovereignty as their external sovereignty comes under increased pressure from external forces. In other words, national and local governments increase their power as their powers are challenged or subdued by transnational or global powers.

[48] McGrew (1998) draws attention to the disjuncture between *de jure* claims to sovereignty and *de facto* practices, and suggests that it is better to express this difference as between sovereignty and autonomy. Even before sovereignty was seriously challenged, many states were already under pressure from other states. And many were weak in the exercise of power over their citizens, while some contemporary states, though subject to transnational legal restrictions, do not seem to have lost much of their political power. The terms 'inter-sovereignty' or 'shared sovereignty' has been suggested to indicate that states are still powerful players, while legislation is increasingly made in concert with other sovereign legislators.

[49] As McGrew (1998: 337–8) notes, 'the consequences of globalisation for any state are mediated by its localisation in the hierarchy of power, domestic institutional structures and the mobilisation of countervailing political and economic strategies'.

VI CONCLUSIONS

In this chapter on the transnationalisation of law, globalisation and legal pluralism, the discussion has mainly drawn on ideas developed in the field of the anthropology of law. A fuller understanding of the immense complexity requires concerted efforts in empirical research and theoretical reflection across the frontiers of traditional academic disciplines. But that would require terminological clarification. We have discussed some of the terminological confusion that exists in the literature. A division of research labour is likely to remain between those who look primarily at transnational legal fields and the complexity of legal forms and processes in these fields and researchers who give more attention to the consequences of such complexity in other social fields. Yet we argue that legal anthropology's sensitivity to these issues makes it an indispensable methodological resource in socio-legal research (of whatever kind) on transnationalisation and globalisation of law.[50] The division of labour between 'macro' studies carried out by sociologists and political scientists and 'micro' studies carried out by anthropologists is a false construct. Our analysis of transnationalising law invites us to reconsider one-dimensional understandings of 'macro' and 'micro', which identify assertions of validity in a given space with its actual operation in that space, in which 'the state' or 'the national level' appears to be 'macro' and villages 'micro'. A spatial analysis shows that the reverse may be the case. Villages form the majority of the nation's land mass and population. 'The national level' on the other hand is primarily a legal representation of political space (Knorr-Cetina, 1988), but the actual spaces in which the national law is valid and significant for actual behaviour may be much smaller than the totality of village areas and their respective populations.[51]

A Homogeneity or Fragmentation?

The way in which the effects of the globalisation of law are conceptualised has consequences. There is a multitude of actors and channels through which the law in nation states, including customary laws and religious law,

[50] We do not agree with Gessner, who suggests that anthropology of law 'with its method of thick description would be in an inferior position to develop propositions on global phenomena than other social sciences that use abstracts from the observation of single cases' (2002: 278). Not all anthropology of law consists of thick descriptions. Nor is it characterised by an unwillingness or inability to abstract from the observation of single instances. Legal anthropology, like anthropology in general, has a varied history of 'macro' inter-cultural and temporal comparison and generalisations. See Gingrich (2002) on macro-comparisons in anthropology.

[51] F von Benda-Beckmann (2001), F and K von Benda-Beckmann (1991, 1998).

is modified by transnational law. As a result of increased transnationalisation of law, we may find an impressive volume of regional and global homogenisation of central state legislation, what Wiener (1999: 190) called a 'transnationally assimilated system of municipal law'. At the same time, transnationalisation may lead to differential glocalisations, that is global forms that obtain a specific local meaning. We have also emphasised the importance of the temporal disjunctures between global processes and local reproductions, the intertwined history of transnationalisation and the history of localities in which transnationalisation has consequences. The difference between a more or less global spread of legal forms, and the spatial and temporal localisation of the various actors who reproduce these legal forms locally, is important for propositions about legal globalisation and forces authors in this field to make more succinct statements about history and presence.

B Global and Local Legal Pluralism

The above reflections are important for the relationship between local, national, and global legal pluralism. From a nation state or intra-state perspective, transnational law adds a 'transnational dimension' to legal pluralism (K von Benda-Beckmann, 2001). This is because it increases the complexity of legal regulations by adding new sources and modes of legitimation to the historical constructions. These sources often lie outside the authority of the law-making agencies of the state.[52] Transnational or global law is not confined to a transnational or global field and destined to live in a space between or beyond states bridged by transnational relations and networks. Transnational transactions take place in contexts that also comprise state law and often also include religious and customary law. For example, the social fields in which *lex mercatoria* is generated and maintained are connected and overlap with social fields of national states as well as the social fields that are within the nation states themselves. Transnational or global social fields are not basically different from Moore's understanding of semi-autonomous social fields as relationship and interaction networks that generate their own rules and sanctioning mechanisms (Moore, 1973) and which merely operate on a different spatial and political scale. The networks and their law are also part of a wider set of local plural legal conditions. In certain interaction contexts, for example, insurance law or joint ventures, the extent of legal pluralism may be minimal. But in other contexts involving transnational actors, relations and law, the extent of legal pluralism may be considerable. This is particularly true, for example, for the conditions of transnational or

[52] See also Teubner (1997a), Günther and Randeria (2001) and Gessner (2002: 279).

multinational enterprises engaged in the exploitation of timber, petroleum and minerals in many Third World nations and even more so when working in resource areas claimed by indigenous peoples as their territories. Transnationalised law, while primarily made for actors engaged in transnational legal relationships, becomes available to actors within states and its usage is extended to govern interactions and agreements within states. For this reason, they are not only a part of global legal pluralism as understood by Teubner, but also of the constellations of legal pluralism within these states. Thus, the analysis would be incomplete without the above constellations of legal pluralism, both for understanding global legal pluralism as a sphere beyond the state, mainly produced and reproduced in transnational social fields, or for understanding the condition of law at global scale.

BIBLIOGRAPHY

ANDERS, G (2002) 'Rechtspluralisme in een internationale context' in E Hey, R de Lange, M A Loth, P A M Mevis and E Swart (eds) *Grensverkenningen in het recht* (SI-EUR reeks 26. Sanders Institute, Erasmus University Rotterdam, Rotterdam).

ANTONS, C (2003) *Law and Development in East and Southeast Asia* (RoutledgeCurzon, London and New York).

APPADURAI, A (1990) 'Disjuncture and Difference in the Global Cultural Economy' in M Featherstone (ed) *Global Culture, Nationalism, Globalization and Modernity* (Sage Publishing, London).

BEDNER, A (2000) *Administrative Courts in Indonesia: A Socio-Legal Study* (University of Leiden, Leiden).

BEITZ, C R (1991) 'Sovereignty and Morality in International Affairs' in D Held (ed) *Political Theory Today* (Polity Press, Oxford).

BENDA-BECKMANN F VON (1979) *Property in Social Continuity: Continuity and Change in the Maintenance of Property Relationships through Time in Minangkabau, West Sumatra* (Martinus Nijhoff, The Hague).

—— (1984) 'Law out of Context: A Comment on the Creation of Customary Law Discussion' 28 *Journal of African Law* 28.

—— (1989) 'Scapegoat or Magic Charm: Law in Development Theory and Practice' 28 *Journal of Legal Pluralism* 129.

—— (1997) 'Citizens, Strangers and Indigenous Peoples: Multiple Constructions and Consequences of Rights, Resources and Peoples' 9 *Law & Anthropology* 1.

—— (1999) 'Multiple Legal Constructions of Socio-Economic Spaces: Resource Management and Conflict in the Central Moluccas' in M Roesler and T Wendl (eds) *Frontiers and Borderlands: Anthropological Perspectives* (Peter Lang, Frankfurt and New York).

—— (2001) 'On the Reproduction of Law: Micro and Macro in the Time Space Geography of Law' in W Fikentscher (ed) *Begegnung und Konflikt – eine kulturanthropologische Bestandsaufnahme* (Verlag der Bayerischen Akademie der Wissenschaften, C H Beck Verlag, München).

—— (2002) 'Who's Afraid of Legal Pluralism?' 47 *Journal of Legal Pluralism* 37.

BENDA-BECKMANN, F VON and BENDA-BECKMANN, K VON (1991) 'Law in Society: From Blindman's Bluff to Multilocal Law' in K von Benda-Beckmann, G C J J van den Bergh, H F M Crombag, A J Hoekema, A Schreiner, B P Sloot, H J L Spiertz, F Strijbosch and H Willekens (eds) *Living Law in the Low Countries* (Vuga, The Hague).

—— (1994) 'Texts in Context: Historical Documents as Political Commodity on Islamic Ambon' in W Marschall (ed) *Texts from the Islands* (Institut für Ethnologie, Bern).

—— (1998) 'Where Structures Merge: State and Off-state Involvement in Rural Social Security on Ambon, Eastern Indonesia' in S Pannell and F von Benda-Beckmann (eds) *Old World Places, New World Problems: Exploring Issues of Resource Management in Eastern Indonesia* (Australian National University, Centre for Resource and Environmental Studies, CRES Publications, Canberra).

—— (1999) 'Community-based Tenurial Rights in Theory and Practice' in H Finkler and K von Benda-Beckmann (eds) *The Papers of the XIth International Congress 'Folk Law and Legal Pluralism: Societies in Transformation' of the Commission on Folk Law and Legal Pluralism and the Institute of Ethnology and Anthropology of the Russian Academy of Sciences* (Russian Academy of Sciences, Moscow).

—— (2005) 'Democracy in Flux: Time, Mobility and Sedentarization of Law in Minangkabau, Indonesia' in F von Benda-Beckmann, K von Benda-Beckmann and A Griffiths (eds) *Mobile People, Mobile Law: Expanding Legal Relations in a Contracting World* (Ashgate, Aldershot, Dartmouth).

BENDA-BECKMANN, K VON (1983) 'The Implementation of State Court Decisions in West Sumatra, Indonesia' in H Finkler (ed) *XIth International Congress of the IUAES, Symposium on the Impact of Folk Law on State Law* (Commission on Folk Law and Legal Pluralism, Ottawa).

—— (1984) *The Broken Stairways to Consensus: Village Justice and State Courts in Minangkabau* (Foris Publications and KITLV Press, Dordrecht and Leiden).

—— (1990) 'Development, Law and Gender-Skewing: An Examination of the Impact of Development on the Socio-Legal Position of Indonesian Women, with Special Reference to Minangkabau', 30/31 *Journal of Legal Pluralism* 87.

—— (1991) 'Developing Families: Moluccan Women and Changing Patterns of Social Security in the Netherlands' in H Claessen, M van den Engel and D Plantenga (eds) *Het Kweekbed Omheind: Opstellen aangeboden aan Els Postel ter gelegenheid van haar afscheid als hoogleraar* (Vakgroep culturele antropologie en VENA, Leiden).

—— (1997) 'The Environmental Protection and Human Rights of Indigenous Peoples: A Tricky Alliance' in F von Benda-Beckmann, K von Benda-Beckmann and A J Hoekema (eds) *Natural Resources, Environment and Legal Pluralism* (Martinus Nijhoff, The Hague).

—— (2001) 'Transnational Dimensions of Legal Pluralism' in W Fikentscher (ed) *Begegnung und Konflikt – eine kulturanthropologische Bestandsaufnahme* (Verlag der Bayerischen Akademie der Wissenschaften, C H Beck Verlag, München).

BRUNNÉE, J (1989) '"Common Interest" – Echoes from an Empty Shell? Some Thoughts on Common Interest and International Environmental Law' 49 *Zeitschrift für Ausländisches Öffentliches Recht und Völkerrecht* 791.

CALLIES, GP (2002) 'Reflexive Transnational Law: On Definition of Transnational Law' 23 *Zeitschrift für Rechtssoziologie* 185.

CHANOCK, M (1985) *Law, Custom and Social Order: The Colonial Experience in Malawi and Zambia* (Cambridge University Press, Cambridge).

COLLIER, J (1973) *Law and Social Change in Zinacantan* (Stanford University Press, Stanford).

DEZALAY, Y and GARTH, BG (1995) 'Merchants of Law as Moral Entrepreneurs: Constructing International Justice from the Competition for Transnational Business Disputes' 29 *Law and Society Review* 27.

—— (1996) *Dealing in Virtue: International Commercial Arbitration and the Construction of a Transnational Legal Order* (University of Chicago Press, Chicago).

FEATHERSTONE, M and LASH, S (1995) 'Globalization, Modernity and the Spatialization of Social Theory' in M Featherstone, S Lash and R Robertson (eds) *Global Modernities* (Sage Publishing, London).

FITZPATRICK, P (1980) *Law and State in Papua New Guinea* (Academic Press, New York).

FOBLETS, M-C (1990) *Justice Civile et Immigration Familiale: Contribution Anthropologique à l'étude des Conflits Culturels* (Universiteit van Leuven, Leuven).

FOBLETS, M-C; GRIFFITHS, A; LAPRAIRIE C and WOODMAN, G (1996) 'Popular Justice: Conflict Resolution within Communities' 36 *Journal of Legal Pluralism.*

GALANTER, M (1981) 'Justice in Many Rooms; Courts, Private Ordering and Indigenous Law' 19 *Journal of Legal Pluralism* 1.

—— (1983) 'Reading the Landscape of Disputes: What We Know and Don't Know (and Think We Know) About Our Allegedly Litigious Society' 31 UCLA Law Review 4.

GESSNER, V (2002) 'Rechtspluralismus und globale soziale Bewegungen' *Zeitschrift für Rechtssoziologie* 277.

GESSNER, V and BUDAK, A C (eds) (1998) *Emerging Legal Certainty: Empirical Studies on the Globalization of Law* (a series published for The Oñati International Institute for the Sociology of Law) (Ashgate, Aldershot, Dartmouth).

GESSNER, V and SCHADE, A (1990) 'Conflicts of Culture in Cross-Border Legal Relations: The Conception of a Research Topic in the Sociology of Law' in M Featherstone (ed) *Global Culture: Nationalism, Globalization and Modernity* (Sage Publishing, London).

GIDDENS, A (1984a) 'Agency, Institution, and Time-Space Analysis' in K Knorr-Cetina and A V Cicourel (eds) *Advances in Social Theory and Methodology. Toward an Integration of Micro and Macro-Sociologies* (Routledge and Kegan Paul, Boston, London and Henley).

—— (1984b) *The Constitution of Society* (Polity Press, Cambridge).

—— (1990) *The Consequences of Modernity* (Stanford University Press, Stanford).

GINGRICH, A (ed) (2002) *Anthropology by Comparison* (Routledge, London).

GRIFFITHS, J (1986) 'What is Legal Pluralism?' (1986) 24 *Journal of Legal Pluralism* 1.

GÜNTHER, K and RANDERIA, S (2001) *Recht, Kultur und Gesellschaft im Prozeß der Globalisierung* (Werner Reimers Stiftung, Bad Homburg).

HANNERZ, U (1992) Cultural Complexity (Columbia Press, New York).

HARVEY, D (1996) *Justice, Nature and the Geography of Difference* (Blackwell Publishers, Oxford).

HELD, D (1995) *Democracy and the Global Order: From the Modern State to Cosmopolitan Governance* (Polity Press, Cambridge).

HELD, D; MCGREW, A; GOLDBLATT, D and PERRATON, J (eds) (1999) *Global Transformations: Politics, Economics and Culture* (Polity Press, Cambridge).

HEYDEBRAND, W (2001) 'From Globalisation of Law to Law under Globalisation' in D Nelken and J Feest (eds) *Adapting Legal Cultures* (Hart Publishing, Oxford and Portland).

HIGGOTT, R A; UNDERHILL, G R D and BIELER, A (eds) (2000) *Non-State Actors and Authority in the Global System* (Routledge, London and New York).

HOLLEMAN, J F (1978) 'Disparities and Uncertainties in African Law and Judicial Authority: A Rhodesian Case Study' 17 *African Law Studies* 1.

KNORR-CETINA, K (1988) 'The Micro-Social Order: Towards a Reconception' in N Fielding (ed) *Actions and Structure: Research Method in Social Theory* (Sage Publishing, London).
LASH, S and URRY, J (1994) *Economies of Signs and Space* (Sage Publishing, London).
LINDSEY, T (1999) *Indonesia: Law and Society* (Federation Press, Leichhardt, NSW).
MAHER, I (2002) 'Competition Law in the International Domain: Networks as a New Form of Governance' 29 *Journal of Law and Society* 111.
MARCUS, G (1992) 'Past, Present and Emergent Identities: Requirements for Ethnographies of Late Twentieth-Century Modernity Worldwide' in S Lash and J Friedmann (eds) *Modernity and Identity* (Blackwell, Oxford, Cambridge).
MCCARTHY, J (2005) 'Contesting decentralization: transnational policy narratives and the emergence of volatile socio-legal configurations in Central Kalimantan, Indonesia' in F von Benda-Beckmann, K von Benda-Beckmann and A Griffiths (eds) *Mobile People, Mobile Law: Expanding Legal Relations in a Contracting World* (Ashgate, Aldershot, Dartmouth).
MCGREW, A (1998) 'Global Legal Interaction and Present-Day Patterns of Globalisation' in V Gessner and AC Budak (eds) *Emerging Global Certainty: Empirical Studies on the Globalization of Law* (Dartmouth Publishing, Aldershot).
MERRY, S E (1997) 'Legal Pluralism and Transnational Culture: The Kaho'okolokolonui Kanaka Maoli Tribunal, Hawai'I' in R A Wilson (ed) *Human Rights, Culture and Context. Anthropological Perspectives* (Pluto Press, London).
MOORE, S F (1970) 'Law and Anthropology' in B Siegel (ed) *Biannual Review of Anthropology* (Stanford University Press, Stanford).
—— (1973) 'Law and Social Change: the Semi-Autonomous Social Field as an Appropriate Subject of Study' 70 *Law and Society Review* 719.
—— (1986) *Social Facts and Fabrications: "Customary" Law on Kilimanjaro 1880–1980* (Cambridge University Press, Cambridge and New York).
NEDERVEEN PIETERSE, J (1995) 'Globalization as Hybridization' in M Featherstone, S Lash and R Robertson (eds) *Global Modernities* (Sage Publishing, London).
NELKEN, D (2001) 'Towards a Sociology of Legal Adaptation' in D Nelken and J Feest (eds) *Adapting Legal Cultures* (Hart Publishing, Oxford and Portland).
NELKEN, D and FEEST, J (eds) (2001) *Adapting Legal Cultures* (Hart Publishing, Oxford and Portland).

OOMEN, B (2002) *Chiefs! Law, Power and Culture in Contemporary South Africa* (University of Leiden, Leiden).

RANDERIA, S (2001) *Local Refractions of Global Governance: Legal Plurality, International Institutions, NGOs and the Post-Colonial State in India* (Free University, Berlin).

—— (2003) 'Glocalization of Law: Environmental Justice, World Bank, NGOs and the Cunning State in India' 51 *Current Sociology* 307.

ROBÉ, J-P (1997) 'Multinational Enterprises: The Constitution of a Pluralistic Legal Order' in G Teubner (ed) *Global Law without a State* (Ashgate, Aldershot, Dartmouth).

ROBERTSON, R (1990) 'Mapping the Global Condition: Globalization as the Central Concept' in M Featherstone (ed) *Global Culture: Nationalism, Globalization and Modernity* (Sage Publishing, London).

—— (1995) 'Glocalization: Time-space and Homogeneity-Heterogeneity' in M Featherstone, S Lash and R Robertson (eds) *Global Modernities* (Sage Publishing, London).

RÖHL, K F and MAGEN, S (1996) 'Die Rolle des Rechts im Prozess der Globalisierung' 1 *Zeitschrift für Rechtssoziologie* 1.

ROSE, CV (1998) 'The "New" Law and Development Movement in the Post-Cold War Era: A Vietnam Case Study' 32 *Law and Society Review* 93.

SANTOS, BOAVENTURA DE SOUSA (1985) 'On Modes of Production of Law and Social Power' 13 *International Journal of the Sociology of Law* 299.

—— (1987) 'A Map of Misreading: Toward a Post-Modern Conception of Law' 14 *Journal of Law and Society* 279.

—— (1995) *Toward a New Common Sense: Law, Science and Politics in the Paradigmatic Transition* (Routledge, London and New York).

SASSEN, S (1991) *The Global City* (Princeton University Press, Princeton).

SEIDMAN, A; SEIDMAN, R B; and WÄLDE, T W (eds) (1999) *Making Development Work. Legislative Reform for Institutional Transformation and Good Governance* (Kluwer Law International, The Hague, London and Boston).

SNYDER, F (1981) *Capitalism and Legal Change: An African Transformation* (Academic Press, New York).

STARR, J and COLLIER, J (eds) (1989) *History and Power in the Study of Law* (Cornell University Press, Ithaca and London).

STRIJBOSCH, F (1984) 'The Concept of Pèla and its Social Significance in the Community of Moluccan Immigrants in the Netherlands' 23 *Journal of Legal Pluralism* 177.

—— (1999) 'Concepts Regarding Legal Pluralism and Their Applicability in the Context of Law Research among Moluccans in the Netherlands' in K von Benda-Beckmann and H Finkler (eds) *Folk Law and Legal Pluralism: Societies in Transition – The Papers of the XIth*

International Congress of the Commission on Folk Law and Legal Pluralism, Ottawa, 1999 (Ottawa: Department of Circumpolar Affairs).

TAMANAHA, B Z (1993) 'The Folly of the Social Scientific Concept of Legal Pluralism' 20 *Journal of Law and Society* 192.

TEUBNER, G (1996) 'Globale Bukowina: Zur Emergenz eines transnationalen Rechtspluralismus' 15 *Rechtshistorisches Journal* 255.

—— (1997a) 'Global Bukowina: Legal Pluralism in the World Society' in G Teubner (ed) *Global Law Without a State* (Ashgate, Aldershot, Dartmouth).

—— (ed) (1997b) *Global Law without a State* (Ashgate, Aldershot, Dartmouth).

TIGAR, M E and LEVY, M R (1977) *Law and the Rise of Capitalism* (Monthly Review Press, New York and London).

URRY, J (2000) *Sociology Beyond Societies: Mobilities for the Twenty-First Century* (Routledge, London).

VANDERLINDEN, J (1989) 'Return to Legal Pluralism: Twenty Years Later' 28 *Journal of Legal Pluralism* 149.

VEL, J (1992) 'Umbu Hapi versus Umbu Vincent: legal pluralism as an arsenal in village combats' in F von Benda-Beckmann and M van der Velde (eds) *Law as a Resource in Agrarian Struggles* (Wageningen University, Wageningen).

VOIGT, R (2000) *Globalisierung des Rechts* (Nomos, Baden-Baden).

WEILENMANN, M (2005) 'Project Law – Normative Orders of Bilateral Development Cooperation and social change: A Case Study From the German Agency for Technical Co-operation' in F von Benda-Beckmann, K von Benda-Beckmann and A Griffiths (eds) *Mobile People, Mobile Law: Expanding Legal Relations in a Contracting World* (Ashgate, Aldershot, Dartmouth).

WIBER, M (1999) 'Caught in the Cross-Hairs: Liberalizing Trade (Post-M.A.I.) and Privatizing the Right to Fish: Implications for Canada's Native Fisheries' 44 *Journal of Legal Pluralism* 33.

—— (2005) 'Mobile Law and Globalism: Epistemic Communities Versus Community-Based Innovation in the Fisheries Sector' in F von Benda-Beckmann, K von Benda-Beckmann and A Griffiths (eds) *Mobile People, Mobile Law: Expanding Legal Relations in a Contracting World* (Ashgate, Aldershot, Dartmouth).

WIENER, J (1999) *Globalization and the Harmonization of Law* (Pinter, London).

YASUDA, N (2003) 'Law and Development from the Southeast Asian Perspective: Methodology, History, and Paradigm Change' in C Antons (ed) *Law and Development in East and Southeast Asia* (RoutledgeCurzon, London and New York).

ZIEGERT, KA (2000) 'Globalisierung des Rechts aus der Sicht der Rechtssoziologie' in R Voigt (ed) *Globalisierung des Rechts* (Nomos, Baden-Baden).

4

Law Reform in the 'Developmental States' of East and Southeast Asia: From the Asian Crisis to September 11, 2001 and Beyond [1]

CHRISTOPH ANTONS

ISSUES OF LEGAL development in Asia[2] have been making unusual headlines for the last few years. At first, this was a result of the Asian Crisis that was blamed among other things on a lack of transparency in the legal infrastructure supporting businesses in various Asian economies. More recently, in the wake of the terrorist attacks in Indonesia and elsewhere in South and Southeast Asia, attention has shifted from economic issues to issues of security. In this context as well, law and law enforcement in Asian developing countries has come under intense scrutiny. One of the prime examples is Indonesia. A frequently-heard view is that Indonesia really is a lawless country, that is, a country that still lacks a functioning legal system. This view is certainly becoming more widespread since the many negative headlines of the past few years, from corruption scandals over the Tommy Suharto trial to the bombings in Bali, Jakarta and other places. Sometimes, observers add a further question: 'Why is it that we are only finding this out now?' This second question could be re-interpreted as meaning: 'How is it that a country that until recently was building airplanes and has been setting up stock markets could do so without a functioning legal system?'

[1] I would like to thank Volkmar Gessner, Jianfu Chen, Andrew Harding and Adriaan Bedner for helpful comments on earlier drafts of this chapter.

[2] 'Asia' in this chapter refers largely to the countries of Pacific Asia, which includes East Asia and Southeast Asia. However, since major policy changes were implemented in India during the 1990s, India is often discussed in this context as well. For a more detailed explanation of the various concepts of 'Asia' in social science disciplines, see Antons and Gessner (chapter 1 of this volume).

In the first part of this chapter, I will try to answer these questions by pointing to the use of law in the development efforts of various countries in Asia. This section provides a departure point for the second part, in which I will summarise the impact of the Asian Crisis and the subsequent law reform debate. My treatment of the reform debate will only be very brief and I will refer for details to other chapters in this volume. In the final part of this chapter, I will raise the question of what the policies after September 11, 2001 will mean for the ongoing debate about both law and globalisation in Asia. The Asian Crisis of 1997 and the events of September 11, 2001 were important events that influenced law-making and law reform in various Asian countries, albeit in different areas of law.

The Oñati workshop on which this book is based was intended as a follow-up to the earlier edited volume, 'Law and Development in East and Southeast Asia' (Antons, 2003a). This earlier book contained updated papers from a conference held at the International Institute of Asian Studies in Leiden immediately after the onset of the Asian Crisis in early 1998. Not surprisingly, most of the papers envisaged a decline of the 'Asian developmental state' and the Asian model of state-led economic development, although some authors concluded that the old concepts and ways of operating would not simply disappear without a major struggle among vested interests. The chapters in this current volume (see in particular Halliday and Carruthers, chapter ten) confirm that this was an accurate prediction. After the initial enthusiasm for law reform, compromises had to be made and many of the transplanted abstract concepts of international business law and 'good governance' proved less practicable 'on the ground'. The recent security crisis has, particularly in Southeast Asia, to some extent overshadowed the older debate about commercial law reform. Bombings and abductions in Indonesia and the Philippines are no longer targeting only Government officials, military and police, but also the Western expatriate and business community and tourists. The subsequent demands of Western nations led by the United States for a strengthening of security have an obvious impact in fields such as criminal and criminal procedural law. However, there is an indirect link between these demands and the economy as well, via bilateral and multilateral aid agencies and their various funding policies.

I LAW IN THE 'ASIAN DEVELOPMENTAL STATE'

One of the most fascinating characteristics of law in the context of Asian development policies is the way Asian governments attempt to achieve continuity by constantly redefining traditional concepts and integrating them into the development process, thereby creating a distinctive form of

Asian modernity (Eisenstadt, 1996). Consideration of this 'path dependency' (Baum, 2003: 148) is not to be neglected in the current reform debate. This part of my chapter will provide some examples of this integration of old and new and of the constant renegotiation of tradition. While many of these examples will be familiar to readers with experience in Asia, they provide readers without such regional knowledge with an important backdrop to understanding the forces that shape law in Asia.

One response to the assertion that a country such as Indonesia has no working legal system is that it actually has too many of them as a result of historical developments and of a conscious policy of the previous Dutch colonial power of keeping the legal rules for various population groups separate (Antons, 2001a). In this way, all the various layers from hundreds of years of Indonesian legal history have been preserved. These layers are traditional customary law or *adat*, going back to the period before the arrival of Islam in the eleventh century[3], Islamic law, Dutch law enacted for the Netherlands East Indies, and Indonesian law after independence, which increasingly reflects a variety of influences including Australian and US ones.[4] The Dutch had enshrined legal apartheid in the quasi-Constitution of the Netherlands East Indies, which provided that European law only applied to Europeans and people from countries with similar legal systems (such as the Japanese) while indigenous customary law and Islamic law applied to Indonesians.[5] Caught between these groups were the foreign trading minorities of Chinese, Indians and Arabs who resided permanently in the colony. Because of their importance to the colonial economy, they became subjected to European commercial law, but remained under their own customary law for family affairs and matters of inheritance.[6] A side-effect of these measures was, of course, that they kept the population not just legally apart, but they also reduced the opportunity for interaction in daily life. The different sets of rules meant that marriages between members of the various groups of the population were difficult,[7] that commercial interactions often required the assistance of lawyers to decide which law was to govern them, and that the various groups tended to remain among themselves in separate quarters of the cities.

[3] On the arrival of Islam in Indonesia, see Ricklefs (1981).

[4] See, for the example of copyright law, Antons (1998).

[5] See Arts 75 and 109 of the *Reglement op het beleid der regering van Nederlandsch-Indië* in *Staatsblad van Nederlandsch-Indië* 1855 No 2 and Arts 131 and 163 of the subsequent *Wet op de staatsinrichting van Nederlandsch-Indië* in *Staatsblad van Nederlandsch-Indië* 1926 No 415.

[6] The classical work on these matters is Gautama (1993). See also Gautama and Hornick (1983).

[7] This issue has recently resurfaced as a result of a restrictive interpretation of the Marriage Law of 1974 by the Indonesian Supreme Court: see Pompe (1991).

The picture is not dissimilar if one looks at other former colonies in Asia (Antons, 2001a). The question of why so many of the freshly independent countries after World War II kept these discriminatory and complicated colonial legal systems instead of changing them immediately remains one of the persistent mysteries for many students of Asian post-colonial history. The reasons for this, however, are purely practical. Immediately after independence, governments had neither the means nor the personnel nor the time for complete law reform. In addition, the various population groups had by then found their interests best served by different parts of the colonial legal order. In countries such as Indonesia and Malaysia, Muslims debated the role of Islamic law and the level of influence from pre-Islamic *adat*, Christians and Chinese hoped for a stronger role of Dutch- or British-derived state law, and non-Christian, non-Islamic communities wanted to maintain their customary systems. Perhaps not surprisingly then, many governments decided to base the new states on compromises and to hope for a solution of the various conflicts of interest at a later stage.

It was particularly hoped that this solution would arrive quasi-automatically with economic development and that people would be more willing to settle on common legal principles once they were better-educated and well-fed. The developmentalist regimes, of Suharto in Indonesia and others in Asia, received their limited legitimacy from this hope. As a result of this legitimacy, based on success in economic development, a particular kind of developmentalist law-making developed that is not specific to Indonesia but can also be found in other countries of Pacific Asia.[8] One of the characteristics of law in the 'Asian developmental state' was the initial concentration of law reform efforts in a few areas of commercial law of immediate relevance to international trade. Intellectual property laws are an excellent example. During the last two decades great pressure has been exerted on Asian developing countries to improve their intellectual property laws. This was initially applied on a bi-lateral basis (Antons, 1991) and, since the conclusion of the WTO Agreement in 1994, via the part of the agreement relating to trade-related aspects of intellectual property rights (TRIPS).[9] There was little change, however, in laws that were only

[8] Compare the 1981 statement of prominent Chinese jurist Zhang Youyu, as cited in J Chen (1999: 41–2):

> Socialist democracy and the legal system are inseparable; both of them are [to be used] to consolidate socialist economic bases and to enhance socialist development. At present, they are powerful tools for promoting the Four Modernisations. Neither of them is an end, but both of them are means.

As for the varieties of capitalism and their effect on the legal systems of the region, see Gessner in chapter 2 of this volume.

[9] Agreement Establishing the World Trade Organization, The Final Act of the 1986–94 Uruguay Round of the Trade Negotiations, and Agreement on Trade-Related Aspects of Intellectual Property Rights, Annex 1C of the Marrakesh Agreement Establishing the World

relevant domestically. One reason for this is that national legislation in such areas is much more difficult to push through politically, as is demonstrated by the strong resistance of the Indonesian Muslim community to a unified national family law in the middle of the 1970s (Katz and Katz, 1975; Cammack, Young and Heaton, 1996). But a second and perhaps more important reason is that indigenous legal traditions are also consciously used by Asian governments to provide a backbone for their development efforts, especially in relation to social security. Principles derived from indigenous moral and religious values provide an alternative system to state-run and -funded welfare systems. These traditions provide a familiar support structure to which (if these traditions and their outworkings are maintained) people can return if they fail to make a living in the big cities of Asia. In societies where all funds are geared towards the 'catching up' process with the West, or with more developed Asian neighbours, social security and financial support at the grass roots level remains the responsibility of the family and of informal credit co-operatives. Malaysian Prime Minister Mahathir, for example, in his landmark speech 'Malaysia: The Way Forward' of 1991,[10] embraced a caring society with a family-based welfare system as one of the fundamental pillars of the Malaysia of the future (Jomo, 2003: 160–1).

Such policies require a heavy emphasis on the collective spirit and social harmony within communities. Accordingly, the assertion of individual rights in court action is often discouraged. In some countries, a major explanation for low litigation rates is simply the neglect of the judicial system and the low esteem in which the courts system is held. However, there are cultural factors as well such as the tendencies in Asian societies to encourage mediation and to avoid the escalation of disputes (Tu, 1996: 9). While such attitudes are partly the result of an education in traditions such as Confucianism, they are also promoted by legal policies. John Owen Haley has shown that in Japan, an outbreak of litigation in the aftermath of the *Meiji* Revolution was soon contained by laws prescribing conciliation processes of an increasingly compulsory character (Haley, 1991: 83–96). These laws did not survive the post-war reforms in Japan, but as Haley points out:

> the attitudes they fostered – that of conciliation as a culturally preferable means of conflict resolution and thus conflict resolution instead of law enforcement as the primary function of the courts in private law cases – were to have enduring impact. (Haley, 1991: 96)

Trade Organization, signed in Marrakesh, Morocco, 15 April 1994. For a survey of developments in Asian intellectual property law, see the essays in Heath (2003).

[10] The speech is often summarized as 'Vision 2020', because Mahathir used it to outline the strategies to achieve developed country status by the year 2020.

Furthermore, while the number of applicants for the Japanese National Legal Examination increased almost ten-fold between 1949 and 1986, the percentage of successful applicants declined from 10.5 per cent in 1949 to only 2 per cent in 1986, which means that the number of practising lawyers has been kept very low (see the statistics in Haley, 1991: 107).

A good example of the continuing importance of alternative social security arrangements outside the state sector is provided by Singapore. The Central Provident Fund, as Singapore's social security system, does not cover roughly one-third of the labour force consisting in particular of casual, part-time and contract workers (Asher, 1993: 155–6). Statistics show that 75.9 per cent of senior Singaporean citizens receive income from their children and 86.2 per cent of those aged 55 and over live with their children. It is against this background that one has to see the *Maintenance of Parents Act* introduced in the mid-1990s that allowed parents to sue their children if the children neglected their Confucian duties to look after their parents in old age (Low and Ngiam, 1999: 241–2; see also Dragsbaek Schmidt, 2000). The example of Singapore's law upholding Confucian tradition also shows that the maintenance of traditional support structures may become problematic once Asian societies become more affluent.

It is important to point out that the approaches of Asian developmental states with regards to law were not really new, but continued an Asian tradition that had defined the relationship between governments and their subjects in terms of duties rather than rights (Ghai, 1998). Many authors, such as Jones (1993), have analysed the role of Confucian thought in East Asian approaches to law and governance and the centrality of a morally superior individual in it, as expressed in the following passage from the Confucian classic *The Great Learning*:

> The ancients who wished to illustrate illustrious virtue throughout the kingdom, first ordered well their own states. Wishing to order well their states, they first regulated their families. Wishing to regulate their families, they first cultivated their persons. Wishing to cultivate their persons they first rectified their hearts. Wishing to rectify their hearts they first sought to be sincere in their thoughts. Wishing to be sincere in their thoughts, they first extended to the utmost their knowledge. Such extension of knowledge lay in the investigation of things. Things being investigated, knowledge became complete. Their knowledge being complete, their thoughts were sincere. Their thoughts being sincere, their hearts were then rectified. Their hearts being rectified, their persons were cultivated. Their persons being cultivated, their families were regulated. Their families being regulated, their states were rightly governed. Their states being rightly governed, the whole kingdom was made tranquil and happy. (J Legge (1893) *The Great*

Learning Vol 1 in *The Chinese Classics* (Oxford University Press, Oxford and London) 131, as cited in Jones (1993).)[11]

What the passage illustrates further is that as a consequence of the personal virtue involved, East Asian political and legal thought does not distinguish between the public and the private domain (Tu, 1996: 8; Jones, 1993: 22). The often criticised blurring of the distinction between public and private law in parts of Asia (Antons, 2003c: 239) may therefore have its roots in this personified understanding of virtuous governance.[12] On the one hand, many institutions that Western law regards as private, such as the family, have public functions in traditional Asian thought. They used to have a certain autonomy in meting out punishment, as is famously illustrated by the execution of an unfaithful concubine in Zhang Yimou's film '*Raise the Red Lantern*'.[13] The family was further regarded as a corporate entity in commercial life, able to hold property and to wield political power (Ebrey, 1984: 37–51). On the other hand, public law and in particular criminal law was also applied by feudal governments in Asia to enforce private obligations, such as contracts (Haley, 1991: 11, 20). Where feudal governments concerned themselves with their subjects in the realm of law, they often did so in a harsh and brutal manner. Different laws applied according to status, evidence was frequently extracted under torture and punishments were severe (Ishii, 1986: 169–70) and even meted out against unsuccessful plaintiffs.[14] Against this background, one can understand the Chinese distinction between *fa* (law) and *li* (virtue[15]) (Bodde and Morris, 1967: 11; P M Chen, 1973: 13) and the traditional dislike of the Chinese for everything that has to do with state law and with lawyers. However, this understanding of law as referring largely to criminal law is by no means confined to East Asia. The term for 'law' in Indonesian is *hukum*, but its verb form *menghukum* means 'to punish'.

Asian developmental states continued this tradition to a considerable degree, although somewhat restrained by the international monitoring of

[11] A more concise summary of these thoughts can be found in Mencius' remark: 'Everyone says "The realm (*t'ien-hsia*), the state (*kuo*), and the family (*chia*)"' (as quoted in Ebrey, 1984: 38).

[12] For a socialist variant of this thinking in the People's Republic of China, see Chen (1995) 52–6.

[13] The death penalty was in particular regarded as appropriate in cases of incest, which included sexual relations with a father's or grandfather's concubine, the wife of one's father's brother, one's own or one's father's sister, a daughter-in-law or granddaughter-in-law, and a brother's daughter: see Ebrey (1993: 252). See also the prescription on the beating of servants in Yüan Ts'ai's 'Precepts for Social Life' in Ebrey (1984: 292–3) and a similar extract from Ssu-ma Kuang's 'Precepts for Family Life' in Ebrey (1984: 49).

[14] See the cases involving unwanted attention from fathers-in-law in Ebrey (1993: 253). In all cases, the sons and daughters-in-law were punished for bringing the accusations in violation of filial piety. In one case, the judge decided not to have the principals tortured into confessions, 'because he knew a woman could not hold out as long as a man'.

[15] *Li* is also often translated as 'correct ceremonial conduct': see Ebrey (1984: 47).

human rights and principles of democracy. Nevertheless, there are numerous examples for this authoritarian understanding of state power, such as the extra-judicial killings of criminals by killing squads in Indonesia in the mid-1980s (Schwarz, 1994: 249). The Internal Security Acts of Malaysia and Singapore also allow for the easy arrest and indefinite detention of suspects (Soesastro, 2003: 74, 77). Human rights activists in Thailand have recently been questioning the killing of about 1,500 'small-time drug suspects by unknown assailants' (*The Bangkok Post*, 14 March 2003). And press reports about new moveable execution vans in China remind readers of the shocking fact that of the 542 Articles in the revised Chinese Criminal Code of 1997, 76 mention the death penalty. As Jianfu Chen points out 'many of these articles deal with more than one offence and many offences in the revised criminal law are punishable by the death penalty' (Chen, 2002: 111–12). A number of further amendments made since 1997 also include the death penalty, adding to the already extremely harsh character of the law.[16]

As far as the political power structure is concerned, attempts at democratisation may run into the problem that political power is often less defined in terms of party programmes than by invoking ethnic, regional or religious ties. Finally, until recently, the idea of an administrative law that would allow citizens to sue officials and the administration was little developed in Asia (Zhang, 1997).[17] In fact, perfectly in keeping with China's legal tradition, Chinese administrative law heavily emphasises 'administrative punishment', which includes such measures as 'detention for review' and 'corrective work'. As a consequence, the distinction between criminal punishment and 'administrative punishment' is not always clear (Zhang, 1997: 84–6). In those Asian countries that were under colonial rule, the law that was introduced by the Western colonial powers was not the same as that in Europe. Instead, it was a crippled, authoritarian version of European law designed to facilitate the running of a colony.[18] It provided for a harsh law and order regime, but not for the constitutional safeguards and individual rights to which Europeans had become accustomed.[19] If it comes to an assessment of the authoritarian nature of Asian legal systems, it is this local institutional history to which close attention must be paid rather than European political ideologies or

[16] Personal communication, Jianfu Chen, 9 August 2003.

[17] See also Ohnesorge, chapter 5 of this volume.

[18] For the example of Singapore, see Carter (2003: 272). More generally Yasuda (2003: 38) and Antons (2001b: 214).

[19] As to colonial legal instruments for the prevention of subversive activities inherited by Indonesia, see 't-Hart (1987: 198–201).

economic policies. In most Asian jurisdictions, developments were in fact too *ad hoc* and too idiosyncratic to allow for easy references to European models.

Instead of the rule of law, many Asian governments showed a marked preference for some form of administrative guidance. Under the Japanese term for the phenomenon, '*gyōsei shidō*', it became a much discussed quasi-legal phenomenon for Japanologists and Japanese law experts[20] and it is one of the reasons often used to explain why a country with very few lawyers can successfully industrialise. The Japanese version of administrative guidance has been described by Young (in Dean, 1997: 221) as:

> nonbinding administrative action that encourages regulated parties to act in a way that furthers an administrative aim. Although compliance with administrative guidance is technically voluntarily, Japanese administrators rely on informal pressure and other means of enforcement to persuade regulated parties to comply. This reliance on informal encouragement as opposed to legal coercion permits the bureaucracy to expand the areas into which they may intrude. It simultaneously limits the extent of those intrusions, however, and requires the bureaucracy to consult and negotiate extensively with the regulated parties.

Matsushita (1993) differentiates between promotional, regulatory and adjudicative administrative guidance, with regulatory administrative guidance being the most controversial. Areas of public life in which administrative guidance is frequently used are building and development permits, environmental regulation and the regulation of the economy. Among the more famous cases from the 1960s and 1970s of successful administrative guidance were the Ministry of International Trade and Industry's (MITI) 'advice' to steel producer Sumitomo to reduce its production, advice that was combined with a threat to cut its import quota for coal; and the request made by the municipal government of the Tokyo suburb of Musashino to a local developer to provide land and money for the construction of schools in exchange for a building permit. In the latter case, the developer only accepted the conditions after the local municipal government threatened to cut its water supply (Foljanty-Jost, 1989: 174–7).[21] However, as Ramseyer and Nakazato have shown (1999: 208–11), by the 1980s the view that administrative guidance remained generally outside judicial review could no longer be maintained. They point to a series of cases, beginning in the late 1970s, in which property developers were successfully suing local governments for not acting on applications or for trying to enforce conditions that had no clearly defined legal basis.

[20] See, for example, Foljanty-Jost (1989), and the extracts from Matsushita (1993), Yamanouchi (1974), Dean (1991) Shindo (1992) and Young (1984) in Dean (1997: 194–221). See further Dean (1997: 156–9) and Ramseyer and Nakazato (1999: 205–11).

[21] Foljanty-Jost (1989: 173) points in this context to the traditional Japanese saying 'to attack Edo in revenge for Nagasaki'.

Nevertheless, they attribute the concentration of cases related to local building permits, and the frequency with which certain municipal governments were involved, to politics. By then, the ruling Liberal Democratic Party (LDP) had lost many local elections and local governments formed from opposition parties found themselves under increased scrutiny from an LDP appointed judiciary (Ramseyer and Nakazato, 1999: 216–18).

Further aspects of law in Asian developmental states that make administrative guidance possible are the open-ended, discretionary nature of much of the legislation, the often unusually large number of implementing administrative decrees and the extended definition of bureaucratic competence. In Japan, administrative guidance is often simply based on an enabling statute that gives the bureaucracy power to regulate a specific field, which may then become redefined as including each and every aspect of it, whether spelled out in the legislation or not (Young in Dean, 1997: 215–16). As for a frequently confusing proliferation of administrative decrees substituting for legislation, Hal Hill's quotation of an Indonesian official describing the Indonesian Foreign Investment Law is instructive:

> The [Foreign Investment] Law is brief and simple, though one should not look at [it] only, but at the 328 kinds of related legislation as well. (Hill, 1996: 100)

Similarly, Vietnam's Law on Land of 1993 refers to nearly 600 implementing regulations (Pham, 2002: 56).

Indonesian intellectual property law is a good example of this mixture of legislation and administrative decrees. Indonesia modernised its intellectual property system during the 1980s and 1990s, mainly as a reaction to pressure from trading partners such as the United States and the European Union (Antons, 1991). However, during much of this period, the government maintained a fairly strong role in the administration of the system. Principles and concepts in the Indonesian intellectual property legislation were often only vaguely defined. For details one had to look further, and the legislation referred to various implementing decrees to be issued by the President, the Government, the Ministry of Justice or the Director of the Patent Office. Many of the most important parts of the Indonesian intellectual property legislation conclude with a section stating that further details will be explained in such a decree.[22] This has several, probably intended, consequences. First, it takes the regulatory power for substantial parts of the law out of the hands of parliament and puts it back into the hands of the executive. Secondly, the actual interpretation of the legislation and the correctness of administrative decision-making is no longer a matter for the courts, but is again supervised by administrators and other parts of the executive, such as patent examiners, the trade mark or copyright

[22] For a more recent survey of these decrees, see Antons (2003b: 392).

registrars, the Director of the Intellectual Property Office,[23] the Minister or the President. Thirdly, this allows the government to meet important international deadlines for new legislation under international agreements, while at the same time giving it an opportunity to provide details and to actually implement the legislation in accordance with its own timetable. Elsewhere in Southeast Asia, Vietnam has shown a similar preference for a large number of implementing decrees to supplement a basic intellectual property framework legislation that until recently was included in the Civil Code (Dang, 2000: 145–50).[24]

A few concrete examples from the area of Indonesian intellectual property law reveal the situation. First, licensing agreements may be concluded in Indonesia, but they need to be registered with the Intellectual Property Office and the officials there need to examine the agreement to ensure that it is free of provisions that could harm the Indonesian economy or impede the capacity of Indonesians to develop technology. But what precisely 'harms the economy' or 'impedes the capacity to develop technology' and how are officials required to decide these issues? The Indonesian intellectual property legislation promises guidelines in the form of government decrees,[25] but these decrees still have to be issued (Antons, 2004: 113–14; Antons, 2003b: 418–19; Antons, 2002: 243). Elsewhere in Southeast Asia, Malaysian officials have to grapple with the questions as to what constitutes 'unfairness' or what amounts to 'excessive' royalties in assessing technology transfer agreements under the Industrial Coordination Act of 1975 (Goon, 2003:332). Secondly, well-known foreign trade marks are protected in Indonesia, but such protection is limited to goods of the same kind as used by the trade mark owner. What is very common in Asia, however, is the use of famous foreign trade marks for completely different kinds of goods (for example, the use of prestigious textile brands for products such as toothbrushes or even motor oil). In many of these cases, it will be difficult to argue that this use will have a diluting effect on the foreign trade mark. Nevertheless, foreign companies have been pressing the government for years to legislate against this practice. Finally, the government provided in the Trade Marks Act of 2001 that such marks

[23] *Direktorat Jenderal Hak Kekayaan Intelektual* (Ditjen HaKI) or the Directorate General of Intellectual Property Rights (DGIP) in *Departemen Hukum dan Hak Asasi Manusia* (the Department of Law and Human Rights), covering patents, trade marks, copyrights, industrial design, integrated circuitry design, trade secrets and traditional knowledge. For updates see the DGIP website: <http://www.dgip.go.id/> and <http://www.dgip.go.id/home.en> (last accessed 30 December 2004).

[24] For a strategic use of implementing and enabling legislation as one of the 'weapons of the weak' in complying with the conditions set by the international financial institutions, see also Halliday and Carruthers, chapter 10 of this volume.

[25] See Arts 72 Patents Act, 43(3) and 4 Trade Marks Act, 47 Copyright Act, 8 Trade Secrets Act, 35 Industrial Designs Act, 27 Integrated Circuit Layout Act: see further Antons (2004: 113–14).

were also protected if used on dissimilar goods, but only if they fulfilled conditions that were to be specified in a government decree. That decree, however, has not yet been issued (Antons, 2003b: 409).[26]

My last example comes from copyright law, where the Indonesian Copyright Act provides that the state holds the copyright to folklore and to so-called 'products of popular culture' (Article 10(2) of the Copyright Act of 2001), a term that refers to traditional artwork of various kinds. With much of such 'folklore' situated in Indonesia's regions, this has quite obviously the potential to come into conflict with the current policy of decentralisation (see F and K von Benda-Beckmann, chapter nine of this volume). When this provision was first included in the Copyright Act of 1982 and various regional communities began to express concerns, the government reacted quickly and inserted a further subsection into the provision explaining that the state would exercise these rights only vis-à-vis foreigners, so that the communities were free to continue using their own folkloristic material. In the new Copyright Act, Article 10(3) now provides that foreigners have to obtain a licence from a relevant state agency. However, apart from the fact that this agency has so far not been set up, the legislation in fact creates a national approach to a question of local cultural identity. For example, would a Balinese artist who moves to Sydney and acquires Australian citizenship no longer be allowed to use motifs from his village in Bali? Furthermore, which institution will decide what precisely constitutes 'traditional art' as opposed to, for example, individual modern calligraphy or dance? And how will such a body be staffed? And last, but not least, which institution will collect and distribute the royalties? These royalties could become an issue under Indonesia's new decentralisation laws that foresee a splitting of resources and tax income between Jakarta and the regions and districts. At the moment the debate still focuses on primary resources such as oil and gas, but it is only a matter of time before biological and cultural resources will become an issue, particularly in those parts of Indonesia that have little else to export. As in the other examples mentioned above, the Indonesian Copyright Act outlines the approach to the issue, but the crucial details are missing and the Act once again refers to a government regulation to be issued in the future. More than twenty years after the provision was introduced in the previous Copyright Act, this implementing decree is still not available (Antons 2000a: 84–8; Antons 2005b: 49).

[26] For a more detailed account of the use and abuse of well-known foreign trade marks in Indonesia, see Antons (2000b).

II LAW REFORM SINCE THE ASIAN CRISIS

With the Asian Crisis, this open-ended, discretionary nature of Asian law has come under pressure and Asian governments have embarked on frenetic activities to reform their legal systems. In line with the 'good governance' doctrine of international financial institutions and with the renewed emphasis on law under the influence of the new institutionalist theories of Douglass North and others (Gessner, chapter two of this volume), transparency and enforcement have been key areas of concern. This required the introduction of more comprehensive legislation, more serious efforts to combat corruption and instructions to judges, prosecutors and police officers to take the letter of the law more seriously than in the past. While much of this originally targeted areas of commercial law, it had spill-over effects in other areas of law. However, these spill-over effects occurred not so much because of a strengthening of the institutions or the overall legislative framework, but rather because, with economic success, developmentalist regimes in Asia had lost the main justification for their existence. Large sections of the population had been willing to tolerate authoritarian governments as long as they were successful in providing double-digit growth rates. With the end of economic success, this tolerance was waning quickly and calls for political liberalisation and changes in government followed in countries such as Korea, Thailand and Indonesia. In chapter six of this volume, Andrew Harding describes the constitutional developments in Thailand and contrasts them with the situation in Malaysia. There, a political and judicial crisis developed after the Malaysian Deputy Prime Minister Anwar Ibrahim challenged his political mentor and Prime Minister, Dr Mahathir, and was subsequently jailed for corruption charges (Wu, 2000/2001; Wu, 1999).

In strongly centralised states such as Indonesia, a period of administrative decentralisation followed the Asian Crisis. Tax revenues and the approval of various types of investment were diverted to the regions and districts (F and K von Benda-Beckmann, chapter nine of this volume). While this originally looked like a realisation of long-standing aspirations to build a more federal structure, it soon became a target of criticism for foreign businesses who suddenly found themselves being confronted with various administrative hurdles at federal and regional level instead of the previously centralised 'one-stop' approval mechanism. In provinces such as Aceh and West Papua active rebel movements felt encouraged in their fight for some form of independence, or at least autonomy, from Jakarta and the conflicts in these regions deepened. As a consequence of greater political freedom, the debate about human rights also intensified and various human rights commissions were established around the region. Apart from local pressure, the emphasis of the Clinton administration on human rights was an important reason for this development.[27]

In spite of these spill-over effects in the areas of constitutional law, administrative law and criminal and criminal procedural law, the bulk of the law reform efforts once again targeted various fields of business law, not only in Indonesia but in other parts of Asia as well. However, while legislation was often changed or newly-enacted, enforcement and the strengthening of the institutional framework remained weak. As a consequence, there has been a tendency, in commercial law in particular, to rely on ad hoc solutions and to set up specialised courts, such as the intellectual property and international trade court in Thailand (Ariyanunantaka, 1999; Kuanpoth, 2003: 342) and the commercial courts in Indonesia that handle bankruptcy and intellectual property cases (Halliday and Carruthers, chapter ten of this volume).[28] Sceptics think that intellectual property reform cannot be divorced from the rest of the legal system (Butt, 2002: 437), and that reform efforts are bound to fail until a more substantial overhaul of the system is achieved. Nevertheless, these efforts might allow a limited number of judges to overcome the limitations of poorly-resourced law libraries and acquire the very specialised knowledge that is now needed to decide cases in fields such as intellectual property law.[29] Of course, appeals from the specialised commercial courts still go to the much less specialised higher courts, but a better working of the system at the bottom might take the pressure off the higher courts as well.

However, crucial parts of the legal infrastructure are often either not yet in place or completely out-dated as a result of years of neglect. Indonesia's civil procedural code (the *Herziene Indonesische Reglement* of 1848)[30] is a prime example. It is still the same, rather paternalistic civil procedural code that the Dutch drafted for the indigenous population of the Netherlands East Indies.[31] This code gave the judge a very strong role and considerably simplified the taking of evidence.[32] For Europeans, or for those people granted the status of Europeans in the colony, a much more sophisticated

[27] For a detailed discussion of the human rights debate in Asia, see the contributions in Bauer and Bell (1999).

[28] For a Thai case similarly controversial to the *Manulife* saga in Indonesia, see Crispin and Zaun (2003: 44–5).

[29] For a survey of these issues see Antons (2005a: 287-99).

[30] During the final years of colonial rule, the Law was originally known as the *Herziene Indische Reglement op de uitoefening van de politie, de burgerlijke regtspleging en de strafvordering onder de Inlanders en vreemde Oosterlingen op Java en Madura.* After independence the reference to '*Indië*' and the discriminating term *inlanders* was replaced by reference to 'Indonesia' and 'Indonesians' respectively.

[31] The HIR as the *Reglement* is abbreviated applies only to Java and Madura. For other islands it is supplemented by the *Rechtsreglement Buitengewesten*: see Soetantio and Oeripkartawinata, 1995: 5.

[32] The French introduced a similar simplified procedural code in the colony of Cochin-China in Vietnam, see Hooker (1978: 159–60).

civil procedural code (the *Reglement op de Burgerlijke Rechtsvordering*) applied that was almost identical with the one in use in the Netherlands. Ironically, the Japanese abolished this more sophisticated code during their brief military rule in World War II, in an attempt to rid the colony of European influences. As a result, the simplified and inadequate legislation for 'indigenous Indonesians' has applied since then to the entire population, although in practice the provisions of the *Reglement op de Burgerlijke Rechtsvordering* may be applied analogously if necessary (Setiawan, 1992: 359–60; Soetantio and Oeripkartawinata, 1995: 6). Again, to provide an ad hoc solution in crucial areas of business law, procedural rules for the newly-created Commercial Court (*Pengadilan Niaga*) are now spread out over the more specialised legislation for bankruptcy and various fields of intellectual property (Antons, 2003b: 396–8).

Areas of commercial law reform other than intellectual property law and bankruptcy law were targeted for reform after the Asian Crisis. They included anti-monopoly and unfair competition legislation, foreign investment law, company law, labour law and banking and financial market regulation. Much of this new legislation concerns key areas of Asian developmentalist policy-making, which was based on close government-business links, cheap labour, cross-shareholding and preferential credit allocation. It was, therefore, hardly surprising that reform-minded governments soon encountered resistance from various factions of the political and business élite that had benefited from the previous practices. However, in almost all countries of East and Southeast Asia, perhaps with the exception of Singapore, the post-Crisis reform also triggered a wider debate about the direction of the countries concerned and their place in the emerging international economic order. Austerity measures imposed by the International Monetary Fund, and deregulation of the economy, led to widespread unemployment and rising prices for crucial commodities such as petrol and electricity, and basic dietary staples such as rice and milk. Governments that were nevertheless willing to implement the requested reforms were accused of 'selling out' to foreign interests and had to find a compromise between their eagerness to attract foreign investment and the need to safeguard the basic requirements of their populations (Dhume, 2003). An interesting example here is the difficult situation that the Thai government is facing with regards to patent protection of pharmaceuticals. Thailand is a country that is severely affected by the AIDS crisis. In common with many other Asian developing countries, it has a pharmaceutical industry specialising in the low cost manufacture of generic drugs (which nevertheless often rely on imported substances, many of which would be patented). As a consequence, Thailand's first Patents Act of 1979 did not provide protection for pharmaceutical patents. Following US trade pressure, such protection was finally introduced in 1992, leaving as the only loopholes the possibility of granting compulsory licences and the parallel importation of generic drugs from elsewhere. However, in spite of strong public demand, the Thai government has so far refused to take these steps for fear of trade sanctions. The government pointed out that, as regrettable as the suffering of the approximately one million AIDS sufferers was, it weighed comparatively less than the consequences of US trade sanctions that would affect the entire Thai population of approximately 60 million people (Kuanpoth, 2003).

III LAW REFORM IN ASIA AFTER SEPTEMBER 11, 2001

In the final part of this chapter I would like to raise the question of what impact the new geopolitical situation and the current focus on security issues by the world's only remaining superpower, the United States, might have on the continuing law reform debate in Asia. At the end of the 1980s, when the discussions about Japan's allegedly superior business practices and its road to economic prosperity were at their peak, the political scientist Ulrich Menzel edited a collection of essays entitled '*Japan – Im Schatten des Siegers*' ('Japan – In the Shadow of the Victorious Power'). The title of the four-volume collection directed the attention of the reader to an often neglected aspect of the so-called 'Asian miracle' of the 1970s and 1980s, namely the extent to which the Asian economic success was also dependent on the realities of the Cold War. Asian industriousness and development strategies notwithstanding, the Asian economic wonderland of those decades consisted of the most important Cold War allies of the West, countries such as Japan, Taiwan, South Korea, Thailand, Malaysia, Singapore and Indonesia that were regarded as front-line states in the battle to stop the advance of communism in Asia. Strategic geopolitical considerations form an important additional factor to explain why so much investment money was pumped into East and Southeast Asia in preference to other parts of the developing world. The Korean War (1950–53) and US assistance in re-establishing commercial ties with Southeast Asia were very important factors in Japan's industrial recovery after World War II (Beasley, 1990: 244–5; Allen 1981: 189–90). In the legal arena in various countries, what became later known as 'Asian business practices'—corruption, lack of democracy and poor human rights and labour standards—attracted relatively little attention, as long as strategic partnership considerations were dominant.

The picture changed after the fall of communism in Eastern Europe and the onset of economic liberalisation in China. Now 'the gloves came off' between previous allies and considerations of economic competition again dominated. Asia's high growth region now saw itself confronted with allegations of unfair trade from Western trading partners (Prestowitz, 1988: 181–217), while foreign investment flows were partly diverted to former ideological foes, such as China, Vietnam and Russia. As for the development of law, foreign investment and financial assistance packages from the major donor organisations became increasingly tied to improvements of the legal framework for business. The Clinton administration in the United States was also a driving force behind the renewed international emphasis on human rights and democratic reform. In Indonesia, the emphasis on democracy as well as a growing range of career alternatives for élite students (Kristiadi, 1999: 107–14) meant that by the end of the 1990s the military that had played such an influential role in the development of the country was in retreat from its double role in defence and politics.[33]

The question that the region now faces after the events of September 11, 2001, and the subsequent war on terrorism (with its military campaigns in Afghanistan and Iraq) is whether the new strategic considerations could lead to a return of 'law and order' policies in parts of Asia, and in economic terms will again allow some countries in Asia to sail 'in the shadow of the victorious power' (Weiss, 2002). Human rights lawyers and activists indeed see indications of such a development. They point, for example, to the debate in Indonesia about an Armed Forces Bill authorising the army to take control in emergency situations (McBeth, 2003: 18–19). After the Marriott Hotel bombing in Jakarta, voices were also raised to revise the newly enacted law on anti-terrorism and give the national security forces greater power. The Indonesian Defence Minister even proposed the introduction of an Internal Security Act similar to the legislation still in force in Malaysia and Singapore (Hari and Suryana, 2003). New anti-terrorism legislation has also been introduced in Nepal, Thailand, India, Hong Kong, China and Japan (Samydorai, 2003: 224–8) (As for India, see Mendelsohn, chapter seven of this volume.) Meanwhile, countries such as Singapore and Malaysia make renewed use of their wide discretionary powers of detention via their existing Internal Security Acts (Harding, chapter six of this volume). Not surprisingly, Lee Kuan Yew in a 2002 interview with the *Far Eastern Economic Review* saw his tight control of politics in Singapore vindicated.[34]

Frequently, the new legislation is the result of bilateral or multilateral economic pressure or the granting of incentives. Asian allies of the United States in the 'war on terror', such as Pakistan and Thailand, have been rewarded with substantial aid packages or the preferential offer of Free

[33] In Indonesia, this double role was ideologically enshrined during the final years of the Sukarno government as the 'dwi fungsi' (dual function) doctrine: see Jenkins (1984: 2–3). The doctrine was only recently abandoned. With it ended also the parliamentary participation of the Armed Forces (McBeth, 2003).

[34] 'Lee Kuan Yew: What went wrong?' *Far Eastern Economic Review* 12 December 2002, 26–7.

Trade Agreements (*Far Eastern Economic Review*, 3 July 2003; Crispin and Wagstaff, 2003: 16; Buckman, 2003: 18–19). In this sense, the war on terrorism can indirectly have a major impact on the economic development efforts of the countries concerned. Ohnesorge (chapter five of this volume) considers these new developments in the bilateral relationships of the United States.

Nevertheless, if all this can be interpreted as leading to a 'turning back of the clock' in terms of democratisation, it will not be easy to achieve. Today the public debate is open and free in countries like Indonesia. At least at this stage, it seems very difficult to imagine that the society could simply return to an environment as restricted as that of the Suharto years. Those voices that advocate a more authoritarian rule must also be reminded that a return to the previous policies would not be without consequences for the economy. It was the constant under-funding of their units and concerns about the loyalty of their troops that led Indonesian army officers to become involved in businesses as early as the 1950s (Kristiadi, 1999: 103–7). In this regard, little appears to have changed. A recent rather bizarre gun battle between military and police units in North Sumatra was apparently triggered by the desire of both units to detain the same drug dealers (Gunawan, 2002). As long as the security apparatus is not properly paid and remains dependent on 'extra income', the fight for transparency and against corrupt practices seems a rather lost battle.[35]

CONCLUSION

During the 1970s and 1980s many governments in East and Southeast Asia achieved high growth rates by offering foreign capital a safe haven for investment. Authoritarian policies guaranteed the safety of the investment environment. The strategy was particularly successful during the Cold War when the choice of investment destinations was rather restricted and Western allies in Asia received preferential treatment. The situation changed after the end of the Cold War in the 1990s, when the same allies had to compete with former Communist foes such as China and Vietnam. At the same time, they were confronted with accusations of unfair trade practices and their labour and human rights standards came under scrutiny. Calls for transparency and improvement of the legal infrastructure intensified after the Asian Crisis of 1997 and were backed by foreign governments and international institutions. The result was a considerable degree of political liberalisation and in some countries the emergence of a more decentralised structure. Law reform proceeded more slowly, however,

[35] See also the remarks of former defence minister Juwono Sudarsono and former Navy intelligence officer Djuanda in the *Jakarta Post* (Unidjaja, 2003).

in the economic arena. While political scientists express concern that the 'war on terror' waged by the Bush administration could reverse many of the achievements in political liberalisation and law reform in Asia, the question remains whether this concern is justified.[36] While such concerns have to be taken seriously, a turning back of the clock and a return to the previous 'law and order' regimes would appear to be difficult to achieve.

BIBLIOGRAPHY

ALLEN, G C (1981) *A Short Economic History of Modern Japan,* 4th edn (Macmillan Press, London).

ANTONS, CHRISTOPH (1991) 'Intellectual Property Law in ASEAN Countries' 13(3) *European Intellectual Property Review* 78.

—— (1998) 'Indonesian Copyright Law after TRIPS: Between Dutch Tradition and Anglo-American Influences' in Jan J C Kabel and Gerard J H M Mom (eds) *Intellectual Property and Information Law: Essays in Honour of Herman Cohen Jehoram* (Kluwer Law International, The Hague/London/Boston).

—— (2000a) *Intellectual Property Law in Indonesia* (Kluwer Law International, London).

—— (2000b) 'The Protection of Well-known Marks in Indonesia' in Christopher Heath and Kung-Chung Liu (eds) *The Protection of Well-known Marks in Asia* (Kluwer Law International, London) 199.

—— (2001a) 'Ethnicity, Law and Development in Southeast Asia' in Frans Hüsken and Dick van der Meij (eds) *Reading Asia: New Research in Asian Studies* (IIAS Asian Studies Series, Curzon, Richmond).

—— (2001b) 'Law and Development Thinking After the Asian Crisis of 1997' in 20(12) *Forum of International Development Studies* 205.

—— (2002) 'Technology Transfer in Indonesia' in Christopher Heath and Kung-Chung Liu (eds) *Legal Rules of Technology Transfer in Asia* (Kluwer Law International, London).

—— (ed) (2003a) *Law and Development in East and Southeast Asia* (RoutledgeCurzon, London).

—— (2003b) 'Indonesia' in Christopher Heath (ed) *Intellectual Property Law in Asia* (Kluwer Law International, London).

—— (2003c) 'Japan as a Model? – Law and Development in Japan, Singapore and Indonesia' in Christoph Antons (ed) *Law and Development in East and Southeast Asia* (RoutledgeCurzon, London).

—— (2004) 'Harmonisation and Selective Adaptation as Intellectual Property Policies in Asia', in Christoph Antons, Michael Blakeney and

[36] See the various papers in Johannen, Smith and Gomez (2003). For a legal perspective and not confined to Asia, see the contributions in Strawson (2002) and the chapter by Fenwick (2002).

Christopher Heath (eds) *Intellectual Property Harmonisation Within ASEAN and APEC* (Kluwer Law International, The Hague).

—— (2005a) 'Specialised Intellectual Property Courts in Southeast Asia', in Annette Kur, Stefan Luginbühl and Eskil Waage (eds) *"...und sie bewegt sich doch!" – Patent Law on the Move, Festschrift für Gert Kolle und Dieter Stauder zum 65. Geburtstag am 25. April 2005 und 20. Oktober 2005* (Carl Heymanns Verlag, Berlin).

—— (2005b) 'Traditional Knowledge and Intellectual Property Rights in Australia and Southeast Asia' in Christopher Heath and Anselm Kamperman Sanders (eds) *New Frontiers of Intellectual Property Law: IP and Cultural Heritage, Geographical Indications, Enforcement and Overprotection* (Hart Publishing, Oxford and Portland, Oregon).

ARIYANUNTAKA, V (1999) 'TRIPS and the Specialised Intellectual Property Court in Thailand' 30 *International Review of Industrial Property and Copyright Law* 360.

ASHER, MUKUL G (1993) 'Planning for the future: the welfare system in a new phase of development' in Garry Rodan (ed) *Singapore Changes Guard: Social, Political and Economic Directions in the 1990s* (Longman Cheshire/St Martin's Press, Melbourne/New York).

BAUER, JOANNE R and BELL, DANIEL A (1999) *The East Asian Challenge for Human Rights* (Cambridge University Press, Cambridge).

BAUM, HARALD (2003) 'Globalization vs. Paternalistic Regulation: Some Thoughts about Economic Success, the Role of Law, and the Regulation of Japan's Financial Markets' in Christoph Antons (ed) *Law and Development in East and Southeast Asia* (RoutledgeCurzon, London).

BEASLEY, W G (1990) *The Rise of Modern Japan* (Weidenfeld and Nicolson, London).

BODDE, D and MORRIS C (1967) *Law in Imperial China: Exemplified by 190 Ch'ing Dynasty Cases* (Harvard University Press, Cambridge, Massachusetts).

BUCKMAN, REBECCA (2003) 'Next U.S. Deal? Try Thailand' *Far Eastern Economic Review* 28 August 2003, 18–19.

BUTT, SIMON (2002) 'Intellectual Property Law in Indonesia: A Problematic Legal Transplant' 24(9) *European Intellectual Property Review* 429.

CAMMACK, MARK; YOUNG, LAWRENCE A and HEATON, TIM (1996) 'Legislating Social Change in an Islamic Society – Indonesia's Marriage Law' in 44 *The American Journal of Comparative Law* 45.

CARTER, CONNIE (2003) 'The Clonability of the Singapore Model of Law and Development: The Case of Suzhou, China' in Christoph Antons (ed) *Law and Development in East and Southeast Asia* (RoutledgeCurzon, London).

CHAROENPO, ANUCHA (2003) 'Kin of dead called on to supply info: Bereaved relatives reluctant to oblige' *The Bangkok Post* 14 March 2003.

CHEN, JIANFU (1995) *From Administrative Authorisation to Private Law: A Comparative Perspective of the Developing Civil Law in the People's Republic of China* (Martinus Nijhoff Publishers, Dordrecht).

—— (1999) *Chinese Law: Towards an Understanding of Chinese Law, Its Nature and Development* (Kluwer Law International, The Hague).

—— (2002) 'A Criminal Justice System for a New Millennium?' in Eduard B Vermeer and Ingrid d'Hooghe (eds) *China's Legal Reforms and Their Political Limits* (Curzon Press, London).

CHEN, PM (1973) *Law and Justice: The Legal System in China 2400 B.C. to 1960 A.D.* (Dunellen Publishing Company, New York and London).

CRISPIN, SHAWN W and WAGSTAFF, JEREMY (2003) 'The Terror's War Next Offensive' *Far Eastern Economic Review* 28 August 2003, 12–16.

CRISPIN, SHAWN W and ZAUN, TODD (2003) 'Courts under the Spotlight' *Far Eastern Economic Review* 4 September 2003, 44-45.

CROUCH, HAROLD (1988) *The Army and Politics in Indonesia* rev edn (Cornell University Press, Ithaca and London).

DANG, T H DUY (2000) 'The Protection of Well-known Marks in Vietnam' in Christopher Heath and Kung-Chung Liu (eds) *The Protection of Well-known Marks in Asia* (Kluwer Law International, The Hague/London/Boston).

DEAN, MERRYL (1991) 'Administrative Guidance in Japanese Law: A Threat to the Rule of Law' *Journal of Business Law* 398–9 and 401–3, reprinted in Dean (1997) 206–8.

—— (1997) *Japanese Legal System: Text and Materials* (Cavendish Publishing, London).

DHUME, SADANAND (2003) 'Calling the IMF' *Far Eastern Economic Review* 23 January 2003, 18.

DRAGSBAEK SCHMIDT, JOHANNES (2000) 'Neoliberal Globalization, Social Welfare and Trade Unions in Southeast Asia' in Barry K Gills *Globalization and the Politics of Resistance* (Houndsmills, Basingstoke and New York).

EBREY, PATRICIA BUCKLEY (1984) *Family and Property in Sung China: Yüan Ts'ai's Precepts for Social Life* (Princeton University Press, Princeton).

—— (1993) *The Inner Quarters: Marriage and the Lives of Chinese Women in the Sung Period* (University of California Press, Berkeley, Los Angeles and London).

EISENSTADT, S N (1996) *Japanese Civilization: A Comparative View* (University of Chicago Press, Chicago and London).

FENWICK, HELEN (2002) 'Responding to 11 September: Detention without Trial under the Anti-Terrorism, Crime and Security Act 2001' in Lawrence Freedman (ed) *Superterrorism: Policy Responses* (Blackwell Publishing, Oxford).

FOLJANTY-JOST, GESINE (1989) 'Informelles Verwaltungshandeln: Schlüssel effizienter Implementation oder Politik ohne Politiker?' in Ulrich Menzel (ed) *Im Schatten des Siegers: Japan, Vol 3: Oekonomie und Politik* (Suhrkamp, Frankfurt am Main).

GAUTAMA, SUDARGO and HORNICK ROBERT N (1983) *An Introduction to Indonesian Law: Unity in Diversity* (Penerbit Alumni, Bandung).

GAUTAMA, SUDARGO (1993) *Hukum Antar Golongan: Suatu Pengantar* (P T Ichtiar Baru Van Hoeve, Jakarta).

GHAI, YASH (1998) 'Rights, Duties and Responsibilities' in Josiane Cauquelin, Paul Lim and Birgit Mayer-König (eds) *Asian Values: Encounter with Diversity* (Curzon Press, Richmond).

GOON, DARRYL (2003) 'Malaysia' in Christopher Heath (ed) *Intellectual Property Law in Asia* (Kluwer Law International, London/The Hague/Boston).

GUNAWAN, APRIADI (2002) 'Soldiers face light sentence for attack' *The Jakarta Post* 21 November 2002.

HALEY, JOHN OWEN (1991) *Authority Without Power: Law and the Japanese Paradox* (Oxford University Press, New York and Oxford).

HARI, KURNIAWAN and SURYANA, A'AN (2003) 'House to revise law on antiterrorism after bombing' *The Jakarta Post* 21 August 2003.

HEATH, CHRISTOPHER (ed) (2003) *Intellectual Property Law in Asia* (Kluwer Law International, London/The Hague/Boston).

HILL, HAL (1996) *The Indonesian Economy Since 1966: Southeast Asia's Emerging Giant*, (Cambridge University Press, Cambridge/New York/Melbourne).

HOOKER, M B (1978) *A Concise Legal History of South-East Asia* (Clarendon Press, Oxford).

ISHII, YONEO (1986) 'The Thai Thammasat (with a Note on the Lao Thammasat)' in M B Hooker (ed) *The Laws of South-East Asia. Volume 1. The Pre-Modern Texts* (Butterworths, Singapore).

JENKINS, DAVID (1984) *Suharto and his Generals. Indonesian Military Politics 1975-1983* (Cornell University Press, Ithaca).

JOHANNEN, UWE; SMITH, ALAN; GOMEZ, JAMES (2003) *September 11 & Political Freedom: Asian Perspectives* (Select Publishing, Singapore).

JOMO, K S (2003) *M Way: Mahathir's Economic Legacy* (Forum, Kuala Lumpur).

JONES, DAVID M (1993) 'The Metamorphosis of Tradition: The Idea of Law and Virtue in East Asian Political Thought' in 21(1) *The Southeast Asian Journal of Social Science* 18.

KATZ, JUNE S and KATZ, RONALD S (1975) 'The New Indonesian Marriage Law: A Mirror of Indonesia's Political, Cultural and Legal Systems' in 23 *The American Journal of Comparative Law* 653.

KRISTIADI, J (1999) 'The Armed Forces' in Richard W Baker, M Hadi Soesastro, J Kristiadi and Douglas E Rampage (eds) *Indonesia: The Challenge of Change* (KITLV Press/Institute of Southeast Asian Studies, Leiden/Singapore).

KUANPOTH, JAKKRIT (2003) 'Thailand' in C Heath (ed) *Intellectual Property Law in Asia* (Kluwer Law International, London/Boston/The Hague).

LOW, LINDA and NGIAM TEE LIANG (1999) 'An underclass among the overclass' in Linda Low (ed) *Singapore: Towards a Developed Status* (Oxford University Press, Singapore).

MATSUSHITA, M (1993) *International Trade and Competition Law in Japan* (Oxford University Press, Oxford) reprinted in Dean (1997).

MCBETH, JOHN (2003) 'The Army Plays Power Politics' *Far Eastern Economic Review* 27 March 2003, 18-19.

MENZEL, ULRICH (1989) *Im Schatten des Siegers: Japan. Band 1: Kultur und Gesellschaft. Band 2: Staat und Gesellschaft. Band 3: Ökonomie und Politik. Band 4: Weltwirtschaft und Weltpolitik* (Suhrkamp, Frankfurt am Main).

PHAM DUY NGHIA (2002) *Vietnamese Business Law in Transition.* (The Gioi Publishers, Hanoi).

POMPE, S (1991) 'A short note on some recent developments with regard to mixed marriages in Indonesia' 147(2/3) *Bijdragen tot de Taal-, Land- en Volkenkunde* 261.

PRESTOWITZ, CLYDE V, Jr (1988) *Trading Places: How we are giving our future to Japan and how to reclaim it* (Basic Books Inc, New York).

RAMSEYER, J MARK and NAKAZATO, MINORU (1999) *Japanese Law: An Economic Approach* (The University of Chicago Press, Chicago and London).

RICKLEFS, M C (1981) *A History of Modern Indonesia: c. 1300 to the present* (Macmillan, London and Basingstoke).

SAMYDORAI, SINAPAN (2003) '9/11 Anti-Terrorist Measures and their Impact on Human Rights in Asia' in U Johannen, A Smith and J Gomez (eds) *September 11 and Political Freedom: Asian Perspectives* (Select Publishing, Singapore).

SCHWARZ, ADAM (1994) *A Nation in Waiting: Indonesia in the 1990s* (Allen and Unwin, St Leonards).

SETIAWAN (1992) *Aneka Masalah Hukum dan Hukum Acara Perdata* (Penerbit Alumni, Bandung).

SHINDO, M (1992) 'Administrative Guidance: Securities Scandals Resulting from Administrative Guidelines' *Japanese Economic Studies* 76–8, 81–6, reprinted in Dean (1997) 208–12.

SOESASTRO, HADI (2003) 'Global Terrorism: Implications for State and Human Security' in Uwe Johannen, Alan Smith and James Gomez (eds) *September 11 and Political Freedom: Asian Perspectives* (Select Publishing, Singapore).

SOETANTIO, RETNOWULAN and OERIPKARTAWINATA, ISKANDAR (1995) *Hukum Acara Perdata Dalam Teori dan Praktek* (Penerbit Mandar Maju, Bandung).

STRAWSON, JOHN (ed) (2002) *Law after Ground Zero* (Glasshouse Press, London).

't-HART, J (1987) 'Aspects of Criminal Justice' in Hans Thoolen (ed) *Indonesia and the Rule of Law: Twenty Years of New Order Government* (Frances Pinter, London).

TU WEI-MING (1996) 'Introduction' in Tu Wei-Ming (ed) *Confucian Traditions in East Asian Modernity: Moral Education and Economic Culture in Japan and the Four Mini-Dragons* (Harvard University Press, Cambridge, Mass/ London).

UNIDJAJA, FABIOLA DESY (2003) 'TNI nothing more than mercenaries: Analysts' *The Jakarta Post* 17 March 2003.

WEISS, STANLEY A (2002) 'Tasks for Russia, China, India and Indonesia' *The International Herald Tribune* 11 July 2002.

WU, MIN AUN (1999) 'The Malaysian Judiciary: Erosion of Confidence' 1(2) *The Australian Journal of Asian Law* 124.

—— (2000/2001) 'Anwar Ibrahim: The Fall and Fall of a Favoured Son' *LAWASIA Journal* 46.

YAMANOUCHI, K (1974) 'Administrative Guidance and the Rule of Law' 7 *Law in Japan* 27–31, reprinted in Dean (1997) 204–6.

YASUDA, NOBUYUKI (2003) 'Law and Development from the Southeast Asian Perspective: Methodology, History and Paradigm Change' in Christoph Antons (ed) *Law and Development in East and Southeast Asia* (RoutledgeCurzon, London).

YOUNG, M (1984) 'Judicial Review of Administrative Guidance: Governmentally Encouraged Consensual Dispute Resolution in Japan' 84 *Columbia Law Review* 926–31, 935–41, 953–9, 982–3, reprinted in Dean (1997) 213–21.

ZHANG, YONG (1997) 'Commentary – Comparisons on the Functions of the Judicial Review System in East and Southeast Asia' in Yong Zhang (ed) *Comparative Studies on the Judicial Review System in East and Southeast Asia* (Kluwer Law International, The Hague).

5

Politics, Ideology and Legal System Reform in Northeast Asia

JOHN K M OHNESORGE

I INTRODUCTION

THIRTY YEARS AGO, in their seminal critique of the law and development movement of the 1960s and 1970s, Trubek and Galanter called for evaluation of law and development projects in a new mode, which they referred to as 'eclectic critique' (Trubek and Galanter, 1974). Eclectic critique called for participants in legal development projects to recognise and leave open to scrutiny their assumptions about law and its complex relationships to politics and society, both at home and in the societies they were trying to assist. Trubek and Galanter focused primarily on challenging over-optimism on the part of law and development practitioners, who uncritically accepted the self-congratulatory story of Western liberal legality, while also being too ready to assume that the same story could be replicated in the Third World. Although Trubek and Galanter focused on over-optimism, the logic of their argument applies equally to criticisms of external efforts to influence national legal systems. To the extent that such criticisms target the substance of law reform efforts rather than the methods by which they are pursued, critics risk making a mistake in the same category as the targets of Trubek and Galanter, ie that of assuming the eventual (negative) impact of law reforms with a greater certainty than is justified.

This chapter is an exercise in eclectic critique, and focuses on two sets of legal reforms that have been under way in Northeast Asia—Japan, South Korea, and Taiwan—for the past several years. Although the importance of foreign influences in bringing about these reforms is a question that will not be focused upon here, these reforms are of the type that the US government and international financial institutions—the World Bank, the IMF, the Asian Development Bank, etc—have been advocating around the world. An eclectic critique of these reforms may be useful then, regardless of the exact confluence of forces, domestic and international, that has brought them about in Northeast Asia. The goal is to provide a framework for exploring the interests and ideologies of those supporting legal reforms in Northeast Asia, and beyond.

II JUDICIALISING REFORMS TO NORTHEAST ASIAN ADMINISTRATIVE LAW AND CORPORATE GOVERNANCE

In terms of legal development initiatives, we seem to be living in an age not merely of legalisation and institution-building, but of *judicialisation*, the tendency to submit greater areas of social and political life not merely to law, but to law as interpreted and enforced by the courts in cases adjudicating private rights. Judicialisation is not synonymous with legal reform, as many reforms involve rule changes or institutional innovations that do not greatly increase the role of the courts in governance. Judicialisation insists instead that courts be at the centre of governance processes, readily available to enforce rights claims put forth by private actors. The hallmark of judicialisation initiatives is that they seek to bring about social change by harnessing the energies of private litigants, channelled through the litigation process.

It would be an exaggeration to say that countries around the world are eager to adopt judicialising legal reforms, because these reforms are often supported by external pressures of substantial force, but a wide range of countries appear at least willing to undertake such reforms. Observers of this trend describe it in different ways. Some speak of a spreading of Western legal culture (Friedman, 1990), while others talk of spreading the rule of law. Some look to invigorated judiciaries as key to facilitating private economic activity, or to enforcing 'credible commitments' to restrain the 'grabbing hands' of government (Ohnesorge, 2003). Well before the Asian Crisis of the late 1990s it was clear that Northeast Asia was not immune to the forces of judicialisation; judicialising legal reforms were well underway in the region by the early 1990s. The Asian Crisis certainly advanced the process, however, as will be shown below.

This chapter explores two areas of judicialising legal reform that appear quite important in Northeast Asia: shareholder derivative litigation and administrative law reforms. Given the centrality of both government agencies and corporate hierarchies in post-World War II Northeast Asia, it would be surprising if the legal regimes that structure and control these hierarchies were not targeted by societal interests seeking political and social change. As is well-known to students of Northeast Asian law, both these areas of law have indeed become targets of legal reform in the last decade. What is seldom explicitly explored, however, is the alignment of foreign and domestic interests that favour reforms in these areas, and the assumptions that underlie the way these interests articulate their visions for reform.

The objective of this chapter is not to map doctrinally the details of these reforms, but to provide a framework for thinking about the interests and ideologies of those supporting the reforms. Legal reforms are by definition attempts at social engineering through law, and it is beyond dispute that the history of such attempts is riddled with failures and unintended consequences. But is there a real alternative to social engineering through law? Even those Americans who yearn for the Anglo-American golden age of common law hegemony (see eg, Epstein, 1995) would, in order to get from here to there (from the existing situation to their ideal), have to undertake a series of concrete reforms which would be as prone to failures and unintended consequences as any other radical attempt at social engineering through law. Those who engage in legal reform efforts enter the process with not only a set of goals but also a set of assumptions, stated or unstated, concerning the likelihood that the concrete legal changes they advocate will result in the social effects they desire. Where legal reforms are supported by societal coalitions that seem to hold substantially differing political views, it is natural to ask which elements within the coalition are likely to achieve their aims, once the social effects of the reforms become clear, and which will be disappointed. In the spirit of eclectic critique this chapter explores this set of questions in the context of Northeast Asia.

The reforms discussed here seek: (i) to invigorate administrative law to provide broader rights for private parties to participate in the administrative process, and enable the use of the courts to challenge administrative activities; and (ii) to invigorate the rights of minority shareholders by increasing shareholder access to the courts. Although in many respects these reforms appear unrelated, they can both be understood as reforms designed to loosen existing power relationships, shifting power from bureaucratically organised hierarchies—government agencies and corporate management—to private interests and to non-management, minority shareholders. More specifically, the private sector/civil society will be empowered vis-à-vis corporate management and government bureaucracies through the creation or enhancement of private rights, enforceable in courts. These power shifts are thus to be facilitated by judicialisation, and to the extent that courts are called upon to define the scope and contours of these newly-created rights, judicialisation also involves a power shift in favour of the judiciary.

A second characteristic these reforms share is that each can be understood as responding to two seemingly distinct sets of concerns or constituencies, a pairing that will be used to structure this chapter. One set of concerns, referred to here as the 'Neoliberal', reflects interests in limiting bureaucratic discretion, limiting government regulation of markets, and maximising the exercise of economic and property rights by private actors. The second set of concerns, here termed 'Populist/Progressive' (P/P), focuses on openness, accountability, and 'voice' in government as well as in corporate behaviour. Such a typology of course represents an over-simplification, as these are ideal-type ideological or rhetorical positions, and particular individuals, as well as groups, may well hold some mixture of these positions, even within themselves. Indeed, the strength of North-east Asia's legal reform agenda may well be the extent to which it is supported not merely by coalitions of groups holding different views, but by groups and individuals to which all of the views are at least somewhat attractive. Notably, it is no objection to this analysis to argue that there is in fact no problem needing to be solved through legal reform, as Professor Ramseyer says of Japanese corporate governance and the rise of derivative litigation there (Ramseyer, 2003). A demonstration that there was no 'real' problem to be addressed would only make the existence of a broad societal coalition supporting legal reform that much more interesting.

Neoliberal and P/P tendencies or commitments tend to be mirrored by, and to mirror, external demands for legal reform. Minority shareholder rights, for example, are championed by foreign equity investors, who want their recently acquired rights to engage in portfolio investment in North-east Asia to give them more than simply an 'exit' option if they are dissatisfied with corporate management. Pursuing this objective are industry-funded groups such as the Asia Corporate Governance Association, formed in 1999 (Asia Corporate Governance Association, 2004), and the Equity Advisory Group of the Institute of International Finance (Institute of International Finance, 2003). The Asian Crisis of the late 1990s provided a strategic opportunity to advance this agenda, as corporate governance reform to protect minority shareholders became a priority of the IMF and other international institutions (Kim, Hwa-Jin, 2001). While this congruence between the interests of foreign institutional investors and the IMF may be simply the natural result of the IMF's policy views, those views themselves are largely shaped by political pressure exerted by the US Treasury (Stiglitz, 2002), which is understandably responsive to the interests of the US financial services industry (see, eg, Stiglitz, 2002: 171–2). The IMF is not the only public institution working to advance the interests of foreign equity investors, however. The Asian Corporate Governance Roundtable, operated by the OECD in collaboration with the World Bank and the Asian Development Bank, pursues a similar shareholder rights agenda (OECD, 2003).

Northeast Asian administrative law reforms have also been supported by external pressures (Oh, 2000), most recently with respect to national regulation of service industries, such as insurance and banking. Northeast Asian 'administrative guidance' has long been criticised by foreign trading partners, who felt that Northeast Asian governments used such informal, unwritten directives to prolong mercantilist industrial policies that they could no longer carry out openly (eg, Johnson, 1982: 242–4). Informal consultative processes between government regulators and the regulated industries were criticised as exclusive and non-transparent, and therefore unfair to outsiders such as foreign investors, and also criticised as vesting too much discretion in government regulators (eg, West, 1992). These concerns were voiced for decades with respect to Japan, South Korea and Taiwan, and are again being heard regarding administrative law issues in relation to China's WTO accession, particularly with respect to the regulation of foreign investment, and with respect to China's commitments to open services markets under the General Agreement on Trade in Services (GATS) (eg, GAO, 2003b; Wilson, 2002).

A Northeast Asian Corporate Governance Reforms: Invigorating Shareholder Derivative Litigation

Derivative actions are actions brought by corporate shareholders to enforce rights belonging to the corporations in which they own shares. They are a mechanism by which minority shareholders can act on behalf of a corporation when corporate management refuses to act, and are especially useful when a corporation has claims against management that management refuses to pursue. In terms of legal doctrine, efforts to invigorate shareholder derivative litigation in Northeast Asia have focused on amending procedural rules in order to make derivative litigation more economically attractive to potential plaintiff shareholders. Because damages awarded in a derivative suit accrue to the corporation instead of to the shareholders who initiate the action, resort to these suits is especially sensitive to costs potentially borne by plaintiffs. In order to make derivative suits economically attractive Japan, for example, changed its rule on court costs so that in derivative suits court costs are a nominal flat fee rather than a fixed percentage of the amount claimed (Aronson, 2003). South Korea addressed a different disincentive to the bringing of derivative suits by lowering the number of shares that a shareholder has to hold in order to have standing to initiate derivative litigation (Kim, Hwa-Jin, 2001). Taiwan has also moved to overcome economic disincentives to shareholder litigation, in part by lowering the minimum shareholding requirement for derivative litigation (Milhaupt, 2003).

The general thrust of these corporate law reforms has been to shift power away from management and towards minority shareholders, and understood at this level of generality it is easy to see why such reforms attract both Neoliberal and P/P constituencies. Neoliberal interest in corporate governance reform is informed by the view that corporate management often enjoys substantial 'slack' in the principal-agent relationship that corporate law envisions as existing between shareholders and management. This view is particularly relevant to Japan, where large corporations often lack a controlling shareholder. In South Korea and Taiwan the Neoliberal interest in derivative litigation is somewhat different, as corporations in these countries are typically controlled by a single shareholder or shareholding family, and thus are not characterised by a separation of ownership and control. In all cases, however, the Neoliberal hope for invigorated derivative litigation is to force management to focus on maximising shareholder value generally, not on the private interests of managers or of controlling shareholders, or on the interests of 'stakeholders' more broadly defined.

This Neoliberal concern receives strong support from foreign interests, bilateral and multilateral. Minority shareholder rights in Japan became a bilateral trade issue in the 1980s, when American investor T Boone Pickens was able to enlist US trade negotiators in his fight with the Koito Corporation. Japan began its legislative effort to invigorate shareholder litigation in the early 1990s, a development that some link to US pressure (eg, Aronson 2003: 24, footnote 56), but it was the Asian Crisis that brought Northeast Asian corporate governance and shareholders' rights into the international spotlight (eg, Claessens et al, 1999). Because it needed IMF assistance during the Crisis, Korea has been subject to the greatest external Neoliberal pressure in this area (Black et al, 2001; Kim, Hwa-Jin, 2001). Taiwan's reforms, while noteworthy, have been the least radical (Milhaupt, 2003).

B Judicialising Northeast Asian Administrative Law

Administrative law reforms can also be understood as driven by a desire to shift power from bureaucratically organised entities to more particular interests, specifically from state agencies to private actors, or to civil society in a collective sense. Recently enacted administrative procedure statutes in Japan, South Korea and Taiwan seek to impose more stringent requirements on how agencies carry out actions affecting private interests, and in particular seek to impose 'rule of law' benchmarks, such as requiring that regulatory decisions be based on specific, pre-existing legal norms. Allowing the courts to enforce these procedural rights on behalf of private plaintiffs is designed to substantially legalise the relationship between regulatory agencies and civil society. New information disclosure laws ('freedom of information' laws in US terms) are designed to give private actors judicially enforceable rights to information held by state agencies, information that is crucial to understanding, and if necessary challenging, administrative action. Like administrative procedure laws, these statutes represent a fundamental shift towards legalisation of the state-civil society interface.

In common with reforms encouraging derivative litigation, administrative law reforms are occurring against a background in which the bureaucratically organised entity, here the government agency, was comparatively unconstrained by law in its dealings with private actors. Students of South Korea and Taiwan would find this claim relatively unremarkable, given that democratisation came only in the late 1980s. Students of Japanese politics will be familiar with Johnson's *MITI and the Japanese Miracle* (Johnson, 1982) and other 'revisionist' analyses of the Japanese 'developmental state', as well as subsequent attempts to demonstrate that the Japanese ministries involved in the formulation and implementation of economic and trade policies were never insulated from social forces, as the revisionists claimed, but were in fact faithful agents of the long-dominant Liberal Democratic Party (LDP) (Ramseyer and Rosenbluth, 1993). This particular debate, though interesting, focuses on questions of power, rather than on legality. Even if one accepts the thesis that Japan's industrial policy ministries simply did the bidding of the ruling LDP, which in turn did the bidding of voters and contributors, that does not mean that a legalisation of the ways in which the ministries interact with the private sector will not matter for Japanese governance. While it must be true that private actors, particularly large commercial interests, always had more influence vis-à-vis Japan's bureaucrats than one might believe from the more ardent admirers of Japan's 'developmental state', even the most strident critics of the developmental state idea do not claim that that influence was exercised through channels created by administrative law. The promise of administrative law reforms in Northeast Asia is not simply to vest power in private actors, but to legalise and render transparent the channels through which such power is exercised. Of course, the creation of legal mechanisms will not mean that political and social channels will no longer operate. Legal channels will simply provide a new set of options to private actors, leveraging the power already exercised through extra-legal channels.

With respect to Japan, the Neoliberal rationale for administrative law reforms centres on Japan's decade-long economic slump, which can only be cured, the argument goes, by deregulation, liberalisation, and a more rights-oriented society (eg, American Chamber of Commerce in Japan, 2002). Re-revisionist arguments notwithstanding, Asian business interests and their lawyers have consistently expressed the view that administrative guidance was often effectively binding on them, even when it lacked a proper legal basis, because the authorities had mechanisms through which they could punish those who ignored or challenged the guidance (see Chu, 1994; Woo, 1991). With economic agencies delegitimised by the Asian Crisis and Japan's decade-long recession, and with politicians running on radical reform platforms (even if rarely carried out), the time has come to alter the legal landscape to prevent the government from attempting to 'muddle through' the Crisis. With respect to Northeast Asia more generally, in the Neoliberal view, economic actors demand a 'rule of law' administrative law regime, which maximises the extent to which regulatory activities are limited to those based upon an organised and transparent system of rules, knowable in advance and which does not change unpredictably.

The P/P rationale for administrative law reforms, on the other hand, stems from a widespread sense that the 'developmental state' sacrificed democracy and responsiveness on the altar of high-speed growth, in a sense agreeing with the re-revisionists that Japan's ministries never governed in the public interest, insulated from political pressures, but in fact served conservative business interests and their political allies. This refrain is familiar to students of US administrative law, who have long noted that both progressives and conservatives (Liberals) accept the agency capture thesis as descriptively accurate. Operating in the absence of effective administrative law oversight mechanisms, Northeast Asia's government agencies engaged in a number of spectacular failures—such as Japan's AIDS-tainted blood imports fiasco, hazardous discharges from nuclear power plants, and failures in banking regulation—while also being seen as conduits for authoritarian political rule, as in Taiwan and South Korea.

III AN AMERICAN CAVEAT

This chapter represents the early stages of a long-term project to understand the potentially enormous changes being made to Northeast Asia's legal systems, changes which go far beyond those discussed here to include fundamental changes to legal education systems and to the make-up of the national bars, among others. This section seeks to present the background to the author's perspective on these issues, which obviously provides the motivation for the project while also colouring all observations.

One of the common reactions to recent Northeast Asian legal reforms is that they represent 'Americanisation', which seems to refer to both the judicialisation of governance and to an invigorated 'rights consciousness' in Northeast Asian societies. Although the degree to which American models have affected the Northeast Asian reforms is not a focus of this chapter, it is beyond dispute that they have been very important. The idea of 'notice-and-comment' rule-making to allow public participation in the making of agency regulations is a specific example (Tang, 2001), as are the region's initiatives to adopt 'US-style' law schools. At a more abstract level, one also encounters the more general idea that becoming a more rights-conscious, rule of law-oriented society will involve learning from the

United States (Asahi, 2003). This arguably puts a special burden on Americans studying these reforms, beyond the normal scholarly obligation to be aware of one's own biases and preconceptions. If these reforms are being sold as 'Americanisation' by at least some of their supporters, then Americans might make a positive contribution by speaking candidly about the American experience. A candid assessment of the state of corporate governance and administrative law in the United States should sound a note of caution with respect to judicialisation and the shift of power from management and government agencies.

First, on a general level, sophisticated Northeast Asian scholars are quite aware of the uncertainties involved in social engineering through law, and US critiques of American legal culture are well known. In conversations with Japanese legal scholars, for example, one regularly encounters the idea that Japan does not really want or need US-style legal culture, but that Japan none the less needs to become more 'American' with respect to law. This stance is somewhat troubling, however, in that it seems to presume a greater precision than experience should tell us is really possible when dealing with society-wide legal reforms. There is reason to doubt that the proposed reforms, once they emerge from the legislative process, will bring Japan to some happy medium, achieving just the right amount of 'rights consciousness', without going 'too far'.

With respect to the idea of invigorating derivative litigation, a US perspective also provides some cause for concern. To really activate shareholder derivative litigation will require economic incentives for plaintiffs and for their lawyers. Getting the incentives right will not be easy, as material incentives are made up of a complex constellation of short and long term interests, and as material incentives are also often intermingled with non-economic motives and affected by social norms. An incentive structure too favourable to shareholder derivative suits may well have perverse consequences, consuming corporate time and resources that could be better spent, distracting management from core concerns and making management too risk-averse, and discouraging qualified people from serving as directors. These are common critiques of derivative litigation in the United States, which is seen as driven by plaintiffs' lawyers seeking contingency fees based upon questionable legal claims that management too often agrees to settle (Romano, 1991). Other reforms currently being tried in Northeast Asia, such as increasing the number of independent directors on corporate boards, or mandating more substantial financial disclosures by corporations, may be far more efficient, while relying less on judicialisation.

In addition, the question remains whether P/P interests would benefit from a broad shift in Northeast Asian corporate governance towards the shareholder primacy norm, the fundamental Neoliberal goal. Workers may not benefit from such a shift, for example, if shareholder primacy results in greater focus on stock price based upon short term financial results. It is easy to imagine that such a focus would lead management to resort more readily to lay-offs than historically has been the case in Northeast Asia, or for management to fail to make long-term investments in productivity-enhancing new technology. In earlier decades, when it was the Northeast Asian corporation that was ascendant globally, these attributes were cited as sources of comparative strength, and it is certainly worth considering whether they would be put at risk by a greater focus on maximising shareholder value.

With respect to administrative law reforms, the judicialising of American administrative law (which took place to a large extent in the 1960s and 1970s) has not decisively served P/P interests, Neoliberal interests, or the public interest generally. The hope that judicialisation, as part of America's 'due process revolution', would legitimate the administrative state in the eyes of the American public does not seem to have been met. Presidential elections are still won by campaigning against the bureaucracy in Washington, and administrative litigation has become a central aspect of the interest group warfare that seems to drive Americans away from politics. Moreover, judicialising administrative law has furthered the politicisation of the American judiciary, as Americans believe, rightly or wrongly, that a judge's position on the left-right political spectrum is a useful predictor of how aggressively that judge will scrutinise administrative actions that come before him or her on judicial review. As a result, some of the most intense judicial nomination battles now accompany nominations to the Court of Appeals for the District of Columbia, the most important appellate court reviewing federal administrative actions.

If enhanced judicialisation has not allowed US administrative law to successfully legitimate the regulatory welfare state, it is also not clear the judicialisation has enhanced the state's ability to regulate rationally and effectively. In the literature comparing national regulatory approaches and outcomes, the 'adversarial legalism' of the United States often compares unfavourably with regulatory cultures characterised by higher degrees of administrative discretion and negotiation between regulator and regulated, and less frequent resort to the courts (Kagan and Axelrad, 2000). Thus while it is far from clear that Americans are better governed than they would be with a more restricted role for private rights and judicial review, one also suspects that decisions and doctrines will tend to benefit anti-regulatory interests over the long term, given that they are likely to be repeat players before the courts, with enormous advantages in terms of resources, and can exercise consistent, targeted focus on the issues important to them.

IV WHO'S GETTING WHAT IN NORTHEAST ASIA: A TENTATIVE SCORECARD

Given the legal changes that have taken place in Northeast Asia, this section seeks to explore which set of interests or concerns, Neoliberal or P/P, has been met more fully as the reforms have functioned to date. With respect to derivative litigation, P/P interests have heartily embraced minority shareholder rights, particularly in Korea, as providing a way to put pressure on corporate management (Milhaupt, 2003; Kim, Jooyoung, 2001). While some Western progressive economists have written favourably about the role of Northeast Asia's corporations (Amsden, 1989), doing so ran the risk of de-emphasising the systematic and often violent suppression of organised labour (Deyo, 1989), and the externalising of enormous environmental costs. To local progressives these corporate faults, together with the tendency of corporate owners to engage in political corruption in support of undemocratic regimes, are all too obvious. If shareholder derivative suits provide a new tool for attacking corporate power when political processes fail, then so much the better. It seems at this stage that derivative litigation is being used more to further P/P interests than to simply influence management to pursue shareholder value. First, many of the suits are being brought by what could be called ideological plaintiffs; that is, by public interest lawyers and shareholder activists such as South Korea's People's Solidarity for Participatory Democracy (PSPD). Second, actions are being brought to punish management for specific types of misbehaviour, such as bribery of government officials, illegal payments to extortionists, or truly fraudulent misuse of corporate assets. For example, Japan's Daiwa Bank case arose out of a scandal in Daiwa's US operations that resulted in the bank pleading guilty to a US federal criminal indictment and losing its US banking licences (Aronson, 2003). Similarly, in Korea the basis of the Korea First Bank case was allegedly illegal loans and bribery, and the Samsung litigation was based in part on illegal political contributions (Jang, 2002). In a sense, derivative litigation is being used as a substitute for the criminal justice process that has failed in these areas. Such uses of derivative litigation fit the P/P agenda well, but seem unlikely to fundamentally reorient management to focus on maximising shareholder value, the primary Neoliberal concern. For although derivative litigation is being encouraged, it does not appear that the rules have been changed enough to make it really attractive to ordinary profit-oriented lawyers. For example, Northeast Asian lawyers do not appear to be financing the bringing of derivative suits, which contingency fee arrangements facilitate in the United States. In addition, the civil discovery rules are still quite restrictive, so the derivative suits tend to depend on information that has already come to light via criminal investigations or public scandals. Furthermore, the exceptional Daiwa

Bank case that resulted in a multi-million dollar damage award against the Japanese bank's directors has led conservative politicians, supported by business, to seek legislative limits on damage awards (Aronson, 2003). Finally, Northeast Asia's judges tend not to be trained in economics, and are not encouraged to see themselves as innovators in decisions with broad political/economic implications. This suggests that the typical P/P cases will be more appealing to them than cases challenging more typical management decisions.

With respect to administrative law reforms, to date these do not appear to have provided business interests, the main focus of Neoliberal concern, with the means to inject the courts into the heart of regulatory governance in the way that administrative law functions in the United States. Business interests are showing an increased tendency towards high-stakes litigation against regulatory agencies, as demonstrated by the suit telecoms carriers have filed challenging a Japanese government rate-setting decision (Aritake, 2003; Belson, 2003). Businesses in Korea, too, are increasingly turning to the courts to challenge specific agency decisions affecting them (Hong, 2000), but such review of licensing and other quasi-adjudicatory decisions is not as challenging to the regulatory agencies as judicially protected rights to participate in the rule-making process. And even in Japan, which has long been a democracy and which began administrative law reforms over a decade ago, companies still complain that they have little legal recourse if a government agency retaliates against them extra-legally (Ibison and Nakamoto, 2003).

On the other hand, individuals have succeeded in cases against their governments that a decade ago would have seemed hopeless. A Taiwanese family claimed a high-profile administrative court victory over Taiwan's Ministry of National Defence (Wu, 2003), and a Korean court has ordered the government to compensate a family that was wronged by the Korean CIA in the late 1980s (Lee, 2003). Civil society groups are also making use of the new administrative law statutes, particularly the information disclosure statutes, to address specific instances of public wrong-doing. While P/P interests are being furthered by the fact that such uses of administrative law are clearly expanding in Northeast Asia, it remains to be seen whether such specific uses can bring about fundamental change to regulatory governance in Northeast Asia. As noted above, major economic actors are still complaining that they lack legal recourse against targeted enforcement by Japan's tax authorities (Ibison and Nakamoto, 2003), a signal that Japanese ministries may still possess some of the leverage they used, in an earlier era, to 'encourage' compliance with administrative guidance.

V THE RETURN OF POLITICS: ENRON AND SEPTEMBER 11

The legal reforms discussed here are part of an ongoing globalisation of law. One of the enduring puzzles of globalisation is whether it is more profitably studied as a general phenomenon or trend, or whether it should be studied as the product of many discrete legal and policy decisions, each the result of a particular amalgam of politics and interests. Working in the former vein we seek the big picture, in order to capture the essence of globalisation, but we do so at the risk of fostering a sense of inevitability or determinism. Working in the latter vein we risk missing the big picture, the fact that for the past decade or so the vast majority of such particular legal and policy battles seems to have been won by the forces of globalisation. The legal reforms discussed in this chapter might be seen as part of a wider, inevitable trend, pushed through by a seemingly unstoppable confluence of internal and external forces. In the past few years, however, two things have happened that should call into question the inevitability of this trend. The first of these two events is captured by the name 'Enron', referring not simply to the collapse of the Enron corporation, but to the general crisis in American corporate governance and securities markets that has been unfolding since early in 2001. The second event was the terrorist attacks of September 11, 2001, particularly as the attacks continue to affect American politics and the administration of President Bush. The following passages consider the effects, if any, of Enron and September 11 on reforms such as those discussed in this chapter.

The possible effects of Enron on Northeast Asian corporate law reforms are still unfolding, but three aspects stand out. First, at the level of law reform rhetoric, Enron should take some of the shine off American models, and some of the hubris from American critics of East Asian 'crony capitalism'. The American model of corporate governance, seen as so successful in the 1990s, was exposed as fundamentally flawed at the individual firm level. Many boards of directors, even those with significant numbers of independent directors, failed to monitor and control management in the interests of shareholders. And the preferred method for obtaining results through a reliance on management self-interest (and the use of stock options in management compensation packages) is now viewed as having induced an *over*-emphasis on stock price, exacerbating the problem of managers inflating corporate earnings figures. One of the features of the Enron crisis has been company after company 'restating' previously announced earnings figures (GAO, 2002), a spectacle that has no doubt contributed to the loss of investor confidence in the US equity markets. This parade of corporate 'restatements' has been matched by a parade of settlement agreements between America's leading financial institutions and state and federal securities regulators. In only one of several such settlements, J P Morgan Chase and Citigroup agreed to pay approximately US$300 million to state and federal prosecutors to settle charges that they helped Enron manipulate its financial statements to mislead investors (SEC, 2003a).

Enron also exposed socially-embedded, non-universal aspects of the US corporate governance system, as the system was shown to depend for its proper functioning on the functioning of a broader corporate governance community made up of accountants, lawyers, securities analysts, investment banks and others (Coffee, 2002). And once the importance of this wider community of actors was highlighted, we were also reminded that many of these actors perform their proper roles in the general corporate governance environment not because of legal mandates that could be easily transplanted abroad, but as a result of highly evolved webs of professional norms, cultures and practices. In fact, precise legal rules in the area of corporate accounting are now seen as having been one of the *causes* of the American crisis, seemingly encouraging professionals to abandon their traditional roles in maintaining the integrity of the system. A common post-Enron view is that precise accounting rules encourage financial engineering to comply with the letter of the rules while escaping their regulatory objectives. Reflecting this view, the Sarbanes-Oxley Act instructed the Securities and Exchange Commission (SEC) to conduct a study on standards-based versus rules-based accounting, and in that study SEC staff recommend a shift to principles-based accounting for corporate financial reporting (SEC, 2003b).

Finally, while corruption was most glaringly demonstrated in the numerous frauds committed against shareholders by corporate insiders, Enron also exposed a corrupt undermining of US regulatory structures. Earlier deregulation of energy markets, for example, had resulted in an environment in which energy traders such as Enron were able to manipulate regional energy markets to create false energy shortages (Krugman, 2003b; Krugman, 2003c). In the area of financial market regulation, Enron exposed the fact that the power and resources of the SEC had been allowed to decline substantially, making it more difficult for the SEC to enact new regulations it felt were necessary, or to adequately investigate possible market misbehaviour.

Given the foregoing, an intellectually honest advocate of corporate governance reforms based upon US models would need, post-Enron, to point out that such corporate governance rules will not function as they do in the United States if removed from the US institutional framework, particularly without the 'gatekeeper' professions, and that the proper functioning of that institutional framework depends upon what are, in essence, cultural norms, expectations and practices. Truly adopting US-style corporate governance thus becomes a matter of importing US business and professional culture more generally. This would be a much more daunting and controversial prospect than simply adopting a few American-style rules, so one effect of Enron might be to undercut further Americanisation.

Viewed from another angle, however, it seems that Enron will only strengthen the corporate governance reform agenda in Northeast Asia. First, the legislative outcome of Enron, Sarbanes-Oxley, will force a round of adjustments in non-US corporate governance systems for companies that wish to access US capital markets. Sarbanes-Oxley is resulting in a major re-working of the US rules, whether promulgated by Congress, the SEC, or the self-governing securities exchanges, and to the extent that the new rules are more specific than those they are replacing, they will force a higher degree of convergence by foreign systems with the US approach, whatever that may be when the current regulatory initiatives are completed.

Secondly, although Enron exposed major weaknesses in US corporate governance, the weaknesses can be understood in the familiar language of minority shareholder rights, and the solutions can be understood to involve strengthened legal protections for minority shareholders. Asian reform advocates will thus be bolstered by Enron, just as it has added fuel to the fire of shareholder rights advocates in the United States, who are often advocates of shareholder rights abroad (Tassell, 2003). And the depressed US stock market that has resulted from Enron only makes this more likely, as US pension funds and other institutional shareholders are forced to look abroad for profitable investment opportunities, in addition to seeking to reduce risk through diversification in additional markets. In other words, while Enron should raise questions about US corporate governance as practised, it will probably only encourage more energetic advocacy for shareholders' rights, in the United States and abroad. US private equity groups such as Cerberus and Ripplewood have obtained rights to take ownership stakes in Northeast Asian financial institutions, and are showing signs of being willing to exercise their rights in ways that will challenge accepted norms and practices (Ibison and Tett, 2003). US investment funds are also bringing their culture of shareholder activism to Northeast Asia. Sometimes they invest directly, as in the case of Sovereign Asset Management's investment in South Korea's S K Global and the Japanese bank UFJ, and sometimes they invest less directly, as the California employee pension fund CALPERS did in investing US$200 million to seed a 'corporate governance' fund operated by Sparx Asset Management, a Japanese fund manager (Tassell, 2003). Thus in terms of the reform impulses discussed in this chapter—the P/P and the Neoliberal—Enron can lend support to both.

While Enron's impact seems to basically reinforce Asian corporate governance reforms, September 11 has had three fairly clear effects limiting US reform pressures. The first, and most direct, is that the Bush administration has clearly decided to focus its attention on its 'war on terror', either because terrorism is the most important issue facing the United

States, or because focusing on terrorism gave Bush the best chance of being re-elected in 2004, a goal which he has now achieved. This focus means that international economic and trade issues are not receiving the attention they did a few years ago. And when the Bush administration does act internationally, it wants to act authoritatively, demanding results, rather than trying to establish institutions and processes that may bring about desired results some time in the future. Trying to bring about desired results in Northeast Asia by encouraging derivative litigation, or more American style administrative law, requires a long-term outlook and a willingness to trust processes and private initiative, rather than demanding results. If it is true that Bush is more inclined than Clinton to demand substantive results, and less likely to accept legal reforms that may eventually lead to those results, American demands for law reforms may become a much less important factor in legislative change in Northeast Asia.

As a result of the resurrection of the importance of strategic interests in US foreign policy, countries that are strategically important to the United States in its 'war on terror' appear to find themselves under somewhat lighter pressure from US trade negotiators, and perhaps from multinational organisations in which the US voice is important. For example, although US authorities found in favour of the first US industry to invoke the new 'market disruption' mechanism for protection against imports from China, President Bush exercised his authority under the statute to deny protection to the complaining industry because he found that protection would not be in the best interests of the United States (US Department of State, 2003). Bush's stated reason for denying the protection was that it would harm other US constituencies, but given that Bush needs China's cooperation in the 'war on terror', this appears to be an instance of strategic interests asserting themselves in trade disputes. Financial commentators, in turn, seem to believe that while Bush is now willing to criticise China for maintaining an overly-weak Renminbi, Japan is able to escape criticism for the manipulation of its currency by virtue of its support for Bush's 'war on terror' (Pilling, 2003). A more controversial example is the new policy of the US Justice Department to challenge law suits brought in US courts by victims of human rights abuses abroad. In the name of preserving relations with our allies, the Justice Department is attempting to block cases brought under the Alien Tort Claims Act and the Torture Victim Protection Act, including a pending case involving slave labour in Burma, prompting public criticism from a Republican member of the Senate Judiciary Committee (Specter, 2003).

A second, less direct, consequence of September 11 has been that it has strengthened the tendencies of the Bush administration towards a conservative, pro-corporate management agenda. This difference between the Bush agenda and the Neoliberalism of the Clinton administration is typified by the fact that Bush has appointed CEOs of large, traditional industries to serve as his two Treasury secretaries, while Clinton's most prominent Treasury secretaries were Robert Rubin, a Wall Street investment banker, and Larry Summers, a market-oriented economics professor. Rubin and Summers reportedly occupied key roles in the Clinton administration, while Bush's Treasury secretaries, and the Treasury department as a whole, have been marginalised (Scheiber, 2003; Krugman, 2003a).

This tone set by the Bush administration may be showing up in recent surveys showing that US corporate boards and managers are increasingly willing to criticise Sarbanes-Oxley and the constraints it puts upon them in the name of shareholder protection (Foley and Lardner, 2003; Michaels, 2003a). The more Bush inclines towards the interests of corporate management the more likely he is to accept their argument that Sarbanes-Oxley and related corporate governance reforms are stifling productive corporate initiative (*Financial Times*, 2004; Michaels, 2004; Buchanan and Donahoe, 2003; Michaels, 2003b; *US Law Week*, 2003), which will make it less likely that the post-Enron momentum for corporate governance reforms will continue. Evidence that this is happening can be seen in the decision of the US Financial Accounting Supervisory Board to delay implementation of a long-sought reform requiring companies to deduct the cost of employee stock options from profits, a decision that appears to be a direct result of political pressure at the behest of industry (Waters, 2004). A conservative, pro-management agenda aligns Bush with Northeast Asia's traditional business elite, who have every reason to be wary about the explosion of derivative litigation. South Korea's Federation of Korean Industries, for example, funds a think-tank called the Center for Free Enterprise, which warns of the dangers of an aggressive, overtly political, minority shareholders' rights movement (Kim, Chung Ho, 1999).

With respect to administrative law, the conservative tendencies of the Bush administration, strengthened by September 11, could also have important implications. The model of American administrative law that has been most influential internationally is a product of the 1960s and 1970s, and is tied to the ideology of political pluralism. In that era, when many no longer accepted that government agencies could be trusted to exercise non-political, scientific expertise to govern in the public interest, US administrative law doctrines greatly expanded opportunities for private parties to participate in the administrative process, opportunities enforceable in the courts. The intended effect of these expanded opportunities was to turn the administrative process into a substitute political process, in which the battle among competing social forces would result in appropriate and politically legitimate social policies.

It is widely believed that this vision of the social function of administrative law was the vision of people who believed in the regulatory, social welfare state, but who needed a new ideology, and a new administrative law, to legitimate such a state once the idea of neutral agency expertise had lost its legitimising power. Such an approach to the regulatory state is anathema to the Bush administration, which is more radical than other Republican administrations in its attempts to roll back the regulatory state, while at the same time rejecting the idea that executive branch processes should be opened up to public scrutiny and contest. In the area of information disclosure, for example, the Homeland Security Act introduced new exceptions to the information disclosure requirements of the Freedom of Information Act (FOIA), ostensibly based upon a desire to keep information about 'critical infrastructure', such as chemical plants, out of the hands of terrorists. Critics, however, have seen these exceptions as an opportunistic, September 11-inspired gift to industry to help it resist environmental activism, prompting Democrats in Congress to introduce legislation to preserve the role of the FOIA (Leahy, 2003; OMB Watch, 2003).

The Bush administration's rejection of the pluralist paradigm has also been apparent in the controversy over the National Energy Policy Development Group (NEPDG), chaired by Vice-President Cheney. Made up of high-level government officials, the NEPDG was directed by President Bush to gather information, deliberate and develop a national energy policy. Rather than soliciting a wide range of views, however, the NEPDG appears to have functioned primarily as a forum for sectors of the energy industry to present their particular proposals with respect to policies affecting them. 'Appears' is the appropriate term, because the administration refuses to disclose who met with the NEPDG, let alone release the minutes of its meetings, even when requested to do so by the General Accounting Office (GAO, subsequently renamed the Government Accountability Office). The GAO was forced to sue the Vice-President under its access-to-records statute, but the suit was dismissed on jurisdictional grounds,[1] and the GAO was relegated to writing a superficial report based on fragments of information it had been able to collect from secondary sources (GAO, 2003a; Sevastopulo, 2003; Seelye, 2003). In its unwillingness to open the NEPDG process to public scrutiny, the administration is demonstrating a fundamental disdain for pluralist assumptions, apparently unconcerned with maintaining even the façade of a pluralist process to legitimate its substantive policy decisions.

In tandem with its tendency to reject pluralist assumptions regarding the transparency of executive branch activities, the Bush administration has also shown itself willing to disregard established understandings in its efforts to bend the administrative agencies to its will. The innocuously titled Data Quality Act of 2000, passed by an uninformed Congress after

[1] *Walker v Cheney*, 230 F Supp 2d 51 (DDC 2002).

being inserted into a massive appropriations bill at the behest of an industry lobbyist (Mooney, 2004; Adams, 2002), is being implemented by officials in the White House Office of Management and Budget in ways that force federal agencies to respond to sometimes spurious private sector challenges to agency science (Weiss, 2004). The perception, driven only in part by controversy over the Data Quality Act, that the Bush administration is willing to subject scientific objectivity within administrative agencies to partisan politics has driven many senior figures in the scientific community into active opposition (Revkin, 2004; Union of Concerned Scientists, 2004). In addition, officials in the Bush administration have twice been publicly rebuked by the GAO for illegally interfering with administrative agencies: once for illegally preventing a Medicare actuary from revealing to Congress the true costs of the administration's Medicare reforms (Pear, 2004; GAO, 2004b), and once for illegally using Medicare funds to produce propaganda for the same reforms disguised as news reports (GAO, 2004b).

In step with the Bush administration, conservative political activists are likewise demonstrating a clear willingness to attack the pluralist assumptions embedded in US administrative law and the regulatory process, launching initiatives such as 'NGO Watch', challenging the legitimacy of consultation with public interest NGOs whose participation in policy-making has been understood as central to pluralist understandings. Finally, to the dismay of even mainstream conservatives such as US Supreme Court Chief Justice Rehnquist, radical conservatives have taken a number of actions to limit judicial discretion in criminal sentencing, actions that in their heavy-handedness challenge the independence of individual federal judges, and thus the judiciary as a whole (Perine, 2004; Walsh and Eggen, 2003; Lore, 2003; Cambanis, 2003).

Whether any of these US developments matters for Northeast Asia is, of course, a different question. One of the fundamental premises of this chapter is that formally similar legal norms and institutions take on lives of their own when adopted in disparate societies. Even if one accepts that US interests have played a large role in supporting Northeast Asia's administrative and corporate law reforms, and did so primarily to further Neoliberal impulses, it is likely that the way these legal fields actually function now in the United States is irrelevant to Northeast Asia. Perhaps the primary way the conservatism of the Bush administration could influence the functioning of these doctrines in Northeast Asia would be by helping conservative, pro-business political parties win national elections. Bush tried but failed to help the conservative candidate in South Korea's December 2002 presidential election, so this sort of US influence is a possibility. Left-leaning Korean President Roh Moo-hyun is currently battling Korean business interests to expand the investigative authority of

Korea's Fair Trade Commission (Park, 2003), and if the Bush administration had been able to tip the election to the conservative candidate this battle might never have been fought. On the whole, though, it is very hard to draw clear connections between developments in the United States and changes in specific legal fields in Northeast Asia.

VI CONCLUSION

Eclectic critique asks us to set aside preconceived notions when we think about law reform. One way to do this is to recognise that legal rules and institutions may carry within them the potential to operate in dramatically different ways, and that we cannot fully evaluate the results of legal reform projects until we can see how newly-adopted norms and institutions function. And reforms that depend upon *judicialisation*, which seek to bring about social change by harnessing private interests channelled through the litigation process, are especially subject to unintended consequences. This chapter has adopted the highly stylised dichotomy of Neoliberal and P/P concerns to help structure an eclectic critique of corporate and administrative law reforms in Northeast Asia. A tentative conclusion reached from applying this structure is that reforms that might well be driven by a Neoliberal agenda can turn out to be very useful to local P/P forces, who may be able to make greater use of such reforms, when these are localised, than could Neoliberal interests. But precisely because the reforms discussed here carry within them the potential to further either Neoliberal or P/P interests, the admonition 'be careful what you wish for' is particularly appropriate. A second conclusion is that September 11 may well slow down the Neoliberal legal agenda globally. Whether that is a good thing depends upon what replaces Neoliberalism, but there is reason to believe that we may look back on the Neoliberal hegemony of the 1990s, with all its faults, as more positive and constructive than what followed.

BIBLIOGRAPHY

ADAMS, REBECCA (2002) 'Federal Regulations Face Assault on Their Foundation' 10 August 2002) 60 *Congressional Quarterly Weekly* 2182.

AMERICAN CHAMBER OF COMMERCE IN JAPAN (October 2002) 'Improve Japan's Civil Judicial Process and Legal Services System' *Viewpoint* (copy on file with author).

AMSDEN, ALICE H (1989) *Asia's Next Giant: South Korea and Late Industrialization* (Oxford University Press, Oxford).

ARITAKE, TOSHIO (2003) 'NTT Carriers Sue Japanese Government on NTT Rate Rise' (24 July 2003) 20 *International Trade Reporter* 1268.

ARONSON, BRUCE E (2003) 'Reconsidering the Importance of Law in Japanese Corporate Governance: Evidence from the Daiwa Bank Shareholder Derivative Case' 36 *Cornell International Law Journal* 11 (2003–2004).

ASAHI SHIMBUN (2003): 'Editorial: Education in Rule of Law' *Asahi Shimbun* (English language Internet edition) 19 August 2003, available at: <http://www.asahi.com/english/op-ed/K2003081900269.html> last accessed 19 August 2003 (copy on file with author).

ASIA CORPORATE GOVERNANCE ASSOCIATION (2004) 'Facilitating Effective Corporate Governance in Asia,' available at: <http://www.acga-asia.org/loadfile.cfm?SITE_FILE_ID=247>, last accessed 15 November 2006.

BELSON, KEN (2003) 'Japan Phone Case to Pit Business Against Bureaucrats' *New York Times* 15 July 2003, W1, col 3.

BLACK, BERNARD ET AL (2001) 'Corporate Governance in Korea at the Millennium: Enhancing International Competitiveness' 26 *Journal of Corporation Law* 546.

BUCHANAN, ROBIN and DONAHOE, JOHN (2003) 'Boards Will be Frozen by Caution's Icy Hand' *Financial Times* 30 July 2003, 13, col 1.

CAMBANIS, THANASSIS (2003) 'Sentencing Law Targets U.S. Judges in Massachusetts' *Boston Globe* 30 May 2003, A1.

CHU, YUN-HAN (1994) 'The Realignment of Business-Government Relations and Regime Transition in Taiwan' in Andrew Macintyre (ed) *Business and Government in Industrialising Asia* (Cornell University, Ithaca, NY).

CLAESSENS, STIJN; DJANKOV, SIMEON; and LANG, LARRY H P (1999) 'Who Controls East Asian Corporations? World Bank Policy Research Working Paper 2054, February, 1999.

COFFEE, JOHN C JR (2002) 'Understanding Enron: It's About the Gatekeepers, Stupid' Columbia Law School, Center for Law and Economic Studies, Working Paper No 207, 30 July 2002, available at: <http://ssrn.com/abstract_it=325240>, last accessed 15 November 2006.

DEYO, FREDERIC C (1989) *Beneath the Miracle: Labor Subordination in the New Asian Industrialism* (University of California, Berkeley, CA).

EPSTEIN, RICHARD A (1995) *Simple Rules for a Complex World* (Harvard University, Cambridge, MA).

Financial Times (2004) 'The boardroom burden: calls for reform are replaced by concern that corporate shake-up has gone too far' *Financial Times* 1 June 2004, 9, col 1.

FOLEY and LARDNER 'Sarbanes-Oxley Shapshot Survey' (2003), available at: <http://view.exacttarget.com/?j=144371&l=72857_HTML&e=tandrlik@webershandwick.com>, last accessed 30 July 2003 (copy on file with author).

FRIEDMAN, LAWRENCE M (1990) *The Republic of Choice* (Harvard University, Cambridge, MA).

GENERAL ACCOUNTING OFFICE (2002) 'Financial Statement Restatements' Report to the Chairman, Committee on Banking, Housing, and Urban Affairs, US Senate, October 2002. GAO-03-138.

—— (2003a) 'Energy Task Force: Process Used to Develop the National Energy Policy' Report to Congressional Requesters, August 2003. GAO-03-894.

—— (2003b) 'World Trade Organization: Ensuring China's Compliance Requires a Sustained and Multifaceted Approach' Statement of Loren Yeger, Director, International Affairs and Trade, October 2003. GAO-04-172T.

—— (2004a) 'Department of Health and Human Services – Chief Actuary's Communications with Congress' Legal Opinion from GAO General Counsel Anthony H Gamboa to members of Congress, 7 September 2004. GAO-B-302-911

—— (2004b) 'Department of Health and Human Services, Centers for Medicare & Medicaid Services—Video News Releases' Decision of the Comptroller General of the United States, 19 May 2004. GAO-B-302710.

HONG, JOON-HYUNG (2000) 'Administrative Law in the Institutionalized Administrative State' in Dae-Kyu Yoon (ed) *Recent Transformations in Korean Law and Society* (Seoul National University, Seoul).

IBISON, DAVID and NAKAMOTO, MICHIYO 'Japanese Tax Bill for Lone Star Worries Foreign Funds' *Financial Times* 17 July 2003, 29.

IBISON, DAVID and TETT, GILLIAN (2003) 'American to Head Japan's Aozora Bank' *Financial Times* 23 July 2003, Companies and Markets 1.

INSTITUTE OF INTERNATIONAL FINANCE, INCORPORATED (2003) 'Corporate Governance in Korea: An Investor Perspective' IIF Equity Advisory Group Task Force Report (July, 2003) (copy on file with author).

JANG, HASUNG (2002) 'Empowering Shareholders Rights: Derivative and Class-Action Lawsuits,' presentation to the OECD Asian Roundtable on Corporate Governance, Mumbai, India (11–12 November 2002) (copy on file with author).

JOHNSON, CHALMERS (1982) *MITI and the Japanese Miracle* (Stanford University, Stanford, CA).

KAGAN, ROBERT A and AXELRAD, LEE (eds) (2000) *Regulatory Encounters: Multinational Corporations and American Adversarial Legalism* (University of California, Berkeley CA).

KIM, CHUNG HO (1999) 'A Thought on Corporate Governance Movements' Center for Free Enterprise Executive Essay, No EE-25, 19 January 1999, available at: <http://www.cfe.org/English/Briefsbbs/essay/content.asp?idx=146>, last accessed 20 October 2004 (copy on file with author).

KIM, HWA-JIN (2001) 'Taking International Soft Law Seriously: Its Implications for Global Convergence in Corporate Governance' 1(1) *Journal of Korean Law* 1.

KIM, JOOYOUNG and KIM, JOONGO (2001) 'Shareholder Activism in Korea: A Review of How PSPD Has Used Legal Measures to Strengthen Korean Corporate Governance' 1(1) *Journal of Korean Law* 51.

KRUGMAN, PAUL (2003a) 'Everything Is Political' *New York Times* 5 August 2003, A15, col 6.

—— (2003b) 'The Road to Ruin' *New York Times* 19 August 2003, A21, col 5.

—— (2003c) 'Another Friday Outrage' *New York Times* 1 September 2003, A23, col 6.

LEAHY, PATRICK (2003a) 'Restoration of Freedom of Information Act ('Restore FOIA') Sectional Analysis' available at: <http://leahy.senate.gov/press/200303/031203c.html>, last accessed 15 November 2006.

LEE, SANG-EON (2003) 'Susie Kim's Retribution' *JoongAng Daily* 15 August 2003.

LORE, MICHELLE (2003) 'Amendment Limiting Judicial Discretion in Sentencing Receives Cool Reception from Judges' *Minnesota Lawyer* 7 July 2003.

MICHAELS, ADRIAN (2003a) 'Reforms Lose Support of Business Leaders' *Financial Times* 28 July 2003, 16, col 1.

—— (2003b) 'Boardroom proposals clash with turn of corporate tide' *Financial Times* 27 August 2003, 14, col 1.

—— (2004) 'AIG chairman bemoans burden of governance' *Financial Times* 20 May 2004, 19, col 6.

MILHAUPT, CURTIS J (2003) *Non-profit Organizations as Investor Protection: Economic Theory, and Evidence from East Asia* (unpublished manuscript, copy on file with author).

MOONEY, CHRIS (2004) 'Paralysis by Analysis' (1 May 2004) 36(5) *Washington Monthly* 23.

NGO WATCH: <http://www.ngowatch.org>, last accessed 15 November 2006.

ORGANISATION FOR ECONOMIC COOPERATION and DEVELOPMENT (2003) 'White Paper on Corporate Governance in Asia', available at: <http://www.oecd.org/dataoecd/48/55/25778905. pdf>, last accessed 15 November 2006.

OH, JUN-GEN (2000) 'The Characteristics and Results of Korea's Administrative Regulations Reform' in Dae-Kyu Yoon (ed) *Recent Transformations in Korean Law and Society* (Seoul National University, Seoul) 73.

—— (2003) 'The Rule of Law, Economic Development, and the Developmental States of Northeast Asia' in Christoph Antons (ed) *Law and Development in East and Southeast Asia* (RoutledgeCurzon, London).

OMB WATCH (2003) 'American Chemistry Council's Comments Demonstrate Need for Public CII Docket' 28 July 2003, available at: <http://www.ombwatch.org/article/articleview/ 1697/1/252?TopicID=1>, last accessed 15 November 2006.

PARK, SANG-SOO (2003) 'New Holding Firm Rule Aims at Simpler Chaebol System' *Korea Herald* 19 August 2003, availlable at: <http: // www.koreaherald.co.kr/SITE/data/html_dir/2003/08/20/200308200051.asp>, last accessed 15 November 2006.

PEAR, ROBERT (2004) 'Inquiry Proposes Penalties for Hiding Medicare Data' *New York Times* 8 September 2004, A16, col 5.

PERINE, KEITH (2004) '"Heightened Tensions" Fray Judicial-Legislative Relations' (18 September 2004) 61 *Congressional Quarterly Weekly* 2148.

PILLING, DAVID (2003) 'Snow Calls on Beijing to Let Currency Float' *Financial Times* 2 September 2003, 1, col 2.

RAMSEYER, MARK (2003) Comment as Panelist, at the *Sharing Scholarship on East Asian Law Conference*, Harvard Law School, Cambridge, Massachusetts, May 2003.

RAMSEYER, MARK, and ROSENBLUTH, FRANCES MCCALL (1993) *Japan's Political Marketplace* (Harvard University, Cambridge, MA).

REVKIN, ANDREW C (2004) "Bush vs. the Laureates: How Science Became a Partisan Issue' *New York Times* 19 October 2004, D1, col 1.

ROMANO, ROBERTA (1991) 'The Shareholder Suit: Litigation without Foundation?' 7 *Journal of Law, Economics and Organization* 55.

SCHEIBER, NOAM (2003) 'Is Snow Worse Than O'Neill?: Buried Treasury' *New Republic* 11 August 2003, 17–21.

SECURITIES and EXCHANGE COMMISSION (2003a) 'SEC Settles Enforcement Proceedings against J.P. Morgan Chase and Citigroup' SEC Press Release, 28 July 2003, available at: <http://www.sec.gov/news/press/2003-87.htm>, last accessed 15 November 2006.

—— (2003b) 'SEC Study on Adoption by the U.S. Financial Reporting System of a Principles-Based Accounting System' SEC Press Release, 25 July 2003, available at: <http://www.sec.gov/news/press/2003-86.htm>, last accessed 15 November 2006.

SEELYE, KATHERINE Q (2003) 'Study Confirms "Stakeholders" Gave Advice to Energy Panel' *New York Times* 26 August 2003, A16, col 5.

SEVASTOPULO, DEMETRI (2003) 'GAO Investigation: Cheney office attacked on energy probe' *Financial Times* 27 August 2003, 2, col 8.

SPECTER, ARLEN (2003) 'The Court of Last Resort' *New York Times* 7 August 2003, A23, col 1.

STIGLITZ, JOSEPH E (2002) *Globalization and its Discontents* (Penguin Books, London and New York).

TANG, DENNIS T C (2001) 'Overview of the Administrative Procedure Act of Taiwan' Presentation to the Alexander von Humbolt Foundation, September, 2001, Taipei, Taiwan, available at: <http://www.avh.de/en/netzwerk/veranstalt/hoersaal/ 2001_taiwan_01.htm>, last accessed 26 July 2002 (copy on file with author).

TASSELL, TONY (2003) 'Japan Gets to Grips with Corporate Governance' *Financial Times* 28 July 2003, 20, col 5.

TRUBEK, DAVID M and GALANTER, MARC (1974) 'Scholars in Self-Estrangement: Some Reflections on the Crisis in Law and Development Studies in the United States' [1974] *Wisconsin Law Review* 1062.

US Law Week (2003) 'SEC Chairman Tries to Allay Concerns That Sarbanes-Oxley Increases Liability' 72(4) *US Law Week* 2056–58.

UNION OF CONCERNED SCIENTISTS (2004) 'Scientific Integrity in Policy Making: Further Investigation of the Bush Administration's Abuse of Science' (July 2004) available at: <http://www.ucsusa.org/global_environment/rsi/page.cfm?pageID=1449>, last accessed 4 November 2004 (copy on file with author).

UNITED STATES DEPARTMENT OF STATE, INTERNATIONAL INFORMATION PROGRAMS (2003) 'Bush Forgoes Action on Imports of Chinese Devices' Washington File, 21 January 2003 available in the Public Diplomacy Query Archive: <http://usinfo.state.gov/products/pdq/wfarchive. htm>, last accessed 31 July 2003 (copy on file with author).

WALSH, EDWARD and EGGEN, DAN (2003) 'Ashcroft Orders Tally of Lighter Sentences; Critics Say He Wants "Blacklist" of Judges' *Washington Post* 7 August 2003, A01.

WATERS, RICHARD (2004) 'FASB postpones stock options rule' *Financial Times* 14 October 2004, 1, col 2.

WEISS, RICK (2004) '"Data Quality" Law is Nemesis of Regulation *Washington Post* 16 August 2004, A01.

WEST, JAMES M (1992) 'Administrative Procedure in Korea' *Journal of the American Chamber of Commerce in Korea* (December 1992)

WILSON, JEFFREY (2002) 'Insurance regime undermines China's WTO credentials' 21 *International Financial Law Review* 35 (February 2002).

WOO, JUNG-EN (1991) *Race to the Swift: State and Finance in Korean Industrialization* (Columbia University, New York).

WU, SOFIA (2003) 'MND Loses Appeal for Return of Pension Paid to Defector's Family' Central News Agency, Taiwan, 6 August 2003.

PART 2:

CONSTITUTIONAL REFORM, THE RULE OF LAW AND HUMAN RIGHTS

6

Southeast Asia, 1997–2003: Two Case Studies on the Politics of Law and Development

ANDREW HARDING

I INTRODUCTION

ONE MAJOR REASON for welcoming this volume and the breadth of the themes outlined in it, is that, as Roman Tomasic in a forerunner of this volume (Tomasic, 2003) and several others, including myself, have been at pains to point out in recent writings on South East Asia, the available literature on law and development issues in East and South East Asia is painfully thin[1] and we are in need of research which is both broad and deep, and searches for what Tomasic calls 'new stories to tell'. Pointing to the period addressed by this book he refers to our subject matter as 'a relatively unploughed field of endeavour', and defines our research tasks as follows:

> Many challenges await socio-legal researchers seeking to make a contribution to improving understanding of major contemporary issues, such as the late 1990s Asian financial crisis, the place of the rule of law, human rights, nation-building, and the effects of globalisation.

Nobuyuki Yasuda (2003) argues for an Asian perspective on law and development studies, and envisages research in this field as 'a kind of policy study mobilising the knowledge of various branches of social sciences to design more suitable legal systems'.

For my own part (Harding, 2002) I have used the relationship between what I call 'global doctrine' and 'local knowledge' as a frame of reference for addressing the issues of current significance that Tomasic, Yasuda and several others have outlined:

[1] This statement in no way takes lightly two very valuable recent contributions, ie, Antons (2003) and Davidson (2002).

> A new phase [of South East Asian legal studies] since about 1990 embraces globalisation-law, which has been driving much of legal development and transplantation in South East Asia in the field of international business and commercial law, for example relating to foreign investment and intellectual property. These developments have had a knock-on effect on organic laws, even public and constitutional law. The interesting outcome of this phase as regards legal studies is a renewed emphasis on culture and society as guides to the analysis and understanding of law. The recent economic crisis in South East Asia has also renewed emphasis on the rule-of-law, civil society and the empowerment of legal institutions as the way forward.

The economic Crisis (Booth, 1999) drew attention, but in a somewhat ambiguous or paradoxical way, to cultural factors: Did cultural factors contribute to the Crisis? If so, why did the Crisis not happen at some time earlier, given that economic growth has been taking place in the region since the mid-1960s? Or are there aspects of culture that were responsible in some way for that very growth?

These approaches seem to have in common the idea of a much thicker type of description and analysis than has often been seen in the age of globalisation.

Since September 11, 2001 much more has been heard about the 'clash of civilisations', and it has been realised that these altered circumstances have put the economic issues surrounding globalisation into a much broader context in which the politics of security, national integrity, and international relations feature much more largely than before. It is not of course that the attacks of September 11, 2001 have brought the process of globalisation to a shuddering halt; however, they have made us much less sanguine about globalisation and have forced us to pay more attention not just to the purely economic problems and possibilities, but also to problems of human rights, security, governance, the rule of law, justice, and cultural difference. The 'end of history' now seems virtually as remote as it did before the end of the Cold War. A future of danger, retrenchment and disintegration seems every bit as possible as a future of peace, progress and global governance.

Thus the effect of the two events that define the period under consideration is to bring to the fore discussion of the political dimensions of legal reform.[2] In this contribution I therefore wish to address the general themes of the book from the perspective of the politics of law and development in relation to two case studies, ie, Thailand and Malaysia. My purpose is to indicate the large differences between these case studies, and to highlight

[2] Both Tomasic and Yasuda discuss the relevance of politics to law and development studies, a factor which is studiously avoided in Pistor and Wellons' study (Pistor and Wellons, 1998). See also the special issue (vol 6, 2002) of the *Singapore Journal of International and Comparative Law*, which contains articles about constitutional change in Thailand, Malaysia, Singapore, Indonesia and Vietnam.

one of the central questions for Asian countries, faced with both the threats and the opportunities of globalisation, which is whether improved conditions of governance are essential to their chances of surviving globalisation and marking out a new path of development. It might be seen that Thailand and Malaysia represent alternative ways of characterising and dealing with these threats and opportunities. Here we may find two 'new stories' of the kind to which Tomasic is referring, stories that leave us with an intriguing paradox, because they appear to lead to opposite conclusions.

II THAILAND, 1997-2003: THE PATH OF POLITICAL REFORM

The case of Thailand is a particularly interesting one, because it involves the pursuit of the path of political reform (Nelson, 2001). The trajectory of events prior to the economic Crisis emphasised the importance of democratic politics to an extent that was already surprising when one compared Thailand with Malaysia, Singapore and Indonesia. The Crisis had the effect of carrying that general trajectory towards root-and-branch reform (McCargo, 2002; Connors, 2003).

In 1991[3] the military government of General Suchinda Kraprakorn was rejected by the public following its brutal suppression of street demonstrations. The democratic government that resulted secured the passage of the constitutional amendments of 1991, which required the drafting of a new Constitution designed to entrench democracy and human rights, exclude military influence in the political process, adopt a zero-tolerance approach to corruption in public life, and make the formation of stable governments less problematical. This was indeed a highly ambitious agenda. To adopt my own description (Harding, 2001), '[i]t is hard to imagine a more comprehensive attempt to change social facts by law'.

Phongpaichit and Baker (1999) have adduced an interesting analysis of Thai dissatisfaction with the previous version of constitutional government:

> First, political goods such as election votes, party loyalty, and ministerial positions [acquired] high and rising prices. Second, the local focus often led to neglect of national issues including economic management and legislation needed in response to the change and modernization in society and economy. The development of this 'money politics' and parochialism had, by the early 1990s, given rise to an urgent debate over the compatibility of capitalism and democracy, and had prompted urban-based reform movements pushing for change.

[3] For the historical background to the recent reforms, see Pinai (2002).

This dissatisfaction became more multi-faceted and pressed the need for reform (Laird, 2000; Hewison, 1997). The reform agenda was taken forward by the governments of Chuan Leekpai (1992–95 and 1997–2001), Banharn Silpa-Archa (1995–96), and Chavalit Yongchaiyudh (1996–97) and a Constitutional Drafting Assembly (CDA) of 99 persons[4] was appointed.[5] The CDA completed its work in April 1997; under the constitutional amendments of 1991 and 1996 the draft Constitution had then to be considered by Parliament, and either adopted without amendment or else totally rejected.

It was into this delicate situation that the Crisis intruded so destructively in the early and middle months of 1997 (Jumbala, 1998). Amid a virtually unprecedented and very alarming collapse of currency values, the Thai people had to decide whether to adopt the most far-reaching raft of constitutional reforms since the institution of constitutional government in 1932, or forgo this unique and critical opportunity in order to deal with their worst economic crisis since the 1930s. Naturally, the arguments were finely balanced. Many Thais felt that the old expedient of relying on the King[6] to deal with constitutional crises was preferable to the uncertainty of reform, and that there were simply more pressing matters than the Constitution at that time. At the same time, many Thais felt that political reforms were an essential prerequisite to economic reforms. It was of particular interest that the draft Constitution involved drastic reforms of both houses of the National Assembly, and considerably demoted parliamentarians in role and status, exposing them to a wide range of new checks and balances related to corruption and abuse of power. It was, ironically, the military that ultimately determined the issue when they made it clear, amid hints of another coup, that the National Assembly should pass the draft without amendment, which was precisely what occurred in September 1997, the King assenting to it the following month.[7] One might

[4] The CDA membership comprised: 76 members, each representing a province, chosen by the Senate from candidates nominated at the provincial level; and 23 'expert' members (consisting of eight lawyers, eight political scientists, and seven civil servants and politicians). See, further, Pinai (2002) and Harding (2001).

[5] Its remit is expressed in the Preamble to the resulting Constitution of 1997, which states that the CDA's duty is 'to prepare a draft of a new Constitution as the fundamental [sic] of political reform . . . with the essential substance lying in additionally promoting and protecting rights and liberties of the people, providing for public participation in the governance and inspecting the exercise of State power as well as improving a political structure to achieve more efficiency and stability, having particular regard to public opinions'.

[6] This expedient clearly still exists. In December 2005 the King intervened in a fierce dispute between the Prime Minister and his leading political opponent, securing the withdrawal of several legal proceedings by the former.

[7] The fact that the regime of governance established by the 1997 Constitution is constantly described in the text (for example, the Preamble, ss 2, 7, 313) as 'democratic government with the King as Head of State' is an acknowledgment that the monarchy is still very popular and necessary to Thai constitutionalism and (as indicated above) the only constant factor in Thai

be surprised that the military played this role; it should be remembered, however, that even the military is not immune from social, political and intellectual developments, and conceivably was convinced that renouncing a political role might even work to its longer-term advantage.

At any rate, by this process Thailand effectively placed political reform ahead of economic reform. If, as Yasuda has said, 'lack of transparency and accountability, nepotism in business and various other political practices including corrupt crony capitalism, and authoritarian forms of government' were the main causes of the Crisis (Yasuda, 2003; see also Gomez and Jomo, 1999), then it would appear that the constitutional reform process in Thailand, even though it commenced some six years before the Crisis, and was brought to conclusion during it, were aimed at precisely the right problems. If this is correct it would follow that, of all the Southeast Asian countries, Thailand was best placed to recover and benefit from subsequent economic and legal reforms, because it had in a sense already 'left the starting blocks' in a flying start whilst others were still deafened or confused by the starter's gun. I am not, of course, arguing that purely economic law reforms are irrelevant to Thailand's recovery. In fact, reforms have occurred in economic law areas such as bankruptcy law (Bankruptcy Act 1998), competition law (Business Competition Act 1999), and foreign investment law (Foreign Business Law 1999), and these have in fact accompanied the constitutional reform process.[8] Official findings criticising the Bank of Thailand have resulted in many changes in banking practices, and a Financial Sector Restructuring Authority has been put in place. The point is simply that, due to the nature and timing of political events, and probably also as a matter of predilection, the constitutional reforms are seen in Thailand as an essential prerequisite for economic recovery as well as for the solution of the problems of corruption, accountability, abuse of power, transparency, military rule, government formation, human rights, and the rule of law. It is a very forbidding agenda, but it is matched by the equally forbidding determination of many Thais to make this reform process succeed. Thailand has now seen 16 Constitutions since 1932,[9] as well as 16 military coups and no fewer than 54 governments. The Constitution of 1997[10] is designed to bring to an end once and for all this cycle of coups and weak, corrupt, coalition governments.

political life over many years. The monarchy is the *only* aspect of constitutional life that has *not* been subjected to reform (Hewison, 1997b).

[8] See, further, Yasuda (2003a). Some laws were introduced in satisfaction of IMF conditions when the IMF advanced a huge loan to Thailand in 1998. Recently, following repayment of the loan, some of these laws have been repealed.

[9] Including an astonishing total of six between the years 1968 and 1978.

[10] Constitution of Thailand, 1997. Government Gazette, 11 October 1997, vol 114, part 55a. Also available at: <http://thailand.ahrchk.net/mainfile.php/docs/133/>.

The next question, then, is how has Thailand proposed to achieve these ambitious objectives by reforming its constitution?

A The Remorseless Logic of the Anti-Corruption Constitution

Although the political spur towards reform was the brutal suppression of opposition to the military government of General Suchinda, the 1997 Constitution itself indicates that corruption (Phongpaichit and Piriyarangsan, 1996) is seen as the source of most of Thailand's ills, and the description of it as an 'anti-corruption constitution' (Borwornsak, 2000) is no exaggeration. There is indeed a deep logic to the reforms that only makes sense if one sees them as an elaborate but carefully honed remedy for the problem of corruption. At the heart of them are a number of related elements.

i The Legislature

Essential to the reforms is the position of the Senate. The Senate is now a wholly elected body of 200 persons, elected on the basis of multi-member constituencies designed to make it widely representative of the people and independent of the executive and the House of Representatives. A candidate for senatorial election may not have been a member of any political party in the previous year, and must hold a university degree (s 126). Further he or she may not hold ministerial office within one year after being a member of the Senate, and enjoys a single term of six years (s 127). The Senate is crucial to the logic of the constitutional reforms, as its job is to guarantee the independence, via the selection and appointment process, of all of the other 'watchdog' bodies set up by the Constitution. The independence of individual senators cannot, of course, be guaranteed; many are thought to have links with political parties, and some are close relatives of disqualified persons.

The House of Representatives, on the other hand, is reformed (ss 98–107) into a body of 500 persons (400 representing single-member constituencies and elected on a 'first past the post' basis; 100 elected on a party-list basis by proportional representation). By contrast, a candidate for election to this House must have been a member of a political party for the 90 days prior to nomination, and must remain so on pain of forfeiting his or her seat in the House. Candidates must also hold a university degree. The term of office for MPs is four years and is renewable. The House of Representatives may be dissolved while the Senate may not. The Constitution also creates a new separation of powers between the executive and the legislature: the Prime Minister and an MP who is appointed as a minister must resign his seat within one month of being appointed (ss 118(7), 204), being replaced in a by-election or by the next person on the party list, as the case may be. This has two important effects: first, there is a natural tendency to prefer ministers appointed from the party-list, as a by-election is thereby avoided; and, secondly, there is a disincentive for ministers to resign, since they have no parliamentary seat to go back to. These effects encourage a greater and welcome degree of governmental stability in a country whose elected governments, invariably coalition governments, have historically lasted for an average of only around 1.2 years.

Following an election the House of Representatives must, within 30 days of convocation for its first sitting, consider and approve the person suitable to be appointed as Prime Minister (s 202), who must be nominated by not less than one-fifth of the total number of MPs. Likewise, his appointment must be approved by the votes of more than half of the total number of MPs. He is then formally appointed Prime Minister by the King. This ensures that, although the Prime Minister then ceases to be a member of the House, he has a working majority in it. However, if the 30-day period expires and no one has been approved for appointment, then the King is to appoint the person who received the highest number of votes (s 203).

Two-fifths of the total number of MPs may submit for debate a motion of no confidence in the Prime Minister; but the motion must name his successor, and if the motion alleges 'unusual wealth', malfeasance in office or violation of law, then a petition for removal from office must also be presented (s 304). This may then be treated as a separate issue from the confidence motion. If the motion is passed, the alternative Prime Minister takes office; if it is not, the MPs submitting the motion may not submit another such motion during that session (s 185). A similar procedure is provided for no-confidence motions in respect of individual ministers. By this means confidence in the government as such is separated from particular corruption charges against ministers. In the past, governmental stability has been compromised by the confusion of these two issues.

A novel provision (s 170) also allows 50,000 electors to submit a petition to the National Assembly to consider a bill, which must be appended to the petition, falling within the area of fundamental rights and directive principles of fundamental state policies prescribed in the Constitution.

The powers of the two Houses are also, of course, somewhat different. While both Houses play a role in legislative procedure, the House of Representatives clearly has the superior role, as one would expect of a lower house. The Senate, however, has the power to appoint important officials: judges of the Supreme and Constitutional Courts, ombudsmen, and members of the Election Commission, the National Counter-Corruption Commission, the State Audit Commission and the National Human Rights Commission. In common with the House of Representatives, it has the formidable power to impeach not only the Prime Minister and other ministers, but also the heads of most state organs defined in the Constitution, as well as MPs and senators. Central to these powers is an obligation of all holders of public office to declare their assets prior to taking office.

The university degree requirement needs explanation. Great importance has been attached to the fact that in consultation sessions the public regarded its legislators as insufficiently qualified for the task. Although from a Western perspective it seems highly elitist to impose such a qualification, from a Thai perspective it is seen as a positive reform. Electing an MP is thought to be seen by many, perhaps especially rural, voters as being similar to choosing a lawyer to represent one in litigation. The interest of would-be politicians in higher education has never been greater.

ii The Watchdogs

As has been indicated, the 1997 Constitution created or reformed a battery of 'watchdog' or independent agencies, designed to provide scrutiny of state organs. These are in addition, of course, to the legislature itself, and the ordinary civil and criminal courts and the administrative courts. The constitution-makers took exceptional care to ensure the genuine independence of all these watchdog bodies—and with good reason. The predecessor of the National Counter-Corruption Commission (NCCC), for example, had been subjected to political oversight and pressures, and since 1981 had secured the dismissal from office of only two people. Vast numbers of cases had been rejected, or else not pursued with alacrity, and few had any positive result (Borwornsak, 2000). Accordingly, care was taken to ensure that the appointment of the watchdog bodies would ensure independence and that these bodies would enjoy guaranteed tenure and budgets.

Since so much of the constitutional architecture depends on the composition of the National Assembly, and electoral corruption has been a sore point with the public for so long, it is not surprising that the Election Commission (ss 138 ff) features largely in the reforms, and in the implementation of the Constitution since 1997. It polices elections[11] with an iron hand and does not shrink from requiring an election to be re-run several times in the event of a breach of electoral law.

A pattern emerges from the constitutional provisions in which the watchdog bodies are chosen by the Senate from candidates (normally numbering twice the required number of members of the watchdog) put forward by a selection committee, which is itself designed to secure

[11] Senate elections were held in 2000 and House of Representatives elections in 2001 and 2005. In the 2005 elections the Thai Rak Thai party obtained an unprecedented 60% of the vote and 375 seats in the House of Representatives.

objectivity by including members representing the various political parties and civil society. The watchdog members (apart from judges) enjoy single, non-renewable, terms of six years and are not permitted to hold certain public and private sector positions during their tenure. Each body enjoys the right to implement its empowering law, the benefit of its own secretariat not subject to civil service rules, and its own constitutionally-guaranteed budget. They also enjoy powers to enforce the assistance of government agencies in performing their functions and in providing evidence. But the watchdog bodies are, of course, themselves subject to anti-corruption rules: in addition to the possibility of impeachment, members must declare their assets and liabilities to the NCCC, whose own members must make their declarations to the Senate and are subject to double the normal criminal penalties. Dubious assets can be confiscated by the Supreme Court and the declaration itself can be verified and used to establish malfeasance, corruption or unusual wealth. In addition, all watchdog bodies are subject to the jurisdiction of the ombudsman with respect to maladministration and to the administrative courts with respect to illegality.

As an illustration of the elaborate approach taken regarding the appointment of the watchdog bodies, it is worth digressing briefly to describe the system for appointing the Election Commission. This system is typical of the care that has been lavished by the constitution-makers to ensure legitimacy. The Commission consists of four persons of apparent political impartiality and integrity appointed by the King on the advice of the Senate. The Senate receives five nominations each from a Selection Committee and from the Supreme Court and then by vote chooses the members of the Commission from the ten nominations: the first five persons obtaining the votes of more than half the Senate are elected, a further vote being held if necessary to fill any shortfall. The Selection Committee consists of ten persons: the presidents of the Constitutional Court and the Supreme Administrative Court; four persons elected from amongst themselves by 'the Rectors of all higher education institutions which are juristic persons'; and four representatives of political parties who are MPs, elected by the parliamentary membership of the parties from amongst themselves. Any nomination must be supported by at least three-quarters of the Committee (s 138). The members of the Commission hold office for only one term of seven years. A complaint supported by one-tenth of the members of the National Assembly that a member of the Commission be disqualified must be referred to the Constitutional Court for determination.

The NCCC is a new body whose independence is also most carefully guaranteed by the Constitution. Its remit is to prosecute cases of corruption, even in relation to very high officials. It has not shrunk, for example, from proceeding against the Prime Minister Thaksin Shinawatra (before he became Prime Minister), and a former Deputy Prime Minister Sanan Kachornprasart on the basis of their declarations of assets. The Prime Minister survived by the narrowest of margins—eight votes to seven—on appeal to the Constitutional Court (August 2001). When Sanan was investigated on corruption charges in 1999, he was the second most important politician in Thailand—Deputy Prime Minister, Minister of the Interior and Secretary-General of the (then) ruling Democrat Party. He resigned his ministerial offices immediately after being indicted in March 2000 for falsification of his declaration of assets and liabilities. In August that year he was found guilty by the Constitutional Court, was barred from political office for five years, and resigned his party political office. These cases are an indication that anti-corruption measures are being taken with the utmost seriousness. As previously indicated, all holders of political office and members of statutory bodies must declare their assets to the NCCC prior to taking up their offices/ appointments. Further, a Criminal Division for Persons Holding Political Positions, a special division of the Supreme Court, has been set up to deal with criminal matters relating to state officials.

The reputation of the NCCC and the entire constitutional apparatus has, however, been somewhat dented by an episode in mid-2005 in which the entire Commission was forced to resign after being found by the Supreme Court to have acted illegally in granting themselves an attendance allowance that was in effect a pay rise. Eventually a constitutional amendment was passed to facilitate the selection of 11 new Commissioners.[12]

iii Justice and Rights

Many new or newly entrenched substantive principles of justice, including an extensive litany of human rights (ss 26–65, 199–200) and rights of accused persons (ss 236–47) appear in the Constitution, which thereby envisages increased judicial activism, or at least increased judicialisation.[13] This provides an opportunity for activism if the judges feel inclined to take that direction. The opening up of the adjudication of constitutional issues to the participation of non-lawyers (ie, political scientists) in the Constitutional Court,[14] and the need for the judges not to be left behind in the rush

[12] See 'Constitutional Conundrums', SEALS website, at: <http://www.law.uvic.ca/seals/forums/showthread.php?t=76>, last accessed 15 November 2006.

[13] See, further, Harding (2005).

[14] The Constitutional Court consists of a President and 14 Judges, appointed by the King on the advice of the Senate, and comprises five Judges elected by the Supreme Court Justices from amongst their own number; two Judges elected by the Supreme Administrative Court from amongst their own number; five persons qualified in law; and three persons qualified in political science. The process for electing the members of the Court in the last two categories is complex. First, a Selective Committee is chosen, consisting of the President of the Supreme

to democratisation and to establish clear credentials may well militate in favour of an increasingly activist approach.[15]

The 1997 Constitution makes a concerted attempt to create conditions of genuine public participation in decision-making (Haller and Patcharee, 2003). In terms of East Asian conceptions of constitutional government, in which even democratic constitutions tend to restrict the participatory nature of decision-making, this attempt is bold and innovative in the extreme, especially considering that principles such as freedom of information are of recent origin even in Western countries. Section 76 states the basic democratic ideology as a state policy:

> The State shall promote and encourage public participation in laying down policies, making decisions on political issues, preparing economic, social and political development plans, and inspecting the exercise of State power at all levels.

Environmental management is especially subjected to the principle of participation, and the Constitution has even been called the 'green constitution'. Not only individuals, but also local traditional (ethnic minority) communities and environmental NGOs, as well as local government organs, are entitled to participate with the state itself in environmental decision-making (ss 46, 56, 79, 290) (Bureekul, 2000, 2006). Environmental rights include a right to participation in decision-making affecting the quality of a person's environment and concerning environmental impact assessment (ss 56, 59). There is also a right of access to information (s 58); a right to present a petition (s 61); a right to sue state agencies (s 62); and a right to natural justice—'the right to participate in the decision-making process . . . in the performance of administrative functions which affect or may affect his or her rights and liberties as provided by law' (s 60).

Space precludes detailed attention to the extensive provisions on fundamental rights, but a few points can be made to illustrate their general character. First, it is worth noting that there is no attempt to construct a notion of rights based on Asian values: none of the rights would be out of place in a European constitution, and no significant right generally enshrined in European constitutions seems to be missing. Indeed, some of the rights are decidedly 'third-generation' in nature. This criticism has been answered by the constitution-makers by emphasising the extent to which

Court, four Deans of law and four Deans of political science chosen from amongst their own number and four MPs representing parliamentary political parties, each party having one representative and such representatives electing four from their own number. The Committee, by a resolution supported by three-quarters of its members, nominates ten persons qualified in law and six qualified in political science. The final choice is made by the Senate, the first five or three on the list, as the case may be, receiving at least one half of the votes. See Klein (2001); Imaizumi (2003).

[15] In the incident mentioned at n 6 above, several of the Prime Minister's legal actions had already been dismissed by the courts, indicating that judicial independence is the norm.

community or group rights are protected, for example, the rights of farmers, indigenous peoples and the disabled. Most of the rights are based on familiar concepts, but have been carefully and broadly drafted. For example, the right to equality before the law prevents discrimination on grounds of 'difference in origin, race, language, sex, age, physical or health condition, personal status, economic or social standing, religious belief, education or constitutionally political view' (s 30).

This broad approach to rights and justice has enormous implications, both in terms of the embracing of a general concept of human rights and in terms of the detailed effect of particular provisions on law, administration and the political process. It may be that the familiar cast of the human rights provisions serves merely to obscure, rather than render irrelevant, the cultural aspects of human rights enforcement. If one regards the inspiration for human-rights observance as being grounded in Buddhist conceptions of human value and obligation—as many Thais will tend to do—then in the implementation and interpretation of human rights one might in due course find that 'Asian values' are of great importance, and indeed positively essential, for the progressive understanding and observance of human rights.

B Some Conclusions

The ultimate political reality is that Thailand is encumbered with a tradition of military coups. It would take only another military intervention to put an end to the constitutional experiment and resurrect some previous version of constitutional rectitude or pragmatism. Such a coup is unlikely, however, in view of the rapidly reducing role of the generals and of the military's own backing of the Constitution in 1997. The 1991 coup was the sixteenth since 1932: twelve years without a coup represents considerable progress. However, it has been noted that Prime Minister Thaksin Shinwatra has secured the appointment of members of his own family to high military office and other key positions. In a process dubbed 'Thaksinisation' in a recent book, the Prime Minister has reversed some of the progress made towards democratisation under the 1997 Constitution (McCargo and Pathmanand, 2005).[16]

Given the historical weaknesses of the Thai legal system it is clear that this kind of social engineering can only succeed if it is backed by immense political will. With the completion of two general and one senate election by early 2005, and the appointment of the members of all the watchdog bodies, the Constitution has, as it were, completed one whole cycle and is

[16] During the events referred to above at n 6 statements by military leaders indicated that they still think they have a political role to play.

now well into a second cycle. Most of the machinery of implementation is now in place and actually operating, albeit not always completely satisfactorily. There are grounds for hoping that a rapid transition to genuine constitutional government can be effected, and in certain respects this can be said to have occurred already. It is clearly too soon, however, to draw any real conclusions. The present Thai Rak Thai government of Thaksin Shinawatra, to judge, for example, by its attitude towards security following September 11, 2001, the response to separatist insurgency in the Muslim South, and the virulence of its anti-drug campaigns, appears little inhibited by the reform-oriented environment. But the real test will come when the limits of its policy space are tested against the constitutional apparatus. This is clearly now happening in several ways.

Consideration of the 1997 Constitution and its implementation indicates strongly that Thai public law reform should be regarded as being of great significance in the context of the development of democracy and constitutional government in Asia and the developing world generally. Perhaps only South Africa has recently undertaken a comparable root-and-branch public law reform; and the Thai effort, it should be recalled, has not been motivated or propelled directly by a political revolution or similar axial event such as the fall of a Marcos or a Suharto. Rather it can be seen as a development of the new Asian constitutionalism, evident notably in some East and Southeast Asian countries during the late 1980s and 1990s. Notable examples are the Philippines, which adopted a new democratic Constitution in 1987 following the fall of President Marcos and is now contemplating further constitutional reform; Indonesia, which embraced democratic reforms after the fall of President Suharto in 1997; Taiwan, which has progressively reformed its Constitution from 1986 following the end of martial law; South Korea, which has reformed its Constitution extensively since the mid-1980s; and Hong Kong, prior to the handover to the People's Republic of China in 1997.

III MALAYSIA: THE PATH OF POLITICAL SURVIVAL

When we turn to Malaysia we find a post-Crisis discourse that could hardly differ more from that of Thailand. The response has been almost the opposite in every respect. Despite the growth of a large *reformasi* movement (a conscious imitation of the Indonesian movement, and lasting just about as long, although rather less effective), it is remarkable to find that, although the Crisis appeared to be a harbinger of enormous and inevitable changes, when the dust finally settled very little appeared to have changed and no far-reaching change is indicated in the near future, despite the retirement in October 2003 of Prime Minister Tun Dr Mahathir Mohamad, who had been in office since 1981. However, the period since the Crisis hit in mid-1997, culminating in the fall and trial on corruption and sodomy charges of the former Deputy Prime Minister and Finance Minister, Anwar Ibrahim (Tey Tsun Hang, 1999; Abbott, 2001; Wu 2001, 2002), has been very turbulent, and the issue of Islamisation (which is not unrelated to issues of constitutional reform: Harding, 2002b) became for a time the crucial issue in political debate.

It is difficult to point to any major or lasting changes that have resulted from the Crisis. The Barisan Nasional (BN) coalition government shaped after 1981 by Dr Mahathir and now led by Datuk Seri Abdullah Badawi is still in office, as it has been since independence in 1957. The opposition is still divided and implausible as an alternative government. Economic policy remains much the same as it was. Demands for governance and constitutional reforms of the kind that emerged in Thailand have been brushed aside in much the same way as they have been at many previous junctures. However, under Badawi the government has given more powers to the Anti-Corruption Agency and made it easier for the general public to reveal corrupt practices. A number of Mahathir-era 'cronies' have also been arrested on corruption charges. Badawi has also brought to the fore an interpretation of Islam known as 'Islam Hadhari', which maintains that Islam and economic and technological progress are not incompatible.

Nationalism (which has been muted, though not entirely absent, in Thailand) remains an official ideology, albeit somewhat muted. Globalisation still evokes contradictory responses, ranging from distrust of Western intentions to excitement at its possibilities for Malaysia. Economic recovery has been slow, and structural reforms have been limited to those required by a policy which maintains that the economic and structural fundamentals are sound, but that the banking sector needs some adjustments, which have been in train for some time

It is worth recounting how this remarkable situation of 'turmoil without movement' came about (Wu 2001, 2002).

Crucially, during the final months of Anwar Ibrahim's tenure of the post of Finance Minister (he was also Deputy Prime Minister and had been selected by Mahathir as heir apparent) he was somewhat at odds with Mahathir's pronouncements on the Crisis. For example, Anwar appeared to think that Malaysia, like Indonesia, Thailand and South Korea, needed IMF intervention in support of its currency, and that the lame ducks among Malaysia's large home-grown companies, which generally have close relations with UMNO, the main BN coalition party, and Mahathir himself, should not receive government bail-outs. Increasingly, Anwar appeared to embrace the very reform agenda that Mahathir was desperate to resist.

The widening gulf between the Prime Minister and his Finance Minister seemed to require some dramatic resolution, and this was hastened by Anwar's ill-timed bid for the leadership of UMNO at the party assembly in

1998. Anwar was shortly afterwards (September 1998) relieved of his posts and arrested on charges of corruption and sodomy. In the subsequent months Mahathir took over the finance portfolio himself and adopted his own controversial method of dealing with the Crisis. He pegged the Malaysian ringgit to the US dollar; required the return of all capital holdings in ringgit outside Malaysia; restricted the export of ringgit; prohibited all transactions in ringgit outside Malaysia; and taxed repatriation of profit in ringgit at 10 per cent. These measures, which were removed on 26 November 2001,[17] were designed to prevent an outflow of capital from Malaysia. Remarkably too, from 31 July 1998 until 31 December 2003, the *bumiputera* equity participation rules that underpin Malaysia's approach to foreign investment and wealth distribution were suspended, with a guarantee that there would be no requirement for equity restructuring after that date. These ethnic preference rules have normally required all new investments to involve 30 per cent ownership by *bumiputera*, that is the indigenous Malays and natives of Sabah and Sarawak. The present government is taking a much more relaxed attitude to this rule and is prepared to make exceptions where appropriate; for example, in the Multimedia Super-Corridor the rule has no application (Likosky, 2005).

Although he was fiercely criticised by both Malaysians and internationally renowned economists, Mahathir resisted calls both for IMF intervention (which occurred both in Indonesia and Thailand) and for extensive political and economic reforms. In the eyes of most Malaysian voters, and not a few economists (some of whom recanted their earlier views), Mahathir was proved right and Anwar wrong concerning the economy. The important point is that he successfully created the appearance of having saved the nation from the worst of the Crisis, and pinned the blame for its occurrence on currency speculators and the West generally, rather than on the policies, or rather practices, of his government, which many insisted were responsible. Thus the debate about the Crisis became personalised, and revolved around the sensational police beating and then trial of Anwar, his inevitable subsequent convictions and appeals, and the 15-year sentence that was imposed on him. All this dominated the news between September 1998 and early 2001. Public disquiet was expressed in huge demonstrations which the police generally dispersed with some degree of brutality. In the end Anwar was set free following a Federal Court decision in September 2004.

Meanwhile, government policy changed only in relatively small ways. There was nothing resembling political will for change. Indeed Mahathir's objective appeared to be to create the nearest thing to China's immobile empire of the eighteenth century that was possible in a modern and

[17] With the exception of the currency peg, now also removed in late 2005.

thriving democracy. He was able to turn the party assembly in his favour. Anwar's supporters left to form their own party (Keadilan, led by Anwar's wife Wan Azizah Wan Ismail) (Case, 1999). He used his control of UMNO to postpone the party elections, with only one of 163 divisions daring to vote against this measure. The Internal Security Act 1960 was used extensively to suppress dissent. Calls for abolition of the policy of ethnic preference in the economy were also rejected. Despite dire predictions of a landslide defeat in the general elections in November 1999, with both Keadilan and the Islamic Party (Parti Islam Se-Malaysia or PAS) gaining support, UMNO and its coalition partners not only won the election, albeit with a reduced majority, but they even retained their prized two-thirds majority, which enabled them to control the constitutional amendment process. Mahathir then secured the succession by appointing the popular Abdullah Badawi as his Deputy Prime Minister and new heir apparent. Sensationally and tearfully, at the party assembly in 2002 Mahathir resigned as party President, only to be immediately 'persuaded' by popular acclaim to revoke his resignation; however, he also announced his intention to step aside in favour of Badawi in October 2003.

Nonetheless, Mahathir's victory over this multi-headed hydra was not as complete as these bare facts might indicate. Despite the majority's apparently calm rejection of calls for reform, the election indicated some surprising developments. Large numbers of Malay/ Muslim voters, traditional supporters of UMNO but angry with the treatment of Anwar and with the fallout from the economic Crisis, defected to PAS, which not only substantially increased its representation in the federal Dewan Rakyat (lower house) from seven to 27 seats, enabling them to lead the parliamentary opposition for the first time in Malaysian history, but also won control of two state governments (the north-eastern and traditionally Muslim states of Kelantan and Terengganu, the former having been controlled by PAS since 1990) on a platform of furthering attempts to create an Islamic state (Harding, 2002b). Other opposition parties also made gains, but although discontent was clearly reflected in declining support for the BN it was not in general reflected in parliamentary representation due to the effects of a 'first past the post' electoral system and other factors such as the weighting of rural constituencies. Ironically, commentators attributed the survival of Mahathir (who swept into power in 1981 as a champion of Malay rights) and the BN to the votes of non-Malays, compensating in effect for the defection of so many Malay voters. These non-Malay voters were clearly disturbed by the prospect of increasing Islamisation, and although they were also disturbed by the implications of the Anwar episode, felt that Mahathir had saved the economy and could handle the ethnic and religious problems: he was, in short, a safe haven in the midst of a storm. BN support, enough at the time merely to hold the line, was triumphantly reasserted in the elections of

September 2004, in which the BN took 198 of 221 seats in Parliament and PAS was decimated, retaining only six seats and losing control of the state government of Terengganu.

Mahathir thus succeeded in a Canute-like resistance to demands for reform. Governance reforms remain principally merely aspects of opposition manifestos. These manifestos do not even say the same thing, as some would adopt an Islamising route towards a redesign of the polity, as they tried to do within the confines of state legislative and executive powers in Kelantan and Terengganu, while others see every piece of tinkering with the original independence Constitution of 1957 as a step in the wrong direction. It does not appear that the empire will remain immobile, but neither will it change its essential character.

IV THE DEEP LOGIC OF ETHNICITY, LAW AND DEVELOPMENT

In order to understand why the outcome has been so different in Malaysia from Thailand, I think we have to understand what Amy Chua (1998) has called the ethnic dimension of law and development, which has been quite absent from our consideration of the Thai case. It is familiar territory that, in order to maintain the good inter-ethnic relations for which Malaysia is known, a social contract was concluded at the time of independence under which special privileges for Malays (or since 1971 all *bumiputera*) were conceded by the non-Malays in return for Malaysian citizenship. These privileges are sanctioned by the Constitution in Article 153 and relate to university places and scholarships, trade and business licences, and positions in the public service, and have been largely accepted by the non-Malays as the price they have to pay for participating in a growing economy and enjoying the protection of their 'legitimate interests', principally their property rights. The social contract is defined in constitutional terms as embracing the special privileges and legitimate interests, citizenship, and the national language, and is protected by entrenched sedition and internal security laws from being questioned (except only as regards its implementation) in any forum, including the floor of Parliament itself (Harding, 1996).

The theory of law and development in Malaysia thus has as an oft-repeated mantra the following propositions. First, the state embodies the social contract, which creates harmonious relations between all the races in a highly pluralistic society. This contract entails affirmative action in favour of the *bumiputera* as the original inhabitants, whose lack of ownership of the economy has to be rectified. Stability depends on preventing, if necessary by detention without trial, racially inflammatory speeches and actions. Economic progress, which over the span of 46 years since independence, and especially since the early 1980s, has been remarkable despite the cataclysm of 1997–98, depends on this stability being maintained. The serious race riots that followed election results in May 1969 are a constant reminder, even if problems in Indonesia are not, of how things would be if this policy were not enforced with rigour and impartiality. Globalisation is an opportunity for Malaysia to continue its path of progress, but, from the Malaysian perspective, its agenda of demanding political changes as well as economic ones must be resisted, and has been successfully resisted.

This is a formula with which it is hard to argue, as it has proved successful, even though from many points of view it is as politically incorrect—in the era of good governance—as the Thai reforms are politically correct. Hence the reluctance of both government and, ultimately, the electorate to embrace fundamental change of the kind Anwar and opposition parties would have imposed on them.

Of course, the effects of globalisation have been great, and in many ways the 'immobile empire' has been agile, imaginative and responsive. Although the government seems to have shelved plans to introduce a competition law (drafted in 1996), it has successfully taken forward its Multimedia Super-Corridor plan, which entailed a raft of legislation called the cyberlaws.[18] The MSC is decidedly a child of globalisation—a bold attempt to create an Asian Silicon Valley in which all obstacles to foreign investment are removed (Likosky 2002, 2005). As was mentioned above, Malaysia has, in the face of a flight of foreign capital, effectively suspended its policy of ethnic preference in equity participation, which was an obstacle to foreign investment.

I have not so far had to deal specifically with the impact of September 11, 2001, but in Malaysia it has had some impact. It has certainly acted as a brake on economic recovery. Groups linked with Al Q'aeda in both Malaysia and Singapore have been broken up, and again use has been made of the Internal Security Act in the process. Given that both the United States and the United Kingdom now have anti-terrorist security laws, and the former has detained its Taliban and Al Q'aeda opponents without trial at Guantanamo Bay, international criticism of Malaysia's security laws has virtually been silenced. Also, PAS's opposition to, and colourful language concerning, the wars in Afghanistan and Iraq, has

[18] Digital Signature Act 1997 (validity of electronic signatures)
Computer Crimes Act 1997 (computer fraud)
Telemedicine Act 1997 (qualifications, liability)
Copyright Amendment Act 1997 (implementation of recent WIPO treaties)
Electronic Government Act 1997 (secrecy and government services)
Multimedia and Communication Act 1997 (facilitation of research and development, streamlining of telecommunications and broadcasting provisions)

seriously undermined its appeal to non-Muslim, and even some Muslim, voters. The total effect has been to lend justification to authoritarian government.

To return to the conventional attribution of causes for the Crisis of 1997–98, these causes are essentially rejected in the Malaysian response. There is certainly 'money politics' which, Mahathir himself said on many occasions and is now echoed by Badawi, must be eradicated. Yet there have been no prominent corruption convictions except that of Anwar, which was politically motivated. There have certainly been human rights abuses, such as police brutality and the beating of Anwar in the famous black-eye incident following his arrest; and Mahathir's government at least created a National Human Rights Commission, as a slight nod in the direction of political rectitude. However, there are dissatisfactions both with its ability to deal effectively with human rights issues and with the government's response to its reports. The repeated concerns about judicial independence and the manipulation of the law and the Constitution have been responded to in some fashion by attempts to bolster judicial standing and performance, for example, in relation to defamation awards, which had been used politically (IBA Report, 2000; SUARAM, 2001; US State Department, 2002). But the independence of the judiciary has not been clearly re-established. The lack of really effective action in all these areas in fact contrasts starkly with the efforts in Thailand to create a new Asian constitutionalism. Malaysia, once the example of democracy and constitutional government in Southeast Asia, and with its many advantages in this field, has largely failed to respond to the call for good governance, let alone lead the way.

V THE CASE STUDIES COMPARED: IS THERE AN EVEN DEEPER LOGIC?

The abrupt change of discourse at the juncture of these two case studies is striking. One is about law and the other is about politics. One is about embracing reform; the other is about resisting it. They lead to apparently opposite conclusions. Which story has the better moral to it will depend on whether it is Thailand's reformist policy or Mahathir's anti-reformist policy that ultimately unravels. The outcome is not readily predictable even seven or eight years after the Crisis, and so far economic recovery is taking place, albeit slowly, in both countries. To say that the Crisis was a result of what the Indonesians call 'KKN' (Korupsi, kolusi, nepotisme'), or 'legal and cultural problems', omits to explain the reasons for what went right for so long in South East Asia. In my view the conjunction of a statist approach to development has probably been justified in terms of its developmental potential and its economic results, but it has borne along with it problems which were always increasing, and which were exposed by the 1997–98 Crisis—a crisis of governance, not simply a currency crisis. The statist approach could not be sustained, and ultimately it will, I think, be proved that good governance is needed to sustain economic growth. There are, however, many other reasons for embracing good governance, which is seen in the Thai case to be a good in and of itself.

Yasuda has identified the use of three kinds of law in South East Asia: indigenous law, imported law and development law. A characteristic of development law in his sense is that it is related to state construction and is characterised by administrative discretion. I believe that development law in this sense has been an essential factor in economic growth and other aspects of development in South East Asia. Malaysia and Singapore (Carter, 2001) afford good examples of this. In this sense the experience of these countries has grated against the all-pervading wisdom of the international agencies and the globalisation gurus (Harding and Carter, 2003). But there is no reason why this situation should continue, and indeed in some respects the globalisers are probably correct (albeit incompletely so) in their analyses. Equally there is no reason why 'globalisation-law' (which could be perhaps stage four of a future Yasuda-style schema?) should prevail without any concession to local knowledge, local circumstance, local politics and local value systems. Yasuda sees stage four as a kind of communitarian / arbitral democracy embracing 'Asian' values. I think there is potential difficulty with the term 'Asian values' in this analysis, but ultimately my case studies reveal that if the fourth stage of legal development is to do with democratisation and human rights, as I agree it is, we can expect that this process will take place in different ways and at different times and with somewhat different results—and even, in some respects, for different reasons. We may expect a degree of legal convergence, but at the same time we may expect a degree of legal divergence. The 'new stories' will not all have the same moral or the same ending.

VI EPILOGUE

On 19 September 2006, during the Prime Minister's absence in New York and following huge demonstrations against the government of Thaksin Shinawatra throughout 2006, the army moved tanks into central Bangkok and took over the government, and, citing widespread corruption and polarisation of society, declared the 1997 Constitution abrogated, and the National Assembly and the Constitutonal Court abolished. It was the seventeenth military coup since 1932. There was no opposition to it, and polls indicate its widespread acceptance. The coup was also quickly endorsed by the King, who ratified an Interim Constitution designed to provide for civilian government and the drafting of a new constitution in

2007, which will be Thailand's eighteenth since 1932. A new Legislative Assembly and a new civilian government were immediately installed and the process for drafting a new constitution is under way as of November 2006. The military junta in its pronouncements embraces the agenda of constitutional reform, but the resolution of the conundrum of Thai democracy, development and good governance remains a matter of some doubt (Kuhonta, 2006).

BIBLIOGRAPHY

ABBOTT, J (2001) 'Vanquishing Banquo's Ghost: the Anwar Ibrahim affair and the Impact on Malaysia's Politics' 25 (3) *Asian Studies Review* 285.

ANTONS, C (ed) (2003) *Law and Development in East and South East Asia* (Routledge/Curzon, London).

BOOTH, A (1999) *The Causes and Consequences of South East Asia's Economic Crisis* (SOAS, London).

BORWORNSAK, UWANNO (2000) *Depoliticising Key Institutions for Combating Corruption: Case Study of the New Thai Constitution* (King Prajadhipok's Institute, Bangkok).

BUREEKUL, THAWILWADEE (2000) *Public Participation in Environmental Management in Thailand* (King Prajadhipok's Institute, Bangkok).

BUREEKUL, THAWILWADEE (2006) 'Access to Environmental Justice and Public Participation in Thailand', ch. 10 of Harding, A J (ed) *Access to Environmental Justice: a Comparative Survey* (Martinus Nijhoff, Leiden).

CARTER, C (2001) *Eyes on the Prize: Law and Economic Development in Singapore, 1959-1999* (Kluwer Law International, The Hague).

CASE, W (1999) 'Politics Beyond Anwar: What's New?' *Asian Journal of Political Science*, June, 1.

CHUA, A (1998) 'Markets, Democrary and Ethnicity: Towards a New Paradigm for Law and Development' 1 *Yale Law Journal* 108.

CONNORS, M K C (2003) *Democracy and National Identity in Thailand* (Routledge Curzon, London).

DAVIDSON, P J (2002) *ASEAN: the Evolving Legal Framework for Economic Cooperation* (Times Publishing, Singapore).

GOMEZ, E T and JOMO, K S (1999) *Malaysia's Political Economy: Politics, Patronage and Profits* (Cambridge University Press, Cambridge).

HALLER, KJ and PATCHAREE, S (2003) (eds) *Legal Foundations for Public Consultation in Government Decision-Making* (Executive Public Administration Foundation, Bangkok).

HARDING, A J (1996) *Law, Government and the Constitution in Malaysia* (Kluwer Law International, The Hague, and MLJ, Kuala Lumpur).

—— (2001), 'May There be Virtue: "New Asian Constitutionalism in Thailand"' 3 *Australian Journal of Asian Law* 24–48.

—— (2002) 'Global doctrine and Local Knowledge: Law in South East Asia' 51 *International and Comparative Law Quarterly* 35–53.

—— (2002b) 'The Keris, the Crescent, and the Blind Goddess: the State, Islam and the Constitution in Malaysia' 6 *Singapore Journal of International and Comparative Law* 154–80.

—— (2005) 'Thailand's Reforms: Human Rights and the National Commission' 1 *Journal of Comparative Law* 1.

HARDING, A J and CARTER, C (2003) 'Cutting Through the Complexity: the Singapore Model of Law and Development', ch 13 of A Perry-Kessaris and J Hatchard *Facing Complexity: Law and Development in the 21st Century* (Cavendish, London) 191-206.

HEWISON, K (ed) (1997) *Political Change in Thailand: Democracy and Participation* (Routledge, London).

—— (1997b) 'The Monarchy and Democratisation' in K Hewison (ed) *Political Change in Thailand: Democracy and Participation* (Routledge, London).

IBA REPORT (2000) *Justice in Jeopardy*, INSAF Special Issue (Kuala Lumpur Bar Council, Malaysia).

IMAZUMI, S (2003) 'Political Reform and the Constitutional Court of Thailand' in N Sakumoto et al (eds) *Law, Development and Socio-Economic Changes in Asia* (Institute of Developing Economies, Chiba).

JUMBALA, P (1998) 'Thailand: Constitutional Reform Amidst Economic Crisis,' in *Southeast Asian Affairs 1998* (ISEAS, Singapore).

KLEIN, JAMES R (2001) 'The Battle for the Rule of Law in Thailand: the Constitutional Court of Thailand' (Asia Foundation Working Paper, Bangkok).

KUHONTA, E M (2006) 'Constitution at the Heart of Thai Coup' *Asia Times* 6 October 2006, available at: <http://www.atimes.com/atimes/Southeast_Asia/HJ06Ae02.html>, last accessed 7 December 2006.

LAIRD, J (2000) *Money Politics, Globalisation and Crisis: The Case of Thailand* (Graham Brash, Singapore).

LIKOSKY, M (2002) 'Cultural Imperialism in the Context of Transnational Commercial Collaboration', in Lowe, V and Likosky, M (ed) *Transnational Legal Processes: Globalisation and Power Disparities* (Cambridge, Cambridge University Press), 221-258.

—— (2005) *Silicon Empire: Law, Culture and Commerce* (Ashgate, Aldershot).

MCCARGO, D (ed) (2002) *Reforming Thai Politics* (NIAS, Copenhagen).

MCCARGO, D and PATHMANAND, U (2005) *The Thaksinisation of Thailand* (NIAS Press, Copenhagen).

NELSON, M H (2001) (ed) *Thailand's New Politics* (KPI Yearbook 2001, Bangkok).

PHONGPAICHIT, P and PIRIYARANGSAN, S (1996) *Corruption and Democracy in Thailand* (Silkworm Books, Chiang Mai).

PHONGPAICHIT, P, and Baker, C (1999) *The Politics of Economic Reform in Thailand* (Carnegie Endowment for International Peace, Washington DC), available at: <http://www. ceip.org/files/pdf/3Phong-Baker.pdf>, last accessed 15 November 2006.

PINAI, N (2002) 'Re-making of the Constitution in Thailand', 6 *Singapore Journal of International and Comparative Law*, 90.

PISTOR, K and WELLONS, P (1998) *The Role of Law and Legal Institutions in Asian Economic Development, 1960-1995* (Oxford University Press, Oxford).

SUARAM (2001) *Malaysian Human Rights Report 2001* (SUARAM, Petaling Jaya).

TEY TSUN HANG (1999) 'Malaysia: the Fierce Politico-Legal Backlash' *Singapore Journal of International and Comparative Law*, 3, 1-25.

TOMASIC, R (2003) 'Asian Economic Crisis and Legal Institutions: A Tale of Two Cities', ch 14 of Antons (2003).

US STATE DEPARTMENT (2002) *Country Reports on Human Rights Practices* (US State Department, Washington DC).

WU MIN AUN (2001) 'Anwar Ibrahim: the Fall and Fall of a Favoured Son' 2000-1 *Lawasia* 46-71.

—— (2002) 'Anwar Ibrahim: Epilogue' 2002 *Lawasia* 45-59.

YASUDA, N (2003) 'Law and Development from a Southeast Asian Perspective: Methodology, History and Paradigm Change', ch 2 of Antons (2003).

7

Law, Terror and the Indian Legal Order

OLIVER MENDELSOHN

I INTRODUCTION

TWO ALMOST PERFECTLY opposed views are ceaselessly presented following the destruction of the World Trade Centre in 2001. The first, predominantly American, view is that, 'everything has changed since 9/11'. This is the position almost daily presented by the Bush administration, which has declared a worldwide 'war on terror'. Arraigned against this view are those who see in the US response to the World Trade Centre attack and in the Iraq war the assertion of a self-interested and aggressive push for still greater American power, not an admirable defence of freedom and civilisation. In the latter account the rhetoric of millenarian anti-terrorism cloaks and rationalises the continuing effort to subordinate the Third World. It is to state the obvious that many of the regimes and much of the population of the Middle East subscribe to a version of the latter position. Situated somewhere between these polar positions are a great number of governments and people, including some overwhelmingly or at least predominantly Muslim nations in Asia—Malaysia, Indonesia and Pakistan are examples—often desperately trying to plot a middle way. Many of the people in these nations subscribe to an aggrieved Islamic perspective on American and western power generally, while the regimes themselves have to manage a more complex world order in which the concerns of the United States must be taken seriously. Moreover, these Asian regimes know all too well that radical Islamic opinion can as easily be directed against themselves as against the United States and the West in general.

The position of India in the months since September 11 is distinctive (Banerjee and Kueck, 2003). India quickly signed up to the US-led 'war against terror'. The government of India was at the time led by the Bharatiya Janata Party (BJP), an aggressively pro-Hindu party, and it made immediate sense to them to join a cause directed against Islamic terrorists. Three months after 9/11, in December 2001, a small band of terrorists penetrated the Indian Parliament and detonated bombs which killed a number of officials. Militants engaged in the long-running military campaign in Indian Kashmir were charged, convicted and ultimately hanged for this attack. The militants' action could reasonably be pronounced to be 'terrorism' and easily linked both to the persistent military actions of Pakistani-backed dissidents in Kashmir and to the World Trade Centre attack. And although Pakistan became an admired assistant to the United States in confronting Al Qaeda and the Taliban in Afghanistan, relations between the United States and India have drawn considerably closer in the three years since September 11. India has succeeded in depicting itself in American eyes as one of the great victims of terrorism, a much more reliable ally for the United States than Pakistan.[1]

The US-led campaign against terror thus suited the BJP-led government of India, since it made their preoccupations more respectable. Indeed, American approval may even have emboldened the government in its descent into opportunistic political violence within India. Thus the most violent Indian event for years was the slaughter of some 2,000 Muslims in Gujarat State in February 2002.[2] This was superficially a spontaneous popular action but the better view is that it was orchestrated, certainly exploited, by elements within the BJP government of Gujarat following the death in a train fire of some 59 Hindu activists (Concerned Citizens' Tribunal, 2002). The activists had been returning by train from a gathering that had sought to revive the movement to dismantle the Babri Masjid, a mosque in the State of Uttar Pradesh that was allegedly built over a pre-existing Hindu temple. A confrontation over the mosque in 1992 had provoked the most bitter political struggle between Muslims and Hindus since partition of the sub-continent in 1947. The death of the Hindu

[1] As with many other countries, India's position on the war in Iraq was equivocal. Prior to the war, if pressed, India declared itself to be against a military solution to the Iraq problem. India, like China and Russia, had intense ambitions in relation to Iraqi oil post-Saddam Hussein, and these ambitions were one factor limiting any Indian criticism of the American invasion. Also, the aggressively Hindu BJP would scarcely have taken the line that an attack on Iraq was an attack on Islam. Following the initial phase of the war the mildness of the Indian position even led to talk of India as a potential contributor to a peacekeeping force in Iraq. But it is also true that the government had to be careful not to senselessly outrage Muslim opinion, both within India and internationally, by its stance in relation to a nation within the heartland of Islam. Solidarity with 'non-aligned nations' like Iraq had been a cornerstone of Indian foreign policy throughout the Cold War, though such policy was now considerably less relevant than before. Ultimately India has stayed clear of any involvement in the war in Iraq.

[2] This is the figure that is regularly cited, though doubts are often cast on its accuracy. For a broad collection of material and sources on the Gujarat riots, see the website of OnlineVolunteers.org available at: <http://www.onlinevolunteers.org/gujarat/reports/index.htm>, last accessed 15 November 2006.

activists in Gujarat in 2002 was claimed to have been deliberately brought about by Muslim zealots, and the official explanation of the ensuing riots was that they were a spontaneous response to the cruel train murders (themselves reminiscent of appalling incidents on trains during partition).[3]

The rise of the BJP as a political force in India at a time of unprecedented international anxiety about 'Islamic terrorism' has led to the public expression of more naked hostility towards Muslims both in India and abroad than has been seen or heard in the country for half-a century. Even where there is no actual violence or hard-edged hostility to Muslims, pejorative valuation of Muslims and of Islam seems to have seeped into the very culture of the Hindu majority of India. This is the dangerous context of the developments discussed in the present chapter. The specific argument here is that powerful elements within India have used the direction of world affairs since September 11 in ways that tend to undermine that strand of the Indian constitutional order that constitutes the libertarian tradition. Opportunistic authoritarianism threatens to work with other developments (such as the increasing criminalisation of politics) so as to undermine some of the fragile supports of Indian democracy. But there have been more heartening developments over recent months. Against virtually every prediction, the BJP won fewer seats in the national election of 2004 than did the Congress party, and the latter has now formed a coalition government in New Delhi. Congress fought the election on a platform of 'secularism' and has proceeded to rescind the most draconian of the anti-terrorist legislation enacted under the BJP government. While it is to be doubted that there has been any deep turning away from anti-Muslim feeling in the country, the election and its aftermath have given new hope to opponents of the drift in national affairs sketched above.

II THE CONSTITUTIONAL BACK-DROP

India has an intensely conflicted Constitution. On the one hand, as still perhaps the longest constitution document in the world, it represents a mid-twentieth century flowering of some of the finest constitutional norms.[4] It contains a bill of judicially enforceable Fundamental Rights, guaranteeing the classic civil and political liberties first enunciated in late

[3] The BJP Chief Minister of Gujarat, Narendra Modi, jumped to the conclusion (still unverified) that the victims of the train fire in Godhra had been murdered by Muslims. His explanation, almost justification, of the ensuing riots throughout Gujarat was to point to Newton's third law: 'every action has an equal and opposite reaction' (*The Times of India* 2 March 2002).

[4] For an accessible account of the making of the Indian Constitution, see Austin (1966). The most authoritative commentary on Indian constitutional law is Seervai (1991).

eighteenth century France and America. It also declares unlawful certain deeply objectionable aspects of historical India, such as untouchability (Article 17) and forced labour (Article 23). Of greater novelty, the Constitution of 1950 goes on to enunciate certain 'Directive Principles of State Policy', not judicially enforceable but designed to guide the government in developing a society fit for the newly independent nation. For example:

> The State shall, within the limits of economic capacity and development, make effective provision for securing the right to work, to education and to public assistance in cases of unemployment, old age, sickness and disablement, and in other cases of undeserved want. (Article 41).

There are to be 'just and humane conditions of work' and 'maternity relief (Article 42). Indeed, workers are to be paid 'a living wage' (Article 43). The state shall 'endeavour' to provide 'free and compulsory education for all children until they complete the age of fourteen years' (Article 45).

The Constitution also lays down the basis of a democratic order, marrying (after the Canadian and Australian examples) the principles of Westminster-style responsible government with US-derived federalism. In addition to specifying the powers and procedures of Parliament and of the (essentially powerless) President, the Constitution establishes a strong Supreme Court. This constitutional basis has enabled the Court to become clearly the most distinguished court in Asia. These, then, are some of the 'progressive' elements of the Indian Constitution. But there is also another tradition of government reflected in and perpetuated by the Constitution. This tradition can be called 'colonial authoritarianism'.

The most basic manifestation of the latter approach to government is the capacity of the President (in effect directed by the Prime Minister of the day) to establish a 'state of emergency' throughout the country. Article 352 authorises the President, if satisfied that the security of India is threatened 'by war or external aggression or internal disturbance', to proclaim an emergency. During its pendency the government can suspend the Fundamental Rights (including freedom of speech and association, and protection against arbitrary arrest) (Article 357). No elections need be held during the emergency (Article 83(2)). Even without a national emergency being declared, the central or Union government can set aside the democratically constituted government of any state (Article 356). During the period of 'President's rule', the federal principle is suspended and all functions of government are directed by the centre through whichever channels it seeks to use. Clearly, then, in the basic design of the Constitution there is sufficient suspicion of the democratic principle to allow for its suspension in difficult times.

This suspicion that democracy may not always be maintainable is clearly rooted in the colonial experience of government and is not limited to providing for the total suspension of democratic principles at particular times. One of the key devices of British rule was preventive detention, anathema to any modern order that embodies a conception of 'due process'. It was often the Collector, the head official of a District, who exercised the power to detain persons deemed to be a threat to order. The Collector doubled as both head of administration, responsible for the maintenance of order, and District Magistrate, thereby confounding any modern conception of the separation of powers. While the framers of the Constitution knew the arguments about where that conception should lead them, they contented themselves with including the goal of separating the judiciary and the executive in the non-enforceable 'Directive Principles of State Policy'. So Article 50 lays down that 'the State shall take steps to separate the judiciary from the executive in the public services of the State'. The higher judiciary and the body of lawyers have taken the principle of the separation of powers seriously, particularly following Indira Gandhi's Emergency of 1975–77, and there has been progressive separation of the lower judiciary from the regular administration. As to preventive detention, however, this has continued to flourish following Independence (Austin, 2000: 53–63; Maiti, 2003).

III THE DIALECTIC BETWEEN LIBERTARIANISM AND AUTHORITARIANISM IN INDEPENDENT INDIA

The internal dialectic of the Constitution in the matter of liberty has been reflected in the constitutional experience of India over more than half a century since Independence. Perhaps unsurprisingly, the darkest periods of authoritarianism have spawned the most vigorous libertarian backlash. India now has a particularly strong civil liberties movement served by lawyers, journalists, academics and a whole range of concerned citizens.[5] Some of these activists direct their activities towards the classic political and civil liberties—speech, association, conscience, due process of law—while many others are concerned with what Isaiah Berlin called the 'positive liberty' of decent standards of living, a clean environment, abatement of sexual oppression, and so on (Berlin, 1969: 118–72). It is doubtful that any nation has more NGOs than does India. Most of these date back no more than 25 years and the whole phenomenon of the rights movement can be seen as a conversation with what has come to be known as Indira Gandhi's State of Emergency of 1975–77 or simply as 'the Emergency'.

[5] One of the strongest organisations is the People's Union for Civil Liberties, formed in the immediate aftermath of Indira Gandhi's Emergency. Its website is at: <http://www.pucl.org>, last accessed 15 November 2006.

Indira Gandhi's Emergency was the first such proclamation to be justified on the basis of 'internal disturbance', as prescribed in Article 352. Previously, Prime Minister Nehru had initiated an emergency proclamation in 1962 in the context of the war with China. Despite the brevity of that war Nehru's emergency lasted six years, and was finally ended only in 1968 by his daughter Indira Gandhi after set-backs in the election of 1967. The explanation for the long duration of this first emergency was that the government had become addicted to the authoritarian powers the device afforded it, particularly under the Defence of India rules. These rules made preventive detention far easier than under other legal instruments. Indira Gandhi again used the device of proclaiming an emergency in 1971, during the war with Pakistan which led to the separation of Bangladesh as an independent nation. This emergency overlapped with her 1975–77 Emergency and was not ended until after the election of 1977, which Indira Gandhi lost.

The 1975–77 Emergency had far more drastic consequences than the two earlier emergency periods. It led to censorship of the press, widespread imprisonment of political opponents, suppression of organised opposition, the implementation of authoritarian programmes such as compulsory vasectomies and brutal slum clearances (Tarlo, 2003). The government had justified its declaration of a state of emergency by the strength of extra-parliamentary opposition to the regime, in particular the movement led by (the non-violent) Jayaprakash Narayan. Whatever the truth as to the 'indiscipline' of Indian political opposition—a favourite refrain of Mrs Gandhi—her proclamation of a constitutional emergency was clearly a desperate response by a Prime Minister who had become embattled on many political fronts.

During the Emergency the Parliament passed the 42nd amendment to the Constitution, which operated to strip the Supreme Court of much of the power it had either been given by the Constitution or won for itself in battles during the first quarter-century following Independence (Dhavan, 1978). Above all, the 42nd amendment purported to prohibit the Court from deliberating on the validity of amendments to the Constitution made by Parliament. Here was a classic contest of executive and judiciary, in the context of a regime busy re-making itself in the image of left-wing authoritarianism (Austin, 2000: 370–88).

When Indira Gandhi lifted the state of emergency in 1977 and held an election she was swept from power. The new Janata government swiftly moved to repeal the 42nd amendment and generally to restore democratic norms. Although the Janata government soon fell apart and Indira Gandhi returned to power in the election of 1980, her Emergency has remained an object of denunciation among the political and civil elites. In the years following the Emergency a great raft of organisations sprang up to expose and challenge arbitrary power in India—the women's movement, for example, is a creation of this era. One of the great arenas of this activity was the courts, above all the Supreme Court of India. 'Public interest' or 'social action' litigation was now positively welcomed by the Supreme Court (Baxi, 1988: 387–415). Despite being chronically over-burdened with litigation, some of it decades old, the Supreme Court now proved itself willing to accept petitions under the Constitution from citizens protesting against their oppression. Sometimes the petitions were written on the meanest scrap of paper. Through its activism—strong in the 1980s then waning for much of the 1990s and renewing itself late in that decade—the Supreme Court reinvented itself as something quite distinct from its early incarnation in the 1950s as a conservative supporter of agrarian property.

The Supreme Court's reinvention of itself over the second quarter-century of its existence has been nothing less than central to the maintenance of the Indian constitutional order and with it a form of liberal democracy. The Court's new jurisprudence has complemented the greatest political achievement of post-Independence India, which is the conduct of competitive elections at national, provincial and even local levels throughout a vast, poor and profoundly unequal country. These elections have on many occasions unseated governments at national and state levels and in the process produced a measure of accountability. Over the same period, however, institutional decay has set in, with habitual lawlessness and violation of due process on the part of officials, the regular infliction of violence on ordinary citizens by police and army personnel, environmental degradation, and the notorious enrichment of many officials at the expense of everyone other than their superiors. The problems have not abated with the now rapid economic development of India—indeed, arguably, deep and rapid change has tended to corrupt and break down government in India. This is the condition that has provided the Supreme Court with its opportunity.

The novelty of the Supreme Court's contribution over the last quarter-century has been to fashion a jurisprudence for a society profoundly different from the nations of the West. To give a simple example, the Court has been asked to consider the interests of a pavement-dweller in the great city of Bombay in the face of the Maharashtra State government's concern to clean up the streets of India's commercial capital. In the case of *Olga Tellis and others v Bombay Municipal Corporation and others* (AIR 1986 SC 180) the argument was that certain pavement- and slum-dwellers were entitled to remain on their patch because they were protected by Article 21 of the Constitution: 'No person shall be deprived of his life or personal liberty except according to procedure established by law'. There were technical arguments as to the lawfulness of methods employed by the Bombay Corporation but the central proposition was that the right to 'life' necessarily encompassed a right to 'livelihood'. The argument was that the pavement- and slum-dwellers should not be seen as voluntary immigrants and unlawful squatters but as impoverished citizens of a vast and poor country who had no options in life. If they were deprived of the capacity to inhabit the pavement or government land, they would be deprived of the capacity to sustain life itself. The Court accepted this argument. So a 'right to life' in Article 21 became by extension a right to sleep on the pavement, if there were no alternative to this.

The early years of public interest litigation were dominated by issues brought by, or on behalf of, the poor or under-privileged (Mendelsohn 1991; Ahuja 1997). There were a number of cases, for example, about the rights of women and children, bonded labourers, prisoners, detainees in psychiatric institutions and sex workers. In the 1990s the strongest flow of cases was on the physical environment, a set of issues that affected everyone. In the late 1990s the Court was even prepared to enter the politically dangerous territory of official corruption, going right up to the highest levels of government. Indeed, the Supreme Court had a procedural part to play in the most spectacular case of judicial confrontation of political corruption at the end of the 1990s. On 29 September 2000 a special court convicted former Prime Minister Narasimha Rao of having taken bribes while Prime Minister and sentenced him to three years gaol. Although Rao ultimately won an appeal on 15 March 2002 in the Delhi High Court on the ground that the conviction was unsafe, the case remains a potent symbol of judicial independence in India.

The Supreme Court's activism and its probity amid the increasing corruption of Indian institutions had by the end of the twentieth century invested it with the status of being the most trusted institution in India (Mendelsohn 2000). It had become a kind of last repository of morality and decency, though there was also a prominent group of objectors to the Court's strong (and, it was argued, undemocratic) activism.[6]

IV TERRORISM AND THE CONSTITUTIONAL ORDER

The new threats to the Indian constitutional order are considerably different from those of the 1970s under Prime Minister Indira Gandhi. Her political problems were those of a declining Congress Party and growing

[6] For example, Andre Beteille, then Professor of Sociology at the University of Delhi, wrote in *The Times of India* on 12 December 1995: 'Judicial activism often stems from the best of motives, the desire to set things right in corrupt and decaying public institutions... But it can also be argued that in a democracy, judicial restraint is a virtue not only in good times but also in bad times.' Nani Palkhivala, one of the most successful lawyers of post-Independence India, wrote about public interest litigation in these terms: 'The real point of issue is not whether the apex court is entitled under the Constitution to decide such issues, but whether democracy can survive this kind of shift in authority' (*The Sunday Times of India* 3 December 1995). For a more recent view, see Shourie (2001).

anti-government mobilisation in the cities of north India, and her response was to assert the power of the executive against both the courts and the westernised middle class who placed a high value on civil liberties. Present circumstances are quite different. There is no political, let alone constitutional, crisis in India today. India appears less fragile in the first decade of the twenty-first century than in any previous decade since Independence. Politics in India now takes the form of an intensely competitive multi-party democracy. The system is neither 'one-party dominance', as it was termed at the height of Congress power,[7] nor is it the two-party system that has evolved in a number of the Western democracies. For a time in the late 1990s and the first years of the present century it appeared as if the BJP had become the pre-eminent Indian party, albeit that it had not become so dominant as Congress was in the early years after Independence. After two brief periods as Prime Minister, Atal Bihari Vajpayee was able to form a government in October 1999 that lasted until the scheduled election in May 2004. This BJP-led government, like its two unstable predecessors, was a coalition rather than a unitary BJP administration, but the party appeared so secure in its grasp of power that virtually every pollster and commentator in the country predicted that it would win the 2004 election. But it was a sharply revived Congress under Sonia Gandhi, widow of Indira Gandhi's son Rajiv, that won marginally more seats than did the BJP, so Congress was able to form a coalition government in May 2004. Sonia Gandhi, controversial by virtue of her Italian origins, stepped aside in favour of Dr Manmohan Singh as Prime Minister. What was impressive about the election was its relative peacefulness and the calm and maturity of the political bargaining that led to the formation of a new coalition government.

If India has developed a distinctive but at least for the time being quite settled political process, this democratic maturity masks political developments of great concern. India now appears less tolerant of difference, particularly religious difference, than at any time since Independence. It has become fashionable to celebrate the death of 'secularism', which for decades has been the term used to describe the religiously uncommitted character of the Indian constitutional regime. And relations between India and Pakistan are in a highly fragile state. In 1999 the two nuclear states fought a border war in Kargil, and in 2002 hundreds of thousands of troops were mobilised on both sides of the border. Within India, during the period of BJP rule in New Delhi, public discourse was full of the simple identification of Indian Muslims with an allegedly rampant Pakistan. The idea of Indian Muslims as a Pakistani 'fifth column' is not new but this

[7] This phrase was first used by W H Morris-Jones (1964) to identify the towering dominance of Congress, despite the system of free elections.

view has never had the legitimacy that it enjoyed during the period of BJP power. More generally, the events of September 11 have played into the hands of those who proclaim the virtues of *Hindutva,* a view that insists that Indian civilisation, and therefore the Indian state, is essentially Hindu and that all policies must be brought into alignment with the country's essentially Hindu nature. Such a doctrine is necessarily anti-Muslim, since it discounts any beneficial effect of Muslims on Indian society and development.[8]

A The Indian Experience of Terrorism

In the Indian case, as elsewhere, it is often difficult to arrive at an objective identification of 'terrorism'. Insurrectionary or separatist movements in India, and even non-political gangsters, have often employed violent tactics that can easily be called 'terrorist'. The validity of such labels depends upon the political position of the parties to the contest. The closer one is to the position of those practising a particular kind of political violence, the less likely it is that one will accept 'terrorist' or any other pejorative label for their activities. Supporters of a movement may identify it by a descriptor which also conveys approbation. So while the 'militants' of Indian Kashmir are often identified by that name or as 'extremists' or more recently, under the influence of American rhetoric as 'terrorists', they are 'freedom fighters' to their supporters in Kashmir itself. But the organs of the state and also majority opinion, which tends to be outraged by the violence of minority groups, are generally not prepared to look behind violent means for political justifications. On the other hand, armed actions taken by the forces of the state against political minorities tend to be reflexively viewed as legitimate force rather than morally equated with the illegitimate violence of the minority. This is now a characteristic of international affairs too. So the present US-led 'war against terror' concentrates exclusively on the violent *means* of the 'terrorists', not their *ends*, while asking us to lay aside doubts about *our* violent means.

India has had a long acquaintance with armed insurrection and with 'terror' or violence as a political tool. Immediately after Indian Independence there was a strong insurrectionary communist movement in the Telengana region of southern India, and this was only suppressed with considerable force (Sundarayya, 1979). In the Himalayan region of Nagaland tribal people have conducted an insurrectionary and separatist movement from virtually the time of Indian Independence up to the present. At one stage in the struggle a favoured tactic was to blow up trains crossing

[8] For a recent discussion of the implications of the Hindutva movement, see Vicziany (2004).

the great Gangetic plain (Kotwal, 2000). In the late 1960s a band of revolutionary Marxists influenced by the writings and experience of Mao Zedong organised violent action in the Naxalbari region of rural West Bengal. The Naxalites, as they came to be called, saw their activities as the beginning of a revolution across India (Banerjee, 1980). Eventually, and with considerable bloodshed, this movement was put down. A decade or so later the movement was re-born in a number of districts of the neighbouring and extremely poor state of Bihar, where it has continued for some 30 years. The character and leadership vehicles of the movement have changed over time but the practice of exemplary violence has persisted. The revolutionaries—or is it 'terrorists', 'extremists' or merely 'representatives of the downtrodden castes/classes of Bihar'?—have sought to spread terror in the countryside by threatening, and occasionally accomplishing, the 'lowering of oppressors by six inches' (the nominal height of a head) (Mendelsohn and Vicziany, 1998: 44–76). It is difficult not to feel a great deal of sympathy for the causes of land reform, social respect and abatement of sexual violence for which many of these people are fighting in India's most unequal and poorest state, even if the tactics seem grotesque. And it should also be pointed out that the violence practised by the other side—some of it meted out by upper caste, landed elements who are defending their hereditary dominance, some of it by the state—has been at least as great as that of the 'revolutionaries'. Indeed, much of this violence can also be seen as 'terrorist' in nature.

In the 1980s the most serious challenge to the Indian state was from militant Sikhs who wanted to establish a separate state to be called 'Khalistan' or the 'land of the pure'. This was undoubtedly a dangerous confrontation of the Indian state but it is also now generally agreed that Prime Minister Indira Gandhi's government handled the conflict very badly. The storming of the Amritsar Golden Temple in 'Operation Bluestar' caused the death of some 1,000 Sikh 'militants' (the term generally used at the time). This event cost the Prime Minister her own life, when one of her Sikh bodyguards murdered her in retribution. The needlessly bloody confrontation of militant Sikhs resonates strongly two decades after the event and also has some parallels with militant Hindu treatment of Muslims at Ayodhya in 1992 (the Babri Masjid affair), in Gujarat in 2002, and more generally for the last 15 years or so. The parallel is a core of sectarianism within the majority Hindu population. But when highly militant and obscurantist representatives of the Hindu majority practise violence in defence of 'mother Hinduism', they are not called 'extremists', 'militants' and certainly not 'terrorists'.

By and large, the Indian state has learnt to live with chronic political violence. The constantly simmering insurrection in Bihar is the longest running example of such conflict, and to a large extent New Delhi manages to ignore what is happening in that state. This is also a grave comment on the importance of Bihar to the nation's capital and on the extent to which that state's problems are taken seriously. The Sikh militancy of the 1980s was taken far more seriously for a number of reasons, including the religious character of the challenge and the proximity of Punjab to the capital.

Given the long experience of violence, the question is why the Kashmiri 'militants' have become so dominant a concern in India today. Why has their 'terrorism' (not always an unreasonable term for their political activities) been taken so seriously? Clearly the answers to these questions have a lot to do with Indian relations with Pakistan, which is identified as a prime provocateur in Kashmir and a source of support for the Kashmiri militants. In terms of the level of violence, it is highly doubtful that the conflict in Kashmir is any worse than other chronically violent situations, notably that of Bihar. The new factor over the last few years has been the advent of September 11 and all its political and military ramifications, which have been highly advantageous to the cause of militant Hindus associated with or supporting the present government of India. There is a high degree of political opportunism in the government of India's enthusiastic association of its own fight against terror with the worldwide 'war against terror' waged primarily by the United States.

B The Legal Regime and Terrorists

Consistent with what has been said earlier about the authoritarian stream in Indian constitutionalism, post-Independence India was quick to enact the Preventive Detention Act of 1950. This Act remained in force until 1970 when it was allowed to lapse, but for a number of years it overlapped the Defence of India rules made under the 1962 Act of the same name. The Act and rules were the legislative response to war breaking out with China, and the rules enabled preventive detention of anyone who had acted or was likely to act in a manner detrimental to public order and national security. The rules were revived in 1971 during the war with Pakistan and its aftermath, and were maintained long enough for the imprisonment of striking rail workers in 1974 (Sherlock, 2001). With an eye more firmly focused on internal disturbances not directly linked to war, the Maintenance of Internal Security Act (MISA) was passed in 1971. This was the principal instrument used for widespread detention of political opponents during Indira Gandhi's Emergency of 1975–77.

After the 1975–77 Emergency the newly-elected Janata government pushed through an amendment to the Constitution which substituted 'armed rebellion' for 'internal disturbance' as a basis for declaring an emergency under Article 352 (though this was later reversed under the Congress Party in 1988.) The Janata government also repealed MISA, as well as the Defence of India rules. But when Indira Gandhi returned to power in 1980, the National Security Act 1980 again allowed preventive detention of anyone suspected of subverting national security, public order and essential economic services.[9] Other decidedly illiberal legislation was passed at this time, including the Essential Services Maintenance Act 1981, providing for the suppression of strikes and lock-outs in key economic sectors.

It was the Sikh situation in the mid-1980s that focused specific attention on what were now called 'terrorists'. The Terrorist and Disruptive Activities (Prevention) Act 1985 (TADA) provided a legislative basis for a range of counter-terrorism surveillance measures (wiretaps etc). It provided for the death penalty in trials which could also be held in camera. On important matters, the burden of proof was reversed. 'Review Committees' were established under the legislation which, it has to be said, did discharge a large number of detainees, as did the Supreme Court upon individual application. Overall tens of thousands of prisoners are said to have been arrested and detained under TADA, although verification of such numbers has always been difficult.[10] There has been no definitive study of the identity of these people but it appears that many of them, probably most, could not by any stretch of the imagination be called 'terrorists'. As is the nature of authoritarian instruments, they come to be used against a far wider sector of the population than was their justification for enactment. TADA allowed detention of anyone who committed or even facilitated the commission of 'disruptive activity', a term only vaguely defined. The Act was finally allowed to lapse by the Congress government in 1995, a rare instance when Congress has been responsible for removing legal instruments which run counter to due process jurisprudence.

When the impossibly fragile Janata coalition was in power (1978–79), it did maintain something of a commitment to opposing the authoritarian thrust of anti-terrorist legislation. With the rise to power of the BJP, the most actively divisive government since Independence, there was a renewed commitment to the approach best represented by MISA and TADA. The BJP proposed a new Prevention of Terrorism Act in 2000 but after sustained opposition by various political parties and the human rights movement the bill did not proceed. Following the World Trade Centre attack, a Prevention of Terrorism Ordinance was rushed through on 24 October, and this was transformed into the Prevention of Terrorism Act

[9] There are a number of websites put up by activist or revolutionary organisations that provide quite useful material on these matters. See, eg, Amnesty International (2000).

[10] In 1997, two years after the repeal of TADA, Amnesty International's annual report on India cited a government source to the effect that in March more than 42,000 people were still detained under the Act pending trial (Amnesty International, 1997). This number had apparently declined by December 1997 to 2,000, following a Supreme Court directive ordering the release on bail of various categories of detainee.

2002 (POTA). When the spokesman for the US State Department, Richard Boucher, was asked to comment on the Ordinance (later Act) in March 2000, he said:

> We do think it is important for governments to take steps against terrorism, to do it in a constitutional way . . . We do believe that that can be done consistent with democratic principles. We have done that. The Europeans have done that. And India seems to have done that as well. (*The Hindu*, 29 March 2000)

The new Act had many features in common with TADA, though in one major respect the later Act was preferable. The vague and obnoxious phrase 'disruptive activity' is not a part of the later Act, which is limited to terrorist acts (including belonging to a terrorist organisation). The punishment for such activities, if they bring about death, was sentence of death or life imprisonment. The Act expanded the range of investigations possible under the ordinary law—for example, there was virtually no limit on what property can be seized (section 7). Special courts could be established to handle offences under the Act, and the trials could be held in camera. Confessions extracted outside the ordinary rules of evidence under the Indian Evidence Act 1872 were deemed admissible (section 32). And, importantly, the burden of proof was in effect reversed if fingerprints or the possession of arms pointed to the involvement of the accused (section 53).

Given the route along which India has passed for thirty years or more, it would not be possible to erect a case on the basis of POTA that India had entered into a new and more draconian phase of legislation justified by the hunt for terrorists. The case against this legislation, as with TADA and MISA before it, was that the most radical aspects were probably not necessary. It is not clear, for example, why proceedings should have been in camera or why there should have been open slather on confessions. The latter is a positive invitation to tyrannical police officers. There were particular concerns about providing a secret regime of trial, conviction and sentence of death. Reversal of onus of proof and other relaxations of the evidentiary burden will almost certainly lead on occasion to wrong conviction. And surely it is not desirable that special courts be established, albeit that the judicial officers are sufficiently qualified. It is true that the Indian court system is inefficient and plagued by delay, and it is therefore possible to sympathise with a government that wishes to bypass these problems in its fight against terrorism. But there are also ways of expediting justice within the regular criminal justice administration without going down the path of a separate apparatus for those accused of terrorism.[11]

[11] There is a large body of literature on the problems in the administration of justice in India. For a recent view, see Galanter and Krishnan (2003).

There was, then, a strong argument that POTA was too authoritarian an instrument, even conceding the legitimacy of the concern to combat terrorism more effectively in what is undoubtedly a dangerous political and security environment for India as well as for many other countries. It was all but inevitable, based on past experience, that if POTA had been richly employed it would quite often have been directed against people who could not by any reasonable definition be thought to be 'terrorists'. In this sense the law was an unwelcome legislative reincarnation of Indian authoritarianism that had been beaten down during the backlash against Indira Gandhi's Emergency.

Of course, India was not alone in having enacted new legal instruments that cut down on the 'luxury' of due process that is maintained, if always under challenge, during 'ordinary' times. In the immediate aftermath of September 11 the United States itself passed the Uniting and Strengthening America by Providing Appropriate Tools Required to Intercept and Obstruct Terrorism Act 2001 (USA PATRIOT Act, 2001). This Act is considerably criticised by civil liberties organisations within the United States for the loss of due process guarantees that are set aside for government agencies in pursuit of terrorists (Chang, 2001). And there is a great deal of international criticism of the long-term incarceration at Guantanamo Bay of hundreds of people from a number of countries in effect declared by the United States to be guilty of terrorism, treason or unlawful warfare but almost all of whom have yet to face a judicial procedure, let alone one that will command the respect of jurists around the world. There are legitimate fears that the American system of justice is being significantly weakened by such measures. And like India, of course, the United States possesses and routinely imposes the death sentence. Australia is another country that has given new powers to its primary security agency following September 11, although the new powers are not so great as those of comparable American agencies.[12]

C The Political Context of Indian Anti-Terror Legislation

The special issue in relation to anti-terrorist legislation in the Indian context is the extent to which it represents a symbolic contributor to the increasingly strained relations between the Hindu majority and the Muslim minority community. Again, the issue of discrimination against Muslims is not an issue confined to India. In the present inflamed world situation there has been ugly discrimination and violence against Muslims and other

[12] Australian Security Intelligence Organisation Legislation Amendment (Terrorism) Act 2003 (Cth).

identifiable 'outsiders' (Sikhs with their highly-visible turbans, for example) in the United States and other western nations (Human Rights Watch, 2002). But the situation in India is especially difficult given the size of the Muslim population, some 130 million.[13]

India developed for more than four decades as a secular state under the Indian Constitution, its modernist first Prime Minister Jawaharlal Nehru and later leaders from both the Congress Party and ruling coalitions that included socialist elements. With the rise of the Bharatiya Janata Party (BJP), the communal landscape of India has changed quite dramatically and the country's commitment to 'secularism' has become a matter of controversy rather than a fundamental commitment. The BJP grew out of an earlier party, the Jana Sangh, which had roots going back to the nineteenth century. Its rationale is its conception of India as 'Hindutva', a land governed by the Hindu view of life in which non-Hindu elements, notably Muslims and Christians, can have only a subsidiary role (Graham, 1990). This is a deeply divisive political position in a country that has a larger Muslim population than any country other than Indonesia.

The BJP Prime Minister from 1998 to 2004, A B Vajpayee, was presented as the moderate face of the party and its front organisations. Indeed, as a former Foreign Minister, Vajpayee knows how to steer a patient passage through the complexities of both domestic and foreign circumstances. But Vajpayee is also someone who has contributed powerfully to the reconstruction of an India that is progressively pushing Muslims to the margins. His New Year's Message, promulgated from Goa at the turn of 2003 (Vajpayee, 2002), represents the vintage Vajpayee approach to politics (Venkatesan, 2002). On the face of it, the message appeared as a strong attack on the right wing of his own party and movement and invoked tolerance in the face of the appalling Gujarat riots of 2002. But closer scrutiny of the speech revealed an approach to society that was more to the taste of his own side and far more insidious from the standpoint of the advocates of a secular India. Vajpayee was at pains to assert that there was no contradiction or even tension between Hindutva and secularism. Hindutva, he suggested, is itself secular by virtue of being tolerant, and therefore India is essentially a tolerant society. Of course, what is controversial about this statement is the view that it is Hindutva that constitutes 'India' and that the good qualities of Indian society arise from that Hindutva and from no other source. The

[13] Although the last Census of India was in 2001, no totals for religious affiliation have been published and may not be until 2005 or later. The delay arises at least in part for political reasons: the figures will immediately become political fodder for both Hindus and Muslims, whose leadership will exploit them for their own ends. The Muslim leadership will use them to claim new facilities for the predominantly poor Muslim population, while Hindus will cite them as evidence of a dangerously rising Muslim population. (For population estimates, see Shahabuddin (2003)).

religion of 130 million Muslims, not to mention Christians and others, is thereby pushed to the margins of irrelevance in terms of the fundamental character of Indian society. In short, the Indian Prime Minister is at the head of a party that is energetically staging a peculiarly Indian version of the culture wars that is profoundly destabilising for the sub-continent. Perhaps the sharpest of the problems faced by Indian Muslims today is the constant suspicion put about that they constitute a fifth column for Pakistan, the nation formerly part of undivided India and composed overwhelmingly of Muslims. So when bombs go off in Mumbai, as they did again on 25 August 2003, killing some 50 people, the forces of Hindutva (including the militant Shiv Sena) are quick to attribute them to 'Muslims', careless of whether they are Indians, Kashmiri separatists or Pakistanis. The object of the exercise is to assert a seamless identity between the enemy nation of Pakistan and Indian Muslims, who are 'really' Pakistanis in Indian clothing.

This, then, was the context of the new Indian security legislation promulgated in the aftermath of the World Trade Centre attack in 2001. There is no denying the existence and potent development of extremist elements among Muslim communities of the sub-continent (mainly in Pakistan, Afghanistan and Kashmir): this is a cause for legitimate concern in Indian security circles. But equally the heightening of tension and distrust between the two largest religious communities of India holds particular danger for the Muslims, who are out-numbered by about 6:1 by the Hindus. For the Muslims attacked in the Gujarat riots of 2002, the terror was brought about by unscrupulous proponents of hatred and intolerance in the majority community. This was no simple popular response to the appalling death of Hindus on the train in Godhra, Gujarat.[14] It was an organised murder of Muslims on a truly massive scale.[15] In these inflamed circumstances, any ratcheting-up of official authoritarianism is to be viewed with suspicion and concern.

[14] It is still unclear just who committed this act, and there are unsubstantiated accounts that point to Hindu provocateurs as the culprits. But it has to be acknowledged that there are extremist elements among Indian Muslims, as there are among Hindus, and that these could have been responsible for the deaths in Godhra. For a collection of reports on the Gujarat massacre in general, see OnlineVolunteers.org (n 2, above).

[15] The progress of one of the major murder cases stemming from the Gujarat riots suggests there is a high degree of fear among witnesses to the atrocities of that period. It is also clear that money is being employed to induce witnesses to change their testimony. In the *Best Bakery* case 21 people were prosecuted for the murder of 14 people during the Gujarat riots. Witnesses gave evidence that some 500 people had attacked the bakery with petrol bombs and that many of the dead had been burnt to death. The accused were originally acquitted on 27 June 2003 by a 'fast track' court set up to bring swift justice in relation to the Gujarat riots. The court found a want of evidence after 37 of the 73 witnesses turned hostile, including a key witness named Zahira Sheikh. So unsatisfactory was this result that the BJP government of Gujarat was forced to appeal to the Gujarat High Court, and a re-trial was ordered. The tragic affair turned into something like a soap opera in late 2004, as Zahira Sheikh changed her position a couple of times more in the lead-up to the re-trial. Her

D The Return of Congress and the Repeal of POTA

The political landscape of India has changed considerably since the victory of Congress in the 2004 election, though it is far too soon to proclaim the reversal of the drift into deeper communal disharmony. Congress ran a campaign that revolved around its claim to represent 'secularism', as opposed to the embrace of 'Hindutva' by the BJP and its allies. As noted earlier, to almost universal surprise Congress ended up with more seats than did the BJP. It is highly doubtful that the result was brought about by any sudden access of commitment to 'secularism' or new-found antipathy to Hindutva on the part of the Hindu majority. The main plank of the BJP's platform for this election was not Hindutva but 'India Shining', a reference to the new prosperity and national prestige being generated by the boom in the ICT and certain other industries. This message turned out to be far from universally attractive. The BJP had forgotten that a large part of India, particularly the rural areas which still comprise over 70 per cent of the population, had benefited little—if at all—from the urban and intensely regional nature of the economic boom. In this and a number of other ways the BJP proved remarkably out of touch with the electorate, which turned back towards Congress and even more towards a range of parties of the left in the different regions.[16]

During the campaign Congress promised to repeal POTA if it won the election. This seeming libertarianism was a newly discovered commitment for a party that had instituted all the anti-democratic emergencies, above all Indira Gandhi's Emergency of 1975–77, since Independence almost 60 years ago. The stance enabled Congress to portray the BJP and its affiliates as dedicated to both sectarianism and authoritarianism. Some four months after its electoral victory the Congress-led government repealed POTA and introduced substitute legislation. Initially both the repeal of POTA and the new law were accomplished in the form of ordinances, and these were converted to Acts during the next session of Parliament.[17]

An early commentary on the new legislation talked in terms of 'three steps forward...two steps back'; the article was headed 'The Reincarnation of POTA' (Human Rights Features 2004). This title was probably overstating the case. Certain key aspects of the Unlawful Activities (Prevention)

community became so outraged that they are reported as having sought to expel her from the community: <http://en.wikipedia.org/wiki/Best_Bakery_Case>, last accessed 15 November 2006. For an analysis of the case, see also People's Union for Civil Liberties (2003).

[16] Two early academic considerations of the 2004 election are Hasan (2004) and Price (2004).

[17] POTA was repealed by the Prevention of Terrorism Act (POTA) Repeal Ordinance 2004 (promulgated on 21 September). On the same day The Unlawful Activities (Prevention) Amendment Ordinance 2004 was promulgated, amending the Unlawful Activities (Prevention) Act 1967. These ordinances were converted to Acts of Parliament on 9 December 2004.

Act 1967 (as amended in 2004) are demonstrable improvements over POTA. For example, POTA (s 32(1)) set aside the hitherto ruling provision of the Indian Evidence Act 1872 whereby confessions to police officers were inadmissible as evidence in court. The new Act restores the bar of admissibility of confessions to police, thereby making torture less rewarding a behaviour of gaolers and police. Under POTA a suspect could be held for up to 180 days without charge (s 49 (2)(b)), whereas now suspects must be produced before the court within 24 hours as prescribed by the ordinary criminal law. Bail could effectively be denied a suspect under POTA for a year without consideration of the court (s 49(6) and (7)), but now the ordinary provisions of the criminal law have been restored in this matter. POTA had authorised the court to draw 'adverse inference' from certain matters (including the finding of fingerprints at the site of an offence: s 53(1)(b)), thereby transferring the burden of proof from prosecution to defence. This too has been removed. And importantly, whereas it was enough for POTA that a person 'belongs or professes to belong to a terrorist organisation (s 20(1)), under the new Act the accused is guilty of an offence only if he (sic) associates himself with the organisation 'with intention to further its activities' (s 38(1)).

On the other hand, as the author of the Human Rights Features (2004) article makes clear, the open-ended definition of terrorist acts persists from TADA, through POTA and into the new Act. The definition is bound to sweep up many oppositional activities that are either dubiously or not at all terrorist in nature. And there remains no procedure for the listing of an organisation as 'involved in terrorism' (s 35(1)(d)) and therefore to be included in the Schedule of the Act. Moreover, proceedings may still be held in camera 'if the court so desires' (s 44(1)).

Overall, however, replacement of the POTA with the new Act is a considerable step in the right direction. The new Congress government has translated its recently found rhetoric of civil liberties into some valuable reform of legal instruments. No doubt this process of reform was aided by the reduced intensity of political pressure from the United States, which is now embroiled in a war in Iraq widely seen to have little to do with its 'war on terror'. The United States too continues to be roundly condemned internationally and at home for its treatment of prisoners in Guantanamo Bay and its torture and mistreatment of prisoners in Iraq. The time was therefore ripe for the new Congress government to show a more civil libertarian face. Whether or not this results in more orderly and careful administration of the criminal law in relation to political opposition remains to be seen.

V CONCLUSION

The broad problem of the post-September 11 anti-terrorism legislation in India, particularly POTA, was that it constituted a significant contraction of due process. Aside from the immensely worrying threats to liberty in general represented by such legislation in India, as well as in a number of other jurisdictions throughout the world, under the BJP government there were realistic fears that authoritarian legislation would be enforced in a discriminatory way. Indian Muslims held particular fears that this would be so, though evidence of practice is insufficient to make a sound judgment as to whether this has actually occurred and if so to what degree. This chapter has sketched a picture of the Indian constitutional order as conflicted, with elements of both the proper observance of human and civil rights and also patterns of authoritarianism inherited from the colonial administration and extended in the years since Independence. A positive account of some aspects of the institutional development of justice in India has been sketched here, particularly the invention of 'social action litigation' by the Supreme Court of India. On the other hand, it cannot be assumed that the Supreme Court, let alone Indian courts in general, will either systematically stand up to, or be effective against, authoritarian rule in the future. Meanwhile, and to the surprise of virtually everyone, political developments within India have to a considerable extent reversed the downward spiral into authoritarianism. Congress is re-born as the party in power at the head of a mildly left-leaning coalition, and this time round it has embraced civil liberties as never before. In the context of the increasingly inflamed character of relations between religious communities in India, this development may be of considerable value.

BIBLIOGRAPHY

AHUJA, SANGEETA (1997) *People, Law and Justice—a casebook of public interest litigation* (Orient Longman, Hyderabad).

AMNESTY INTERNATIONAL (1997) *AI Report 1997: India,* available at: <http://www.amnesty.org /ailib/aireport/ar97/ASA20.htm>, last accessed 15 November 2006.

—— (2000) 'India: The Prevention of Terrorism Bill. Past abuses revisited' (23 June 2000) available at: <http://web.amnesty.org/library/index/ENGASA200222000>, last accessed 15 November 2006.

AUSTIN, GRANVILLE (1966) *The Indian Constitution: Cornerstone of a Nation* (Clarendon Press, Oxford).

—— (2000) *Working a Democratic Constitution – the Indian Experience* (Oxford University Press, New Delhi).

BANERJEE, S (1980) *In the Wake of Naxalbari: a History of the Naxalite Movement in India* (Subarnekha, Calcutta).

BANERJEE, DIPANKAR and KUECK, GERT W (2003) *South Asia and the War on Terrorism — analysing the implications of 11 September* (India Research Press, New Delhi).

BAXI, UPENDRA (1988) 'Taking Suffering Seriously: Social Action Litigation in the Supreme Court of India' in U Baxi (ed) *Law and Poverty – critical essay* (Tripathi, Bombay).

BERLIN, ISAIAH (1969) 'Two Concepts of Liberty' in I Berlin *Four Essays on Liberty* (Oxford University Press, London).

CHANG, NANCY (2001) 'The US PATRIOT Act. What's So Patriotic About Trampling on the Bill of Rights?' available from the Center for Constitutional Rights at: <http://www.ccr-ny.org/v2/reports/docs/USA_PATRIOT_ACT.pdf>, last accessed 15 November 2006.

CONCERNED CITIZENS' TRIBUNAL (2002) *Crime Against Humanity: an inquiry into the carnage in Gujarat. Vol II Findings and Recommendations* (Citizens for Justice and Peace, Mumbai).

DHAVAN, RAJEEV (1978) *The Amendment: conspiracy or revolution?* (Wheeler, Allahabad).

GALANTER, MARC and JAYANTH K KRISHNAN (2004) 'Debased Informalism: *Lok Adalats* and Legal Rights in Modern India' in Thomas Heller and Erik Jensen (eds) *Beyond Common Knowledge: Empirical Approaches to the Rule of Law* (Stanford University Press, Stanford).

GRAHAM, BRUCE (1990) *Hindu Nationalism and Indian Politics: the origins and development of the Bharatiya Jana Sangh* (Cambridge University Press, Cambridge).

HASAN, ZOYA (2004) 'Indian Election 2004: A Setback for the BJP's Exclusivist Agenda' available at: <http://www.ceri-sciences-po.org/archive/sept04/artzh.pdf>, last accessed 15 November 2006.

HUMAN RIGHTS FEATURES (2004) *The Reincarnation of POTA* (Voice of the Asia Pacific Human Rights Network, New Delhi) available at: <http://www.hrdc.net/sahrdc/hrfeatures/ HRF106.htm>, last accessed 15 November 2006.

HUMAN RIGHTS WATCH (2002) '"We are not the enemy" Hate Crimes Against Arabs, Muslims and Those Perceived to be Arab or Muslim after September 11' Report by Amardeep Singh for HRW (14 November 2002) HRW Index No G1406 (see especially Part V 'The September 11 Backlash') available at <http://www.hrw.org/reports/2002/usahate/ usa1102-04.htm>, last accessed 15 November 2006.

KOTWAL, DINESH (2000) 'The Naga Insurgency: the Past and the Future', *Strategic Analysis: a monthly journal of the IDSA* (July, Vol XXIV No 4) avail <http://www.ciaonet.org>, last accessed 15 November 2006.

MAITI, PRASENJIT (2003) 'On Civil Liberties and Society in India' formerly available at: <http://www.e11th-hour.org/security/india.society.html>

(as at 28 March 2003), but relocated at: <http://www.poetryrepairs.com/v01/144.html>, last accessed 15 November 2006.

MENDELSOHN, OLIVER (1991) 'Life and Struggles in the Stone Quarries of India' 29(1) *Journal of Commonwealth and Comparative Politics* 44.

—— (2000) 'The Supreme Court as the Most Trusted Public Institution in India' 23 *South Asia* 103.

MENDELSOHN, OLIVER and VICZIANY, MARIKA (1998) *The Untouchables — Subordination, Poverty and the State in Modern India* (Cambridge University Press, Cambridge).

MORRIS-JONES, W H (1964) 'Parliament and Dominant Party: Indian Experience' 17 (1964) *Parliamentary Affairs* 206-307.

ONLINEVOLUNTEERS.ORG (2003) 'Gujarat Carnage: The Aftermath' (collection of resources, links March 2002 to December 2003) available at: <http://www.onlinevolunteers.org/gujarat/ reports/index.htm>, last accessed 15 November 2006.

PRICE, GARETH (2004) 'How the 2004 Lok Sabha Election was Lost' Chatham House Briefing Note (Royal Institute of International Affairs) July 2004 available at: <http://www. chathamhouse.org.uk/pdf/research/asia/BNgp0704.pdf>, last accessed 15 November 2006.

PEOPLES UNION FOR CIVIL LIBERTIES (PUCL) (2003) 'Best bakery case – PUCL demands fresh trial' Press Release 7 July 2003 available at: <http://www.pucl.org/Topics/Religion-communalism/2003/best-bakery.htm>, last accessed 15 November 2006.

SEERVAI, H M (1991) *Constitutional Law of India* (Tripathi, Bombay).

SHAHABUDDIN, SYED (2003) 'Approximate Muslim population in India [2001]' *Milli Gazette* 28 October 2003 available at: <http://www.milligazette.com/Archives/15092001/29.htm>, last accessed 15 November 2006.

SHERLOCK, STEPHEN (2001) *The Indian Railways Strike of 1974: A Study of Power and Organised Labour* (Rupa, New Delhi).

SHOURIE, ARUN (2001) *Courts and Their Judgments* (Rupa, New Delhi).

SUNDARAYYA, P (1979) 'Telengana' in A R Desai (ed) *Peasant Struggles in* India (Oxford University Press, Bombay).

TARLO, E (2003) *Unsettling Memories: narratives of the emergency in Delhi* (University of California Press, Berkeley).

VAJPAYEE, AB (2002) http://www.indianembassy.org/pm/vajpayee/pm_dec_31_2002.htm (consulted March 27 2007).

VENKATESAN, V (2003) 'A Secular Veneer', *Frontline* 20 (2), Jan 18-31, 2003, http://www.hinduonnet.com/fline/fl2002/stories/20030131005103700.htm (consulted March 27 2007).

VICZIANY, MARIKA (2004) 'Globalization and *Hindutva*: India's Experience with Global Economic and Political Integration' in Gloria Davies and Chris Nyland (eds) *Globalization in the Asian Region: impacts and consequences* (Edward Elgar, Cheltenham).

8

Role/Rule of Law in China Reconsidered

JIANFU CHEN

I INTRODUCTION

AT THE FIRST workshop of this series in 1998, which also coincided with the twentieth anniversary of the formal launch of post-Mao reform programmes,[1] I argued that the pragmatic use of law under the leadership of Deng Xiaoping fell well within the notion of rule *by* law, not the rule *of* law, and law—phrased in general and vague statements—served more as policy statements than providing practical guidance (J Chen, 2003). Since then, several significant developments, at global and domestic levels, have occurred, each of which demands some re-thinking about the rule of law in China and elsewhere.

First, a series of analyses of the Asian financial Crisis from an economic-legal perspective has been undertaken and become available for study. While opinions still differ as to the causes of the Crisis, its impact on the legal system, and the direction of future legal reforms in Asia, a consensus seems to have emerged that, if law is a factor that contributed to the Crisis or an element that is needed to avoid the repetition of such a crisis, it is not the law per se but the effectiveness of the law in action that needs to be examined carefully and to be improved for the future stability of society in general and financial security in particular. It is also clear that if rule of law is to have any meaning or effect in a society, however it is defined, equal application of law to all, meaningful independence of the judiciary, and accountability of government actions are indispensable, despite the fact that many of these studies challenge economics/economist-driven theories of the rule of law promoted by the World Bank, IMF and other Western powers (see Glazebrook, 1999).

[1] The Third Plenary Session of the Eleventh Central Committee of the Communist Party of China (CPC), held in late December 1978, is generally seen as the event that formally launched the post-Mao reforms.

Secondly, the Washington-pronounced and widely-followed 'war on terror' has now produced many draconian measures and laws in many countries, both in the West and in Asia. These measures and laws pose some direct challenges to the upholding of some very basic elements of the rule of law in the countries concerned. Inevitably, people must reconsider the strength of the rule of law in a given society, if not a total reconsideration of the notion of the rule of law and its role in society.

Thirdly, in the case of China, the phrase *Yifa zhiguo, jianshe shehuizhui fazhiguo* (Ruling the Country According to Law and Building a Socialist Rule of Law Country, 依法治国,建设社会主义法治国家), initially pronounced at the Fourth Plenary Session of the Eighth National People's Congress (NPC) (1996) as a long-term development strategy (*Guangming Daily,* 1996: 1), has now been incorporated into both the State and Party Constitutions through constitutional amendments in 1999 and 2002 respectively (J Chen, 2004). Further, China's efforts to join the World Trade Organisation (WTO) and, since December 2001, China's membership obligations in the WTO have led to some rapid legal development that continues today.

This chapter re-visits the debate about the role of law (and hence the rule of law) in China. It is argued that while the Chinese legal system, its laws and institutions, have improved significantly since 1978, a clear transition from rule by law to rule of law is yet to emerge *in practice*, and the Chinese legal system remains problematic when assessed against basic requirements for the rule of law (on basic requirements, see Section III below). In this argument, it is emphasised that academic discussions and views must not be confused with official policies on the rule of law, and official or academic views must be distinguished from practical reality. The emphasis on practical reality also suggests that economic development does not necessarily depend on the rule of law, contrary to what the World Bank, IMF, etc have often asserted.

II 'THIRD WAVE' OF LEGAL REFORM IN CHINA

The most recent legal reform efforts, largely required by WTO membership, are seen by some as a new, third wave of legal reform, following up the 'first wave' of law reform from 1978 to the early 1990s and the 'second wave' from the mid-1990s (Cohen, 2001). This 'third wave' will no doubt necessitate some major legal and institutional reforms so as to ensure that Chinese laws and regulations are, in the language of the WTO, transparent, readily accessible, relatively stable and universal in their application, and that Chinese judicial and other dispute resolution mechanisms are independent, impartial and transparent. Specifically, while the WTO does not lay down comprehensive and systematic requirements on law and the administration of law, WTO rules contain various ad hoc requirements in specific areas, such as Article X (Publication and administration of trade regulations) of the General Agreement on Tariffs and Trade (GATT), and Articles III (Transparency) and VI (Domestic regulation) of the General Agreement on Trade in Services (GATS), with the most comprehensive requirements being contained in the Agreement on Trade-Related Aspects of Intellectual Property Rights (TRIPS), including, for example, Part III (Articles 41–61) on enforcement of intellectual property rights and Part V (Articles 63–64) on dispute prevention and settlement (see Cohen, 2001; Clarke, 2002). As a country could not be expected to maintain a legal system which only guarantees fairness and justice in one area not in others, these ad hoc requirements are often seen as requirements for a whole legal system in WTO members (see Clarke, 2002). On China's membership specifically, Article 2 (Administration of the Trade Regime) of the Protocol on the Accession of the People's Republic of China does provide some basic principles on transparency of law, reasonable administration of law, and effectiveness of judicial review (for a more detailed discussion on WTO and legal reform requirements for China, see Lubman, 2002a).

Since China became the WTO's 143rd member on 11 December 2001, the number of articles and books published in China on legal reforms demanded by its membership has indeed mushroomed and the Chinese authorities have made some very substantial and rapid efforts to review and revise laws and regulations that would otherwise be inconsistent with WTO rules and principles (see J Chen, 2001 and 2002b; Yang, 2001; Y Zhang, 2003).

If law reform in post-Mao China is to be divided into three waves, this present wave of reform could be very different from the previous two and could have a more direct and greater actual impact of law on the ordinary people and on the future of the rule of law in China. And this third wave of reform will be the most difficult one, demanding not just law reform but also fundamental reforms in the politico-economic system in China. Due to the politico-economic implications, many Chinese scholars have argued that the WTO demands the establishment of the rule of law in China (see Section VI of the present chapter).

A number of more optimistic scholars have asserted that China is already in the transition from rule by law to a certain version of the rule of law. Peerenboom, for example, takes the view that the Chinese government has moved away from a purely instrumental conception of law towards a conception of the rule of law where law is meant to bind both government officials and citizens (Peerenboom, 2002: xii). Though he concedes (at 23, footnote 23) that the goal of the Chinese legal system to bind the state and its actors is often not realised in practice, he nevertheless argues that the

Chinese legal system is moving towards a regime that complies with the basic elements of a thin rule of law (at 6 and 558). Many other scholars, however, remain sceptical (see Orts, 2001).

Since rule of law is a contested notion, in China and elsewhere, any discussion of the notion of the rule of law makes sense only if it is discussed in a specific context. Thus it is necessary to first set out the context in which the rule of law in China is discussed here.

III RULE OF LAW AS A CONTESTED NOTION

Evidencing the contested nature of the concept, a clear and concise definition of 'rule of law' has proved elusive. *The Oxford Companion to Law*, for instance, describes 'rule of law' as 'a concept of the utmost importance but having no defined, nor readily definable, content' (1980: 1093). The concept, as pointed out by Orts, is 'notoriously difficult as a matter of jurisprudence, and different people can mean very different things by the rule of law, especially when they are speaking in different languages and from the perspectives of different cultures' (Orts, 2001: 47). Others have also asserted that it 'has been glimpsed, sketched in practice, unreflectively and intermittently enjoyed, half-understood, [and] left indistinct' (Oakeshott, 1975: 120, quoted in Orts, 2001: 47).

There is no shortage of scholarship on the notion of the rule of law nor is there any lack of practical variations. As to scholarship, there are not only disagreements, sometimes academic views are diametrically opposed (for detailed discussions, see the various sources listed in the references). As regards variation in practice, while it is generally accepted that there is rule of law in developed Western countries, it would be naïve to think that there is uniform practice of the rule of law in these countries. Even at a very superficial level, one can easily see the difference between common law and civil law jurisdictions. No one could claim that rule of law practice is identical even within one general legal family—such as the United Kingdom and the United States, or France and Germany.

As an idea, it can easily be traced back to the ancient Greeks. Plato and Aristotle, among others, discussed the rule of law (or perhaps more precisely, rule by law) extensively. As a constitutional doctrine and practice, it has a relatively short and varied history and has been largely developed through the common law systems. However, greater controversies emerged, at a much later stage, when the notion of the rule of law was linked to political orders in the Western (liberal) developed countries. This was especially so when proponents of critical legal studies or a post-modernist approach to law began their fierce attack on the rule of law as an idea and as a practice (for further discussion of these harsh criticisms of the rule of law, see Orts, 2001: 79–81). Most recently, it has been argued by some scholars that there is a need to develop alternative conceptions of the rule of law in the context of the analysis and understanding of Asian legal development (see Jayasuriya, 1999; Peerenboom, 2002). Clearly, the notion of the rule of law more often attracts disagreement than agreement, and it is fair to say that it is not a static concept, but one developed and continuing to develop in various historical and geopolitical contexts.

Rule of law thus means different things to different people, in different contexts, at different times, and for different purposes. To law and development scholars, it means the security of property rights and the functioning of legal institutions. To philosophers, it is a question of defining law and politico-legal systems. To political scientists, it is a complementary mechanism to democracy and the political system. To constitutional lawyers and other legal practitioners, it is a mechanism of checks and balances. Though these are, of course, over-simplified generalisations of the much more sophisticated views among scholars of different disciplines, they indicate some vastly different understandings of the rule of law among scholars and practitioners. Some treat a country as having the rule of law because of the existence of certain elements in its legal system and others see the rule of law as something which 'manifests itself more as an *absence* than a presence' (Walker, 1988: 3). Still, it is contested whether the rule of law requires some moral assessment about the virtue of the rules of law and how they are used so as to distinguish the rule *of* law from rule *by* law (Orts, 2001: 97–99). Rule of law is therefore variously treated as an idea/ideal, a legal doctrine, a mechanism or institution, a tool or instrument, or an all-embracing legal notion devoid of specific content or containing all ('good' or 'positive') aspects of a liberal democratic system. It means different things in different contexts.

Neither scholarly disagreement nor practical variation, however, should distract us from the existence of certain common understandings as to the minimum requirements or core meaning of the rule of law. It is generally agreed that, at least as a constitutional doctrine, the rule of law means certain limitations being imposed on government, its governing élites as well as the governed (Walker, 1988: 3). Peerenboom summarises this well when he states:

> At its most basic, rule of law refers to a system in which law is able to impose meaningful restraints on the state and individual members of the ruling elite, as captured in the rhetorically powerful if overly simplistic notion of a government of laws, the supremacy of the law, and equality of all before the law. (Peerenboom, 2002: 2)

In the case of China, and contrary to what would be expected by law and development theorists or proponents, the Chinese economy since 1979 has developed continuously and grown rapidly in the absence of the rule of law, and the present pressure for reform towards democracy and the rule of law came less from the need for market reform or the emergence of a middle class civil society, than from a strong resentment of the so far seemingly uncontrollable epidemic of corruption (Pan, 2003: 3–4). In other words, if the rule of law is to have any practical value, rather than be just a beautiful but empty promise, as an instrument for economic development, the expectation is that it will involve the establishment of some basic checks and balances in the running (or ruling) of a country, hence the upholding of government of law, supremacy of law and equality before the law. Indeed, those who were among the 200,000 or so people who responded to a recent Internet survey conducted by the country's national newspaper nominated anti-corruption and the establishment of checks and balances as the top issue that people expect the Tenth National People's Congress (NPC) (2003–8) to address (see *People's Daily*, 2003a). Albeit instrumentalist in attitude towards law, the survey result points to a popular demand on the rule of law in China that must be addressed if democracy is to have any meaning in real life.

Thus both much scholarly and popular evidence points to the basic practical need for checks and balances that drives demand for the rule of law in China. It is in this context that this chapter will examine whether there is rule of law in China.

IV RULE OF LAW AS AN OFFICIAL POLICY

The present debate on the rule of law in China focuses on legal development under the 'Third Generation of Communist Party (CPC) Leadership with Jiang Zemin as Its Core' since the official adoption of 'Ruling the Country According to Law' as a long-term development strategy, and implicitly suggests that China under Deng Xiaoping was a country under rule *by* law, not the rule *of* law (J Chen, 2003: 257–9). This artificial distinction between Deng's China and China under Jiang Zemin (and, since 2003, under the Fourth Generation of Communist Party Leadership headed by CPC Secretary-General Hu Jintao) is, to say the least, questionable.

I have discussed the role of law in China under the leadership of Deng Xiaoping in an earlier paper (J Chen, 2003) and to avoid repetition, I shall but briefly summarise those arguments here. First, legal development has always been part and parcel of modernisation in the sense of economic development and, this being so, legal development has always been limited by the politico-economic parameters which are largely defined by the Party. Secondly, law was initially seen, and largely used, as a tool for institutionalising and generalising ad hoc policies for economic reforms. Thirdly, the politico-economic parameters had evolved from those of a command economy to those of a socialist planned commodity economy and, finally, to those of a 'socialist market economy'. With these changes, the perceived needs for law had also changed, but the attitude towards the law remains largely the same, that is, the law is often still viewed as a tool to create and maintain an environment of social stability conducive to economic development. However, changes in politico-economic parameters had significantly liberalised the extent of tolerance towards introducing reform measures (including legal ones) and debating the role of law, as well as brought about the potential for more fundamental politico-economic and legal reform.

If the above represents the understanding of 'rule of law' in China under Deng Xiaoping, what then was introduced in 1996 that has been described as the 'biggest event in the evolution of the rule of law in China' (Peerenboom, 2003: 58) and one capable of changing the nature of law in China?

Again, I explained the background to the renewed discussion of the rule of law in my earlier paper. Put simply, in 1996 the Party (through its Secretary-General, Jiang Zemin) started the talk about 'Ruling the Country According to Law' (*Yifa zhiguo*, , 依法治国). Although little elaboration was offered by the Party, the phrase was declared a long-term development strategy and incorporated into the Ninth Five Year National Economic and Social Development Plan and the Outline of Goals by Year 2010, adopted by the Fourth Plenary Session of the 8th NPC on 17 March 1996 (for text, see *Guangming Daily*, 1996: 1).

In the absence of any concrete substance, one may be puzzled by the excitement aroused by the introduction of yet another political slogan. However, in the Chinese context, this new slogan involved a change of terminology from 法制 to 法治 (both romanised as *fazhi*),[2] the former having been used since 1978. This terminological change, as I also pointed out in my earlier paper, was one of the principal reasons for the renewed discussion of and enthusiasm for the rule of law. The principal Party document which authoritatively laid down the Party policy on 'Ruling the Country According to Law' was the Political Report delivered to the 15th Party Congress in September 1997 (1997 Political Report). It said very little about the rule of law: the supremacy of law (over and above the Party and its policies), the independence of the judiciary, and, most importantly, checks and balances were all missing. The 1997 Political Report was talking about rule by law, not the rule of law, in that the focus remained on using law 'to secure long-term stability' (*baozhang changzhi jiu'an*, 保障长治久安) for economic development. Despite the ambiguities and vagueness inherent in the phrase 'Ruling the Country According to Law,' it

[2] Linguistically, 法制 means legal system, and 法治 means to rule by law. Historically, the two terms have been used inter-changeably, referring to the Western notion of 'rule of law'. See also note 4 below.

was formally incorporated into Article 5 of the state Constitution during its 1999 revision.[3] The incorporation of this phrase is again emphasised as being an important guarantee for the country's long term stability (Tian, 1999).

If China were to move from rule by law to the rule of law, the Communist Party—the real authority which determines the direction of national development—must clarify the ambiguities inherent in the 1997 Political Report, but little effort has been made to elaborate the notion or to establish specific mechanisms for checks and balances since 1997, other than the continuation of the rhetoric. Five years after the initial proclamation on establishing 'Ruling the Country According to Law', the 2002 Political Report, delivered at the 16th CPC Congress, managed to say very little on this issue:

> Leadership by the Party is the fundamental guarantee that the people are the masters of the country and that the country is ruled according to law. The people being the masters of the country constitutes the essential requirement of socialist democracy. Ruling the Country according to Law is the basic strategy the Party pursues in leading the people in running the country. The Party is the core of leadership for the cause of socialism with Chinese characteristics.[4] (2002 Political Report, Section V)

Here the phrase 'basic strategy' clearly means 'a method', 'a means to an end', and that end is the guarantee of Party leadership and economic development. Despite the lack of details, the 16th CPC Congress nevertheless added 'Ruling the Country According to Law' to the Party Constitution. According to a CPC spokesman, the revision of the Party Constitution was to establish a 'unity' of leadership of the CPC, 'the people being the masters of the country' and 'Ruling the Country According to Law' (CPC Constitution Revision Explanation, 2002). To this effect, Paragraph 12 of the Preamble of the revised Party Constitution now states:

> The Communist Party of China leads the people in promoting socialist democracy and building socialist political civilisation. It keeps expanding socialist democracy, strengthens the socialist legal system, rules the country according to law, builds a socialist country ruled according to law, and consolidates the people's democratic dictatorship.[5]

[3] The 1999 revision of the Constitution added the following to Article 5: 'The People's Republic of China practise Ruling the Country according to Law and builds a socialist country governed by law'. For a discussion of the 1999 constitutional revision see J Chen (1999a).

[4] It should be pointed out that *yifa zhiguo* has been consistently translated by the *China Daily* as 'ruling the country by law' instead of 'ruling the country according to law'.

[5] An English version of the CPC Constitution was published in the *China Daily*, 6 December 2002. A Chinese text of the Party Constitution is available from the *People's Daily*, 19 November 2002. The English translation (above) has been modified to better accord with the original Chinese texts.

The same revision of the CPC Constitution also declares in Paragraph 13 that:

> [t]he Communist Party of China leads the people in their efforts to build spiritual civilisation as well as material and political civilisations and to combine ruling the country according to law with ruling the country by virtue.

The 2002 revision also added Jiang Zemin's 'Three Represents'[6] as an important 'Thought' which shall guide the action of the Party (paragraph 2 of the CPC Constitution). Similarly, the state Constitution was also revised in 2004 to incorporate the 'Three Represents', thus ensuring that both the Party and the state Constitutions uphold what I have termed 'Six Fundamental Principles'—that is, the Four Fundamental Principles,[7] Deng Xiaoping Theory, and the 'Three Represents' (see J Chen, 1999a and 2004)—with Party leadership as their very essence. The new insertion of 'ruling the country by virtue' adds more confusion, if not signifiying a retreat to the 'rule of man' as understood in traditional China, and reinforces the conception of law as more or less an instrument of the governing elites.

The most recent Party policy document on this topic, under the Fourth Generation of the Party Leadership, is the Decision on Strengthening the Capacity Building of the Ruling Party, adopted by the Central Committee of the CPC on 19 September 2004. Because it is a Party document, specifically on capacity-building, one would expect it to outline some concrete measures not only on strengthening the ruling capacity of the Party, but also on controlling the Party's power and its exercise if the Party were to take the rule of law seriously. Indeed, there is a specific section (Section 5) on the rule of law and Party leadership. It talks about democratic election, decision-making, management and supervision, and about supporting legal construction and judicial work as well as guaranteeing basic rights to the people while maintaining and strengthening Party leadership in political and legal work. It goes on to declare the need to strengthen the control and supervision of political powers and their exercise. However, the document contains hardly any concrete measures or mechanisms for realising these goals or any specific timetables for achieving any of them. In short, it is rich in rhetoric but poor in measures and mechanisms. And the actual practice in political reform, press freedom, tolerance of intellectual freedom, and regulation of the Internet, under the

[6] 'The Three Represents' means that the Party represents 'the development trend of China's advanced productive forces, the orientation of China's advanced culture and the fundamental interests of the overwhelming majority of the Chinese People'. See para 1 of the CPC Constitution.

[7] The 'Four Fundamental Principles' are loosely stated in para 7 of the Preamble of the 1982 Constitution, which provides that 'The Chinese people of all nationalities will continue to be led by the Communist Party of China, guided by Marxism-Leninism and Mao Zedong Thought, adhere to the people's democratic dictatorship and follow the socialist road.'

leadership of Hu Jintao so far seems to have crushed, rather than raised, expectations of political observers who initially gave the generous benefit of doubt to the new leadership when the change-over occurred in 2002-03 (see Lynch, 2005).

If there is any clear message from these documents, it is this: the Party is genuine in pursuing economic modernisation and development with specific measures and innovations, as such a development is clearly seen as a foundation for the legitimacy of its leadership. The Party however has so far only offered rhetoric without specific actions for the rule of law as it is still struggling to find specific measures that would uphold the idea of rule of law whilst not undermining or threatening its leadership position. As such, one must not read too much into these frequent changes or additions of political phrases. Otherwise, we may well fall into the trap of taking at face value what a prominent Chinese legal scholar has termed 'the tendency to rule the country by slogans' (He, 2003).

V RULE OF LAW AS AN ACADEMIC TOPIC

Rule of law as an academic topic in China must not be confused with practical reality, nor with its being an official policy (Chen, 2002c: 39; see also Liang, 2000: 1). Indeed, in academic discussion, theories on the rule of law largely mirror those in the West and quite often bear little relationship to social reality or official practice. Given this, it is not surprising that such discourse seems 'abstract' to outsiders (see Dworkin, 2002). This does not suggest that academic discourse on the rule of law is meaningless or totally insignificant (see below). However, caution is urged when writers are tempted to reach optimistic conclusions based on academic writings in China.

There is no difficulty in finding references to *fazhi* 法制 or 法治) in the Chinese historical texts, especially those from the late Qing period when modern law reform began, and those of the era of the Republic (1911–49). In communist China the topic was one of the most extensively and intensively contested academic issues in the 1950s and late 1970s (see Guo, Li and Hao, 1998; Editorial Group, 1981; Keith, 1994). These academic debates were largely centred on contention between the rule of man and the rule of law. Both terms, 法制 and 法治, were used in the debate and there was no clear preference for either. The debate did not lead to any substantial consensus among Chinese scholars, nor did it provide much guidance for legal development. Nevertheless, the phrase *fazhi* (法制) was later adopted in official documents and consistently used by scholars referring to the need to establish a modern legal system in China.

As mentioned earlier, legal development in post-Mao China has largely been constrained by politico-economic parameters set by the CPC. This is also true in terms of academic discussion and debate. Not surprisingly, the CPC's decision to establish a 'socialist market economy' as a long-term direction of economic reform in 1992 has been a turning-point (see 1992 Political Report). Lively discussions in legal circles regarding the reform of legal ideologies and legal development began to spring up, as that decision finally threw off the shackles of the orthodox ideologies and gave some relative freedom to academic discussion and debate as long as the CPC leadership is not directly challenged.

The fundamental argument by Chinese scholars is that market economy demands 'rational' law in the sense defined by Max Weber. A socialist market economy, it is then asserted, is an economy under rule of law (*fazhi jingji*) (see Xiao, 1994; S Chen, 1994; Min, 1994; but compare Lin, 1994). The establishment and perfecting of a socialist market economy is thus a process of establishing the rule of law (J Wang et al, 1996). To establish a market economy in China thus demands a revolution in legal theory and legal thought (see Guo, 1994; H Xie, 1994b; Wen, 1995; W Zhang, 1995).

Though far short of a revolution in legal theory and legal thought and though the ideas advocated by the Chinese scholars are neither 'intellectually sophisticated, theoretically refined or rich in philosophical depth', nor are they original (A Chen, 2000: 163), the 'second tide of academic thoughts' in post Mao-China[8] swept all areas of Chinese law and led to some practical manifestations (see A Chen, 2000; Peerenboom, 2002). In jurisprudence, rights (including rights against the state) began to be emphasised and traditional notions of duties, status and dictatorship began to be rejected (Jurisprudential Debate, 1991). In relation to law-making, jurists began to openly demand that law, not policy, must be relied upon to legitimise economic and social reforms (Gan, 1991), and that the 'traditional doctrines', based on those of A Y Vyshinsky and imported in the 1950s from the Soviet Union,[9] must be abandoned and any vestige removed (Project Group, 1993; J Zhang, 1994).[10] In civil law, it began to be strongly urged that all economic participants must be treated equally and that law must be made universally applicable to all kinds of economic actors (see Market Economy Symposium, *1992*; J Wang et al, 1996; Lu, 1994; Zhou, 1993). Further, some scholars held that, if public property is upheld as sacred and not to be violated, then private property must also be

[8] Chinese scholars often refer to an academic debate and discussion as a 'tide of academic thoughts' or a 'liberation of thoughts'. In post-Mao China, the debate in the late 1970s is seen as the first 'liberation of thoughts', the second as starting in 1992 and the third as dating from 1996-97 onwards. Scholars are now anticipating a fourth 'liberation of thoughts', pending a CPC decision to deepen political reforms (see Guo, Li and Hao 1998: 1).

[9] The 'doctrines' developed by Vyshinsky emphasised the class nature of law and law as a weapon for class struggle.

[10] Some scholars have, however, offered some qualified defence for Vyshinsky (see Sun and Zeng 1996).

elevated to the same level for protection, and not just be allowed to have 'lawful existence' (see Market Economy Symposium, 1992; W Zhang, 1993). In the important areas of law for the protection of human rights and individual liberties, that is, the criminal law and criminal procedure law, the debate on several long-rejected criminal justice principles—such as the presumption of innocence, timely and adequate access to legal counsel, *nullum crimen, nulla poena sine lege* (and the consequential Abolition of Analogy in criminal law), judicial independence, equality before the law (thus rejecting the class nature of the criminal law), and proportionality—resumed their much deserved prominence in legal discourse, as did the debate on counter-revolutionary crimes, and on the reform of trial processes and strict application of the death penalty (see J Chen, 1997 and 2002a; Chen and Ke, 2000). And in the most important area for checks and balances, scholars in administrative law began to advocate strongly the idea of administrative law as being first and foremost a law for controlling government and its activities, rather than merely providing a legal basis for government control and management or for legitimising government actions. Administrative justice, it was argued, entails much more than substantive justice; procedural justice is equally, if not more, important in securing justice and equality for all and in controlling government behaviour (see J Chen, 1998).

In light of the ideological breakthrough in academic discourse since 1992, the 'renewed' discussions (and the third wave of 'liberation of thoughts' since 1996) on the notion of the rule of law offer very little that is new. To define 1996 as a 'landmark', and the 'beginning of a new era', as it is commonly described in the Chinese official media, is to severely overstate the significance of the linguistic changes, even though such changes of terminology may have helped the more cautious scholars to openly accept Western liberal ideas and legal notions. The present debate is best seen as a continuing discourse since 1992. Indeed, the catchwords used in the Chinese discussions of the phrase 'Ruling the Country According to Law', such as 'supremacy of law', 'judicial independence', 'equality before the law', 'separation of powers', 'humanity', and the emphasis on the need for checks and balances, a parliamentary system and the protection of human rights, have all emerged and been extensively used and debated since 1992 (Liu, Li and Li, 1996).

VI ACHIEVEMENTS IN, AND FUNDAMENTAL OBSTACLES TO, THE RULE OF LAW IN PRESENT-DAY CHINA

It is perhaps fair to say that, if 'rule of law' as an official policy has any concrete substance, it remains that '[t]here must be laws for people to follow; these laws must be observed; their enforcement must be strict; and law-breakers must be dealt with' as pronounced in 1978. Indeed, it is seen as the basic reference in the understanding of the 'rule of law' as pursued in China (see 2002 Political Report, Item 2, Section V; see also *People's Daily*, 2002).

In relation to the goals (law-making, observation of law, enforcement of law and sanctions against violation of law), as set out in the above 'rule of law' formulation, it is understandable that the initial emphasis was heavily on law-making in the post-Mao legal reform. To this end, massive law-making programmes were undertaken and their achievement has been impressive if not spectacular. For example, within one five-year term of the Eighth NPC (1992–97), the NPC set itself a target of drafting 152 laws with 125 of them to be guaranteed for adoption. To facilitate such an ambitious task, a massive programme of transplanting foreign laws—in the name of 'internationalising Chinese law' or 'doing things according to international practice' but in a fashion similar to the Qing and Kuo Min Tang (KMT) legal reforms—was restored after an interruption of some 35 years (see J Chen, 1999b). Through such efforts, the majority of the planned laws were adopted and the planned revisions of laws passed. The Ninth NPC (1998–2003) continued this effort: in the space of five years 113 pieces of law, legislative interpretations or decisions were adopted or revised, including a constitutional amendment, the adoption of the Legislation Law, Administrative Reconsideration Law, Trust Law, Securities Law, Contract Law, Government Procurement Law, several revisions of the Criminal Law, revisions of laws on judges, prosecutors and lawyers, and the revision of all principal foreign investment laws as a result of WTO membership compliance requirements (for the full list, see *People's Daily*, 2003c). During that same period, the State Council initiated 50 pieces of law and issued 150 sets of administrative regulations. It also reviewed 756 administrative laws that it had issued by the end of 2002, which resulted in 71 being abolished and 80 declared ineffective. The ministries and commissions under the State Council also reviewed some 2,300 sets of governmental rules, and of these 830 were abolished and 325 revised in accordance with WTO membership requirements (see *People's Daily*, 2003b). Equally, local governments have also reviewed, revised, and sometimes abolished, thousands of local rules (J Chen, 2001). The current, Tenth NPC (2003–08) has plans to enact or revise no fewer than 130 laws so as to ensure that a 'complete socialist legal system' will be established by 2010 (Tenth NPC Legislative Plan). As of June 2004, the NPC and its Standing Committee had in total adopted 323 laws (212 of them currently effective), 138 resolutions and 10 sets of legislative interpretation. The State Council had issued 970 administrative regulations (650 of them currently effective). At the same time, local legislatures at the provincial level had issued more than 10,000 local rules (7,500 of them currently effective), and some 480 sets of autonomous regulations had been issued by the various autonomous regions (X Li, 2004).

In establishing the rule of law in China, however it is understood, no-one denies the need for institutional reform of the politico-legal system. Once again, the achievement in this area should be acknowledged. Indeed, massive measures have been taken in the areas of administrative and judicial reform (see Lam and Cheung, 1998; van Rooij, 2002; Y Li, 2002; J Chen, 2002d). Until very recently, the underlying rationale for administrative reform had been centred around the improvement of bureaucratic productivity and efficiency, rather than accountability. The promulgation of the Administrative Penalty Law in 1996 and the Administrative Permit Law in 2003 began the government's efforts to reduce and restrict powers that might be exercised by administrative authorities, in part as measures to curb widespread corruption and abuse of power. These measures introduce some checks on administrative powers, but not so much in terms of balances. Judicial reform, on the other hand, has been largely ad hoc and experimental. While many measures taken by the Supreme People's Court, the Supreme People's Procuratorate, or their local authorities are indeed innovative and admirable, few have achieved their intended objectives due to the lack of fundamental political reform that cannot be initiated by the judiciary nor carried out without authorisation from the Party (see J Chen, 2002d).

We should not be too dismissive of Chinese legal development and its achievements. However, having law is one thing but having rule of law another. Most importantly, we must not overlook the fundamental flaws in the movement towards establishing a 'socialist' rule of law in China. First, the above 'rule of law' formulation is not without some fundamental flaws: there are no requirements regarding how laws are to be made, whether the rulers are to observe the law, whether enforcement must also be impartial and independent, or how law-breakers are to be dealt with, other than strictly. Even in law-making, the underlying rationale relates more, though not exclusively, to law as an instrument for economic modernisation than as part and parcel of the rule of law per se; this explains why the great majority of the laws and regulations enacted and revised in post-Mao China have been related to the establishment and regulation of a socialist market economy. And, more often than not, there has been a tendency to use the more flexible and ad hoc legislation to deal with specific situations or targets identified for various political and economic campaigns. Thus, under the guidelines for establishing a 'socialist market economy', although Marxism may be out of fashion, 'socialism' is not—at least when it is useful. The adoption of 'Ruling the Country According to Law' does not change these fundamental principles. The phrase 'Ruling the Country

According to Law' in the Chinese Constitution must, therefore, be understood in the context of its co-existence with the Four Fundamental Principles centred around the leadership of the CPC (see J Chen, 1999a: 70–2). In this context, Chinese scholars are rightly concerned that China might end up with a rule by man in the name of the rule of law (D Guo, 1994). Chinese scholars are also rightly concerned that, without firmly and explicitly rejecting the ideology of legal instrumentalism, it would be very difficult for the rule of law to be realised in China (Yu, 1989; H Xie, 1994a).

In light of the massive and very impressive development in law-making and the continuous institutional reform in post-Mao China, a good indication of the actual realisation of the rule of law in China is the implementation and enforcement of law. Despite very admirable efforts by the Chinese judicial institutions, the problems in this area are not minor, but massive and deeply rooted in the fundamental politico-economic system. Legal scholars have no difficulties in identifying many fundamental problems in institutions and in performance by power-bearers (see Chen, Li and Otto, 2002). I myself have summarised the problems in terms of some fundamental contradictions within the Chinese politico-legal system and its practice: politicisation versus professionalisation, judicial independence versus economic fragmentation, and internal efforts versus external constraints (J Chen, 2002d). The tremendous difficulties experienced by Chinese courts in enforcing court judgments or decisions are but one example of such consequences. But the root of these problems is power, or, more precisely, the inability of the judiciary to exercise any checks and balances. One Chinese economist described the problem as the 'privatisation of public powers' (Tang, 2002: 105), to which we may add the 'localisation of power', more often referred to as 'local protectionism' (for detailed discussion on local protectionism in China, see J Chen, 2002d). If, as one Chinese scholar has questioned, the law cannot be independently enforced, it is doubtful whether it is important to have law at all (Zhao, 1994: 5).

The 'privatisation of public powers' is no doubt responsible for the epidemic of largely uncontrollable corruption[11]—commonly referred to by many Chinese people as a cancer in the society and in the political system—in China today (see Yan, 1998; Liu, 2002; Ye, 2002). From the many interviews I have had with Chinese scholars, it seems that many Chinese are now resigned to the proposition that corruption is inevitably part and parcel of social and economic transition and modernisation. This,

[11] According to the OECD, in monetary terms, corruption represented some 3-5% of China's GDP, that is, between US$50–84 billion, and despite significant efforts from the Party and the government, corruption is far from being contained (see OECD, 2005: 101-32, and *The Australian*, 30 September 2005).

however, need not be—at least, there is no evidence to suggest that, should checks and balances have been established in China, corruption would have continued to be so widely spread and deeply rooted. There is no doubt that efforts have been made to deal with the problems of corruption and many high ranking officials have been severely punished, but much of this effort has been made through political campaigns, though using law as a penalty mechanism. Again, from my many interviews conducted in China over many years, it has been clear to me that corruption is far from under control. It is equally clear to me that many Chinese scholars and practitioners agree that the lack of any meaningful mechanism for checks and balances is the greatest obstacle to the fight against corruption.

If we agree that the desire for the rule of law in China stems largely from the sentiment against corruption, and hence the need for checks and balances (and, logically, fundamental political reforms), then the latter is precisely where the fundamental obstacles to the rule of law in China lie and remain to be seriously addressed by the Party and state authorities.

VII SOME CONCLUDING REMARKS

Taking academic discourse in China at face value, one has little difficulty in asserting that the rule of law is emerging from the heavy shadow of the rule of man and rule by law. However, caution should be taken in relation to these theoretical efforts and we must not confuse theoretical efforts among academics with practical reality, for the rule of law—just like the notion of human rights—must first of all be concerned with and related to the daily life of ordinary people. Although it is not very accurate to say that these theoretical debates are abstract, concerning only abstract jurisprudential issues (Dworkin, 2002), it is equally unrealistic to claim that they all address real problems in contemporary social and political life (A Chen, 2000: 163). These academic debates have had some limited success in that some of their theories have been translated into law and institutional reforms, thus leading to some practical achievement, particularly in areas of civil and administrative laws (see J Chen, 1995 and 1998). But overall their success has been limited, and certainly far from leading to the establishment of the supremacy of law, equality and, more importantly, a meaningful degree of judicial independence and checks and balances in the political and legal spheres. Detailed examinations of the extent of academic contribution to legal advancement in the three most important areas for human rights protection and, more generally, for the rule of law (namely criminal law, criminal procedural law and administrative law) reveal that, in all important issues, the resulting laws (or amendments) adopted contained only a number of the proposals advocated by scholars, and then only compromised versions of those proposals (see J Chen, 1997, 1998, and 2002a). In this context, it is equally premature to declare that China has entered the era of the rule of law. We must remember that 'a glass half full' is nevertheless 'a glass half empty'. This having been said, it should not blind us to the fact that China has achieved a great deal in moving towards a society guided and governed by law.

The establishment of checks and balances requires some fundamental reforms in the politico-legal system in the direction of democratisation. This explains why democracy is as appealing to those seeking relief from the arbitrary exercise of power as to those seeking the rule of law (Shapiro, 1994: 2). In the case of China, however, it would be unrealistic to expect any major breakthrough in terms of democratisation, however it is understood, in the foreseeable future (see Lynch, 2005). Though WTO membership requires China to allow foreign investment in state-owned enterprises and reform in the economic system can be expected to deepen, any political or democratic reform which would challenge Party dominance is unlikely to be allowed in the foreseeable future. We must therefore seriously consider the relationship between democracy and the rule of law.

It has been suggested, and appears to be a viewpoint endorsed by Chinese scholars, that the rule of law is legitimate only if it is the product of democratic government, which is supposed to represent the people as a whole (see Orts, 2001: 102; A Chen, 2000: 134). This implies that democracy and the rule of law must be developed 'hand in hand'. This indeed would be ideal. This being so, a sharp separation of the two is not desirable because, on the one hand, without the rule of law democracy will not bring in its desired effect to all the governed, especially the minority groups (which by definition will never have a majority in any legislature). Indeed, recent experience of the 'anti-terrorism' campaigns waged by Western democratic governments, while revealing the weakness of democracy and the vulnerability of the notion of the rule of law, reinforces the importance of the rule of law in democratic societies, as the final bulwark against various draconian laws—often enacted with bipartisan support in the name of protecting personal and national security at the cost of individual civil liberties—whose practice will be played out in the courts of law.[12] On the other hand, the rule of law does not function well without democracy either. A government through law without democracy is at best a government of rule by law, not rule of law. The rule of law necessarily

[12] For various reports on anti-terrorism law being enacted in Western countries and their severe impact on civil liberties and the rule of law requirement (eg, differentiated treatment of terrorist suspects, denial of access to lawyers and judicial oversight, and detention without charge), see Amnesty International: <http://www.amnesty.org>. The website of the UN Security Council's Counter Terrorism Committee (<http://www.un. org/terrorism>) also contains comprehensive materials on this subject. It is worth pointing out that the 'war on terror' has so far been conducted in the absence of an internationally accepted definition of 'terrorism'.

demands certain checks and balances not just in the implementation and enforcement of law, but also the making of law. One must not forget that checks and balances are established through man-made law, that is, the supreme law (constitutions) or ordinary laws. This is not to deny, however, that there are tensions between the two ideals. Indeed, democracy is, at least theoretically, about authorising the elected with the power to rule or infusing the law with the will of the majority, while the rule of law relates to the regulation or control of government and its conduct (Shapiro, 1994: 2; Pan, 2003: 9). This suggests that democracy and the rule of law can be conceptually distinguished, yet they reinforce each other. Thus, for practical purposes, it is not completely impossible to distinguish democracy as an internal constitutional check on political rulers, and the rule of law as an institutional and structural limit on government (Orts, 2001: 88). In other words, the two ideas may develop in different timeframes (Peerenboom, 2002: 513), but not at the expense of one another. Most importantly, neither democracy nor the rule of law makes any sense unless they are centred around the idea of establishing checks and balances. In this, democracy and the rule of law must be assessed by their end results, not the particular forms adopted. After all, in practice democracy has as many variations as the rule of law.

Two recent legal developments in China illustrate well the lack of democracy in law-making and highlight the continuing attitude of treating law as largely a tool for the perceived needs of the ruling élites. One involves an amendment to the 1997 Criminal Law while the second relates to the recent revision of the state Constitution.

First, as mentioned above, many Western countries have recently enacted draconian laws in the name of 'anti-terrorism' and in violation of basic civil liberties and minimum rule of law requirements. In many countries, though not all, such laws have only been enacted after considerable debate among the citizens and some of them will sooner or later be challenged in a court of law. In China, however, such a law was enacted very quickly and without any public consultation at all.[13] The relevant Amendment significantly expands the scope of the crime of endangering public safety, as well as the application of the death penalty. Once again, it is a naked use of law as a government instrument to suit its own perceived needs. As a result, it is now much easier for the authorities to suppress and punish various activities in the name of 'anti-terrorism' (see IFEX 2003). Indeed, one

[13] This was done through an amendment to the 1997 Criminal Law, adopted by the 25th Meeting of the 9th NPC on 29 December 2001. It is not suggested here that a more democratic law-making process would necessarily ensure that draconian laws will not be adopted. However, a democratic process does ensure that the potential dangers of such laws in undermining the rule of law and the protection of civil liberties are better understood and, hence, safeguards (such as a sunset clause) are incorporated into the law.

prominent US-based Chinese dissident has already been sentenced to life imprisonment for engaging in 'terrorist' activities, and other actions have been taken by the authorities in labelling 'separatists' as 'terrorists' in the Xinjiang Uighur Autonomous Region (see BBC News, 2003; Becquelin, 2004; Amnesty International, 2004).

The second example of the lack of democracy in law-making is the recent revision of the state Constitution. Although the NPC is the only authority having the power to revise the Constitution, the Party apparently sees no problems in establishing its own secret committee to make 'recommendations' for constitutional revision. The Committee had apparently been established not long after the 16th CPC Congress in December 2002, but we only knew of its existence from academic journals and, from these journals, we also knew that a small group of selected experts were consulted on the revision of the Constitution in June 2003. A formal announcement by the Politburo in August 2003 on the convening of a plenary session of the Central Committee of the CPC to be held in October 2003 again failed to mention the existence of such a committee, even though it said that the plenary session would discuss the proposals for constitutional reform.[14] As in the previous constitutional revision, the Party made its 'Suggestions on Amending Certain Contents of the Constitution' to the NPC, and the NPC dutifully and faithfully adopted the 'recommendations' from the Party (the Standing Committee adopted them in December 2003, and the full NPC did so in March 2004). In this whole exercise, the full text of the Party 'Suggestions' was only issued to the public on 22 December 2003, leaving little time for discussion and debate before they were finally adopted by the NPC on 14 March 2004. While the merit of the various amendments is a separate subject-matter for academic debate (see J Chen, 2004), the process is clearly non-democratic. If the people have no right to participate in such fundamentally important political matters, it is perhaps unrealistic, if not insulting, to tell the people that they enjoy democracy and the rule of law.

A further query that needs to be addressed is whether I have been too harsh in my assessment of Chinese legal development by imposing Western values upon the Chinese legal system. I believe that there is a need for cultural sensitivity in the study of laws and legal development in different cultural settings, but the movement towards the rule of law in China and the assessment of it should be made on the basis of a commonly understood conception of the rule of law, one capable of embracing the core meanings of the rule of law widely accepted among Chinese and Western scholars and practitioners. This is to say that any use of an

[14] These announcements were published in the *People's Daily* (*Renmin Ribao*) 12 August 2003, 1.

existing label must correspond to the commonly understood tenets of the label, even though such tenets may be minimal and contain variations. True, the spectacular economic growth in China in the last 25 years or so in the absence of a genuine rule of law and, in particular, in the absence of a clear system of property rights, challenges the notion that a market economy goes hand in hand with the rule of law. At the same time, the seemingly unstoppable and ever-increasing corruption phenomenon, despite a series of efforts by the Party and the government to curb it, and increasingly severe punishments imposed on corruption, points up the desperate need for checks and balances, independent judicial oversight of government actions, and equality of law, all of which are essential ingredients of a genuine rule of law. It is fine to call the Chinese legal practice 'Chinese socialist legality', in accordance with whatever that is understood to be, but if China declares that it is moving towards the establishment of the rule of law—a label largely originated and developed in the West—then a commonly-understood core meaning of that label must apply. We should not deny China the right to use that label, and we should accommodate and encourage a 'home-grown' concept built upon the existing understanding of the rule of law in China. However, a completely new 'Asian' or 'Chinese' conception that is so alien as to render any comparison and assessment meaningless is not a helpful solution. Indeed, a prominent Chinese scholar has rightly pointed out that, with the official 'rule of law' version emphasising the definitional word 'socialist', and hence one-party domination, there is a danger of '*socialist* rule of law' being used to reject any possibility of the rule of law having any universal value and the 'rule of law *with Chinese characteristics*' being used to reject any Western theories and practice of the rule of law (Liang, 2000: 1). Put simply, while we should not impose Western liberal ideas and values on a wholesale scale upon China or any other non-Western countries, we need not be too ready to discard the idea that some values are universal. After all, no Chinese would ever deny the truth that 'power without checks and balances is destined to corrupt'.[15]

Finally, what is the exact status of the rule of law in China? In light of the rapid legislative development, continuing improvement of the legal institutions, the increasing awareness of law and rights among citizens, and the ever-vigorous academic debates among Chinese intellectuals, it is perhaps fair to say that a foundation for establishing the rule of law has been laid in China, and the old foundations supporting an authoritarian state have been undermined and challenged by the accumulated forces brought about by the various legal and economic developments in the last

[15] A paraphrase of Lord Acton's famous dictum that has been widely used by Chinese scholars. See *People's Daily*, 1997a.

two decades. The actual establishment of the rule of law in China will be a long process, at least until the Party agrees that political reforms towards democratisation and the establishment of checks and balances work more with, rather than against, its interests and the interests of society in general.

BIBLIOGRAPHY

10th Anniversary Symposium (1992): 'Further Emancipating Minds and Making Great Efforts for the Prosperity of Legal Science – A Discussion in Commemorating the 10th Anniversary of the Re-establishment of the China Law Society' 4 *Legal Science in China* (*Zhongguo Faxue*) 13.

1992 Political Report: Jiang Zemin (1992) 'Accelerating the Reform, the Opening to the Outside World and the Drive for Modernisation, so as to Achieve Great Successes in Building Socialism with Chinese Characteristics. A Political Report to the 14th Congress of the CPC' *People's Daily* (*Renmin Ribao*) (overseas edition) 21 October 1992, 1–3.

1997 Political Report: Jiang Zemin (1997) 'Holding High the Great Banner of Deng Xiaoping Theory for an All-round Advancement of the Cause of Building Socialism with Chinese Characteristics to the 21st Century. A Political Report to the 15th National Congress of the Communist Party of China' *People's Daily* (*Renmin Ribao*) 25 September 1997, 1.

2002 Political Report: Jiang Zemin (2002) 'Building a Well-off Society in an All-Round Way and Create a New Situation in Building Socialism with Chinese Characteristics – a Political Report delivered by Jiang Zemin at the 16th Party Congress, 8 November 2002'. A Chinese version is available from the People's Daily at: <http://www.peopledaily.com.cn/GB/shizheng/16/20021117/868414.html>, last accessed 15 November 2006. An English text was available from *China Daily*, Internet edition, 6 December 2002 at: <http://www.chinadaily.com.cn/highlights/party16/news/1118full .htm>, last accessed 12 June 2002 (copy on file with author).

AMNESTY INTERNATIONAL (2004) *People's Republic of China: Uighurs fleeing persecution as China wages its 'war on terror'* AI Index: ASA 17/021/2004.

ANTONS, CHRISTOPH (ed) (2003) *Law and Development in East and Southeast Asia* (RoutledgeCurzon, London/New York).

BBC NEWS, 2003: BBC NEWS WORLD EDITION, 'Chinese dissident [Wang Bingzhang] jailed for life' 10 February 2003, available at: <http://news.bbc.co.uk/2/hi/asia-pacific/2743445.stm>, last accessed 15 November 2006.

BEACH, SOPHIE (2004) 'In China: New Journalism, and New Threats' (Committee to Protect Journalists: Special reports from around the world), available at: <http://www.cpj.org/ Briefings/2004/China_8_04/ China_8_04.html>, last accessed 15 November 2006.

BECQUELIN, NICOLAS (2004) 'Criminalizing ethnicity: political repression in Xinjiang' [2004] 1 China Rights Forum 39–46. Also available at: <http://iso.hrichina.org/fs/ downloadables/pdf/downloadableresources/ b1_Criminalizing1.2004.pdf?revision_id=8744>, last accessed 15 November 2006.

CHEN, ALBERT (2000) 'Towards a Legal Enlightenment: Discussions in Contemporary China on the Rule of Law' 17 *UCLA Pacific Basin Law Journal* 125.

CHEN, JIANFU (1995) *From Administrative Authorisation to Private Law* (Martinus Nijhoff Publishers, Dordrecht/Boston/London).

—— (1997) 'A Moderate Step in a Right Direction – The revision of the Criminal Procedural Law in the PRC' [1997] 3 (1) *Journal of Chinese and Comparative Law* 139.

—— (1998) 'The Development and Conception of Administrative Law in the PRC' [1998] 16 (2) *Law in Context* 72.

—— (1999a) 'The Revision of the Constitution in the PRC – Conceptual Evolution of "Socialism with Chinese Characteristics"' [1999] 24 *China Perspectives* 66.

—— (1999b) 'Market Economy and Internationalisation of Civil and Commercial Law in the PRC' in Kanishka Jayasuriya (1999).

—— (2001) 'China and the WTO: Legal Implications and Challenges' [2001] 4 (11) *China Law Update* 7.

—— (2002a) 'A Criminal Justice System for a New Millennium?' in E B Vermeer and I d'Hooghe (eds) *China's Legal Reforms and Their Political Limits* (Curzon Press, London).

—— (2002b) 'An Emerging New Legal Framework on Foreign Trade' [2002] 5 (4) *China Law Update* 7.

—— (2002c) 'Implementation of Law as a Politico-Legal Battle in China' [2002] 43 *China Perspectives* 26.

—— (2002d) 'Mission Impossible: Judicial Efforts to Enforce Civil Judgements and Rulings' in Chen, Li, and Otto (2002).

—— (2003) 'Policy as Law and Law as Policy: The Role of Law in China's Development Strategy' in Antons (2003).

—— (2004) 'The Revision of the Constitution in the PRC: A great leap forward or a symbolic gesture?' [2004] 53 *China Perspectives* 15.

CHEN, JIANFU and KE, SUIWA (2000) *China Criminal Law: Commentary and Legislation* (CCH Asia, Singapore).

CHEN, JIANFU; LI, YUWEN; and OTTO, JAN MICHIEL (eds) (2002) *Implementation of Law in the People's Republic of China* (Kluwer Law International, London/Boston/The Hague).

CHEN, SHIXI (1994) 'Our Legislative Trend in the 1990s' *Guangming Daily* (*Guangming Ribao*) 9 March 1994, 5.

CHEN, SHOUYI (1988) 'A Review of Thirty Years of Legal Studies in New China' 2 *Journal of Chinese Law* 181.

CHINA LAW SOCIETY (1995) 'Summary of the 1992 Annual Conference of the Institute of Civil and Economic Law of the China Law Society' [1995] 5 *Legal Science in China (Zhongguo Faxue)* 119.

CIVIL LAW SYMPOSIUM (1993) 'A Summary Report of the Symposium on New Topics for Civil and Economic Law in a Socialist Market Economy' [1993] 4 *Legal Science in China* (*Zhongguo Faxue*) 119.

CLARKE, DONALD C (2002) 'Statement Before the US-China Security Review Commission', Washington DC, 18 January 2002 (copy on file with the author).

COHEN, JEROME A (2001) 'Opening Statement Before the First Public Hearing of the US-China Security Review Commission', Washington, DC, 14 June 2001 (copy on file with author).

CPC CONSTITUTION REVISION EXPLANATION (2002): 'Explanations on amendment of the CPC Constitution', *China Daily*, available at: <http://www.chinadaily.com.cn/highlights/ party16/news/ 1118explain.htm>, last accessed 6 December 2002 (copy on file with author). A Chinese version of the Explanation was available from *People's Daily*, <http://www.peopledaily.com.cn/shizheng/19/ 20021118/869077.htm>, last accessed 19 November 2002 (copy on file with author).

DENG, XIAOPING (1984) 'Implement the Policy of Readjustment, Ensure Stability and Unity' in *Selected Works of Deng Xiaoping (1975-82)* (Foreign Languages Press, Beijing).

DWORKIN, RONALD (1985) *A Matter of Principle* (Harvard University Press, Cambridge).

DWORKIN, RONALD (2002) 'Taking Rights Seriously in Beijing' *The New York Review of Books*, 26 September 2002, 64–7, republished in (2002) 3 (7) *Perspectives*, available at <http://www.oycf.org/ Perspectives/19_123102/takingRights.htm>, last accessed 2 October 2003 (copy on file with author).

EDITORIAL GROUP (ed) (1981) *A Collection on Debates on the Question of Rule of Law and Rule of Man* (*fazhi yu renzhi wenti daolunji*) (Press of the Masses, Beijing).

FANG, SHAOKUN (1993) 'On Correcting Civil Legislation Deficiencies' [1993] 1 *Legal Science in China* (*Zhongguo Faxue*) 30.

FINNIS, JOHN (1979) *Natural Law and Natural Rights* (Clarendon Press, Oxford).

FOSTER, FRANCES HOAR (1982) 'Codification in Post-Mao China' [1982] 30 *American Journal of Comparative Law* 395.

FRIEND, JAMES HUGO (2000) Foreword to 'The Rocky Road towards the Rule of Law in China: 1979–2000' [2000] 20 *Northwestern Journal of International Law and Business* 369.

FULLER, LON (1969) *The Morality of Law* (Yale University Press, New Haven).

GAN, ZANGCHUAN (1991) 'How to Secure the Legitimacy of Reform – From Reliance on Policy to Reliance on Law' [1991] 6 *Studies in Law* (*Faxue Yanjiu*) 3.

GAO, LU (1993) 'The Emergence of the Notion of "Socialist Market Economy"' [1993] 1 *Xinhua Digest* (*Xinhau Wenzhai*) 40.

GLAZEBROOK, SUSAN (1999) 'The Role of the Rule of Law in the Asian Economic Crisis', available at: <http://www.ipba.org/membersonly/papers/documents/glazebrook.pdf>, last accessed 15 November 2006.

GU, ANGRAN (1989) *Socialist Legal System and Legislative Work (Shehui Zhuyi Fazhi He Lifa Gongzuo) (China University of Political Science and Law Press, Beijing).*

Guangming Daily (1996): 'The Ninth Five Year National Economic and Social Development Plan and the Outline of Goals by Year 2010' *Guangming Daily (Guangming Ribao)* 20 March 1996, 1.

GUO, DAOXU (1994) 'Market Economy and the Changes in Legal Theory and Legal Thought' [1994] 2 *Jurisprudence* (*Faxue*) 2.

GUO, DAOHUI; LI, BUYUN; and HAO, TIECHUAN (eds) (1998) *A Record of the Contention on the Science of Law in Contemporary China* (*zhongguo dangdai faxue zhengming shilu*) (Hunan People's Press, Changsha).

HE, WEIFANG (2003) 'Difficulties in Establishing Rule of Law and Solutions' available at: <http://www.sinoliberal.com/hwf/hwf2003010502.htm>, last accessed 6 March 2003.

HUTCHINSON, ALLAN C and MONAHAN, PATRICK (eds) (1987) *The Rule of Law: Ideal or Ideology* (Carswell, Toronto/Calgary/Vancouver).

IFEX (2003): International Freedom of Expression eXchange, 'UN Rights Experts Urge Respect for Civil Liberties in Fight Against Terrorism' (a joint statement of the Special Rapporteurs/Representatives, Experts and Chairpersons of the Working Groups of the Special Procedures of the United Nations Commission on Human Rights) issued 30 June 2003, available at: <http://www.ifex.org/en/content/view/full/52000/>, last accessed 15 November 2006.

JAYASURIYA, KANISHKA (ed) (1999) *Law, Capitalism and Power in Asia: The Rule of Law and Legal Institutions* (Routledge, London/New York).

JURISPRUDENTIAL DEBATE (1991): 'Jurisprudential Debate on the Relationship Between Rights and Duties' [1991] 4 *Xinhua Digest* (*Xinhua Wenzhai*) 16.

KEITH, RONALD C (1994) *China's Struggle for the Rule of Law* (St. Martin's Press, New York).

KELLER, PERRY (1989) 'Legislation in the People's Republic of China' [1989] 23 (3) *University of British Colombia Law Review* 643.

LAM, L and CHEUNG K (1998) 'The Rise and Challenge of Administrative Reform in China: Post-Mao and Beyond' in J Y S Cheng (ed) (1998) *China in the Post-Deng Era* (The Chinese University of Press, Hong Kong).

LI, BUYUN (1998) *Towards a Rule of Law* (*Zouxiang Fazhi*) (Hunan People's Press, Changsha).

LI, MAOGUAN (1995) 'The Legal Controversy Concerning the Separation of Public and Private Law' [1995] 22 *Seeking Truth* (*Qiushi*) 44.

LI, XINHUI (2004) 'Fifty Years of Remarkable Legislative Process' *Legal Daily* (*Fazhi Ribao*) 14 October 2004, 14.

LI, YUWEN (2002) 'Court Reform in China: Problems, Progress and Prospects' in Chen, Li and Otto (2002).

LIANG, ZHIPING (2000) 'Rule of Law: Institutional Construction in Periods of Social Transition' originally published in [2000] 2 Studies in Contemporary China (*Dandai Zhongguo Yanjiu*), reproduced on the Chinese University of Hong Kong website: <http://www.usc.chhk.edu.hk/wk_wzdetails.asp?id=243>, last accessed 30 October 2003.

LIN, CHENGDONG (1997) 'The Development of Democracy Must Be Closely Linked with the Improvement of Legal System' *People's Daily* (*Renmin Ribao*) 18 October 1997, 3.

LIN, JIE (1994) 'A Question on the Proposition "Market Economy Is an Economy Under the Rule of Law"' [1994] 1 *Legal Science in China* (*Zhongguo Faxue*) 68.

LIU, HAINIAN; LI, BUYUAN and LI, LIN (eds) (1996) *To Rule the Country according to Law and to Establish a Socialist Country Ruled by Law* (*Yifa Zhiguo Jianshe Shehui Zhuyi Fazhi Guojia*) (Press of Chinese Legal System, Beijing).

LIU, JINGHUA (1995) 'Globalisation: An Historical Process Full of Paradoxes' [1995] 1 *Pacific Studies* (*Taipingyan Xuebao*) 70.

LIU, S and WU, Q (eds) (1986) *China's Socialist Economy: an Outline History (1949–1982)* (Beijing Review Press, Beijing).

LIU, SHENGPING *et al (1993)* 'Market Economy and Changes in Legal Ideologies' [1993] 4 *Legal Science in China* (*Zhongguo Faxue*) 9.

LIU, YU (2002) *The Struggle Between Red and Black: A Record of Anti-Corruption in the People's Republic* (*Hong yu he de jiaolian: gongheguo fangfu shilu*) (Qingdao Press, Qingdao).

LU, YUN (1994) 'The Transformation of Legal Models: A Deep Revolutionary Change' [1994] 1 *Legal Science in China* (*Zhongguo Faxue*) 27.

LUBMAN, STANLEY (2002a) 'Keynote Speech' (delivered at the international conference *Legal and Political Reform in the People's Republic of China,* Lund, Sweden, 3–4 June 2002) (copy on file with author).

—— (2002b) 'Statement submitted to the Congressional-Executive Commission on China, February 6, 2002', available at: <http://www.cecc.gov.papers.hearings/020702> (copy on file with author).

LYNCH, DAVID J (2005) 'Retreat in China', *USA Today* (10 August), available at: <http://www. usatoday.com/news/opinion/editorials/2005-08-10-forum-china_x.htm.>, last accessed 15 November 2006.

MARKET ECONOMY SYMPOSIUM (1992): 'Market Economy and the Modernisation of a Legal System – Speeches Given at the Symposium on a Market Economy and the Modernisation of the Legal System' *[1992] 6 Studies in Law (Faxue Yanjiu) 1.*

MIN, XIANWEI (1994) 'Socialist Market Economy Is Naturally an Economy Under the Rule of Law' [Special Issue, 1994] *Journal of Shandong Normal University* (*Shandong Shifan Daxuebao*) 93.

NEUMANN, FRANZ (1986) *The Rule of Law: Political Theory and the Legal System in Modern Society* (Berg, Leamington Spa/Dover).

OECD (2005), *Governance in China* (OECD Publishing, Paris).

ORTS, ERIC W (2001) 'The Rule of Law in China' [2001] 34 *Vanderbilt Journal of Transnational Law* 43.

OTTO, J M; POLAK, M V; CHEN, J; and LI, Y (eds) (2000) *Law-making in the People's Republic of China* (Kluwer Law International, London/Boston/The Hague).

PAN, WEI (2003) 'Toward a Consultative Rule of Law Regime in China' [2003] 12 (34) *Journal of Contemporary China* 3.

PEERENBOOM, RANDALL (2002) *China's Long March toward Rule of Law* (Cambridge University Press, New York).

PENG, ZHEN (1984) 'Several Issues Concerning Socialist Legality' in *Selected Materials on Introduction to Law* (*Faxue Gailun Ziliao Xuanbian*) (Publishing House of Law, Beijing).

People's Daily (1997a) 'The Road to Rule of Law – A Summary of Legal Construction and Democratic Developments since the 14th Congress' *People's Daily* (*Renmin Ribao*) 3 September 1997, 9.

People's Daily (1997b) 'To Greatly Push the Process of Ruling a Country according to Law' *People's Daily* (*Renmin Ribao*) Editorial, 17 October 1997, 9.

People's Daily (2002) 'There Must Be Some "References" for Implementation of Law' *People's Daily* (*Renmin Ribao*) 20 February 2002, 9.

People's Daily (2003a) 'Top ten issues selected by netizens for the NPC to address' *People's Daily* (*Renmin Ribao*) 26 February 2003, Chinese Internet edition <http://www. peopledaily.com.cn/GB/it/20030226/931243.html>, last accessed 15 November 2006.

People's Daily (2003b) 'State Council Government Work Report delivered to the First Session of the Tenth NPC on 5 March 2003' *People's Daily* (Renmin Ribao) 20 March 2003, 1.

People's Daily (2003c) 'Work Report of the Standing Committee, delivered to the First Session of the Tenth NPC on 10 March 2003' (Appendix I) *People's Daily* (*Renmin Ribao*) 22 March 2003, 1.

POLITICAL REPORT BACKGROUND 'Great Practice, Bright Chapter – the Birth of the Political Report of the 14th Congress of the Party' *People's Daily* (*Renmin Ribao*) (overseas edition) 24 October 1992, 1 and 3.

PROJECT GROUP (1993): Project Group (Law Institute, Chinese Academy of Social Sciences), 'Some Theoretical Considerations and Practical Suggestions Regarding the Establishment of a Legal System for a Socialist Market Economy' 6 *Studies in Law* (*Faxue Yanjiu*) 19.

QIAO, SHI 'Speech at the 2nd Session of the 8th NPC, delivered by Qiao Shi on 22 March 1994' *Economic Daily* (*Jingji Ribao*) 23 March 1994, 1.

RAWLS, JOHN (1971) *A Theory of Justice* (Harvard University Press, Cambridge, MA).

RAZ, JOSEPH (1979) *The Authority of Law* (Clarendon Press, Oxford).

SHAPIRO, IAN (ed) (1994) *The Rule of Law* (New York University Press, New York/London).

SUN, GUOHUA and ZENG, BING (1996) 'On the Definition of Law by Vyshinsky' [1996] 2 *Jurists* (*Faxue Jia*) 38.

TANG, XIAOTIAN (2002) '"Strictly Rule the Party" and the Constitutional Litigation' [2002] 2 *Journal of Jiangsu Administrative College* (*Jiangsu Xingzhen Xueyuan Xuebao*) 104.

TENTH NPC LEGISLATIVE PLAN: 'Legislative plan for the Tenth NPC emerged' available on the website of the Legislative Office of the State Council: <http://www.chinalaw.gov.cn>, last accessed 7 July 2003.

The Australian (2005) 'Graft a partner of Chinese boom' *The Australian* 30 September 2005, 10.

TIAN, J (1999) 'Explanation on the Constitutional Amendment Bill' *People's Daily* (*Renmin Ribao*) 9 March 1999, 7.

TURNER, KAREN G; FEINERMAN, JAMES V; and GUY, R KENT (eds) (2000) *The Limits of the Rule of Law in China* (University of Washington Press, Seattle & London).

VAN ROOIJ, BENJAMIN (2002) 'China's System of Public Administration', in Chen, Li and Otto (2002).

WALKER, GEOFFREY DE Q (1988) *The Rule of Law: Foundation of Constitutional Democracy* (Melbourne University Press, Melbourne).

WANG, CHENGGUANG and LIU, WEN (1993) 'Market Economy and the Distinction between Public and Private Law' [1993] 4 *Legal Science in China* (*Zhongguo Faxue*) 28.

WANG, JIAFU ET AL (1996) 'On the Rule of Law' [1996] 2 *Studies in Law* (*Faxue Yanjiu*) 3.

WEN, ZHENGBANG (1995) 'Some Legal and Philosophical Thoughts on Market Economy' [1995] 4 *Legal System and Social Development* (*Fazhi Yu Shehui Fazhang*) 1.

XIA, YONG (2000) 'What is the Rule of Law: Source, Precept and Value' [2000] 2 *Public Law Review* (*Gongfa*) 1.

XIAO, YANG (1994) *Market Economy and Legal Construction* (Publishing House of Law, Beijing).

XIE, GUISHENG (1994) 'Market Economy and the Separation of Public and Private Law' [1994] 1 *Studies in Finance* (*Caimao Yanjiu*) 62.

XIE, HUAISHI (1993) 'On Establishing a Civil-Economic Law System Appropriate to the Needs of Socialist Market Economy' [1993] 1 *Studies in Law* (*Faxue Yanjiu*) 12.

XIE, HUI (1994a) 'An Analysis and Comment on Legal Instrumentalism' [1994] 1 *Legal Science in China* (*Zhongguo Faxue*) 50.

—— (1994b) 'From a Planned Economy to a Market Economy: A Revolution in Legal Theory' [1994] 4 *Gansu Journal of Theoretical Research* (*Gansu Lilun Xuekang*) 53.

XUE, JU and WANG, JIAFU (1997) 'Towards Ruling the Country according to Law' *People's Daily* (*Renmin Ribao*) 1 November 1997, 9.

YAN, SHI (ed) (1998), *Twenty Years of Anti-Corruption in China* (*zhongguo fangfu ershi nian*), (Helongjian People's Press, Herbin).

YANG, JINYU (2001) 'Accession to the WTO and Legal Construction in Our Country', being a seminar presented to the 24 Session of the Standing Committee of the Ninth NPC, 27 October 2001, available at: <http://www.people.om.cn/GB/14576/15097/2369614. html>, last accessed 8 November 2004.

YE, FENG (2002) 'The Chinese Procuratorates and the Anti-Corruption Campaigns in the PRC' in Chen, Li and Otto (2002).

YU, XINGZHONG (1989) 'Legal Pragmatism in the People's Republic of China' [1989] 3 *Journal of Chinese Law* 29.

ZHANG, JUNHAO (1994) 'Market System and Private Law in China' [1994] 6 *Journal of China University of Political Science and Law* (*Zhangfa Luntan*) 34.

ZHANG, WENXIAN (1993) 'Three Points on Market Economy and Legal Construction' [1993] 3 *Legal Science in China* (*Zhongguo Faxue*) 19.

—— (1995) 'Market-oriented Economy and the Spirit of Modern Law' (paper presented to the 1995 International Sociological Association Conference, Tokyo, 1–4 August 1995) (copy on file with the author).

ZHANG, YUXIN (2003) 'Improving the Legal System to Protect the Opening to the Outside', available at: <http://www.fdi.gov/cn/common/info.jsp?id=ABC00000000000012234>, last accessed 8 November 2004.

ZHAO, SANYING (1994) 'On Rule of Law in Market Economy' *Economic Daily* (*Jingji Ribao*) 2 May 1994, 5.

ZHOU, YONGKUN (1993) 'Market Economy Demands Equality in Legislation' [1993] 4 *Legal Science in China* (*Zhongguo Faxue*) 16.

ZHU, SULI (1997) 'Modernisation of China and the Rule of Law in the 20th Century', available at: <http://www.usa.cuhk.edu.hk/wk.asp>, last accessed 6 September 2005.

PART 3:

ADMINISTRATIVE REFORM AND DECENTRALISATION

9

Between Global Forces and Local Politics: Decentralisation and Reorganisation of Village Government in Indonesia

FRANZ AND KEEBET VON BENDA-BECKMANN

I INTRODUCTION

DECENTRALISATION IS CURRENTLY regarded as one of the most important means to create more democratic societies and transparent and accountable government accessible to citizens.[1] It is expected to lead to political participation and to enable regional or local communities to have a stronger say over their own affairs that reflects their interests and aspirations. It has become a central objective in the world-wide movement to bring about the good governance that is encouraged by the World Bank and other important donor agencies, and by non-governmental organisations (NGOs) and citizen initiatives. There is a large body of literature on the topic, yet little systematic research has been done on how it works out at lower levels of political organisation. Indonesia, which has embarked on a 'big bang'-style decentralisation (Asia Research Centre, 2001: 18), after the fall of the autocratic Suharto regime in 1998, offers an excellent opportunity to study these processes.

This chapter offers the results of a long-term study on how decentralisation operates in the province of West Sumatra, where we have followed the

[1] Asia Research Centre (2001). Bünte (2002) gives a good discussion of the various elements of state organisation that are summarised under the umbrella concept of decentralisation. See Rösel and Von Trotha (1999) and Rüland (1993) for a critique of decentralisation policies and discourses. On Indonesia, see also Holland (1999), Linnan (1999), Malley (1999), Manor (1999), Rüland (2000), UNDP and Government of Germany (1999), Aspinall and Fealy (2003), Schulte-Nordholt and Asnan (2003) and Kingsbury and Aveling (2003).

development since it began in 1999.[2] West Sumatra has been one of the regions to be most actively engaged in decentralisation in Indonesia. Moreover, in addition to the Indonesia-wide reorganisation of the administrative and financial relationships between the centre, the provinces and the districts, West Sumatra has used decentralisation to embark on a far-reaching reorganisation of the village government that forms the lowest administrative unit of the state organisation. This reorganisation is characterised by a return to the 'traditional Minangkabau village' or *nagari,* following a period from 1983 when smaller essentially administrative units or *desa* had been the lowest administrative unit of the state administration. Looking at the process of decentralisation from its inception and over a longer period of time provides insights into the dilemmas it poses at various levels of the state administration and in the local responses. What emerges are highly diverse and contested processes with as yet uncertain outcomes that do not correspond with the optimistic picture associated with decentralisation policies, nor with the pessimistic expectations of the critics. We argue that the political and economic relationships between the new villages and higher administrative levels have changed considerably in West Sumatra, despite the uncertainties accompanying the process. While decentralisation was given shape through 'top-down' processes, it was also actively taken up by lower level political organisations. In villages that have actively responded to the new opportunities, it has led to a wider participation by the village population. At the same time, it has led to the re-emergence of social differences rooted in traditional or customary Minangkabau law, called *adat* or *adat law*. The West Sumatran experience also shows that the new village organisation has to be understood against the background of shifting relationships between state, *adat* and Islamic notions of legitimacy of political offices and of representation. Ever since Minangkabau was Islamised in the sixteenth century, there have been tensions between Minangkabau *adat* and its matrilineal institutions and the *syari'ah*, called *syarak* in Minangkabau, with its patrilineally-biased blueprint for social organisation. These relationships have shaped the ways in which notions of decentralisation, democracy and participation have been taken up at local level. In this process, decentralisation—and the '*kembali ke nagari*' or 'return to the *nagari*' in particular—has increased the significance of both *adat* and western principles of democracy.

[2] Our research was carried out in co-operation with Andalas University in Padang. We gratefully acknowledge the help and stimulating suggestions of Alfan Miko MA, Erwin MA, Prof Dr Syahmunir, Prof Dr Syofyan Thalib, MA, Dr Takdir Rahmadi, Tasman SH and the late Prof Dr Aziz Saleh Narullah Dt. Parpatiah nan Tuo SH, MA. We also thank Leontien Visser and Christoph Antons for comments. For more detailed information, see F and K von Benda-Beckmann (2001a).

We first give a brief overview of the decentralisation policy at national level, followed by a sketch of the historical background of the *nagari* and village government in West Sumatra. We then trace the processes that led to the adoption of a provincial regulation on village government, and show how this framework was elaborated in more specific regulations at district and village levels that formed the new institutional structure for village governance. Then follows a description of the social processes through which villages were reconstituted and village governments formed. Although information on economic decentralisation is still scarce, we shall describe the emerging trends in the relationship between districts and the newly-formed villages.

II DECENTRALISATION IN INDONESIA

Decentralisation as a policy objective is not new in Indonesia. The *Deutsche Gesellschaft für Technische Zusammenarbeit* (GTZ, German Technical Co-operation, an agency of the German Ministry of Home Affairs) has been advising the central government on this issue since 1992. In 1995 President Suharto set the issue on the agenda of national politics and initiated a pilot project in 26 districts (see Bünte, 2002; Holland, 1999; and Linnan (1999). These first attempts, however, were confined to purely administrative decentralisation and did not involve a restructuring of political rights. Moreover, the central ministries did not cede any of their authority (Bünte, 2002: 86).

Since 1998, Indonesia has embarked upon a political and legal process of restructuring its state administration.[3] The greater political freedom and the adoption of a renewed and arguably far stronger policy of decentralisation resulted from a combination of external and internal factors. In the past international financial institutions believed economic development and a stable political system were possible in an autocratic political structure, and that national and international financial relations could be dealt with adequately without political restructuring. But in the 1990s the World Bank and the IMF reconsidered their lending policies, and adopted a policy in which sustainable ecology and good governance were treated as preconditions for a well-functioning economy (F von Benda-Beckmann, 1994). During the late 1990s Indonesia's economic and fiscal crisis had become so desperate that the government finally had to accept the advice and conditionalities of World Bank and IMF who made financial and

[3] This has attracted much attention in Indonesian politics and in (inter)national academic debates. See Usman (2001), Hidayat (2001), Booth (2001), Bünte (2002) and Anwar (2001). The *Decentralisation Newsletter* of the GTZ provides regular information on decentralisation, available at: <http://www.gtzsfdm.or.id>, last accessed 15 November 2006.

judicial reform—as well as democracy, human rights and decentralisation—a condition for financial support (see Bünte, 2002). This involved a series of far-reaching political, administrative and judicial changes as well as a reorganisation of the public and private economic sectors.

Calls for more democracy, good governance and human rights had also increased during the 1990s via foreign governmental organisations, such as the GTZ, the United States Agency for International Development (USAID), the Australian Agency for International Development (AUSAID), and NGOs such as the Ford Foundation. The bilateral donor agencies joined forces under a newly established umbrella of the United Nations Development Program (UNDP) 'partnership for governance'. These agencies not only advise the central government, but also operate at regional and district levels, often co-operating with Indonesian NGOs.[4] Such activities tie the external to internal pressures on Indonesia. Indonesian NGOs, many of them internationally well-connected, had long fought for greater democracy, as had previous generations of politicians and citizens (Uhlin, 1997). After 1998 there was suddenly more room for political activism and there were more well-endowed foreign donor agencies who had not only the capacity but also the will to support these activities financially and through technical and intellectual advice. These help organise and finance seminars and training sessions, at which the meaning of concepts or slogans—such as 'good governance', 'development from below', 'community participation', 'transparency' and 'accountability'—is explained and their importance for the reform stressed to local politicians and administrators at provincial and district levels. Apart from these externally-generated pressures for more democracy and the curbing of corruption, there were also pressures from the regions themselves, especially from resource-rich regions, for greater political and economic autonomy vis-à-vis the central government.

In 1999 the Indonesian government enacted two major pieces of decentralisation legislation. One (Law 22 of 1999) deals with the decentralisation of the administrative structure. The other (Law 25, 1999) rearranges the financial relations and redistributes revenues and taxes between the central government and the more autonomous regions. The laws name the provinces and the districts and towns as the new autonomous regions, but the focus is clearly on the districts and towns. The provinces have been deliberately put into a relatively weak position with little fiscal autonomy, for fear of secession of powerful and rich provinces (see Usman, 2001: 4). Some of the earlier centralised powers have been transferred to the districts and towns, though there is disagreement about

[4] For a good overview of all foreign and international donor activities, see GTZ (2001).

the precise scope and some of the powerful and wealthy ministries offer strong resistance. In the new structure, only five major central ministries were to be maintained: Foreign Policy, Monetary and Fiscal Policy, Justice, Religious Affairs, and Defence. In addition, some other services and functions were retained at the central level, such as national administration, national macro-economic development planning, the policy for strategic technological development, the development of human resources, and national resource conservation. The other ministries at central level were to be dissolved, and their regional offices transformed and fused with the administrative civil services (*DINAS*) of the regions. The sub-districts (*Kecamatan*) have been dissolved as separate territorial organisations; the sub-district heads and their administration have been placed under the districts to co-ordinate the latter's tasks with the villages. The foreign institutions favoured the provinces as the focal level of decentralised administration. They did not view districts as economically and politically viable units.[5]

Decentralisation is an ongoing and contested process, and its consequences are still uncertain. As yet, it is not clear to what extent decentralisation and regional autonomy contribute to the wider political ideals that are associated with these policies. Critics have pointed out that the process has been too hasty and without sufficient preparation. There has been too little implementing legislation at the central level, so that the legal structure is seriously deficient, giving rise to much uncertainty. The process has been likened to the poetic imagery of 'building a ship while sailing'.[6] Responses to these uncertainties range from lethargy to drafting legislation before higher legislative bodies do and, as often as not, in contradiction to central legislation.

A second point of critique is that the quality of local administrative officials is inadequate to deal with the new challenges. The transfer of civil servants from hierarchical departmental line agencies (branches of central administrative offices under direct control from the central office) to new provincial and district offices (operating under the control of the governor or district head respectively) has created immense problems. Thirdly, there is serious doubt whether the financial means of decentralised administration match the range of responsibilities devolved to them. In addition, there seems to be an upsurge of ethnic and localist attitudes. It is suspected that one of the major effects of decentralisation is the decentralisation of corruption, collusion and nepotism (*Korupsi, Kolusi, Nepotisme* or KKN)

[5] In 2004 the decentralisation laws were revised by Law No 32/2004 on Regional Government and Law No 33/2004 on Fiscal Balance between Central Government and the Regions. The period covered by our contribution does not encompass these recent legislative changes.

[6] *Jakarta Post*, 21 December 2000. See also Bünte (2002: 154).

to local levels. Administrative controls on 'money politics' are not yet strong enough to counter these tendencies. One major fear is that instead of the 'big *rajas*' in Jakarta, many new little *rajas* will emerge in districts and villages who will treat regional resources as their own private property and parcel them out to the highest bidder, much like Suharto and his cronies used to do.[7] A final point of critique is that decision-making at lower administrative levels does not necessarily mean that there is also wider citizen participation in government.

Uncertainty continues for a number of reasons. Some important ministerial responsibilities that should have been decentralised according to Law 22 of 1999, such as the National Land Board, have been exempted from decentralisation by presidential decree (*Keputusan Presiden* 62 of 2001). According to legal experts, this is unconstitutional. There are continuing efforts to revise the decentralisation laws and create better regulations for their implementation. The Indonesian government is under constant pressure from the donor community to revise and improve the decentralisation legislation and to enact further legislation for the implementation of the general laws (see GTZ newsletters). In the regions, such attempts at determining the nature and extent of implementation are decried as 're-centralisation'. Some provinces and districts have been officially divided, and many more lobby for similar division—usually the resource rich parts of provinces or districts wanting to establish their own administrative and economic unit. Such district divisions have to be decided first by the district parliament and then by the provincial parliament, and ultimately authorised by Indonesian parliamentary legislation. Indeed, newspapers report that there are more provincial and district lobbyists at the parliament in Jakarta than MPs having to pass the respective laws.[8]

While the foreign donor community, which closely monitors the process at the national and at regional levels, presses for decentralisation of political power and fiscal-economic decentralisation, there are also pressures from inside the administration at various levels. At the provincial level, the Association of Governors lobbies to reinstate most of the authority of the provincial governments. There are countervailing pressures from the Association of District and Township Heads and Parliaments to prevent such changes.

The general opinion is that decentralisation has not yet been a great success. However, there are some definite and significant changes in Indonesian political society. The strong vertical relations of power have not disappeared but they have weakened considerably. In political practice, districts in particular have started to make their own policies largely

[7] *Jakarta Post*, 21 December 2000.
[8] See *Kompas*, 28 January 2003.

independently of the central or provincial governments. Moreover, more and more horizontal political linkages and associations, both within and outside the state apparatus, are being formed. Largely stimulated, advised and financed by the foreign donor agencies, all-Indonesian associations or forums have been established of the provincial governors, district heads, town mayors, district and town parliaments, with these associations holding regular meetings, organising seminars, publishing newsletters and lobbying for their political objectives.[9] In the national parliament a faction (*Fraksi Utusan Daerah* or FUD) has been established that promotes regional interests across political party lines. There has also been a strengthening of the NGO sector and representatives of (self-proclaimed) *adat* law communities have also formed an alliance: *Alliansi Masyarakat Adat Nasional* or AMAN (see Acciaioli, 2001). There is also the Consultative Forum on Oil Producing Districts (or FKDPM), an alliance of some 48 district governments. And elected women at all levels of regional government in Indonesia have established an All Indonesia Women Councillors' Forum. Such organisations are not strictly district or provincial as their members are able to act collectively to pursue their shared agendas, for example, the FKDPM agitating for the revocation of a decree that restricted oil revenues to district governments (in whose areas those revenues are produced) to just one to two per cent. Following the organisation's sustained protests, that figure is now 15 per cent (Sangkoyo, 2003: 18).

While there is considerable political debate about the future course of decentralisation and great insecurity about its present state, decentralisation has acquired its own momentum in the provinces, districts and villages. Provincial and district governments have reconstituted themselves in line with the general principles of decentralisation, redistributed civil servants, and begun implementing the new rules concerning the redistribution of revenues. These processes are further complicated by regional political dynamics, especially by attempted and actual subdivisions of provinces and districts. During the first years of decentralisation there was hardly any systematic information on how decentralisation was taken up by the various actors at provincial, district and village levels and to what extent the hopes and fears surrounding decentralisation have eventuated (Antlöv, 2001). In particular there were few studies of the *process* of decentralisation itself. Since 2001 Indonesian and foreign scholars have initiated research in many regions, and research results are disseminated at conferences and seminars. From the information available so far, it is clear that there is considerable variation both between and within regions.

[9] These are closely monitored in the press. The GTZ *Decentralisation Newsletter* is an excellent publication reporting on these developments (see n 3, above).

In West Sumatra, the process of decentralisation is particularly dynamic and interesting. It was the first province that began the process of decentralisation. In contrast to other provinces, it also took the opportunity to reorganise village government. In 2000 it enacted a provincial regulation on local government which was then further developed in district regulations and finally in new village governance organisations in 2001 and 2002. The central government's decentralisation law itself only makes a short reference to village government. It only later issued a Government Regulation (*Peraturan Pemerintah*, PP 76 of 2001) delineating the general principles of village autonomy and village government under decentralisation. It allows for the creation of new villages. Any further regulation concerning the creation, abolition or fusion of villages has to be made by district regulation (PP 76-2001, Article 4(1)). But after two decades of Indonesia-wide uniform village government, local government in West Sumatra is again based on the traditional units of Minangkabau political organisation, the *nagari* or village republic. Despite considerable changes during the colonial and post-colonial history, these villages and their government have remained firmly associated with Minangkabau culture, political identity and traditional law or *adat*. What has become known as 'the Minangkabau way' of decentralisation has attracted much attention from outside West Sumatra, from representatives of other regions as well as from the international donor community. It is regarded as the most successful example of the new trend towards a government along traditional lines that is supposed to be more democratic, participatory and accountable (Asia Research Centre, 2001: Appendix F). Donor agencies are also following the process with keen interest. These agencies include the GTZ, USAID and the UNDP Partnership for Governance which facilitate the transition to the new government structure with training programmes. In order to understand these processes, we shall first turn to an historical reconstruction of village government in Minangkabau.

III THE HISTORICAL BACKGROUND OF THE NAGARI

Historically, the main socio-political units were the *nagari*, or village republics. These territorial units were associations of localised Minangkabau wide matriclans (*suku*), usually sub-divided into a larger number of major matrilineages headed by a titled lineage head (*panghulu*). The council of the lineage heads of the founding matrilineages formed the village government.[10] Authority and decision-making processes were dominated by two major principles. One was the principle of consensual decision-making, the reaching of consensus after a process of common deliberation (*musyawarah untuk mupakat* or *sakato*). The other one was more hierarchical and stressed the line of authority between clan and lineage heads and their lineage members (Benda-Beckmann, 1981). There were important differences in social, economic and political status between the members of a *nagari,* expressed as the 'four kinds of nephews and nieces' (*kemanakan*): the descendants of the founding lineages, formally-adopted group members, 'newcomers' comprising emigrants from other *nagari* (known as *perantau*), and descendants of former slaves (*kamanakan dibawah lutuih,* literally 'nephews and nieces below the knee'). Only the first two had full economic and political rights in *adat.* The latter two could be incorporated into a lineage, but had lesser rights (see F von Benda-Beckmann, 1979: 62).[11] After Islamisation, religious officials were incorporated into the matriclan organisation. The matriclan system had been challenged at the beginning of the nineteenth century by those aligned with a group of orthodox Muslims *hajjis* who, having come under the influence of the orthodox Wahabi movement during their pilgrimage to traditional sites (located in the then Ottoman Empire), gave fresh impetus to the Padri movement for greater Islamic orthodoxy. Having returned to Minangkabau, they strove for the abolition of the un-Islamic form of village government and the property and inheritance system that was based on principles of matrilineal descent. The conflict erupted in civil-religious war between traditional leaders or *panghulu* and their supporters, and the Padri religious leaders, the *tuanka*, and their followers. During the so-called Padri war of the 1820s and 1830s, theocratic forms of government were established in villages under Padri control. The Dutch intervened in the war, defeated the Padri forces, and gradually incorporated West Sumatra into their colonial empire. They suppressed Islamic political aspirations and strongly supported the traditionalist *adat* parties. Their system of indirect rule largely built upon the *nagari* structure. However, they reshaped the *adat* system in several ways. They introduced a head-*panghulu* as village head, fixed the number of recognised lineage heads, and reconstituted the councils of lineage heads as *nagari* government.[12]

[10] See F von Benda-Beckmann (1979) for the two major types of pre-colonial *nagari* government. For further details of Minangakabau history, see Schrieke (1955), Kahin (1999), F von Benda-Beckmann (1979), Manan (1984), Kahn (1993), Oki (1977) and Kato (1982).

[11] On the status of the descendants of former slaves, see also Verkerk Pistorius (1868).

[12] Between 1874 and 1919 the Dutch also created a new 'native' territorial unit (*laras*) under a Minangkabau *laras* head, and during the period of forced cultivation (from the mid-1850s to 1908, when local villagers had to cultivate coffee and deliver it to the government) they also created a new type of lineage head who was responsible for the cultivation and delivery of coffee (*panghulu rodi*).

With this, the dualistic government structure of the village was firmly established: on the one hand the state-imposed *nagari* government including *adat* leaders, and on the other the *adat* government with the council of lineage heads, Village Adat Council or Council of *Panghulu*, as the highest organ. In 1918 village councils formally recognised the 'three pillars' or 'the heart with three legs' as the basis of village leadership, that is, the *adat* lineage heads, the religious officials (*alim ulama*) and a third group, the *cerdik pandai*, usually translated as 'intelligentsia' or 'intellectuals'. In the struggle for independence, the urge for party politics and representative democracy gained in importance. During the Japanese occupation, a new tripartite division of village government emerged: *adat* leaders, religious officials and nationalists (Manan, 1984: 219). After the Declaration of Independence, the composition of the village councils was again changed. Now there were to be five different groups/categories: *adat* elders, religious officials, a village national committee of 100 men, another of 100 women, and representatives of political parties. After the regional secessionist movement in West Sumatra had been quashed in the late 1950s, there was another major change in village government, in line with the policy of guided democracy introduced by Sukarno (president, 1945–67). Membership and representation was no longer organised along party lines, but was once again based on membership of functional groups. Regulations stipulated 10 such groups: *adat* elders, religious officials, the national front, village social development, co-operatives, women, farmers and fishermen, workers, youths, and veterans (Manan, 1984: 232). Sukarno had introduced the system of functional groups as a means of mass mobilisation, but it was later adopted by Suharto and transformed into the well-oiled system of political patronage and tight political control over the civil service that characterised his regime.

Under Suharto (1967–98) the first 'New Order' (*Orde Baru*) regulations stipulated elections by popular vote from the different groups. But in the following years the village constitutions moved back to the earlier, tripartite system with a lower democratic content. A 1968 regulation again instituted a 'classical' tripartite deliberative council as advisor to the village head. And with the 1974 Regulation of Local Government, with a village mayor and a legislative council of *adat* elders, religious officials and intellectuals, the status of the traditional village leadership was fully restored (Manan, 1984: 234). In the late 1970s the Indonesian central government started to homogenise the plurality of laws on its territory, consolidate centralist rule and standardise the regionally diverse local government. The Javanese model of the village (*desa*) as the lowest local government unit became standard throughout Indonesia under the Law on Local Government of 1979. In West Sumatra this law was effectively implemented in 1983. The relatively smooth adoption of this new structure was due to the new law allocating a fixed yearly development grant to each village, irrespective of its size or population. As the *nagari* were substantially larger than villages elsewhere in Indonesia, West Sumatra would have been severely disadvantaged financially had one *nagari* been simply converted into one *desa*. Splitting each *nagari* into several *desa* initially multiplied the amount of funds by nearly seven. The 543 *nagari* in West Sumatra (including the islands of Mentawai) became 3,516 *desa*. The number was later reduced when a number of *desa*, too small and having too few inhabitants to be feasible management units, were merged (1988–89). After a period of reshuffling, approximately 1,700 *desa* had replaced the original 543 *nagari*.[13]

With the implementation of the Law on Local Government of 1979, the *nagari* had ceased to be an official administrative unit. However, Provincial Regulation 13 of 1983 allowed for the *nagari* as an 'adat law community' and acknowledged the Village Adat Council as the institution representing this community.[14] A number of implementing regulations gave detailed instructions as to how the Village Adat Council was to be constituted according to *adat*, and how it was to exercise its main tasks: strengthening traditional values, maintaining the unity of the *nagari* population, and settling disputes on *adat* matters. Of special importance was the task given to the Village Adat Council in managing the *nagari*'s wealth by Instruction No 102/GSB/1985 of the Governor of West Sumatra. *Nagari* wealth includes the natural resources of the *nagari* territory, the market, and the revenues the *nagari* receives as part of the *nagari* revenues managed by the district or provincial administration (Article 2). These resources were to be managed by the chairman of the Village Adat Council, assisted by the secretary and accountable to the full Village Adat Council (Article 3). A West Sumatran Appellate Court circular stated that *adat* disputes would not be accepted unless the Village Adat Council had passed a decision.

The *nagari*, as adat law community and the Village Adat Council were, paradoxically, formally regulated as 'informal law and institutions'. Once more there was a dualistic structure: an official village administration at *desa* level, and a traditional *adat* council at *nagari* level. These new Village Adat Councils, however, mostly had a different character from that of the unrecognised Village Adat Councils of the 1970s. They were more strongly controlled by the (Golkar) party and rather bureaucratic in their functioning. Golkar, the ruling state party under the Suharto regime, had originally been established as a body of representatives of 'functional groups' (*golongan karya*). Representation of the clan and lineage heads that in *adat* formed the legitimate *nagari* government declined. Although information on the period is scarce, it seems that they continued to work as authorities

[13] For other regions in Sumatra, see Galizia (1996) and Kato (1989).
[14] On the details and significance of that regulation, see Sjahmunir (1996).

over lineage land, their people, and in dispute management. Conflicts between the Village Adat Councils and *adat* leaders in general and the *desa* heads (*kepala desa*) seem to have been common, especially over the authority of *adat* leaders in matters of marriage and divorce, and over the distribution of fees and the village development funds. In many *nagari*, the Village Adat Council still had considerable influence in village politics, as shown in an incident where opposition from the head of a Village Adat Council of the *nagari* Batipuh effectively blocked the dismissal of an elderly official whom the people had thought no longer able to effectively perform his duties as the administrative official responsible for the registration of marriage and divorce. The *desa* head, together with the religious leaders and the youth organisation, had decided to replace him with a new official. Although the decision was supported by the whole village and the sub-district head of the Office for Religious Affairs (to whom the official was responsible), the Adat Council head argued that such a dismissal was 'unethical' and also in contravention of the adat of the Koto Piliang system of the *nagari* Batipuh which dictates that a leader cannot be replaced during his lifetime, only after his death. His view prevailed. (Sjahmunir, 1996: 184ff).

IV REGIONAL AUTONOMY AND THE RETURN TO THE *NAGARI* POLICY

The problematic relation between *desa* and *nagari*, and especially the role of communal land (*ulayat*) of a village or matriclan, was intensely debated in West Sumatra during the 1980s and 1990s in a number of journals devoted to Minangkabau politics, history and the role of *adat*.[15] In several former *nagari*, the *desa*—or the *adat* leaders in the *desa*—had attempted to reunite the *desa* belonging to the former *nagari*. As the *nagari* no longer existed as administrative units of local government such re-organisation led to an amalgamation of the five or so *desa* into one large *desa* within the boundaries of the former *nagari*. Sjahmunir (1996: 242, 243) reports that by 1993, 92 *desa* had reunited with other *desa*. In the cases described, migrants (*perantau*) played an important role in supporting these developments. There were more attempts at reunification, but some were blocked by *desa* that did not support the proposals.

With greater political freedom and regional autonomy emerging, discussions of the possible implications for Minangkabau intensified among politicians, engaged citizens, and in the provincial and regional political

[15] See Abdullah (1996) and Naim (1990). For more details, see F and K von Benda-Beckmann (2001a).

arenas as well as in the villages. In West Sumatra the governor commissioned a research team to investigate and make recommendations regarding the desirability of, and support for, a return to the *nagari*. The team had concluded that by far the majority of the community favoured a return to the *nagari*. Those in favour emphasised that it was not simply the strengthening of *adat* that was important to them, but also that the cross-*desa* family ties and feelings of belonging to the same clan were important elements fostering co-operation. The team reported that the *adat* leaders were usually strong supporters of the return to the *nagari*, and recommended that the Village Adat Council should remain and play a role as a village court, as well as develop into an organisation active in the economic field, managing *nagari* resources. But there were also doubts. Many had welcomed the division into smaller units because it brought the administration closer to the people, especially in very large *nagari*. On 7 December 1998 the governor sent his deliberations, based on the findings and recommendations of the research team, to the Minister of the Interior. He stated that the imposition of the *desa*-village model had not worked well in West Sumatra because it was 'not in accordance with the socio-cultural system'. The province wanted to return to the *nagari* as the smallest unit of local government.[16]

West Sumatra officially adopted the 'back to the *nagari*' policy before the 1999 general elections and the enactment of the national decentralisation laws, pre-empting the move towards decentralisation by the central government, which only made a Government Regulation (No 76 of 2001) in November 2001. As a result, West Sumatra had made a regulation that did not conform to the Central Government Regulation, which stated that further regulation should be made by the districts and not by the provinces.

Altogether there were 20 provincial draft regulations on local government which were intensely discussed in and outside the provincial parliament, in consultations with non-governmental *adat* and Islamic organisations, prominent Minangkabau migrants in Jakarta and in the local newspapers. The influential provincial Association of Adat Councils (*Lembaga Kerapatan Adat Alam Minangkabau* or LKAAM) took an active role in the debates. Established with government support to contain political *adat* aspirations, the LKAAM had been part of the ruling state party Golkar, but its position had become increasingly independent. Before the 1999 general elections it had dissociated itself from the state and from Golkar. Its most important members were former high officials in the

[16] Additional legislation was to follow, dealing with the question of whether and how current municipalities could also become *nagari* again, and with the situation on the non-Minangkabau Mentawai islands under the administration of the province. There is general consensus that Mentawai has a different *adat* from Minangkabau and should be allowed its own village structure.

provincial and regional administration (some of whom were to return to district administrative positions after the regional elections), and some academics who were also *adat* leaders in their own villages. The provincial and district associations organised recurring all-Minangkabau meetings at which important issues related to *adat* were discussed among *adat* leaders from the whole province. The LKAAM has propagated the most far-reaching form of returning to the *adat* structure of the *nagari*.

There was broad consensus on the general principles but differences in opinion over the details of what the *nagari* is and should be, and on the appropriate place the three main value systems—state regulation, *adat* and religion—should have in the new *nagari* constitutions. The return to the *nagari* clearly involved reconstituting the village territory and the village population as an *adat* law community. But different political value systems provide different answers to the question of what constitutes a *nagari*. According to national and international notions of democratic polities, a village population consists of formally equal citizens, that is, those having acquired resident status (usually after six months, according to local government laws). Political participation and elections would normally proceed via political party representation.

In the most traditional *adat* conception of the village, at a minimum it consists of four matriclans and their lineages, headed by a *panghulu* with authority over the lineage members. In the colonial period and following Independence, the 'ideal-type' composition of the population, representation and leadership changed to accommodate Islamic functionaries and modern educated élites in the village structure, which led to changing categories of functional groups (*unsur* or *golongan*). Finally, donor agencies and NGOs that organise workshops and training sessions on village government introduced a new political rhetoric and village leaders rapidly familiarised themselves with terms like 'sense of ownership', 'social capital', 'democracy', 'good governance', 'open society', 'accountability', 'transparency', 'efficiency', 'development from below', that is, with the whole 'brave new world of concepts', as Bourdieu and Wacquant (2000: 7) have called it.

Many local politicians, intellectuals and especially the younger generation are afraid that the selection process will be dominated by the old and new élites in the villages, and that reinstating the *nagari* means returning to an old-fashioned way of life. In their view, the new village parliament as the highest village authority should be a democratic body elected by secret ballot. Others vehemently deny that traditional consensual procedures could be regarded as undemocratic. This view is most strongly expressed by the *adat* lobby claiming to be the guardians of the true, Minangkabau type of democracy. Minangkabau democracy, with its strong emphasis on processes of common deliberation until consensus is reached is considered superior to the 'western style 50+1 voting democracy'. 'We have come back to the *nagari* and to *adat*, and in *adat* we do not vote', one designated Mayor told us. But it is not just the traditionalist *adat* lobby that is in favour of introducing Minangkabau principles of democracy. In the public sphere, many politicians praise the Minangkabau consensus democracy. The district head of Solok declared:

> Democracy of the Minangkabau type [is] to be valued higher than 'western' democracy, for the *nagari* had been republics. Actually, the western countries had learnt democracy from Minangkabau . . . in Minangkabau, democracy is based on the principle that '*Adat* is based on religious law, religious law is based on the Koran'. And *adat* has clear standards for the election of its leaders. (*Haluan*, 5 June 2001).

Professor Marlis Rahman, Rector of Andalas University, stated that the selection of the members of the Village Parliament, the *Adat* and the Religious Consultative Council must proceed according to the Minangkabau philosophy, that '*Adat* is based on religious law, religious law is based on the Koran' (*Haluan*, 8 June 2001). According to this view, balanced representation can only be reached by means of *adat*.

Proponents of both *adat* and 'modern' democracy play to the ears of the donors. The former emphasise that *adat* is indeed 'bottom-up' development, participatory, and community-based. The latter stress the value of free elections and democratic decision-making processes. The donor agencies themselves are ambivalent as to how to evaluate the competing principles of democracy. A brochure of the UNDP partnership for governance presents the Minangkabau *nagari* as good governance *avant la lettre*, indicating that this present push for good government is nothing new, but rather represents a desire to restore traditional values (UNDP, 2001: 6). The Minangkabau consensus type of democracy appeals to their notion of participatory and community-based development. But the donor agencies also press for free and general elections conducted by secret ballot. On the whole, they tend to support the combinations that are being employed.

The debate about the character of the *nagari* was not just a discourse about Minangkabau identity. It had political and institutional implications of which everybody was very much aware. Of all village institutions, the name, status and functions of what was to be the Village Adat organisation was most intensively debated. By choosing to use the designation Village Adat Institution (*Lembaga Adat Nagari*) and not Village Adat Council (*Kerapatan Adat Nagari*) in the relevant legislation, provincial parliamentarians wanted to emphasise their intention of dissociating this body from the Village Adat Councils of the period where the establishment of the councils was associated by the New Order government of Suharto.[17] Others favoured the term 'Council' for similar reasons.

The other major issue was the recognition of *adat* rights to the village commons (*ulayat*) that had largely been treated as state domain by the state, a status that had always been contested by villagers who considered it *adat* land. There is consensus that issues concerning village commons should be regulated by a Provincial Regulation. By early 2002 several drafts were circulating, one proposed by the Association of Adat Councils, another by the National Land Office (*Badan Pertanahan Nasional*). It is generally assumed that the village commons are property of the *nagari*, but opinions diverge radically concerning those parts of the village commons over which the state has granted temporary rights of usage. According to *adat*, these rights become obsolete after the period set for the right has elapsed, and the resource will be village commons again. Under the other interpretation, mainly held by administrative officials, once state rights have been vested in village commons, the resource remains state land.[18]

After lengthy discussions, the province enacted Provincial Regulation No 9 on *Nagari* Government in December 2000, which came into effect in January 2001. The language of the regulation is full of references to *adat* and to the unity of *adat* and religion.[19] It provides for an initial return to the *nagari* in their pre-1979 territorial boundaries and, furthermore, makes mention of the *nagari* resources: a market, village field, council hall, mosque and prayer houses, land, forest, rivers, ponds, lakes and part of the sea which used to be common *nagari* resources (*ulayat nagari*), public buildings and movable and other properties. So resolution of the issue of *nagari* commons is no small matter. While the regulation refers to the 'riches' of the *nagari*, the issue of rights to the commons is not resolved. In 1999 the central government issued a regulation on village commons containing a partial recognition. This led to vehement reactions in Minangkabau, by common people, NGOs and university lecturers (see F and K von Benda-Beckmann, 2001a). This issue has to be negotiated with the central government, and discussions of draft regulations continue to this very day. Provincial regulation sets a general framework regulating local

[17] Whilst the Village Adat Council had been mentioned in the very first draft, it had disappeared in later drafts, but the consultant team and the Association of Adat Councils pressed successfully for its reintroduction into the final draft.

[18] For a more detailed description of the legal background and the discussions in West Sumatra, see F and K von Benda-Beckmann (2001a). See also Haverfield (1999), Fitzpatrick (1999) and Slaats (2000).

[19] The preamble states that West Sumatra is going back to *nagari* government, followed by the formula: *Adat basandi syarak, syarak basandi kitabullah. Syarak mangato adat memakai alam tabang jadi guru.* ('*Adat* is based on Islam, Islam is based on the holy Koran; religious law orders, *adat* is used; nature is the teacher of mankind.') Characteristically, this is now abbreviated as ABSSBK.

government, leaving the details to the districts. The village government consists of an elected mayor, his staff, and an elected legislative body.

The mayor (*wali nagari*) is the head of the village government. He represents the *nagari* internally and externally and is accountable to the village parliament. His task is to guide the social and economic development, preserve law and order, draft village regulations and enact them together with the village parliament.

The village parliament is called the Representative Council of Village Citizens (*Badan Perwakilan Anak Nagari* or BPAN). Its task is to discuss and enact village regulations and the village budget, and to control their implementation. It consists of members chosen in free and general elections by the *nagari* village population.

Besides this official village government, two further institutions are regulated. The Adat and Religion Consultative Council (*Badan Musyawarah Adat dan Syarak*) advises the mayor and village parliament on *adat* and religious matters. It is composed of representatives of four or more categories, that is, *adat* leaders, religious leaders, intellectuals and women. The Village Adat Institution (*Lembaga Adat Nagari*) is, as before, regulated but it is not part of the official *nagari* government. Its main task is to mediate in disputes relating to lineage property and to protect *adat* in general. It is left to the districts and *nagari* to choose another name.

V DISTRICT AND VILLAGE REGULATIONS

The response to the new regulations and political debates at district and village levels has been quite diverse, both in pace and content. In two districts, Solok and Limapuluh Kota, district regulations on village government were made within two or three months (February and March 2001), and the district heads pushed for speedy formation of *nagari*, establishment of the new village parliaments and elections of the new mayors. Most other districts followed suit at a slower pace and only finalised their regulations between six and eight months after the provincial regulation was enacted (June and September 2001). Political discussions continued in administrative circles, the NGO community and the general public, now focussing on the progress, the district regulations enacted and the first elections. In the local newspapers, draft regulations and election politics at district and village levels were closely followed and commented upon. In a curious mixture of 'top down' regulation and participation of districts and villages, the drafts and plans were discussed at numerous meetings where officials explained the (draft) law to the population and allowed for questions and comments. It shows that, after decades of authoritarian rule, the administration is not yet used to this new mode of participatory communication. Whenever their proposals encounter opposition, the standard reaction is that those expressing opposition have not yet been 'socialised' (*disosialisasikan*), or that the issue needs further 'socialisation' (*sosialisasi*). However, occasionally these consultative rounds have actually led to changes in the regulations. The draft of district Sawah Lunto-Sijunjung, for example, had been the least *adat* minded regulation. It only focused on the village mayor and parliament and then proceeded to regulate 'other institutions'. However the final regulation, following local consultative processes, devoted quite extensive regulation to the Village Adat Council (Articles 56, 57).

The weakening of the hierarchical relationship with the provincial government gave district heads considerable leeway to design their own village government regulations that were more adapted to their own political vision and the specific political constellations within their districts. As a consequence, there are a number of differences between the (eight) district regulations. Some are mainly symbolic, while those concerning the range of governance institutions, the prescribed representation of the village population and election procedures are more substantial.

A The Mayor

The position of the mayor is quite uniformly regulated throughout the province, though set at district and village local level. District and village regulations set the criteria a candidate must fulfil. He must be competent, know and respect *adat* and religion, be neutral in terms of party politics and not have been involved in the 1965 communist coup. There are some minor differences, for instance in the minimum age (often 30 years, sometimes 25) and residency requirements. Some demand prior residence in the *nagari* of two years to prevent influential migrants returning from Jakarta or other big cities from immediately assuming control in the village. The gender of candidates is left open, but it is an issue discussed in some circles. The great majority of mayors are men. In early 2002 only three or four female mayors had been elected and a few were expected to be elected in the near future. Nobody expected the number to rise above a handful. As a member of the West Sumatran provincial parliament declared:

> the exclusion of women should not be seen as being contrary to human rights. Rather it is in accordance with Minangkabau *adat*, where women for instance cannot be installed as lineage head and bear the title of *Datuk*. Despite the important position of women in Minangkabau, there are limits. (*Haluan*, 20 June 2001)[20]

[20] See F and K von Benda-Beckmann (2001b).

B The Village Parliament

While district and village regulations have remained within the framework of the provincial regulation in most respects, they have not done so for the composition of the village parliament. The provincial regulation speaks of a Representative Council of Village Citizens, indicating representation of the village population without further qualifications. The districts of Limapuluh Kota, Sawahlunto Sijunjung and Pasaman, for example, have adopted that designation while Agam and Tanah Datar speak of a *Badan Perwakilan Rakyat Nagari,* Solok of *Badan Perwakilan Nagari* and Pesisir Selatan of a *Dewan Perwakilan Nagari.* Representation along political party lines is disapproved of by both the state administration and *adat* élites. Members are to be chosen—in general and free elections—by the *nagari* population. In contrast, all district regulations state in different formulations that the parliament has to 'consist of', is 'chosen from' or 'mirrors' the population as differentiated along the functional categories / groups (described earlier). In the district of Solok's Regulation 4-2000, for example, the relevant categories are *adat* elders, religious leaders, intellectuals, women and the young (Article 76). In Tanah Datar all members represent their village ward and are to be chosen from the categories *adat*, religion, professionals or other eminent local persons. Some villages, such as Padang Sibusuek, have more official organisations of each of the categories (*lembaga unsur*). The individual district regulations allow for some variation in the regulation of the village parliament, regarding age, number of members, and in the procedure for selection. Most village regulations combine geographical and *adat* principles and require representation both by ward and by category. In some cases, the details of the nomination and election process are left to village regulations. But the districts Tanah Datar and Solok state that 'the election of the members of the village parliament is carried out according to common deliberations leading to consensus, which is facilitated by the ward heads' (Article 15.3) while Sawahlunto Sijunjung prescribes elections by secret ballots (a point discussed below under election procedures).

The combination of *adat* elders, religious leaders, and the 'intellectuals' appears in all regulations relating to the composition of village parliaments. In addition, two other categories are always used: 'the women' (*bundo kanduang*)[21] and 'the young'. Sometimes 'local leaders', 'professionals', 'farmer's groups' are added to the list of categories. In a number of cases there is a separate category of 'migrants', people originating from the village, who have migrated to one of the towns or cities. This suggests

[21] Named after a mythical Minangkabau female figure, *Bundo Kanduang,* which had formerly been the name for an *adat* women's association created in parallel to the (male) Association of Village Adat Councils (LKAAM) in 1966.

a concept of village community that includes non-resident members. Such a concept is new. Traditionally, village members who had migrated out remained only dormant members, unable to exert any rights in the village as long as they were not residents. Upon their return they would resume their full citizens' rights. However, Minangkabau migrants have in the past exerted influence on the politics of their *nagari*.

C The Village Adat Council or Institution

As in earlier times, the Village Adat Council maintains its ambiguous position in the new village governance structure. It is not a body of the official *nagari* government, yet it is regulated and its functions are circumscribed and authorised in the official regulation, down to the committees the Council is to have and its financial support. Yet there is one significant difference. Provincial Regulation 13 of 1983 that had given the Village Adat Council control over *nagari* resources has been repealed, and this has left the question of who now controls these resources somewhat open and contested (see below).

Most district regulations have reverted to the name Village Adat 'Council', as happened in Agam, Tanah Datar, Sawahlunto Sijunjung, and Solok districts. Only Limapuluh Koto and Pasaman retain references to the Village Adat 'Institution' in their district and most village regulations. In Solok, the council is simply 'recognised' under the heading of 'other institutions'. Its organisation and working methods are to be decided by the *nagari* in accordance with existing *adat*. The regulation of Tanah Datar defines the competence of the Village Adat Council in more detail than the other regulations. It is to maintain, develop and strengthen *adat* and Islamic law, and to settle disputes on *adat* titles and family property, and to del with violations of *adat* and Islamic law. Decisions on *adat* titles are final, whilst the Village Adat Council can only mediate on other issues. Limapuluh Kota and Tanah Datar stress the adjudicative function in particular. The District regulation of Pesisir Selatan takes an extreme position and does not mention a Village Adat Council or Institution at all.

D The Adat and Religious Consultative Council

The provincial regulation states that this body, that is to advise on *adat* and religious matters, consists of representatives of adat elders, intellectuals, religious leaders, adat women and other components of society. The district and village regulations show considerable variety in name and composition. In the district regulation of Solok the institution is called the Council of the Three Pillars (*Majelis Tungku Tigo Sajarangan* or MTTS), a designation adopted by most village regulations within the district. Its members are to be chosen from among the *adat* elders, religious leaders and intellectuals. Some villages have chosen to give representatives from migrants living in the urban centres of Indonesia a formal position on this body. (For more details, see F and K von Benda-Beckmann, 2001a). *Nagari* Koto Baru has perhaps the most elaborate composition: six members from among *adat* elders, one member from each of the former *desa*, four intellectuals who have migrated to Padang, with one such migrant from Jakarta, one from Medan and one from Bandung. The district head of Tanah Datar, however, has refused to cater for the creation of such a council in his district regulation altogether. According to him the Village Adat Council is the appropriate consultative forum for *adat* and religious matters. He sees no need for an additional institution.

E Religious Councils

Differences in the political representation of *adat* and Islam show most clearly where district regulations set up special Religious Councils.[22] Their tasks overlap with those of the *Adat* and Religious Consultative Council. Some districts and villages have opted for combined *adat* and religious councils, while the districts Agam and Limapuluh Kota, for example, installed separate councils,[23] representing *adat* and religion as separate spheres. The Religious Councils have to promote and strengthen the spiritual and religious values in the villages according to the principle that '*adat* is based on religious law and religious law is based on the Koran'.[24] Behind these choices are political considerations: attempts to emphasise or de-emphasise the role of religious parties. Whilst the administration discourages party politics from entering village level politics, the institution of a separate religious advisory council enhances the overall influence of religious politics. According to some commentators, this is a political

[22] District regulations show another difference in the emphasis accorded to *adat* as against a purely state legitimation of the members of the village parliaments. This concerns the oath of office the elected members have to take. Whilst the oath is a standard text, there are differences in the procedure. In Sawahlunto Sijunjung, the oath is made in front of the district head or a civil servant (Art 12). In 50 Koto, however, the oath has to be taken in a ceremony led by the Head of the Village Adat Institution, that is, the *Pucuk Adat* (head of *adat*) or *Panghulu Kaampek Suku* (head of the four clans) (Art 30, Explanation).

[23] Called *Lembaga Syarak Nagari*, 'Religious *Nagari* Institution', in Limapuluh Koto, and *Majelis Ulama Nagari*, 'Council of *Nagari* Religious Leaders' in Agam.

[24] In Limapuluh Kota, the Religious Council also has the task of pronouncing *fatwa* for the village population. In Agam, the Religious Council has the task of explaining and familiarising the population with *fatwa* in Islamic law as the Council is the official *fatwa*-issuing institution of the *nagari*.

manoeuvre of the Islamic PAN party, having the majority in districts like Agam, to set up an institutional basis for party politics.[25]

VI THE REORGANISATION OF VILLAGE GOVERNANCE

The reunification of the *nagari* and the imminent reorganisation of village government have led to new dynamics in village politics. The expected greater significance of *adat* and *adat* leadership has motivated many Minangkabau, villagers and urban residents, to become lineage heads. In recent years, a great number of long-vacant positions of lineage heads have been filled again, often in 'wholesale processes' in which several lineage heads were installed on the same day.[26] The position of Chairman of the Village Adat Council has become interesting again. The chairmen were expected to take a leading role in the preparation and implementation of the elections of the village parliament and the mayor. Moreover, the prospect of greater economic autonomy of the *nagari,* increased revenue streams and more control over the village riches made people interested in that position. In addition, there was a hope of better remuneration of elected village officials and working funds for the Village Adat Council. The position of chairman of the Village Adat Council might be a good springboard for the election of mayor, a position that was coveted for the same reasons. In addition, the question of whether or not all *desa* indeed wanted to reunite also became an important issue in the early phase. In many villages, migrants took a very active part in these processes. For those living in the provincial capital Padang this was not difficult, given the good infrastructure of the region. But modern communication had made contacts over longer distances far more intensive and frequent. The return to the *nagari* rekindled an interest in their home village of wealthier and influential migrants living in Jakarta, Medan, and other major cities, who had found it difficult to identify with their village since the introduction of the desa structure. This interest shows in the many migrants running for mayor, and in migrants who offer financial support and have taken on more or less formal consultative roles.

A The Formation of the New Village Institutions

The reconstitution of the new village organisation is a prolonged process. It usually follows two phases. In the first phase, a series of public meetings

[25] Narullah Dt Parpatiah nan Tuo, SH, Lecturer at the Faculty of Law, Andalas University (Padang), personal communication.

[26] On 10 March 2001 we witnessed how 43 *panghulu* were installed in *nagari* Talang Anau, Limapuluh Koto.

is held in which representatives of the *desa* concerned deliberate as to whether or not they want to reunite as *nagari*. If this is the case, a Preliminary *Nagari* Council is constituted that organises the election of a Preliminary Mayor (*pejabat jabat sementara* or PJS) for the transitional period until the official elections of village parliament and mayor take place. These processes had already begun before the official regulations of village government at provincial and district levels had been finalised. The Talago PJS, for example, was elected just days before the Provincial Regulation had been enacted and received his letter of appointment from the district head before the District Regulation came into force. The second phase, with the official elections of the village parliament and the official mayor, started after the respective district regulations had become effective. The process ended with the official installation of the mayor by the district head, usually in a big ceremony attended by the district head together with his higher staff, *adat* elders and religious leaders and the village population.

In most cases the chairman of the Village Adat Council took the initiative to start the discussions about unification, regulations and elections. Usually, all *desa* concerned selected an equal number of representatives to these meetings. In some villages the chairman organised meetings in each of the wards (as in Alahan Panjang and Selayo), or with representatives of the wards (as in Candung Kota Lawas), to discuss the procedures to be followed. In other villages he initiated meetings with each of the clans (as in Saning Bakar). These initial meetings were all characterised by common deliberations among male leaders. They then decided on the way in which the preliminary *nagari* council should be constituted, and who should sit on it.[27] These councils then elected, mostly by voting, the preliminary mayor who was then officially appointed by the district head. At the same time, the district head would revoke the letters of appointment of the *desa* heads. The next step was to appoint an Election Board, with members from the different wards or clans that would organise the official elections of the village parliament. These election boards all consisted of leading men and were selected in a process of common deliberation. The main task of the preliminary mayor was to organise the election processes.

Because the districts enacted their regulations at quite different speeds, the years 2001 and 2002 showed a patchwork of *nagari*, some of which had been recognised as new *nagari*, some in which reunification still was under discussion, some with a preliminary mayor, and others with an already-elected parliaments and mayors.[28] The experiences in the 'faster'

[27] This was the process leading to the election of the preliminary mayor in *nagari* Talago, Limapuluh Kota in early 2001.

[28] In the districts Solok, Limapuluh Kota, Pasaman and Sawah Lunto Sijunjung, the process was more or less completed in March 2002. In Agam and Padang Pariaman, no

districts and villages were widely known, compared and discussed in those lagging behind. Only in 2003 was the process of *nagari* formation and election of village parliaments and mayors concluded province-wide.[29]

B Representation

Because district regulations left villages relatively free to design their own procedures, villages had to discuss the proper mode of representation, an issue that is of immediate relevance for the power relationships within the village. Most *desa* heads were of the opinion that the wards were the appropriate units to be represented in the *nagari*. Being the legitimate administrative authorities until the new village administration was in place, they claimed a leading role in the election process in the hope of being able to influence the selection of candidates. They argued for a nomination process in each ward, to be followed by general elections by secret ballot in the *nagari*. But in many villages *adat* leaders asserted their primary place in the process and claimed that the clan-segments should be the primary units to be represented. Most villages eventually opted for a combination of a territorial (ward), a genealogical (clan) and a functional (category) principle. Usually each ward is accorded one representative on the village council, and the other seats are distributed acoss the relevant categories. *Adat* leaders, religious leaders, intellectuals, women and youths are standard, but there are differences in the relative weight (number of seats) the categories have. While most district regulations offer some leeway for village regulations, the district regulation of Sawahlunto Sijunjung prescribes how many seats must be reserved for each of the categories.

C Nomination and Election Procedures

Having decided on the distribution of seats, the next step was to design the procedure for nominating candidates. The procedures for the mayor's

mayors had yet been elected: all *nagari* worked with a preliminary mayor. Most village parliaments, however, had been elected. The district of Padang Pariaman was last and only finished its regulation on 6 March 2002: no village parliament or mayor had been elected, and in only 24 of the 52 *nagari* was there a preliminary mayor. In Tanah Datar and Pesisir Selatan districts, the process had been partially concluded. In some districts, some *nagari* had been divided. In Limapuluh Koto, the original number of 70 *nagari* has risen to 75 as a result of *nagari* having been divided.

[29] By March 2002, 461 of the 498 *nagari* had been recognised in their new form, and 303 mayors elected. In 137 *nagari*, the preliminary mayors were still in office and the remaining villages still had the old *desa* heads. And a total of 428 villages had officially elected their parliaments (*Kepala Biro Pemerintahan Nagari/kelurahan, Propinsi Sumatera Barat*, March 2002). By 20 November of the same year, 421 *nagari* had fully completed the reorganisation (same source, quoted in *Haluan* 21 November 2002).

election and the village parliament were slightly different, but nomination of candidates followed more or less the same pattern. The Election Board instructed the wards, the clans, and, as in Padang Sibusuk, the organisations of each of the categories (*lembaga unsur*) to nominate candidates. As there was considerable overlap in the classifications, many persons could theoretically be nominated under different categories. Some men could be classified as religious leaders or as intellectuals, as lineage heads or youths, while women could be classified as youths, women or intellectuals.[30] Nomination invariably occurred in processes of common deliberation. It was said that in theory all members of the ward, clan, or category participated. In practice, the discussions were heavily dominated by leading men. Most villages followed a two- or three-stage process to finalise the list of candidates. Some district regulations mentioned age, education and leadership criteria. For the position of mayor, there were some additional formalities. All candidates for mayor had to be screened on these criteria. In many villages, one could protest against candidates and some had a letter-box for complaints. In a last round of deliberations the final list was made. This list then had to be sanctioned by the sub-district head and the district head.

There was no formal screening for the candidates for the village parliament, though some villages gave further specifications.[31] Generally, each of the clans or wards proposed their own list, the wards or clans having been asked to propose twice as many candidates as there were positions for each category. These lists were all made in the same process of common deliberations as the lists of candidates for the mayor, albeit that some formalities were not deemed necessary here. Although most people we talked to agreed that common deliberation was the best way of organising this nomination process, there were also critical voices. Several young people complained that the youths had been completely left out of the process. Others complained that the same people who had always run the village dominated the deliberations.[32] This was not only a concern for

[30] It is not quite clear when youth becomes too old for that category. There are men of 40 years of age who are considered youths.

[31] These vary markedly. In Saning Bakar each clan appoints a representative for each of three functional groups: one *adat* leader (also representing the intellectuals), one religious leader and one woman; the migrant organisation appoints three candidates and the Village Adat Council appoints six members. In Selayo, clans may decide on candidates for the functional group of *adat* leaders while the wards appoint candidates from the other four categories. In other villages, such as Padang Ganting, each of the wards is to come up with a specified number of candidates. The candidates should represent all categories, but there are no specific instructions as to how this is to be achieved.

[32] These processes are closely followed and reported in the local newspapers. Some villagers of *nagari* Limbanang in Limapuluh Kota, for instance, protested that the members of the village parliament had been selected via appointment and not through voting (*Padang Ekspres* 17 March 2001). One mayoral election in Agam district was claimed to be invalid

urban intellectuals; this opinion was also voiced in villages. Yet others complained that this procedure was very open to manipulation.

The mayors were all elected through secret ballot, on the basis of a list of candidates screened by the village parliament and by the district. The procedures for the final election of the members of the village parliament varied among and within districts. Some villages (eg, in Saning Bakar) opted for a process of common deliberation within each of the clans and each of the wards. Others (eg, Alahan Panjang) opted for secret ballots. There could even be variation within one *nagari*. Selayo, for example, left it to each ward to organise its own elections. Two opted for secret ballots, one for common deliberations. The fourth ward, which opposed the reunification of the *nagari* refused to co-operate altogether and the Village Adat Council finally decided to appoint five persons to represent this ward until it appointed its own representatives. (Two migrants were also appointed, one representing the Sumatran migrants, and the other the migrants from outside Sumatra: F and K von Benda-Beckmann, 2001a).

According to the district regulations, the mayor has the authority to appoint the ward heads and the heads of his staff. In practice, most mayors have opted for election of ward heads by secret ballot. They felt this would signal to the ward heads and the population that they valued the ward heads and considered them to be a crucial part of the village administration.

Although representative data are not yet available, the end of the Suharto era seems to be clearly reflected in the elections of new village officers. It seems that only a few of the old *desa* heads have been elected as mayor. Many new mayors, especially the former migrants, are highly educated with at least secondary education and often more. They have been elected because they are expected to have a good grasp of the economy and know their way around in the administration, and because they do not have too close ties to the old regime.

D Struggles over Reunification

Before the provincial regulation had been enacted, the re-creation of the *nagari* had been very controversial. In some former *nagari*, the *desa* had already pre-empted reunification by joining together into one *desa*. Here, conversion into a *nagari* was particularly easy (see Sjahmunir, 1996: 242). In others, there were protracted discussions about the advantages and disadvantages, but after the reorganisation had become a *fait accompli*,

(*Haluan* 26 August 2002) and in *nagari* Kumanga, Tanah Datar, the mayor was installed without the villagers attending (*Padang Ekspres* 6 November 2002).

most *desa*-villages have accepted the policy, and the process of reunification has proceeded without major difficulties. Reunification is problematic, however, in a few cases where *desa* do not want to rejoin the *nagari*. The provincial regulation states that fusions and divisions of the former *nagari* are not impossible, but can only occur after the *nagari* has been unified in its pre-1983 boundaries. A *nagari* can be divided only after intensive consultation of the whole *adat* law community. For this the Village Adat Institution and other social leaders have to seek consensus after a process of common deliberation and the decision has to be confirmed by the district head.[33]

If the former *nagari* are simply too large, splitting into two *nagari* does not create great problems. However, several *desa* wanting to establish an independent *nagari* against the explicit wish of the other *desa* within the former *nagari* creates intense conflict within the *nagari*. Autonomy forces villages to look for revenues and to exploit the economic development potential of village resources. It then becomes of great economic and political interest who has control over property within the *nagari* (F and K von Benda-Beckmann, 2001a). Opposition to joining the former *nagari* is strongest for *desa* that had originally been settlements of migrants or descendants of slaves because in *adat* they have fewer political and economic rights than the original lineages. Most of these settler groups are ethnic Minangkabau themselves and have lived there for more than a century, but there are also traders or Javanese and Tapanuli transmigrants, who have settled relatively recently.[34] In *adat* terms, they cannot become full *nagari* citizens. The territory on which they live is usually part of the inherited property of certain older clans or lineages that has been 'given' to the newcomers under *adat*. While this property has become inherited property (*pusako*) for the newcomers, some residual rights of control remain with the original titleholders. It follows from their status as newcomers that the rights of the original lineages and lineage heads should be recognised and that they have to obtain the consent of these original lineages to sell land. Politically such newcomers cannot become a lineage head and member of the Village Adat Council with the same status as the heads of the original lineages. Some of these groups live in a more or less separate ward within the old *nagari* and form a *desa* of their own. Under

[33] There are three different degrees of independence: (1) full independence as a *nagari* with a mayor and parliament as well as in *adat* terms with an independent Village Council (subject to the agreement of the mother *nagari*); (2) the formation of a new *nagari* with its own mayor and parliament but without an independent Village Adat Institution; and (3) a village independent in terms of the state administration, with a mayor and parliament only. In matters of *adat* and village commons, *nagari* of the second and third type would still be under the authority of the Adat Council of the mother *nagari*.

[34] Tapanuli is the region north of West Sumatra, between Minangkabau and the Batak region, with a mixed Islamic and Christian population.

the *desa* structure the newcomer-*desa* had obtained a certain amount of autonomy, cherished by these settlements and resented by the old lineages who felt that the *desa* system had weakened their authority. Newcomer-*desa* are afraid that under the new regime the heads of the old lineages, who mainly reside in the older parts of the *nagari* and who dominate the Village Adat Council, will reassert their rights in *adat* after reversion to the *nagari*. Many urban intellectuals support this view and fear that under the new system former inequalities, which had been largely equalised under the *desa* regime, might re-emerge.[35] This fear is all the more pressing in view of the perspective that *nagari* wealth may indeed generate resources on a scale not possible under the *desa* system and the authoritarian Suharto regime. *Adat* leaders of the original village for the same reason strongly oppose the *desa* becoming an independent *nagari*. They are afraid that they would now lose even more than under the *desa* system, and at a time when control would regain some of its practical meaning. They want to retain or resume their say over their land and in potential lucrative economic developments that have emerged with the new autonomy. In some *nagari*, such as Padang Sibusuk and Selayo, this has led to a serious impasse in the reorganisation of the village.[36] Reunification politics are not confined to the village context. In some cases, parties stage public demonstrations and lobby the district administration for support in their struggle for, or against, independence. In other cases, the district administration itself interferes in this process, contrary to the district regulation that requires consensus at village level.[37]

VII FINANCIAL DECENTRALISATION AND *NAGARI* AUTONOMY

Financial decentralisation has two major components, the transfer of responsibilities and competences, and the redirection of financial flows. It

[35] Yonariza, Research Associate, Andalas University (Padang), personal communication.

[36] See F and K von Benda-Beckmann (2001a) for a description of these cases. In Selayo, there had already been an attempt to reunite the *desa* into one in 1993, a process blocked by one *desa* (Sjahmunir, 1996: 211). After the reorganisation law, the unwilling *desa* even organised its own elections of a *nagari* mayor. Towards the end of 2004 there were indications that the *desa* no longer opposed reunification.

[37] *Desa*, however, can also become objects of a centralisation process of a different kind, ie when the re-establishment of *nagari* comes into confrontation with expanding municipalities that want to incorporate neighbouring *desa* as municipal districts (*kelurahan*). The most notable case at present is the expansion of the town of Bukit Tinggi, whose mayor unilaterally declared some *desa* of *nagari* in the district of Agam part of Bukit Tinggi. This led to protracted political struggles involving the district head and the mayor, the respective parliaments, the media, *adat* representatives of the *nagari* concerned and mass demonstrations of the village populations. A similar problem may occur with the expansion of the city of Padang Panjang in relation to district Tanah Datar. These examples are beyond the scope of this paper.

started much later than the political-administrative reorganisation of the Indonesian state. Regulation and implementation of new economic flows and redistribution of taxes and revenues took a long time and is still highly controversial and subject to intense lobbying.[38] It is a complex and painful process, in particular as it coincides with a contracting state apparatus. There were no clear directions as to how the fusion of central governmental line agencies with provincial and district offices was to take place and all feared a disproportionately heavy burden from the incorporation of the former line agencies' staff (who cannot be dismissed).[39] As a result of this lack of direction, by 2002 some of the main central governmental line agencies, such as the (former) Department of Social Affairs, had ceased to function in the provinces for lack of structural funds and *Inpres*[40] project funding from the central government, but they had not been incorporated into the new structure. And no one really knew how responsibilities would be assigned, or how and when funding would start flowing again (see F and K von Benda-Beckmann, 1998; and Bünte, 2002). The process has been further complicated by the politics of splitting up regional autonomous areas.[41] So, at the moment, the question of how much decentralisation and autonomy is effectively taking place is difficult to answer.

A District Autonomy

The different pace at which districts and newly-formed villages dealt with decentralisation of economic and fiscal resources mirrors the differences that had characterised the transformation of the village government structures. While there has been little progress at the provincial level, some districts (notably Solok) have made a serious start with the incorporation of the central governmental line agencies into its general staff. But it encountered a serious problem in one of the main areas of its new

[38] Law 34/2000 regulates the sharing of regional taxes and fees. Regions and districts continue to demand revision of this distribution and claim larger shares, also from state-owned enterprises: see GTZ Newsletter 31 (2002): 3 and 37 (2002): 2. The law is currently under review. Districts have made a large number of new local taxes and retributions. See GTZ Newsletter 17 (2001): 5.

[39] Although unable to be dismissed, civil servants can be put on reserve, in which case they only earn their basic salary without the additional income from participating in projects, which may comprise one-third or more of their usual monthly income. A civil servant living only on his basic salary is unable to pay for education for his children and has serious problems paying for healthcare: see F and K von Benda-Beckmann (1998). On the redistribution of civil servants in the municipality of Padang, the capital of West Sumatra, see Bünte (2002).

[40] Much of Indonesia's infrastructure was centrally financed via *Inpres* (*Instruksi President*) funding. See F and K von Benda-Beckmann (1998).

[41] In West Sumatra, initiatives for splitting districts have been developed in the districts of Solok, Pasaman and Sawah Lunto-Sijunjung. The division of Solok seems to have already received the agreement of the Minister of Home Affairs (*Haluan* 16 September 2002).

competence: land issues, including land taxation. Contrary to the decentralisation law of 1999 and local expectations, the National Land Administration Board has not been decentralised. The district head of Solok had established his district land office administration but then realised that it would not work, and the line agency was re-instituted.

Nevertheless, the districts have obtained a considerable level of autonomy when compared to the period under Suharto. They receive a yearly block grant and no longer depend on project money under the presidential *Inpres* programme. They have also gained more competences for generating additional income, though the opportunities are unequally distributed across the province. On the other hand, they have more responsibilities than before and this has not always been matched by appropriate funding. District heads have responded differently to these new challenges and responsibilities. In a number of districts the new freedom has invigorated the district administration. Instead of waiting for directives from the province and central state, they have initiated innovative ways of generating income. It is too early to establish how enduring these initiatives are, but district officers, now more likely to be members of the local population, have a far better comprehension of the region's economic potential than their predecessors, who did not need to design their own development planning but almost completely depended on orders from the provincial and national administration. Other districts have remained more passive. Their district heads feel uncomfortable without the old familiar paths and known political links through which they formerly generated project funds from the central and provincial government. They seem to hope that decentralisation will 'blow over' and centralisation soon reappear. Signals from the National Land Office and the Ministry of Forestry, two of the most powerful and wealthy ministries opposing decentralisation, confirm that view. The difference in attitude among the districts cannot be explained by economic potential, because the wealthiest districts in the coastal regions, with their palm oil plantations, are among the most reluctant. The differences probably have more to do with the personal economic interests of the district élites and their ties with the old economic élites in Padang and Jakarta.

B Relations between District and Nagari

In the new organisational arrangement, the *nagari* in most districts will get a block grant (*dana alokasi umum nagari* or DAUN), once they have established their new village government. The amount varies according to a set of criteria, including *nagari* population, the size of its territory, and developmental status of both the *nagari* and its infrastructure. The grant varies between 75 and 150 million rupiah per year.[42] The block grant is two or three times more than what the now reuniting *desa* used to receive as development funds towards the end of the *desa* period. Apart from the salaries for the village government paid out of the block grant, the *nagari* can use the grant as they see fit.

The block grant, however, is only one part of the future village budget. Districts can also give contributions to development projects (*dana partisipatif*) based on plans of the villages specifying their own contribution in money, labour or kind. In addition, *nagari* receive shares of the revenues, fees and taxes from the exploitation of their natural resources such as sand, stones, timber, water and fisheries, and from tourism and agriculture and forestry, which higher-level administration, the district in particular, collects. They also collect levies, such as market dues, fees for resident passes, business permits and marriage permits, which have been transferred to the *nagari*. Often a fixed share of such levies has to be given to the district administration. The *nagari* may also create their own sources of revenue, which may not, however, duplicate those of the district or province or the central administration.[43] Contributions from migrants are an important new source.[44]

Much of this, however, is still theory, for the new financial arrangements are just starting to function. What happens in practice is rather difficult to grasp. At the moment, there is still considerable variation in district policies. In the two fastest-moving districts, Solok and Limapuluh Kota, nearly all *nagari* received their block grant for 2002, and some for the months in 2001 in which the new village government operated. In districts where the village organisation was not yet established, the *nagari* at first received a preliminary grant, apparently at a very low level (in Agam, for example, this is reported to have been 10 million rupiah per *nagari*.) Quite a different policy is followed in Tanah Datar. Here the district head does not want to give block grants at all. The district pays village officials their salaries directly. For the remainder of their funding, the district head demands that the villages put forward project proposals for which they have calculated their own contribution. Only on this basis is he inclined to

[42] In 2002, US$1 was worth approximately 10,000 rupiah.

[43] By spring 2002 the Ministry of Finance had identified 123 regional taxes which were not in line with Law 34/2000: GTZ Newsletter 27 (2002: 3).

[44] According to rumours some rich migrants contribute significantly to the village budget and in one case (Sulit Air) are said to have wanted to pay for the office car of the mayor, who is a returned migrant himself. It was reported later that they have already given a truck to the village government (*Haluan* 5 November 2002). The cooperation of the migrants and their villages in the process of reorganizing *nagari* government is strongly encouraged by the district heads: *Haluan* 12 December 2002. Some villages (eg, Saning Bakar) organise big meetings for village leaders and successful migrants: *Padang Ekspres* 11 December 2002.

allocate district funds to village projects. His main reason is that experience from Solok and Limapuluh Kota shows that the people became too 'block grant-crazy' and have adopted more or less the same attitude towards the government as had been common under the Suharto's New Order regime: waiting for the government to give them money. He also contends that the mayors who had received block grants had become 'little kings'.

District policies vary considerably on how block grants may be used for routine activities (including village officials' salaries and village administration working expenditures), development activities, and the financing of the functioning of the village parliament. Most district regulations allow villages to set aside 10 per cent for the functioning of the village parliament. In Solok this was recently raised to between 15 and 20 per cent. In Solok 40 per cent is allocated to development expenditures, and a maximum of 60 per cent to routine expenditures for the village government, although even this appears flexible.[45] In Sawahlunto Sijunjung, the distribution is 70 per cent for development, and only 30 per cent for routine expenditure. In Limapuluh Kota and Pasaman, the proportion is 40 per cent for routine and 60 per cent for development expenditures. Generally, the mayor will receive 400,000–500,000 rupiah per month, the village secretary 300,000–350,000 rupiah, and the Ward Heads and Heads of Village Administrative Departments 200,000 rupiah.[46] Contributions for the functioning of the Village Adat Council also vary.[47]

Revenue sharing and the extent to which revenue collection has actually been transferred to the villages also vary among districts. Administrative fees for residential passes, permits for marriage and building permits used to fall under the competence of the sub-district heads. In some villages the sub-district head still gets a share of the fees for his co-ordinating activity. Markets are a special case. They used to be *nagari* property.[48] However,

[45] At a meeting with village officials, in March 2002, the district head stated that (as a maximum) even 75% could be used for routine expenditures.

[46] There is a special regulation for those mayors who had been active civil servants. They remain civil servants and retain their salaries, but up to 50% of the official salary rate for mayors may be added to their salary. Village officials complain about the low salaries, given the important new tasks they have which take up their time. District officials are eager to point out that the present salaries are in any case much higher than the honorary payments of 30,000 or 50,000 rupiah given to the former *desa* heads. Moreover, villages are free to make village regulations and raise the income of village functionaries from their other financial sources.

[47] The district head of Solok announced that he would give 600,000 rupiah per year for the functioning of the council.

[48] On Minangkabau markets, see Effendi (2003), Kahn (1993) and Oki (1977). When the *desa* system was introduced, *nagari* markets (in accordance with the Governor's Decree 103/GSB/1985) were managed by a market committee that collected the market tax. After deducting 10% for wages, the revenue was to be given to the Village Adat Council that had been instituted in 1983 (see Effendi, 2003: 73, 77).

most markets today were built or modernised under the Presidential programme *Inpres* and came under district authority, which collected market fees (Effendi, 2003: 77). According to the new village autonomy, the markets, including the right to collect and control market fees, should be handed over to the villages. Solok has handed over all markets to the villages, but other districts have not yet done so. Because many markets were joint markets of several *nagari*, a new problem emerges around the distribution of market fees among villages. It seems that in practice the *nagari* in which the market is located controls the fees.

Gradually, villages have started making yearly budgets. In Limapuluh Koto the district head has experimented with some *nagari* who were to formulate their own budgets, including other sources of revenue. Several have come up with a budget between double and four times the level of their block grant. The most striking case is a *nagari* that is allocated 97 million rupiah and which came up with a budget of 660 million rupiah. Whether these budgets are realistic is difficult to assess at this stage. Others, however, have not yet created a good regulatory budget framework. It is the district head's responsibility to create a district regulation that should serve as a framework containing guiding principles for budget formulation.

C New Tensions in the Nagari

At this stage it is difficult to come to any clear conclusions about the economic prospects of the new *nagari*. Much still is in flux; much will depend on the emerging patterns of revenue sharing between villages and districts. As the villages vary greatly in natural resources and business possibilities, the new arrangements will lead to considerable inequalities among villages. It is not, however, clear to us yet whether these are really *new* imbalances or a continuation of older ones. Given that the index for the block grant allocation does not really leave much leeway to the district heads, they will find it difficult to equalise the differences in prosperity between villages. The possibility of participative funding, however, allows them to balance out the worst inequalities.

The economic prospects of the *nagari* to a large degree will depend on the extent to which they will control and exploit the natural resources on the *nagari* territory, in particular the village commons (*ulayat*). This is a matter relevant both for relationships between *nagari* and district, and for relationships within the *nagari*. As long as there is no Provincial Regulation, the districts adopt various ad hoc strategies to deal with this issue. Some district heads have started to hand over some of the village commons to the *nagari*. Others fear that opening up the village commons problem will turn out to be a 'can of worms' and avoid this issue. Some districts intend to make their own regulation on village commons. In other districts previous expropriation of village commons under the Suharto regime may be seen as having largely relieved them of the responsibility or, at the very least, complicated the issue.[49]

Control over economic rights and obligations under decentralisation and the expected greater control of common village resources also causes new tensions within the *nagari*. The mayor, as the head of village government, competes with the Village Adat Council as holder of traditional *adat* authority. And it is as yet unclear whether the *nagari* will be entitled to receive revenues under their traditional authority over these *nagari* resources and thus from activities conducted in relation to them (for example, collecting forest products, logging, coal and gravel mining and market fees). The issue remains contested, and is further complicated because there are not only village commons (*ulayat nagari*) but also commons of clans and lineages, which are not under village control. While such commons may in external relations be considered a *nagari* resource, within the *nagari* the rights are held by clans or lineages. Outside investors interested in exploiting sand or stone on clan or lineage land would therefore have to negotiate directly with the representatives of the clan or lineage, bypassing the *nagari* government and the Village Adat Council. This is likely to generate conflicts about interpretation and actual control over the nature and holders of rights to commons. Apart from the authority over *nagari* resources, there are also some struggles over the distribution of the assets of the former *desa*.[50]

The dominant trend seems to be that the mayor, as the official village government, takes control over all *nagari* resources, though there is some variation. Solok district government holds that all resources fall under the village government, while the district Association of Adat Councils (LKAAM) and several villages distinguish between village government assets and village assets, the latter remaining under the control of the Village Adat Council. Actual practice varies. In some villages, the authority has officially been handed over by the chairman of the Village Adat Council to the village government. In other *nagari*, compromises between

[49] The Sawahlunto-Sijunjung district administration and parliament see no need for making such regulation because in their opinion there are no more village commons in the district. Here huge resource areas had been 'freed' of commons' rights during the Suharto era and given to regime- and family-friendly enterprises via licences and concessions.

[50] It is not contested that the buildings of the *desa* administration now fall under the *nagari*. But it is contested what should happen to the motorcycles of the *Desa* heads, and their office land (*tanah bengkok*). Government office land in West Sumatra, in contrast to that of Javanese villages, was a recent, post-1983 invention and never had great economic significance.

the two are negotiated. However, many new mayors have had difficulties taking over actual control of the resources controlled by the *adat* elders or the Village Adat Council.[51]

VIII CONCLUSIONS

Decentralisation is a process riddled with ambiguous and contradictory effects. As a general policy, it has been forcefully disseminated by the international financial world and foreign donor agencies, but it has now become a largely autonomous process within Indonesia, with great regional differences. As is constantly emphasised by officials and researchers at public meetings and in the newspapers, decentralisation has not as yet fulfilled the high hopes often attached to it.[52] Research on the process of implementation is increasingly demanded.[53] In our view, some preliminary conclusions can be drawn. Decentralisation has already led to some positive changes in West Sumatra, but it also has some serious shortcomings. It has weakened the hierarchical ties that bound the districts and provinces to the centre, considerably widening the scope for political action at district level, albeit that it has also led to great uncertainty at all administrative levels about competences, responsibilities and means of tapping into resources. Decentralisation has increased interest in the economic potential of districts and villages, and people in the districts and in villages have started to consider what they can do themselves without waiting for the central government to tell them what to do. However, both levels tend to become over-burdened by responsibilities without appropriate funding. The process through which the *nagari* were formed was initially top-down but over time it also obtained characteristics of a bottom-up process, in the relations between the district and the provincial and central government, between the villages and the districts, and within villages. Though the framework regulations firmly structured the process, local politics has given it its own, often highly variable, face. In villages where decentralisation has been taken seriously the circle of involved citizens has widened and there is a remarkable involvement of highly-educated village members who had migrated to the large Indonesian cities. However, cynical voices throughout all social strata of Minangkabau say that the whole process is just a new version of containing village élites

[51] Some 39 mayors, of the Forum *Warga Agam*, have complained about this problem, stating that the *nagari* riches belong to the *nagari* and should be under the control of the *nagari* government, not of the *adat* elders (*Haluan* 31 August 2002).

[52] See, eg, statements by the Chairman of the University Research Centre on Regional Autonomy (*Haluan* 29 November 2002).

[53] The district parliament of Limapuluh Kota demanded research into the implementation (*Padang Ekspres* 4 September 2002).

under the firm control of the government. The younger generation has not experienced what living in a *nagari* was like, and most do not find attractive the prospect of a system that is likely to strengthen the old-fashioned authority of the *adat*-minded among the older generation. However, this scepticism seems only partly justified.

The new village structure has to be understood against the background of shifting relationships between the state, *adat* and religion. At the provincial level, *adat* is a powerful resource for mobilising and legitimising opposition to the Javanistic political centre of the nation state. A return to the *nagari* structure is thus a symbolic act within the wider national political debate. At local government level, the return to the *nagari* has increased the significance of both *adat* and western principles of democracy compared with the purely administrative structure of the *desa*-village. Reunification gives greater significance to *adat* in several respects. It re-establishes some *adat* control mechanisms over land issues and revitalises older social *adat* differentials between categories of villagers. Most importantly, it reproduces the political territory in *adat* terms, thereby significantly enlarging the territory of these new villages as compared with the old *desa*-villages. The boundaries of the present *nagari* are largely the same as in colonial times. In this sense the old *adat* constitutions largely define the 'new' territorial boundaries. At local level, the return to the *nagari* thus forms a centralising element in the general decentralisation process.

If the *nagari* and *desa* administration systems are compared, the changes are considerable. If the *nagari* are compared to the situation before 1983, however, apart from the more democratic checks and balances between village mayor and village parliament, the village government looks very similar to the form it had under the earlier Suharto regime. The Adat Council is once more not part of the official village government. Thus the village government remains firmly embedded in the state legal system, despite some very strong lobbying by *adat* organisations. Some claim that the *adat* sector has actually lost out, though our findings do not support this view. This becomes particularly evident when looking at decision-making processes within the village government. It was mainly *adat* leaders and the chairmen of the Village Adat Councils, and not the *desa* heads, who shaped the reorganisation of village government. And *adat* procedures of decision-making and election are important again, albeit in combination with Western principles. The district and village regulations and the practices of the village administration reflect the uneasy relationship between the various principles of legitimation and modes of democracy underlying these new processes of village government. All villages have opted for a combination of genealogical, territorial and functional principles for organising representation. As a result, the process is heavily dominated by a relatively small group of older men. Young men and women have little influence apart from the very last stage of formal elections. But what is seen as giving weight to *adat* principles, and outright rejection of party politics of Suharto's 'New Order', can also in some respects be understood as a continuation of that by now old order policy of distinguishing and representing 'functional groups'. The same categories that are now employed as *adat* categories and form an important basis for representation also figured in the various bodies of village government throughout the Suharto era, an era that is now generally seen as having been utterly undemocratic. What is more, the state party Golkar was originally established as a body of representatives of 'functional groups'. So what is meant to be a rejection of the undemocratic New Order of Suharto, is taking over precisely the principles upon which that regime's main political support was founded. That being said—and despite the fact that the procedure is subject to manipulation—the results show a clear break with the past. Very few former *desa* heads seem to have been elected as mayor.

The strongest, and at the same time most strongly-contested and least government controlled revitalisation of *adat*, is in the field of rights to natural resources on the village territory. Claims to a wider validity of *adat* rights over the (former) village commons have a strong lobby in *adat* intellectuals and village leaders. State agencies and those who continue to profit from state control over these resources have not accepted these claims very gracefully. People have gone to court over these issues, resorted to self-help and engaged in negotiations with state agencies and private companies who hold concessions in these resources. The first successes suggest that *adat* has regained some of its force in these issues (see F and K von Benda-Beckmann, 2001a).

The problematic relationship between *adat* with its matrilineal principles for structuring group formation, economic relations and political power, and Islam is re-balanced as well.[54] Underneath the rhetorical unity of *adat* and Islam, old struggles over their relative superiority continue. Regional differences within West Sumatra become visible, especially at district levels where some district heads clearly favour the traditional *adat* dominance in internal village affairs whilst others have created a sharper division by introducing a separate Council of Religious Elders parallel to the Village Adat Council. The return to the *nagari* is clearly an issue that enhances the status of *adat*. For most local politicians, village leaders and NGOs, the relevant community under debate is the *adat* community of the *nagari*, not the Islamic community of believers. The response of Islamic leaders was a parallel discourse on 'the return to the *surau*', stressing the importance of

[54] On the relationship between *adat* and religion see Abdullah (1966, 1971), Kato (1982), Kahn (1993) and F and K von Benda-Beckmann (1988).

Minangkabau moral values, and the need to defend them, when they are so strongly confronted with the forces of cultural and economic globalisation.[55] In political and economic terms, *adat* has a greater prominence again, while Islam is mobilised more strongly for specific moral issues.[56]

The pressure of international and transnational institutions, and the political and legal ideas promoted by them, together with the internal pressure for regional autonomy, have been vital for the greater political freedom at national and local levels at which such political ideals can be realised. Locally, however, these transnational actors have primarily enriched ideological debate. Ideas related to democracy and good governance have reached far into the Indonesian population, and the training workshops provided by the transnational actors are important occasions at which these ideas can be discussed. Yet we think that their influence on local political practice is, as yet, modest. Donor agencies seem to follow political developments rather than actively shaping them. The politics leading to the actual regulations for village government are dominated by the old struggles between state, *adat* and Islam. In these struggles, transnational actors can be valuable allies and their notions welcome as additional legitimating resources. And the many training programmes show how readily local actors appropriate these ideas and make them subservient to their designs or strategies. If the process makes one thing clear, it is the intimate and interactive links between the main moral and regulatory orders—state, *adat* and religion— which remain entwined in an uneasy embrace, combined and recombined with transnational legal forms and concepts in an on-going search for alternative legalities.

BIBLIOGRAPHY

ABDULLAH, TAUFIK (1966) 'Adat and Islam: An examination of conflict in Minangkabau' *Indonesia* 2:1-24.

—— (1971) *Schools and Politics: The Kaum Muda Movement in West Sumatra* (Cornell University Modern Indonesia Project, Ithaca, N.Y).

—— (1996) 'Adat, nasionalisme dan strategi kultural baru' *Jurnal Genta Budaya* 52.

ACCIAIOLI, GREG (2001) 'Memberdayakan kembali "Kesenian Totua": Revitalisasi adat masyarakat To Lindu di Sulawesi Tengah' *Antropologi Indonesia* 60.

[55] *Surau* or small mosques were originally the sleeping places for unmarried Minangkabau men who had no place to stay in their maternal homes under the system of matrilineal social organisation and post-marital uxorilocal residence. Following Islamisation they were also the place where instruction in *adat* and Islam was given, and later often simply worship spaces. (see Kartikawening, 2002: 11).

[56] Islamic pressure in the Provincial Parliament led to the adoption of a hotly-discussed regulation (11 of 2001) on 'social illnesses' (*penyakit masyarakat*, PEKAT).

ANTLÖV, HANS (2001) *Village governance and local politics in Indonesia* Paper presented at the 3rd EUROSEAS Conference, London, 6–8 September 2001.

ANWAR, DEWI FORTUNA (2001) *The fall of Suharto: Understanding the politics of the global* Paper presented at the 3rd EUROSEAS Conference, London, 6–8 September 2001.

ASIA RESEARCH CENTRE (2001) *Decentralisation and development cooperation: Issues for donors* Asian Research Centre, Murdoch University for the Australian Agency for International Development (AUSAID) of the Department of Foreign Affairs and Trade.

ASPINALL, EDWARD and FEALY, GREG (eds) (2003) *Local Power and Politics in Indonesia: Decentralisation and Democratisation* (Institute of Southeast Asian Studies, Singapore).

BENDA-BECKMANN, F VON (1994) 'Good governance, law, and social reality: Problematic relationships' *Knowledge and policy* 55.

—— (1979) *Property in social continuity: continuity and change in the maintenance of property relationships through time in Minangkabau, West Sumatra* (Martinus Nijhoff, The Hague).

BENDA-BECKMANN, FRANZ VON and BENDA-BECKMANN, KEEBET VON (1988) 'Adat and religion in Minangkabau and Ambon' in Franz von Benda-Beckmann, and Keebet von Benda-Beckmann (eds) *Adat and religion in Minangkabau and Ambon* (Foris, Dordrecht).

—— (1998) 'Where structures merge: State and off-state involvement in rural social security on Ambon, Indonesia' in Franz von Benda-Beckmann and Keebet von Benda-Beckmann (eds) *Where structures merge: State and off-state involvement in rural social security on Ambon, Indonesia* (The Australian National University, Centre for Resource and Environmental Studies, Canberra).

—— (2001a) *Recreating the nagari: Decentralisation in West Sumatra.* Working Paper No 31 (Max Planck Institute, Halle).

—— (2001b) 'Actualising history for binding the future: Decentralisation in Minangkabau' in Franz von Benda-Beckmann and Keebet von Benda-Beckmann (eds) *Actualising history for binding the future: Decentralisation in Minangkabau* (van Gorcum, Assen).

BENDA-BECKMANN, K VON (1981) 'Forum shopping and shopping forums; dispute processing in a Minangkabau village' *Journal of Legal Pluralism* 117.

BOOTH, A (2001) *Indonesia: Will decentralisation lead to disintegration?* Paper presented at the 3rd EUROSEAS Conference, London, 6–8 September 2001.

BOURDIEU, P and L WACQUANT (2000) 'Schöne neue Begriffswelt' *Le Monde diplomatique* (5–6 May) 7.

BÜNTE, M (2002) *Regionale Autonomie in Indonesien. Bedingungsfaktoren erfolgreicher Dezentralisierung* (Westfälische Wilhelms-Universität, Münster).

EFFENDI, NURSYIRWAN (2003) 'Nagari markets: Social management of local economic resources in Minangkabau, Indonesia' in R Pradhan (ed) *Legal Pluralism and Unofficial Law in Social, Economic and Political Development* Papers of the XIIIth International Congress of the Commission on Folk Law and Legal Pluralism in Chiang Mai, Thailand, 7–10 April 2002 (International Centre for the Study of Nature, Environment and Culture, Kathmandu).

FITZPATRICK, DANIEL (1999) 'Beyond dualism: Land acquisition and law in Indonesia' in Timothy Lindsey (ed) *Indonesia: Law and society* (The Federation Press Annandale).

GALIZIA, MICHAELE (1996) 'Village institutions after the law No. 5/1979' *Archipel* 135.

GTZ (2001) *Donor activities related to decentralisation and local governance capacity building in Indonesia* (GTZ, Jakarta).

HAVERFIELD, R (1999) 'Hak ulayat and the state: Land reform in Indonesia' in Timothy Lindsey (ed), *Indonesia: Law and society* (The Federation Press, Annandale).

HIDAYAT, S (2001) *Local state elites and the practice of local autonomy in Indonesia* Paper presented at the 3rd EUROSEAS Conference, London, 6-8 September 2001.

HOLLAND, P (1999) 'Regional governments and central authority in Indonesia' in P Holland (ed) *Regional governments and central authority in Indonesia* (The Federation Press, Annandale).

KAHIN, AUDREY (1999) *Rebellion to integration. West Sumatra and the Indonesian polity 1926–1998* (Amsterdam University Press, Amsterdam).

KAHN, JOEL (1993) *Constituting the Minangkabau: peasants, culture, and modernity in Colonial Indonesia* (Berg, Providence/Oxford).

KARTIKAWENING, D (2002) *Public Space Dynamic in Minangkabau Rural Area Indonesia*, available at: <http://www.design.asu.edu/apa/proceedings02/S-KARTI/s-karti.htm>, last accessed 15 November 2006.

KATO, T (1982) *Matriliny and migration. Evolving Minangkabau traditions in Indonesia* (Cornell University Press, Ithaca/London).

—— (1989) 'Different fields, similar locusts' 47 *Indonesia* 89.

KINGSBURY, DAMIEN and AVELING, HARRY (eds) (2003) *Autonomy and Disintegration in Indonesia* (RoutledgeCurzon, London/New York).

LINNAN, DAVID (1999) 'Decentralisation versus administrative courts: Which path holds greater promise?' in T Lindsey (ed) *Indonesia: Law and Society* (The Federation Press, Annandale).

MALLEY, MICHAEL (1999) 'Regions: Centralisation and resistance' in D K Emerson (ed) *Indonesia beyond Suharto: Polity, economy, society* (Sharpe, Armonk, NY).

MANAN, I (1984) *A traditional elite in continuity and change: the chiefs of the matrilineal lineages of the Minangkabau of West Sumatra, Indonesia* (University of Illinois, Urbana-Champaign).

MANOR, JAMES (1999) *The political economy of democratic decentralisation* (World Bank, Washington).

NAIM, MOCHTAR (1990) 'Nagari versus desa: sebuah kerancuan struktural' in Mohamad Hasbi, Mochtar Naim and Damciwar (eds) *Nagari, desa, dan pembangunan pedesaan di Sumatera Barat* (Yayasan Genta Budaya, Padang).

OKI, A (1977) *Social change in the West Sumatran Village: 1908-1945* (Australian National University, Canberra).

RÖSEL, JACOB and VON TROTHA, TRUTZ (eds) (1999) *Dezentralisierung, Demokratisierung und die lokale Repräsentation des Staates* (Rüdiger Köppe Verlag, Köln).

RÜLAND, JÜRGEN (1993) 'Politisch-institutionelle Reformen und Dezentralisierung: Thesen zum Forschungsstand' in K Simon, A Stockmayer, H Fuhr (eds) *Subsidiarität in der Entwicklungszusammenarbeit: Dezentralisierung und Verwaltungsreformen zwischen Strukturanpassung und Selbsthilfe* (Nomos, Baden-Baden).

—— (2000) 'Demokratisierung in Südostasien: die Asienkrise als Motor politischen Wandels?' *Zeitschrift für Politik* 3.

SANGKOYO, HENDRO 'Indonesia: The Coming Demise of a Ludicrous Carbocracy' paper presented at the Berkeley Centres for African and Southeast Asian Studies Workshop on Human Rights and Oil in Southeast Asia and Africa, University of California, 31 January 2003 available at: <http://ias.berkeley.edu/africa/Events/OilHR/HENDRO-OILFIN-FINAL%20PAPER.pdf>, last accessed 15 November 2006.

SCHRIEKE, BERNHARD (1955) 'The causes and effects of communism on the West Coast of Sumatra' in Bernhard Schrieke *Indonesian Sociological Studies: Selected Writings of B. Schrieke, Vol. 1* (Van Hoeve, The Hague/Bandung).

SCHULTE-NORDHOLT, HENK and ASNAN, GUSTI (eds) (2003) *Indonesia in Transition: Work in Progress* (Pustaka Pelajar, Yogyakarta).

SLAATS, HERMAN (2000) 'Aardverschuivingen in het Indonesische denken over grondenrecht' *Recht der Werkelijkheid* 41.

SJAHMUNIR, AM (1996) *Kedudukan dan peranan Peraturan Daerah No. 13 Tahun 1983 dalam proses pengambilan keputusan pada pemerintahan desa di Sumatera Barat.* PhD dissertation (Universitas Gadjah Mada, Yogyakarta).

UHLIN, A (1997) *Indonesia and the "Third wave of democratization": The Indonesian pro-democracy movement in a changing world* (Curzon, Richmond).

UNDP (2001) *Good governance for the people involving the people: Partnership for governance reform* (Partnership for Governance Reform Secretariat, Jakarta).

UNDP and GOVERNMENT OF GERMANY (1999) *Decentralisation: A sampling of definitions* (UNDP, Jakarta).

USMAN, S (2001) *Indonesia's decentralisation policy: Initial experiences and merging problems* Paper presented at the 3rd EUROSEAS Conference, London, 6–8 September 2001.

VERKERK PISTORIUS, A W P (1868) 'Iets over de slaven en afstammelingen van slaven in de Padangsche Bovenlanden' *Tijdschrift Nederlandsch-Indië,* derde serie 2:423-43.

Newspapers

Haluan (West Sumatra)

Padang Ekspres (West Sumatra)

Kompas (Indonesia)

Jakarta Post (Indonesia)

PART 4:

COMMERCIAL LAW REFORM

10

Foiling the Financial Hegemons: Limits to the Globalisation of Corporate Insolvency Regimes in Indonesia, Korea and China*

TERENCE C HALLIDAY AND BRUCE G CARRUTHERS

I INTRODUCTION

THE ASIAN FINANCIAL Crisis in late 1997 and early 1998 ('the Crisis') precipitated a wave of institution-building and law-making within those countries that suffered the deepest fiscal distress, most notably Thailand, Indonesia and Korea. Indeed, emergency assistance to those economies from the International Monetary Fund (IMF) was conditional upon their making substantial changes to legislation governing or regulating their economies (see Letters of Intent signed by the governments of Thailand, Indonesia and Korea.) In countries such as China, which rode out the Crisis relatively unscarred, the Crisis was nevertheless sobering. Agents of global economic development intensified their efforts to inoculate countries against prospective economic downturns, again through

* This chapter is based on a revised version of a paper presented originally at the 'Workshop on Globalization and Law in Asia', Oñati, Spain, 10–11 April 2003.The authors are grateful for the research support of Gibb Pritchard, Hayun Kang and Teri Caraway, and for funding from the American Bar Foundation and the National Science Foundation Project SES-0214301. We are indebted to the participants in the Oñati conference for their reactions and to Christoph Antons, Michael Burawoy, and Sebastiaan Pompe for their comments. We have also benefited from seminars presented at the International Monetary Fund and the University of Arizona. This chapter draws from a larger research project on the globalisation of bankruptcy law that includes (a) a time-series analysis of all bankruptcy reforms worldwide from 1973 to 1998; (b) participation observation, several hundred interviews and documentary analysis of international financial institutions (IMF, World Bank, Asian Development Bank and European Bank for Reconstruction and Development), international professional associations (International Bar Association and International Federation of Insolvency Practitioners), and world governance organizations (OECD and United Nations Commission on International Trade Law); and (c) case studies of Indonesia, Korea and China.

pressure for institutional and legal reforms. China, for example, facing widespread bankruptcy of state-owned enterprises committed itself to continuing large-scale corporate reorganisation (see World Bank, 2000) and welcomed the technical assistance given the legislative drafting committees by the German Government. In all cases, bankruptcy law and corporate restructuring regimes[1] were integral to the intensive negotiations and discussions between powerful global actors and national governments that led to market reconstruction via legal reformation.

These events offer a 'prime site' in which to address a major puzzle about the globalisation of law. Given the enormous coercive powers of global financial actors, why has the implantation of new bankruptcy regimes proved so difficult? Conversely, how do developing nations foil such legal 'transplants'? A solution to this puzzle would help define the limits to law-making by the world's financial hegemons, particularly in circumstances of financial crisis. It would also take us a step further towards a contingent theory of globalization of law (Halliday and Osinsky, 2006).

Reform of bankruptcy law in Asia since the Crisis presents a 'prime site' for analysis precisely because the circumstances should have been optimal for effective transplantation. On the one side, nations such as Indonesia and Korea confronted financial meltdown and desperately required massive infusions of credit that they could obtain from no source other than international financial institutions. On the other side, the world's financial powers could exercise maximal leverage as they controlled the conditions under which credit would flow. Economic coercion could not have been more intensive. In short, the enormous asymmetry in financial power presented conditions that were optimal for the adoption of transplanted law and institutions. Further, since commercial law is generally thought to be more readily transplantable than other areas of law (Harding, 2002), the combination of external pressure and internal need should have ensured ready conformity with global models of bankruptcy law and institutions.

We analyse three countries where adoption has been neither smooth nor certain—Indonesia, Korea and China. These countries lie on a continuum of proximate coercion. Indonesia represents an extreme case since the international financial institutions (IFIs) and the US government responded to its need with a series of explicit expectations for bankruptcy reforms,

[1] In this chapter we distinguish (a) the reform of substantive and procedural corporate bankruptcy law, from (b) the reform or formation of institutions to implement substantive law, such as courts, professions, and out-of-court agencies, and (c) broader initiatives at corporate debt restructuring, whether informal or formal, that influence and are influenced by bankruptcy law. We adopt the short-hand of 'bankruptcy law' to cover all three elements of a complete bankruptcy regime and distinguish among them only when the argument requires it.

codified in successive Letters of Intent delivered to the International Monetary Fund (IMF) by the Government of Indonesia (GOI), and which served as conditions for release of successive tranches of credit from early 1998 to the present. Korea represents an intermediate case of constraint, since the IMF compelled the Government of Korea (GOK) to incorporate into its first Letter of Intent a general commitment to reform bankruptcy law, but thereafter has relied on suasion of various sorts to effect reform up to the present. China represents the case of least coercion since its insulation from the Crisis did not expose it to the leverage of the IMF, although it has mostly welcomed technical assistance from the Asian Development Bank, the International Bank for Reconstruction and Development (hereafter, the World Bank) and the German government, all of which have relied on suasion to effect reform.

The three countries are similarly arrayed on a continuum of extensive to limited reform. Indonesia lies at one extreme. Here the IMF sought to create an entire bankruptcy system and debt-restructuring regime. Korea lies in the middle, where the IMF has principally sought reform of its substantive law, although it has encouraged some reform of the courts and the creation of other mechanisms for debt restructuring. China lies at the other extreme. Here most foreign influence is directed to its substantive bankruptcy law, although the World Bank has attended closely to the administrative initiatives of the government agency that regulates state-owned enterprises (SOEs).

The degree of success enjoyed by IFIs does not correlate perfectly with the intensity of external pressure. At one extreme, the Indonesian initiatives by the IMF have been the most ambitious but also the least successful, at least by an absolute standard. The World Bank and IMF have had some success in Korea, although it has been slow and mixed. And the influences of foreign and global actors on China have been perceptible in various drafts of its proposed bankruptcy law, but the influence is diffuse and success is uncertain.

We begin this chapter by considering what the literatures on globalisation and transplantation might have predicted or have subsequently concluded about the reformist aftermath of the Crisis. We then analyse each case, observing in turn the initiatives undertaken at the behest of global agents, the failures or successes of the reforms, and the mechanisms, strategies and processes that help explain why the transplants did or did not work. We approach the cases from the developing country's perspective to ask what capacities developing nations have to resist the power of the world's financial hegemons, even under the most extreme circumstances. We shall show that nation states can deploy many weapons of resistance. In conclusion, we reflect on some solutions to the puzzle of why legal transplants do not take root readily, even under extreme asymmetries of global power. Those reflections, in turn, will indicate some limits to the globalisation of law.[2]

A Global Bankruptcy Reforms and the Asian Financial Crisis

While the Crisis dramatically focused the world's financial hegemons on market-making and institution-building, their concern with bankruptcy regimes was not without precedent. A global movement of insolvency reforms has been developing since the mid-1970s. Most of the world's leading economies, such as the United States (1978), England (1985), France (1985 and again in 1994), Japan (1992), and Germany (1994), have substantially reformed their approaches to corporate bankruptcy. All countries making a transition from a planned to a market economy have been compelled either to resurrect and amend a pre-Communist law, or, more commonly, to create a bankruptcy law de novo. Developing countries in Latin America, such as Chile (1987), Columbia (1988-89), and Argentina (1995), or in Asia, such as India (1985) and Singapore (1995), and all the countries of Francophone Africa, have similarly undertaken substantial changes. Common to most reforms has been a shift from a strict emphasis on liquidating weak companies, frequently through the unilateral action of major banks, to a softer landing for distressed companies through mechanisms for debt restructuring and corporate reorganisation. The principle of rehabilitation, as embodied in Chapter 11 of the US Bankruptcy Code enacted in 1978 (Carruthers and Halliday, 1998), has echoed around the world in one manifestation or another. And it is no accident that this rehabilitative turn has appealed to many countries precisely because it offers a convenient trade-off between the hard budget constraints demanded by the neo-liberal economics of the Washington Consensus and the demands of domestic political constituencies for protection of jobs and businesses (Carruthers, Babb and Halliday, 2001).

The Crisis stunned international institutions into a qualitatively different orientation towards market-making through commercial law reform. In response, the world's financial hegemons mobilised in unprecedented fashion. The Clinton administration (1992-2000) called for a new 'international financial architecture' (Gilpin, 2000:327). The 'G22', a coalition of

[2] We recognise that there are severe temporal constraints in our approach, as only some eight years have elapsed since the onset of the Crisis. By any standard, this is not a long time for any law to take root and flourish, especially if it demands fundamental changes in commercial and legal practice and culture, not to mention the creation and operation of new institutions. However, as this chapter seeks to demonstrate, all of the reforms stimulated by the IFIs exist in a longer context of anticipated or actual reforms. In some cases, the Crisis triggered what was already being put forward by governments.

22 of the world's most 'significant' economies, specified that that architecture include robust debtor-creditor regimes that would forestall crises by swiftly and effectively enabling work-outs of troubled firms. Substantive bankruptcy law must be accompanied, said the G22, by effective enforcement mechanisms and competent professions.[3] The G7 and G22 turned to the international financial institutions (IFIs) to begin building the new order. The Asian Development Bank (ADB) rated the bankruptcy systems of 11 Asian nations against 33 criteria and subsequently initiated technical assistance projects to correct problems (Asian Development Bank, 2000:3).[4] The IMF and the World Bank for the first time used the maximal leverage of their emergency lending agreements to demand bankruptcy reforms as a condition of new credit. Both institutions also initiated more comprehensive, long-term projects to create models or principles of good bankruptcy systems that any country might adopt (IMF 1999; Halliday and Carruthers, 2007).[5]

The interventions of the IFIs in the countries of East and Southeast Asia therefore mark a turning point in the globalisation of insolvency regimes. IFIs escalated their leverage through conditionalities for loan agreements. The legal departments of the IMF and World Bank embarked on an unprecedented level of intervention and institution-building; for the first time in emergency situations they were included in the initial wave of teams sent from Washington and so were involved at the onset of international responses to the Crisis. The IFIs sought to sustain their direct leverage over country bankruptcy reforms after the Crisis through a variety of expedients, ranging from persuasion to assistance. Global financial institutions muster enormous resources for economic coercion (Braithwaite and Drahos, 2000). IFIs can maintain continuing leverage through sequences of conditionalities for subsequent loan disbursements, through monthly or quarterly monitoring of progress (Interview 2278),[6] through the setting of strict deadlines for reforms, and through public shaming by releasing Letters of Intent signed by debtor nations which effectively amount to progress reports. In addition, the IMF has increasingly been using its mandated annual Article IV consultations on the economy of each

[3] Finance ministers and central bankers from, amongst others, England, Hong Kong, Argentina, Australia, Brazil, Canada, France, Germany, Japan, Malaysia, Thailand and the United States participated in the G22 (G22, October 1998a; G22, October 1998b).

[4] Hereafter, ADB Report.

[5] The United Nations Commission on International Trade Law (UNCITRAL), fresh from its success in creating a Model Law on Cross-Border Insolvency, also appears poised for further success in the production of the much more demanding task of a Legislative Guide for Insolvency—a three-year collaborative effort involving 30 to 40 countries and the world's leading expert bodies on bankruptcy law (Halliday and Carruthers, 2003b).

[6] To protect the anonymity of our sources, we cite interviewees by an arbitrary interview number.

country to put pressure on recalcitrant governments (Stiglitz, 2002), which pressure it relieves and focuses through technical assistance programmes (Interview 2305).

B Transplants and their Disconnects

Under circumstances of concerted global financial power, it follows that mandated law reform, especially in crisis circumstances, should be readily adopted and implemented. Some scholarship on legal transplants would predict just such an outcome. Watson (1974) and his followers maintain that legal transplants can readily be lifted from one legal system and embedded in another. Since law has some autonomy from social and cultural institutions, it is portable, and commercial law more so than areas of domestic legislation such as family law (Harding, 2002; Heydebrand, 2002). If this is so in general, it should be even more the case under the extreme circumstances witnessed following the onset of the Crisis.

In addition to negative incentives, such as withholding access to requisite capital if change is not implemented, there are also positive inducements for foreign capital inflow. Some research indicates that those countries that have adopted the property rights and corporate governance standards considered normative by creditor nations, and which are effectively enforced, attract significantly more foreign direct investment (FDI) or weather financial crises more successfully (Pistor et al, 2002:3; 2000). This creates domestic demand for laws that will speed the flow of foreign credit, and it is reinforced when IFIs press for changes that are consistent with the models or practices of the 'suppliers' of a country's capital (Pistor, 2000). Indeed it should be noted that whether better law does increase FDI and subsequent economic development remains contested. Clearly, China, or the Asian Tigers before 1997, offer striking counter-examples. Countries manifestly lacking in the very rule of law championed by leading creditor nations and IFIs nonetheless managed to attract, and in China's case continue to attract, massive overseas investment. The statistical evidence, also, is far from definitive.

A substantially larger body of scholarship, supported by the indifferent experiences of some of those global practitioners who must deal with transplants, remains wary—if not sceptical—of any assumptions that importation and implementation of laws and institutions will be easy. While the debate over legal transplants has been declared 'tired and often confused' in an Oñati volume (Nelken and Feest, 2002), new empirical scholarship in law and finance, heavily influenced by the experiences of legal transplants in the 1990s, has reinvigorated work on the concept. Initial work demonstrated a strong empirical association between property rights and economic development (Schleifer and, Vishny 1997). It seemed a short step to conclude that the enactment of rights would produce immediate, effective implementation and, in response, that flows of capital, successful privatisation and the emergence of effective corporate governance regimes would follow.

More sophisticated subsequent work, however, casts significant doubt on whether transplants can be taken for granted. Indeed, Katharina Pistor[7] and her colleagues, who have undertaken extensive historical and cross-sectional empirical work on law and development, have coined the term 'transplant effect' to label ineffective transplants. There are two aspects to the transplant effect—demand and context.

On the *demand* side, the evidence suggests that laws will not be effective unless there is demand from within a country. That implies that there are strong interest groups who want change, and that they have the capacity to select what they want. Legal professionals are critical: lawyers, judges and related professionals must understand the new rules, the concepts behind the rules, and the compatibilities between those rules and concepts and others extant in current law. There must be a sufficient supply of professionals to satisfy the demand (Berkowitz et al, 2003). Yet the status and qualifications, not to mention reputation, of most lawyers in countries into which transplantation is being considered mean that the professional constituency able to command attention for reform will be quite limited in size and probably also quite limited in its capacity to satisfy demand, should reforms succeed (Lev, 1996).

On the *context* side, evidence supports the proposition that transplanted laws will not work if they are (i) not adapted to local circumstances, (ii) unfamiliar to the population, and (iii) bear little resemblance to the recipient country's own laws or practices. Familiarity might arise from geographic proximity, a shared history or immigration (Pistor et al, 2000). Context also relates to culture and institutions. It is probable that an imported law must in some manner be related to the myths and narratives of the recipient country's identity, both national and legal (Nelken, 2002). Unless an imported law can be conformed to a country's 'invented traditions' or 'imagined communities', and given its own local cultural warrants, it may be viewed as culturally alien (Heydebrand, 2002). Effective transplants require not only that the new law fits that immediate

[7] Pistor, herself, has extensive experience consulting with the Asian Development Bank, the European Bank, and the World Bank, among others. Her scholarship therefore reflects both intimate knowledge of reforms from the perspective of global actors and an extensive historical and comparative research enterprise in numbers of areas of law that are supposed by IFIs to be related to the flow of FDI. While Pistor and Wellons (1999) can be criticised for failure to integrate politics into the analysis of South and East Asia, Pistor's later empirical papers show a far greater sensitivity to local cultural and institutional variability and the political climate into which transplants are introduced.

moment, but that there are sufficiently creative and authoritative institutions to undertake the adaptations that will necessarily result from the law's incompleteness (Pistor and Xu, 2002).

Moreover, choice requires alternatives. This implies that alternatives exist and that a country's political leaders have had the chance to review and select what laws seem best suited to the country's exigencies (Pistor, 2002). Context also implies institutional affinities, since transplants will not work if the institutions that are to implement them are weak or absent (Pistor et al, 2002; Berkowitz et al, 2003).

The local story is invariably more complex than this, for domestic demand for reform is frequently contested, just as a variety of strategies may be deployed to 'manage' foreign imports (Halliday and Karpik, 1997; Nelken, 2002). Local contestants—elites excluded from power versus entrenched elites, entrenched professionals versus insurgent professionals, locals versus cosmopolitans—may play out their own struggles for influence on the international stage (Lev, 1996), just as international organisations and countries may re-enact their global competition on the national scene (Dezalay and Garth, 2001; 2002). Struggles ramify at the centre, at the periphery, and between centre and periphery. Thus the indeterminacy of successful legal transplants stems substantially from the outcomes of contests in multiple arenas, themselves unpredictable.

In sum, transplant scholarship offers extremes with many points along the continuum. Optimists would predict that IFI initiatives in commercial law will be readily transplanted (Watson, 1974). Pessimists hold that wholesale transplantation is simply impossible because law is always so deeply embedded in a social and cultural situation and in an interpretative community. Many other views are arrayed between these extremes. Harding (2002: 208, 219), for instance, accepts the Watson thesis that 'the idea of law can be readily transplanted' because historically 'western law has been digested by South East Asian societies'. A 'great battle-for-legality' is being played out across the region and contradictions abound. Thus it may be more constructive to view legal transplants and imports into South East Asia as 'an accretion of layers of law'. Pistor and her colleagues appear in their writings as moderately pessimistic: 'copying statutory law from foreign sources has only rarely resulted in a self-sustainable process of legal change and innovation' (Pistor et al, 2002: 37). And Dezalay and Garth (2002) observe that over a decade of effort by IFIs in Latin America has had no significant effect on developing effective courts. Yet support for the possibility of successful transplants may also vary by the degree of coercion and length of time given to transplants to take root. Harding's greater optimism may reflect his longer temporal horizon and the force of colonial power.

II THE FATES OF IFI REFORMS IN ASIA

The general parameters of the Crisis are well-known. On 2 July 1997, the Thai baht crumbled under assaults from global currency speculators. In relatively short order, speculators also attacked the currencies of Malaysia, Korea, the Philippines and Indonesia. By late 1997 what began as a currency crisis had escalated into full-scale economic crises: in each country, a 'domino effect' of crumbling companies led to collapsing banks and brought the entire financial system to the brink of failure (Carruthers and Halliday, forthcoming).

The IMF response in each country followed a broadly similar formula. The Fund negotiated massive rescue packages so governments might support their currencies and, not coincidentally, enable partial repayment to foreign creditors. Loan packages depended on extensive conditionalities—higher interest rates, reduced government spending and higher taxes. The conditions, codified in public agreements between each country and the Fund, included commitments by loan recipients to extensive institutional restructuring of the market, including the banking system and corporate governance. Integral to all loan agreements were commitments by governments to reform mechanisms for handling corporate failures, both in the emergency and in the longer term (Stiglitz, 2002; Wade, 2000). The devastating effects of the Crisis and the initial 'medicine' to cure it can be seen in plunging GDPs (for example, Indonesia's GDP dropped by 13.1 per cent in 1998), widespread failure of companies (for example, up to three-quarters of all Indonesian firms experienced some kind of financial distress) and deepening poverty.

III INDONESIA

Lawyers from the IMF and the World Bank descended on Jakarta in late 1997 to confront a legal system that had become effectively moribund and discredited. While Indonesia had a bankruptcy law on the books which it had inherited from the Dutch, the law had scarcely been used. Indeed, law in general had fallen into a heavy decline in use since the 1950s and had been broadly domesticated and corrupted by the Sukarno and Suharto regimes. Commercial litigants avoided the courts. Judges were thought to have little independence from either the state or the market (Lev, 2000). Commercial disputes of any consequence were settled privately or through interventions by politicians and officials.

The enactment and implementation of law reforms, substantive and institutional, occurred in a context fraught with conflict. IFIs differed fundamentally with each other. Creditor nations took sharply contrasting positions about how to restructure corporate debt. Foreign creditors confronted national resentments and recalcitrant debtors. And entrenched interests in the justice system resisted reformist impulses. All of the reforms, therefore, reflected initial and continuing differences in policy, institutional prerogatives, economic interests, and even ethnic or regional tensions. Part of the political dynamic inhered in alliances formed between parties from the North and South as they confronted each other and those national interests fighting a rearguard action against the world's financial hegemons.

On 31 October 1997, the Government of Indonesia (GOI) signed the first of many Letters of Intent with the IMF to include substantive reforms in the extant bankruptcy law and the creation of new institutions. We focus on the three most important reforms which sharpened lines of conflict among institutions, elites and professionals: the courts, the out-of-court initiative, and the new receiver's profession.

A Founding of the Commercial Court

While the IFIs agreed that extensive reforms were warranted if the law was to serve a central regulatory role in reconstructed Indonesian financial and other markets, they could not agree on the architecture of the new system, particularly on the role of courts (Halliday and Carruthers, 2003a). On the grounds that the court system could not be fixed, the US Agency for International Development (USAID), and subsequently the World Bank, together with some Indonesian reformers and expatriates, favoured a retreat from the judiciary altogether and its replacement by a government bankruptcy agency. The IMF and its Indonesian supporters, by contrast, believed that the Crisis provided an opening for a new specialist court that would serve as an exemplar for the entire court system. It was hoped that, by providing a 'wedge' in the court system, reformers might solve two problems—administration of bankruptcy law and generic court reform—by a single stroke. Yet others believed that a radical cleansing of the court system would occur only through a decisive purge of all sitting Supreme Court judges, an overhaul of court administration (including the employment of new staff), and the establishment of a new commercial court with 'clean', competent judges (Interviews 2273, 2276, 2249). Thus solutions arrayed along a continuum from gradualist and incremental to dramatic and jolting.

Final adjudication of the dispute occurred in Washington. The US Treasury lent its support to the IMF, and its solution—the creation of the new Commercial Court—was formalised as a commitment to international lenders by the GOI in June 1998 (GOI, Memorandum to IMF, 24 June 1998). A cluster of Indonesian reformers had high expectations of the new court. They hoped that it would be a model court, 'clean, open, accountable, and also modern', a court comparable to those of Singapore, Thailand, and Malaysia, demonstrating to investors that they could expect fairness and competence. They were led to believe that the Commercial Court would have its own modern facilities, competent staffing, up-to-date equipment, and hand-picked judges (Interview 2265).

Almost immediately, limited resources and lack of political will began to compromise the initial concept. The first problem was money: the GOI made no new funds available to house a model court with modern equipment. Instead, the court was housed at the Jakarta Central Court in an old down-town building, where judges were packed, five or six at a time, into a single room with no computers and few staff. Even courtrooms were in short supply. Symbolically, the placement signified business as usual—this would be just another court. Moreover, the new court was embedded within the old court system. Instead of a clean slate, judges were compelled to rely on an 'arthritic', compromised bureaucracy. And rather than being a 'carve-out' within the court system, appeals went directly to the Supreme Court, itself an institution with limited experience in sophisticated commercial cases and of doubtful probity.

A great deal, therefore, rested on the selection of judges. Reformers had floated many ideas: finding clean, competent judges in Indonesia; recruiting judges from the Netherlands; relying on expatriates; or seconding first-rate commercial lawyers to the bench for a limited period. However the Ministry of Justice and Supreme Court prevailed upon the GOI to follow established procedures for judicial selection. It was politically unacceptable to employ foreigners and too radical to second private practitioners. Instead, the Supreme Court set up some selection criteria (for example, at least ten years' experience on the bench) and proceeded to maintain its own (compromised) control by selecting lawyers from the general courts. Most of the judges were ill-prepared, with little significant commercial and virtually no bankruptcy experience. The Japanese, Australian and Dutch governments did provide some funding for a crash training course in bankruptcy law, but that lasted only a few weeks (Interviews 2279, 2277, 2265; GOI, Letter of Intent, 29 July 1998).

Since the authoritarian regimes had never invested in law, and neither *pribumi* (ethnic or non-Chinese Indonesians) nor upwardly mobile Chinese saw legal administration as a channel of opportunity, recruits to the judiciary ranked low in the prestige hierarchy of legal professionals. High salaries might have provided an incentive for a career on the commercial court, but that hope, too, was frustrated by the GOI, which decided there were too many bureaucratic hurdles to surmount in order to get pay increases that, in any event, would create problems of equity with the rest of the judiciary (Interview 2265).

In short, the disturbance that a powerful and independent commercial court might have produced for the political elite, accustomed to a subservient court, or for the judicial elite, entrenched in a comfortable patronage system of mild expropriation, never eventuated. The entire infrastructure of the new court was effectively subverted by a collusion of political and legal elites before the first case was heard.

A reformist minister in the short-lived Wahid Government pleaded with the new judges 'to regain the trust of the people in the judicial and legal institution' and decide just three 'celebratory' cases free of corruption (Interview 2257). But their agreement rang hollow since the initial cases, brought to the court precisely because of the prominence of the creditors (including a World Bank affiliate) and the strength of the cases, were decided in ways that fulfilled the worst fears of the optimists and the cynical expectations of the realists (Interviews 2273, 2256, 2269).

Despite these early setbacks, the IMF did not retreat but pushed on with a series of measures to remedy the court's faults. In November 1998 the GOI announced the creation of ad hoc judges, experts from outside the judiciary who would sit on panels of judges and provide some insulation from external pressures (GOI, Letter of Intent, 12 November 1998). But when the GOI rejected the requests for procedures that might protect the reputations of ad hoc appointees, this reform ground to a halt. Only one ad hoc judge sat on a handful of cases, even though some lawyers for creditors said they always request an ad hoc judge on any case they take.

A further initiative, announced in March 1999, proposed legislation to combat corruption in the public sector, including the courts (GOI, Letter of Intent, 16 March 1999). Court watchers were put in place to monitor all cases closely and provide confidential reports to the IMF. Essentially staffed by foreign lawyers, and therefore politically explosive, they offered a source of valuable intelligence for the IMF (Interview 2250). Subsequently, an IMF grant enabled Pappenas, a government department, to appoint a team of seven Indonesian lawyers and retired judges to review and publicise all court decisions in order to keep the courts and judges in the spotlight (Interview 2278). The team reviewed every case from the beginning of the Commercial Court (approximately 300), created a concordance of the cases with the case law, digested the cases and for each offered a summary with their evaluation of the case. Essentially they asked of every case—is the decision good? Does it meet the law? If not, why not? Are there differences between similar cases? What is the reasoning of the judges? And is there consistency between decisions of the Commercial Court and Supreme Court on bankruptcy? For cases whose reasoning was hard to fathom, the team tried to suggest how it might better have been decided. The analysis was published as a report and forwarded to judges and the Supreme Court, all in an effort to improve consistency and accountability (Interviews 2318, 4110). Regulatory and judicial clarifications of the new bankruptcy amendments continued, with the intention of tightening definitions, clarifying interpretations, increasing transparency, altering time limits, and specifying the method for setting professional fees (Interview 2278).

Despite these strenuous efforts, the principal constituency for the new court—creditors—remained profoundly frustrated. What went wrong? The incompetence of judges and counsel is one possibility. The most benign interpreters of the decisions blame incomprehension, lack of English, lack of experience and lack of confidence (Interviews 2274, 2265). Cynics or realists blame corruption. Judges are susceptible to bribes, particularly in a commercial court, says one of the lawyers most often alleged to corrupt the system. When judges earn US$200 a month on cases where the lawyers are earning US$200 an hour, he says, and where it is worth the while of business owners to spend millions to save control of their companies, then judges will be vulnerable to extra-legal considerations (Interview 2259). Is it logical, said a lawyer from the Indonesian Bank Restructuring Agency (IBRA), which lost most of the cases it took to the court as a creditor, that a given lawyer would win 100 per cent of his cases? Or is it something other than logic? (Interviews 2259, 2249, 2270, 2277, 2257).

The Commercial Court is an arena of struggle that reproduces in microcosm the contest between, on the one side, the giant conglomerates that led much of the Indonesian state developmental economy and, on the other, the mostly foreign credit institutions that fuelled the last years of the Indonesian economic bubble. The foreign lenders sought the repayment of loans, or the transfer to them of property that had collateralized their failed loans, or the exchange of debt for equity (and often control) of major Indonesian firms. In this contest, local 'debtors outgunned mostly foreign creditors'. The debtor corporations had much more at stake—control of their enterprises and conglomerates—than the foreign creditors who could write off or write down bad debt, or maintain the fiction in their balance sheets that one day the debt would be repaid. Debtors in control of major local corporations, by contrast, stood to lose everything. Because the stakes for them were high, and because their resources were extensive, they could fight their battles on the turf of the local courts by buying the 'best' counsel and using extra-legal means to get a favourable outcome, even if it meant enabling 'money to change hands' (Interview 2259).

Furthermore, debtors' lawyers could justify some of their extra-legal approaches to judges as an ideologically valid means of resisting illicit economic coercion by foreign interests. Judges, too, may find ideological solace in decisions that reflect resistance of many Indonesians to a law and court that seemed to exploit Indonesia's weakness during the Crisis. 'Someone wants to close this country' was the suspicion. Foreign creditors, it was alleged, sought to force their will on a weakened economic and political system. And even if judges did not act for such grand nationalist ideals, they might exhibit a resistance to following a legally correct solution when that ruling would throw workers out of their jobs or when it would alienate senior politicians with financial interests in the company. Inexplicable legal decisions, therefore, could reflect a coincidence of personal economic interest, nationalist sentiment, social consciousness and plain political expediency (Interviews 2278, 2265).

B The Jakarta Initiative Task Force

The World Bank and the IMF also sought to reproduce in Indonesia an out-of-court restructuring scheme similar to those implemented in other situations of crisis, such as Ecuador and Thailand. The out-of-court mechanism existed alongside, and was intended to complement, the Commercial Court. The GOI launched the Jakarta Initiative in September, 1998, with assistance from the World Bank and the Asian Development Bank (GOI, Letter of Intent, 19 October 1998). It was envisaged that the Jakarta Initiative Task Force (JITF) would relieve the pressure on the courts by providing a forum in which companies with more than US$10 million in assets would obtain expert mediation in reaching agreement with their creditors on debt restructuring. Successful work-outs would result in a Memorandum of Understanding (MOU) among the parties, although the JITF did not have any powers to enforce the MOUs. Housed in the Ministry of Finance and staffed substantially by experienced expatriates from Australia, the United States, and other countries, the JITF was handling some 125 companies with US$17.5 billion in foreign currency debt and 7.8 trillion rupiah in domestic currency debt by March 1999 (GOI, Letter of Intent, 16 March 1999).

Yet again, however, the GOI frustrated the design offered by the World Bank by creating an entity that possessed few positive incentives and fewer negative sanctions. A World Bank architect for the Jakarta Initiative 'believed a voluntary scheme would never work unless there was a hammer to make people reasonable' (Interview 3002). In the initial drafts of the JITF legislation, both the World Bank and the IMF pressed for coercive measures potentially against recalcitrant debtors (Interviews 2277, 2251). But, according to an IFI official, the GOI deliberately backed down on its political commitment to include negative sanctions in the initial drafts of the enabling legislation. Many GOI ministers had financial interests in the largest debtors and therefore resisted disclosure to the JITF of their interests (Interview 2277).

The consequences of mediation 'without teeth' quickly became apparent. Debtors immediately understood that they could resist creditors and the

JITF with considerable impunity. The JITF had no powers to bring them to mediation in the first place. And once there, JITF officials had only persuasion to produce a result. Creditors, too, realised they were completely at the mercy of debtors who feared neither the Commercial Court nor the criminal system. Consequently, debtors employed every possible delaying tactic, both in getting to JITF and in agreeing to an MOU once there. To get closure, creditors felt compelled to take extraordinary 'haircuts' or loan reductions, frequently approaching 90 per cent, in order to get an agreement. To save face, creditors also offered long-term bonds with generous terms, never expecting to see them mature (Interviews 2260, 2277, 2251).

Whilst the GOI could therefore report to the IMF that some US$12 billion debt owed by 54 companies had been restructured by June 2001 (GOI, Letter of Intent, 27 August 2001), and at the closing of the JITF that it had restructured 96 companies with an aggregate debt of $20.5 billion, these figures need to be interpreted with caution. Creditors essentially had lost most of the value of their loans. And, in any event, MOUs were documents of intent, not of effect.[8] Further, the debt restructuring amounted to financial restructuring only. It included no operational restructuring to enhance a company's managerial effectiveness or efficiency.

The IFIs sought another corrective iteration of legislative amendments that would provide more effective positive and negative sanctions. On the one hand, if parties dealt in good faith they might become eligible for tax incentives, banking incentives, and capital incentives, while debt-to-equity swaps were made tax-neutral. And companies would be protected from being de-listed on the Jakarta Stock Exchange.[9] On the other hand, several negative sanctions were proposed by IFI officials. These included publishing the names of uncooperative debtors and taking away the licences of companies that failed to negotiate in good faith. Neither was accepted by political authorities. The former seemed too modest; the latter removed a form of government patronage. Some government ministers were sceptical that the state had any role to play in private negotiations between parties to commercial transactions (Interviews 2251, 2253).

C The Receivers' Profession

Effective corporate bankruptcy regimes require skilled professionals. Since corporate bankruptcy work can be highly lucrative, decisions over which professionals obtain 'jurisdictional rights' from state authorities frequently

[8] JITF had no statistics on what proportion of its MOUs were closed in what timeframe.

[9] Some 25 per cent of 60 cases brought to an MOU had taken advantage of tax incentives (Interview 2260).

lead to contests of several sorts—between state officials and private professionals who covet work; between different professions, such as lawyers and accountants; and between resident and non-resident professionals in a jurisdiction (Carruthers and Halliday, 1998). The stakes become higher with economic globalisation as new markets open and old markets are transformed, often at the behest of IFIs. When IFIs encounter national professions, they become potential allies for local professional elites who seek to maintain current perquisites or endeavour to open up new opportunities (Dezalay and Garth, 2002; Halliday and Carruthers, 2000).

At the outset of their engagement with the Crisis in Indonesia, IFIs and USAID confronted a confusing and inadequate division of labour for corporate restructuring. While Jakarta could boast some excellent corporate law firms, lawyers could not hope to handle the massive volume of bankruptcy work themselves, in part because so much of the restructuring would rely on valuations where accountants were needed. International accounting firms and major local firms also had a notable presence in Jakarta, but they did not have the experience of acting as bankruptcy receivers or administrators as is common in Britain and many other Commonwealth countries. Receivers in the GOI were too few and knew little about modern business or international transactions.

The IFIs considered several options. The Dutch and civil law tradition leaned towards lawyers. Australian and Commonwealth professionals in Jakarta preferred the English-style reliance on accountants. The IMF wanted to let the market choose either accountants or lawyers. The IFIs and USAID also intended that experienced foreigners could enter the professional services market and train indigenous professionals. Finally, the GOI agreed with the IFIs to create a new profession of receivers. These might be either lawyers or accountants, but they would need to be trained in bankruptcy law and practice, to qualify through examination, and to become members of a self-regulating professional association, the last of these a particularly critical condition given the susceptibility of bankruptcy professionals to economic or political corruption (Interviews 2273, 2256, 2266).

Implementation went less smoothly. The GOI committed itself in June 1998 to create a new system of receivers and administrators to be drawn from the private profession (GOI, Memorandum to IMF, 24 June 1998). Yet, in response to the fierce protectionism of the Indonesian legal and accounting professions, and aware of nationalist sentiment about foreign influence, the Ministry of Justice issued implementing regulations that required oral and written examinations in *Bahasa Indonesia,* thereby at a single stroke excluding virtually all foreign professionals, except the handful of long-time expatriate residents who spoke *Bahasa Indonesia.*

The regulations required that receivers be members of the Receivers Association, thus placing it in a gatekeeping and self-regulating role (Interviews 2273, 2266, 2258).

The merits of the GOI's move can readily be debated. Importing judges from a former colonial overlord would inflame nationalist sentiment. And given the significance of *Bahasa Indonesia* as a defining linguistic characteristic of post-colonial Indonesian society, its abandonment as a necessary condition of membership in a public profession would undoubtedly be politically awkward, especially at a time when foreign influence seems unusually intrusive.[10] Nonetheless, the understandable retreat by the GOI from facilitating participation by foreign professionals had the effect of subverting an approach that might have gone some way to overcoming a dearth of expert services in an area critical to corporate reorganisation.

From the beginning, the new profession ran into difficulties. Little time was available for training the first cohort. Methods of appointing receivers by the court quickly became suspect. Although the regulations envisaged that receivers would be appointed by the court, it had been mandated and expected in practice that creditors could nominate receivers for court confirmation. In fact, many sources reported that Commercial Court judges frequently rejected creditors' nominees and selected alternative receivers without adequate explanation. While some qualified receivers got no cases (for example, one experienced lawyer had been proposed eight times by creditors and never accepted by the court), other firms got many. Such arbitrariness and concentration of appointments fuelled conjecture that a 'bankruptcy ring' of collusion had formed between judges, debtors, and receivers, where judges received a kick-back from receivers and/or debtors in order to appoint debtor-friendly receivers (Interviews 2265, 2268, 2266, 2305).

In sum, the Indonesian pattern is consistent. In each case—the Commercial Court, the Jakarta Initiative and the receivers' profession—the IFIs were able to get a law on the books which reflected some of the principal elements of the IMF design. In each case, however, in either the law or the regulations implementing the law, the GOI managed to subvert the overall intent by opening each institution to the very attacks the IFIs were intent on avoiding. As a result, the GOI and the IMF engaged in a series of skirmishes in which the IMF sought to plug a gap or fill a hole or add another check or balance, and the GOI acceded formally but proceeded half-heartedly or incompletely. And even when formal assurances were implemented, the GOI could rely on disabling institutionalised practices to

[10] We are indebted to Christoph Antons for pointing out the political sensitivity of implementing what on its face seemed a plausible instrumental solution to a vexing problem of limited supply of expert services.

permeate the new institutions as they have the old. In this condition of maximal leverage, therefore, even the largest multilateral lenders found themselves substantially foiled.

Reasons for the extent of this resistance inhere in the magnitude of the challenge implied by the bankruptcy reforms to fundamental institutions and interests in Indonesian society. In systemic crises, when a large proportion of companies and conglomerates are in severe financial difficulty, massive shifts may occur in ownership and control of entire sectors of the economy. Where the shift occurs from control by Indonesians to control by foreign banks, and then the subsequent sale of Indonesian assets to foreign corporations, a forced internationalisation of the national economy readily stirs nationalist reactions.

If the shift of control effectively takes the commanding heights of the Indonesian economy away from the Chinese commercial elite, a dual threat emerges: at best, a reluctance by Chinese business leaders to bring back into Indonesia any of the enormous assets they are alleged to have removed from the country at the onset of the Crisis; and, at worst, a recurrence of the intense *pribumi*-Chinese conflicts that produced civil strife and economic disaster in the 1960s.[11] The post-Suharto governments sent no clear signal to the Chinese business community that a new social 'contract' would give them the same security as the relationship built up between the Chinese merchants and Indonesian political elite during the Sukarno and Suharto regimes, or would at least protect their assets (Interview 2255).

The strategic response of Chinese entrepreneurs was to play for time. They dragged out debt restructuring. They fought to maintain control of their companies. They kept most of their money out of the country. They cooperated just as much as they must, to save face and to save their companies. Until clear political signals emerged that gave them confidence in renewed economic opportunity, they had little incentive to play a game in which they could only be the losers, as entrepreneurs and as a vulnerable ethnic minority (Interviews 2255, 2264, 2260).

Confronted with such intractable constraints, therefore, it is not surprising that many in Indonesia wrote off an initiative such as the JITF as 'an abysmal failure'. But then, again, precisely because the JITF faced such long odds, with 'no legal system to enforce rights, with 'no leverage' itself and with no leverage for creditors who have nowhere else to go, a JITF

[11] One of Indonesia's most perceptive commentators believes that the most fundamental question confronting Indonesia is the incipient tension between the Chinese and *pribumi*. 'Can a pribumi-led democratically elected government find a peaceful sustainable relationship with a Chinese-led entrepreneurial economy?' (Interview 2255)

staff person might have been justified in his conclusion that 'given its resources, the JITF has done bloody well' (Interviews 2260, 2251).[12]

Moreover, the successive iterations of court reforms, each one attempting to close the gap between law and practice, sought in effect to re-institutionalise courts as a new centre of power in the state and market. The difficulties in this exercise appear to vindicate the pessimism of Dezalay and Garth (2001) about IFI reforms of courts on other continents. As the problems in the courts mounted, evidence appeared that both the World Bank and the IMF had encouraged the Litigation Division of IBRA, the state debt restructuring agency, to seek to solve its problems outside the bankruptcy courts. If so, this signalled some recognition that institutional reconstruction might be beyond even the formidable pressures of the IMF (Interview 2275).

IV KOREA

While superficially similar—two countries in crisis requiring immense infusions of capital—Korea entered the Crisis with a much stronger economy than Indonesia, a transforming polity, a technocratically sophisticated state, and the foundations of a robust legal system (Carruthers and Halliday, forthcoming). Only one year earlier, in 1996, Korea had signalled its economic 'coming-of-age' by being admitted to the OECD, the club of the world's richest nations. On all counts, Korea bounced back rapidly, and within four years of its massive bailout was already repaying its multilateral creditors.

At the moment of crisis, however, its indebtedness and dependency on foreign creditors far exceeded those of Thailand and Indonesia. In principle, IFIs had the Korean government at their mercy and could exact strict conditions for the release of the bail-out package the Government of Korea (GOK) negotiated with the World Bank, the IMF, and the wealthiest creditors nations, including the United States and Japan. In fact, the economists and lawyers of the IFIs did descend on Seoul in October and November 1997 and quickly thereafter a succession of Letters of Intent and Memorandums issued every three or four months from the GOK, promising an array of financial and regulatory reforms, most directed to a reconstruction of the financial system.

IFIs entered Korea under quite different conditions from Indonesia. On the one hand, because Korea's economy was so developed, neither the

[12] At the time of its closure, in December 2003, the Chairman of the JITFreported that it had successfully financially restructured 96 companies with debts that totaled US$20.5 billion. Companies reduced their debt by approximately 50 per cent. (JITF Press Release, 18 December 2003).

World Bank nor the IMF had offices in Seoul or personnel on the ground on whom they could draw for immediate expert insight. On the other hand, Korea boasted a government and 'an already vibrant, semi-independent research community' that had produced significant data and analysis that could immediately inform IFI interventions (Interview 2040). More importantly, the Ministry of Finance and Economy (MOFE), which had driven Korea's state development model of economic advancement, had successfully recruited Korea's most outstanding economists, significant numbers of whom had taken advanced degrees from the best research universities in the west, and a critical few of whom had worked for the IMF in Washington.

And therein lay much of the deeper problem confronting the IFIs. Their concern was much less a solution of the liquidity crisis and much more a bold venture to restructure the Korean economy. This, in effect, presupposed a restructuring of much more—the depth of government intervention into the market, the shift of power from technocrat ministries to the National Assembly and the Blue House,[13] and an enhanced carrying capacity for law as the principal medium of market relations. Not least, to implement these institutional restructurings of Korean society, MOFE, the locus of the best and brightest technocrats, would need to yield its pervasive presence in the market to other institutions, including law. The underlying scope of IFI ambitions, therefore, integrated bankruptcy reforms into broad systemic restructurings in the balance of power in control of the economy (Halliday and Carruthers, 2004).

When the IMF and World Bank lawyers reached Seoul at the outset of the Crisis, they knew that law had an ambivalent status in Korean society. While prestigious and competent, the tiny size of the legal profession[14] intimated that the preponderance of commercial activity bypassed private, corporate law practice. If a technocratically-regulated market rendered lawyers relatively marginal, it did no less to the judiciary. The judiciary valorised the generalist judge. No judges had direct experience of private commercial practice. Few major commercial disputes entered the courts. And, in particular, as the IFI lawyers discovered, corporate debtors and

[13] The Blue House is the Presidential residence in Seoul (the equivalent of the US White House).

[14] The approximately 500 Korean lawyers and a handful of first-rate corporate law firms fought strenuously to keep their numbers low and competitors out of what was a lucrative professional services monopoly.

creditors avoided courts, not least because public proceedings over corporate failure would intensify the loss of face and shaming of a company's management (Interview 3002).[15]

The paradox of legal competence and institutional marginality played itself out through the Crisis in a veiled struggle between economists at MOFE, commanding the heights of Korean technocratic power, and lawyers, whether in the conservative, weak Ministry of Justice, or in the private bar, long sheltered in its lucrative and comfortable practice. Each profession premised its actions in response to the Crisis on epistemologies that sharply conflicted over how law works (Halliday and Carruthers, 2004). Economists believed rapid iterations of law reform would produce immediate efficiencies and effective restructuring. Lawyers believed the law needed little revision and the real problems lay outside it. The Washington architects of Korean institutional restructuring not surprisingly discovered a greater affinity with the MOFE economists than with the Ministry of Justice. The substantive and institutional reforms that flowed from the Crisis were therefore driven principally by a working relationship between IFI economists and lawyers, on the one side, and MOFE economists, on the other side, with the Ministry of Justice and private and academic legal experts and the Supreme Court reluctantly following (Interview 2040).

The IFIs pressed for reforms that occurred in rapid succession. The Korean response to IFI intervention appears as a complicated mix of swift compliance by the economists impatient for quick results, and 'foot-dragging' by the lawyers, who never ceased doubting that substantive reforms were needed at all or, if so, not on the scale they were occurring. The cycles proceeded along two, intertwined tracks: in-court, law-based initiatives alongside out-of-court, market-based experiments. The two tracks reflected the continuing ambivalence of different reformers over the belief that more law is necessary for a sophisticated market but that law might not be ready yet for such a responsibility or that legal solutions themselves rely on effective out-of-court mechanisms that nonetheless work only in the shadow of the law.

IFI lawyers concurred with their economist colleagues that the bankruptcy reforms should support the wider structural and institutional aims of reducing the intrusion of government agencies into market behaviour, compelling banks to act more like profit-maximising market actors than instruments of government policy, encouraging corporations to engage in genuine restructurings, and employing law to take up the burden, efficiently and fairly, of regulating market transactions.

[15] In 1996, for instance, in the whole of Korea, 18 individual estates and companies were liquidated under the Bankruptcy Act, 9 individuals and companies entered proceedings under the Composition Act, and 81 companies made use of the Corporate Reorganization Act (Nam and Oh, 2000: 37, Table IV-1).

A Producing Legal Efficiency: 1998 and 1999 Reforms

The Government of Korea (GOK) committed right away, in October 1997, to revising bankruptcy procedures in line with 'international best practices,' and it followed up this general commitment with a more expansive pledge to undertake 'a thorough review' of liquidation regulations and bankruptcy law (GOK, Letter of Intent, 31 October 1997; GOK, Memorandum to IMF, 15 January 1998). Apparently, behind the scenes the GOK went so far as to accept that its three different laws governing bankruptcy would be combined into one harmonised statute, a promise perhaps rashly given at a time of emergency and subsequently weakened.

Experts and the IFIs agreed that the courts had limited expertise and moved too slowly. Debtors abused reorganisation proceedings in order to escape loss of control and liquidation of their firms. Courts treated debtors and shareholders too leniently. And creditor-banks often colluded with debtors not to liquidate firms, since the debt write-offs would adversely affect their balance sheets (Nam and Oh, 2000: 55–6). Within months, the GOK introduced regulations and amendments. A 1998 amendment reduced judges' discretion and overrode creditors' preferences by pushing companies into liquidation if they failed a 'simple' economic test of having a liquidation value higher than a going concern value (Oh 2002, 2003).[16] Procedural rules sought to speed up the disposition of cases so that reorganisations not completed in a year consigned firms to liquidation. Amendments made it easier to move a corporation from one track—reorganisation—to liquidation and they took measures to forestall delays caused by appeals (Nam and Oh, 2000; GOK, Letter of Intent 24 June 1998; Oh, 2002, 2003; Interviews 2280, 2281, 2285).

Significant institutional reforms were mooted. To increase transparency and expertise in the courts, the amendments created a new entity, the Management Committee, which would permit experts from the private sector to sit with judges and advise them on the complexities of corporate finance. In addition, the GOK indicated that it would create a specialised bankruptcy court or bankruptcy division within the Commercial Court (Nam and Oh, 2000; GOK, Letter of Intent 24 June 1998; Oh, 2002, 2003; Interviews 2280, 2281, 2285).

Some in the legal community viewed the 1998 amendment as an 'economising' of a legal domain, since several provisions directly attacked the judicial discretion that lawyers avowed must always be available to a court, given the complexity of real-world situations. Observers disagreed over the success of the Management Committee. Some applauded the

[16] Simply put, 'liquidation' refers to a breaking-up of the company and the piecemeal selling of its assets; 'going concern' refers to the sale of the company as a functioning entity.

expertise they brought; others said they added delay. The Budget Office rejected as too expensive the proposal for a separate bankruptcy court and so the Supreme Court instead created a bankruptcy division within the Seoul District Court.

Later amendments refined the earlier adjustments with measures to return more discretion to judges; to give judges new powers to send a company into liquidation; to speed up decision-making; and to push debtors into real restructurings. The MOFE-led reforms aimed no less than to compel banks to confront the magnitude of their non-performing loans and recognise that they must take steep write-offs, even if it adversely affected their own balance sheets. It limited the ability of debtor/owners to avoid liquidation when no hope of reorganisation remained. And it pressured courts to act more expeditiously and ruthlessly when the facts and circumstances warranted it (GOK, Memorandum/Letter of Intent 12 July 2000; Nam and Oh, 2000: 35ff, 48).

B Invoking Market Efficiencies: The Creation of Debt-Restructuring Mechanisms

While the GOK was pursuing one track of reform within the courts, it pursued another track out-of-court. MOFE officials continued to believe that the courts could not handle the largest reorganisation cases. In any event, it was better to catch cases of corporate failure at a stage before technical insolvency. MOFE therefore tried to adapt the London Approach[17] in a peculiarly Korean form. In June 1998, the GOK compelled all major financial institutions in Korea to enter into an agreement to implement a work-out programme for the largest *chaebols*.[18] When a large firm or conglomerate got into difficulty, a lead bank would bring together the major creditors and hammer out a Memorandum of Understanding with the debtor (Nam and Oh, 2000: ch V).

Though beguiling in its simplicity, the programme ran into unforeseen difficulties. In the first place, while the IFIs pressed hard to keep the government from interfering in the market, the Corporate Restructuring Agreement institutionalised such interference. While the banks controlled the work-outs, the GOK had a controlling interest in many of the largest banks. Secondly, the work-out procedure produced a significant free-rider

[17] The London Approach is an out-of-court technique employed by the Bank of England, bringing together major creditor banks in order to produce a consensual debt restructuring plan for major companies in distress. Variants on the London Approach have been tried in many Asian countries, although there are questions as to their effectiveness: see Flood (2001) and Meyerman (2000).

[18] *Chaebols* are large conglomerates of companies where control is centralised and ownership is closely held by families (Steers et al, 1989).

problem where foreign banks and trade creditors who had not signed the Agreement were not bound by it. And thirdly, the work-out scheme did not solve the problem of large creditors and debtors who colluded to avoid meaningful restructuring. Large banks did not want to write off massive amounts of debt that would expose their weak balance sheets and shareholders of large debtors did not want to exchange debt for equity, since they might lose control of their companies (Nam and Oh 2000: 72, 83–4).

The work-out scheme seemed successful on paper, and presumably saved transaction costs incurred in legal processes.[19] But much of the requisite information for calculating their success is not in the public domain. Thus we cannot know how completely the scheme was foiled. But we do know that three parties within the scheme—debtors, creditors, government—as well as excluded parties from the scheme, all had reasons to undermine it.

That the scheme also paid a price for avoiding law and the courts was manifest, among other things, in its limited ability to bind various parties in a way necessary to make a restructuring work in practice. MOFE therefore tried to borrow a concept from US bankruptcy law and yoke the out-of-court, private negotiations among leading creditors with the powers of a court. However, its Korean-variant of the US model had several deficiencies that made it unattractive to lawyers and judges alike, so it was scarcely ever used (Interviews 2294, 2282).

In its place, MOFE tried again, over the objections of the Ministry of Justice, this time with the Corporate Restructuring Promotion Act (CRPA) enacted in July 2001. The Act mandated that when a leading bank creditor saw that a client was ailing, it must call together the major creditors and prepare a restructuring plan. The plan could be passed by 75 per cent of creditors. Effectively, the Act allowed banks to force a restructuring plan on minority and dissenting creditors so they were bound by the decision of the majority (Interview 2290; MOFE 2001; Oh, 2002).

What looked like more efficiency to the MOFE economists, however, appeared to be inequity to lawyers and foreign bankers. For lawyers, it was inequitable because it discriminated against minorities and on those grounds might even be unconstitutional. Since it applied only to domestic banks and foreign resident banks, it let foreign creditors off the hook and thus discriminated against domestic banks. And in practical terms, by excluding certain creditors from a binding decision, even voting against their interests, the inequity readily converted into inefficiency, for those creditors (for example, trade suppliers) in the longer term would have the

[19] Nam and Oh (2000: 76) report that 'as of October 1999 a total of 93 firms, of which 54 belong to the top 6-64 chaebols and 39 not affiliated with the top 64 chaebols, were in workout programs'. The 81 firms with an approved plan had loans totalling 38.4 trillion won.

capacity to unravel the deal and thus frustrate the purpose. Short-term inequity buys long-term inefficiency. Foreign banks resident in Korea, which by definition are almost always minority creditors, viewed themselves as 'victims' of an edict that reduced a creditor to an 'asterisk' when it was told ex cathedra, 'this is what we decided for you.' Even the IMF wondered if the design might be flawed since it did not make court protections available to minority creditors (Interviews 2299, 2305).[20]

Consequently, lawyers resisted it and stayed away from it. Foreign investors didn't like it and adopted stalling mechanisms to keep it at bay: 'if you are a smart creditor ... and CPRA hits, you ignore it, hold onto to your security ... and play a waiting game' until the Act expires in 2005 (Interviews 2299, 2303). And even senior MOFE technocrats were divided over whether the out-of-court or in-court options worked better (Interviews 2290, 2293).

C Unification of Law as a Legal Efficiency

Korean bankruptcy law—borrowed from the Japanese, who in turn borrowed from the United States in the 1950s—was divided until 2005 among three separate acts, as was US bankruptcy law before its unification in 1978. At the time of the Crisis it was inconceivable that something so radical as a complete unification of these three pieces of legislation could be accomplished right away, but the GOK indicated a willingness to consider unification at a later time. After a World Bank report to the GOK recommended unification in 2000, the IMF also encouraged the GOK to unify and harmonise its law, which it committed to do in its last Letter of Intent/Memorandum in July 2000.

It is notable that the World Bank and the IMF could no longer apply economic pressure, for Korea had rebounded so fast it was now repaying its loans. Indeed, the rapidity of its rebound allowed Korea, according to the IFIs, to drag its feet on earlier commitments. Instead, the IMF from 2000 through 2004 kept up a steady moral suasion, in part through its regular Article IV reviews of Korea's economy. Reportedly, the IMF approach was to play to Korea's intense desire to meet the highest global standards by steadily calling for a modernised bankruptcy law (GOK, Letter of Intent, 12 July 2000; Interview 2305).

The unification of the three laws pitted lawyers, judges and legal academics against powerful proponents. MOFE wanted unification because it supposed that the blending of three laws into one would create efficiencies in smoothly switching from one track (for example, reorganisation) to another (for example, liquidation). The Blue House supported this

[20] Some dissensus existed within MOFE among senior officials on the impact of the Act.

view, partly because it accepted the efficiency argument, partly because it wanted to respond positively to IFI recommendations, partly because it seemed modern and reflected a global fashion, and partly because there seemed to be some public sentiment for holding corporate managers accountable (Interviews 2281, 2290, 2293). The Ministry of Justice also supported the concept and took the lead in its development.

Despite the consensus among MOFE, the Ministry of Justice, the Blue House and the IFIs, a significant current of opinion in the legal community remained strongly opposed. It might be that lawyers are inherently conservative, as proponents of unification asserted. Most lawyers remained to be convinced that a consolidation of three acts into one would produce any efficiencies. They saw no 'cry from the marketplace' (Interview 2280). And judges feared that it would raise false expectations of an assertiveness by courts that many judges were reluctant to provide. Even professionals quite intimately involved in the preparation of the legislation were not all persuaded that it represented an advance.

Despite lawyers' resistance, a draft bill was completed by the drafting team and sent to the IMF for review. The IMF in turn sent it to one of their principal consultants.[21] His reservations were passed on to the Minister of Justice, who introduced the bill to the National Assembly on 20 February 2003 where it wound a twisted path until enactment and promulgation in 2005.[22] With some 660 articles, the Act is one of the biggest pieces of statutory law in Korea. However, it is unlikely that adoption of the Act will entirely satisfy either the IMF or MOFE. Already there is discussion over substantive amendments, most notably to change current composition provisions which allow owners/managers to stay in control of their firms without undertaking substantial restructuring. Thus the recursivity of law continues (Carruthers and Halliday, 1998; Oh, 2003; Interviews 2298, 2305).

Foiling IFIs in Korea took a more subtle form than in Indonesia. The IFIs did have a strong internal partner inside Korea—MOFE, which welcomed IFI leverage to maintain its own threatened influence on the institutional restructuring of the Korean economy. In this sense, many aspects of the IMF programme for Korea were championed by its internal proxy, which was a great advantage to the IFIs.[23] The IFI/MOFE alliance has effectively pushed through reforms in the face of broad opposition.

[21] The consultant was Manfred Balz, drafter of the current German Bankruptcy Code. Balz has worked on the insolvency laws of several countries, most recently of Cambodia.

[22] The Debtor Rehabilitation and Bankruptcy Act was passed on 2 March 2005 by the National Assembly, was proclaimed on 31 March 2005 by the President, and will become effective on 1 April 2006.

[23] This proxy is by no means a cipher, since the IMF aims to *diminish* MOFE's direct interventions in the economy. Their interests, therefore, are by no means identical, although their orientations converge.

Other parties, however, resisted. The foiling of reforms in the Korean case ultimately reflected the strong inertial tendencies long institutionalised in the GOK, markets, and law. Government agencies and technocrats found it difficult to withdraw from their close interventions in economic life, which extended all the way from broad policy to directives for credit to particular firms. The banking industry was long unaccustomed to decision-making on commercial criteria alone, and banks remained defensive about their balance sheet vulnerabilities if government was too vigilant in enacting reforms. Major corporations fought rearguard battles to preserve their ownership and control. Segments of the state and market remained ambivalent about the capacity of law to undertake a task so critical to the economic well-being of Korea. And the judiciary and legal profession only reluctantly greeted the new institutional responsibilities of autonomous law.

Change occurred, therefore, but in the face of stolid resistance. It is too early to tell whether reforms in the form and substance of law or the creation and refinement of agencies and organisations will achieve the surface goals of effective corporate debt restructuring. Even less can it predicted whether the cluster of all IFI-stimulated or supported reforms since the Crisis will realise the fundamental goals of institutional restructuring.

V CHINA

Just as Indonesia was a situation where IFI powers to transplant law should have been most effective, China was the opposite, where those powers should have been least effective. In that respect China helps specify the limits of globalising agents on the law of developing countries (Halliday and Carruthers, 2001). Because IFI influence has been less direct and intrusive in China, we sketch only some broad outlines of its significance for our thesis.

China escaped the direct impact of the Crisis that brought other Asian economies to their knees (Stiglitz, 2002). Partly for this reason, IFIs have had no direct financial leverage over China and instead have relied on invitations by the Chinese government to provide technical assistance, albeit on China's terms. Another source of potential influence, foreign creditors, remains diffuse since the orientation of global creditors towards China appears fundamentally different from virtually any other country. While China relies heavily on foreign direct investment,[24] those creditors

[24] In 2003 FDI to mainland China reached approximately US$55 billion and in 2004 US$47 billion (OECD, 2005). However, per capita China's FDI is considerably lower than some other leading developing countries such as Brazil (OECD, 2003).

who take a long-term view seem prepared to accept short-term losses as a price of entry to long-term access to prospectively the world's largest single market. Consequently, while the Chinese are aware that rolling law reform is necessary to attract the massive quantity of capital they believe necessary to fuel growth, the evidence of continuing overseas investment probably conveys to Chinese law-makers that there is no urgency for them to provide effective mechanisms (such as bankruptcy law) that will allow foreign investors to protect their investments.[25] Given China's sense of dignity, and its awareness of its attraction as a trading power to the world's leading economies, it has also limited the visibility of other sovereign nations in the construction of its market regulatory institutions.

The institutionalisation of bankruptcy regimes in China has proceeded in three stages (Halliday and Carruthers, 2001). The first stage began in the middle 1980s when a remarkable moral entrepreneur, Cao Siyuan, managed to build a groundswell of political support to implement China's first post-Mao bankruptcy law in 1986. Since the initial law applied only to state-owned enterprises (SOEs), a second stage, initiated in the early 1990s, saw a patchwork of special bankruptcy laws, regulations, and procedures erected for particular categories of companies or regions so that all enterprises of any kind in China were covered. The third stage began in 1994 when the State Council charged the Finance and Economic Committee of the National People's Congress with the responsibility for creating a single, integrated bankruptcy law for all China.

On a quite independent track, in response to a commission from the State Economic and Trade Commission (SETC), which administered China's state-owned enterprises,[26] the Asian Development Bank (ADB) in 1996 issued a report with extensive recommendations about how to reform China's bankruptcy system—or, more accurately, how to erect such a system *de novo* (Asian Development Bank, 1996). The ADB Report recommended the drafting of a unified substantive bankruptcy law which included a strong regime for rehabilitating companies. It urged the creation of specialised bankruptcy courts that were independent of government intervention and staffed by thoroughly trained judges. It called for the

[25] Fragmentary evidence indicates that most large foreign companies take a quite realistic view of the protection of their investments in China. On the one hand, they do not expect that if investments turn bad they will have any legal basis on which to protect their assets inside China. On the other hand, they use forms of informal insurance within China (eg, building relationships with government officials) and conventional forms of loan protection outside China (eg, obtaining collateral on assets of Chinese companies which are located *outside* China and therefore subject to enforceable legal remedies).

[26] The SETC was abolished in 2003 and its responsibilities distributed principally to a newly formed Ministry of Commerce and a new state agency, the State-Owned Assets Supervision and Administration Commission of the State Council (SASAC). SASAC has responsibility for the administration of approximately 200 of the most important state-owned enterprises in China (Interview 2308).

formation of an insolvency practitioners' profession and the application of 'recognized accounting standards'. And it proposed that the government consider a bankruptcy agency to handle 'hopelessly insolvent' cases (Asian Development Bank, 1996: 2–3).

The ADB Report gracefully but directly indicated the problems the implementation of the recommendations would confront. It pointed to the government's vexing problem of developing a *socialist* market economy. It anticipated that the state would withdraw from direct intervention in the economic affairs of firms. It also recognised the challenge of creating independent institutions and professions, all of which were alien to post-revolutionary China. Not least, it recognised the necessity of a new system of welfare for unemployed workers.

In the event, the ADB Report effectively disappeared from sight. It was not made public by the government. Five years later senior officials at SETC were still unaware of its existence. And, most remarkable of all, the drafting committee of the new bankruptcy law had neither seen it nor knew it was available, even though it set out the most complete template for an entire bankruptcy system of any document on China (Interviews 2001:107, 2001:108). Evidence does not enable us to conclude whether this involved deliberate burying of unwelcome advice or the hapless result of inter-ministerial rivalries or bureaucratic incompetence.

By contrast, a World Bank Report released in 2001, and also commissioned by the former SETC, had a higher profile. Whereas the ADB Report was prepared by lawyers specialised in insolvency affairs, the World Bank Report was written principally by economists and it drew on extensive data and research the World Bank itself undertook at many experimental sites in different parts of China. The World Bank Report described and appraised in detail the various schemes that the Chinese government had tried, step by step, at increasing scale, to liquidate or rehabilitate SOEs. It applauded the gradualist and experimental approach undertaken in first a handful, then in hundreds, of jurisdictions and it recommended which of these to continue, extend or revise (World Bank, 2001).

Above all, the World Bank urged the Chinese government to enact its draft bankruptcy law quickly. It sang the praises of the current draft law which, it pronounced, 'largely resembles the bankruptcy laws of developed market economies' (World Bank, 2001: 34). But it also reflected, and stated plainly, the political realisms that reforms would need to surmount, including fears of local authorities that they would lose their powers, fears of workers that they would lose the social welfare system intertwined with SOEs, and the sustained fear expressed by the Chinese Communist Party that social unrest caused by displaced workers could lead to political instability (World Bank, 2001: ii, 15, 22–4, 29, 34).

In the meantime, the German aid mission in Beijing (GTZ) provided steady and extensive expert assistance for reform of Chinese commercial law, including bankruptcy. The GTZ hosted several conferences to which they brought bankruptcy experts from many parts of the world—and a scattering of 'legal families'—to provide critical and constructive comments on each successive draft of the bankruptcy law. The cumulative effect was to provide the Chinese drafting committee with comparative reference points for every Article in the draft code.[27] The World Bank's insolvency specialist consulted with the Chinese and compared the draft law to the standards the Bank has been developing for insolvency systems everywhere. And the Asian Development Bank brought together experts at the penultimate stage to advise the Legal Affairs Committee of the National Peoples Congress.

Despite ample expert and IFI advice, however, the Chinese government resisted the urgings of the World Bank for rapid enactment and repeatedly delayed putting the bill before the Standing Committee of the National People's Congress (NPC) until 2003. It moved stop-and-start through successive readings until enactment suddenly took place in August 2006 to become effective in July 2007. The twelve-year marathon demonstrated simultaneously the overwhelming influence of domestic issues and the comparative weakness of international influence. The top leadership of the Chinese government knew it faced proximate opposition from many quarters: SOEs, which might be exposed to the harsh currents of the market; banks, which became accustomed to avoiding responsibility for bad loans, since they were directed and cushioned by the central government; provincial and municipal leaders, who often had and continue to have well-entrenched patronage relationships with local industry; and workers, whose low wages had traditionally been compensated for by a cradle-to-grave welfare system.

Two deeper reasons for the delays come from the bureaucracy and the Party. Bankruptcy reform efforts proceeded on two parallel tracks. The National People's Congress drafting team pushed forward its bankruptcy law mostly independent of the extensive administrative solutions to failing SOEs that had been attempted by the SETC since 1994. If SOEs were to be included within a new bankruptcy law, it would sharply diminish the powers of the SETC,[28] long one of China's most powerful government ministries. A loose coalition of SOE managers, provincial leaders, and senior SETC administrators viewed the diminution of the SETC's leading role with anxiety.

[27] See, for instance, Symposium of the Foreign Experts on the Law of Enterprise Bankruptcy and Restructure of the People's Republic of China (Draft, June 2000), hosted by GTZ, Changsha, 1–8 July 2000.

[28] In 2003 the SETC was abolished, its several functions divided among several government agencies and ministries. Some 190 major SOEs, often corporate groups, were placed under the supervision of the new State-owned Assets Supervision and Administration Commission (SASAC) of the State Council.

The SETC resistance coincided with the complex problem a market-based bankruptcy system posed for the Party. Reforms presuppose a successful ideological project to adopt a manifestly capitalist institution whilst preserving distinctively socialist attributes. The 1986 law ran into heavy ideological opposition, some of which remains. And solving the ideological problem by maintaining distinctively socialist characteristics might practically subvert the value of the law.[29] It is no surprise that the final road-block to enactment came in the form of a struggle between factions that supported the priority of workers versus those who favoured secured creditors and banks. Most fundamentally, to implement the ADB and World Bank reports presupposed institutions China does not yet have (such as a comprehensive welfare safety net for unemployed workers) and entailed political risks (such as large-scale economic disaster and social unrest) that the Party will not tolerate.[30].

VI LIMITATIONS OF THE FINANCIAL HEGEMONS

We began with a puzzle—how can the world's most powerful economic actors, especially in crisis situations, be foiled by comparatively weak developing countries? Answers to this question should suggest some limits to globalisation and specify some conditions under which transplants will not succeed.

A Bridled Power

Global actors mobilise enormous financial powers, especially in crisis circumstances, as they control the disbursement of tens of billions of dollars in initial bail-out packages. Any one category of actor—a multilateral institution, a sovereign creditor nation, international private banks—would be influential on its own terms. In crisis circumstances, they act collectively and thereby unify and concentrate their powers, ensuring a coherent approach and forestalling any recipient country's proclivities to divide and conquer. The flow of capital is thereby channelled through a single outlet. This monopoly of supply sends clear signals to global

[29] The two most distinctively socialist provisions in an earlier version of the draft law were to give both (a) the wages and benefits of workers and (b) state tax claims for unpaid taxes an unlimited priority above all other creditors, a priority that would doom most reorganisations since it would drain the cash needed to jump-start a reorganised firm.

[30] A lively debate among legal scholars turns on whether China has, or is likely to have in the foreseeable future, a legal infrastructure, of which courts are the most important, that can handle commercial cases such as bankruptcy competently and independently. Contrast Lubman's (1999) pessimism with Peerenboom's (2002) optimism.

financial markets, since private capital markets will price their risk, and thus future investments, on the terms of the deal reached between the IFI-led bail-out consortium and the distressed country.

We have seen that IFIs exercise initial and continuing powers from conditionalities for loans to close monitoring and surveillance through periodic reviews (Article IV), technical assistance and aid programmes. Yet successes appear incommensurate with leverage. In Indonesia, laws were amended, institutions constructed, processes initiated, and the new Commercial Court, the Jakarta Initiative, the new receivers' profession, and the substantive and procedural law reforms produced flattering statistics (for example, number of cases coming to court, speed of disposition, extent of assets restructured in JITF MOUs, numbers of qualified receivers) but also widespread disappointment. In Korea, the government undertook formal reforms consistent with IFI preferences, albeit on its own schedule, but those reforms still confronted a wall of inertia and resistance from affected parties. In China, experiments widened and deepen to reform SOEs, but the decade-long momentum for the creation of a comprehensive bankruptcy system remained incomplete as late as mid-2006.

B Weapons of the Weak

How does the asymmetry between enormous financial power and manifest vulnerability lead to partial success for the subordinate party? Or in the memorable title of Scott (1985), what are the 'weapons of the weak'? As importantly, in what circumstances are particular strategies of resistance likely to be most effective?

i Avoidance of Conditional Foreign Capital and Aid

There are two notable instances in recent years where nations have refused the terms of the IMF, or have not been dependent on IFI interventions. In contrast to its neighbors in Thailand and Indonesia, Malaysia in 1997 refused to accept the IMF bail-out package. Its judgment was courageous, for its economic risk and its exceptionalism, but in hindsight it is arguable that its decision was defensible and the results acceptable because Malaysia did not suffer such drastic domestic reversals in its economy as its neighbours (Stiglitz, 2002).[31] China was somewhat inoculated against the Crisis and it therefore had no need to expose itself to pressures from the IFIs, although the repercussions of the Crisis elsewhere led to numerous domestic reforms on China's own terms.

[31] It continues to be a matter of debate whether Malaysia paid a subsequent price in a reduction of foreign investment.

The ability to reject pressure from the IFIs therefore appears more likely in three circumstances: when there is no crisis and thus no desperate internal demand for capital and therefore less external leverage for suppliers of capital; when there is a crisis, but capital can be found elsewhere or a country is prepared to ride out the crisis while sustaining domestic economic damage (cf, Argentina since 2003); and when there is a powerful, entrenched national leadership that can speak to outside institutions cohesively and remains in control domestically.

ii Outright Refusal

On occasions a country may accept IFI-led bail-outs, but will refuse explicitly to implement major recommendations of international agencies. It simply says 'no'. More common is the practice of accepting some recommendations but obtaining relief from others. Korea engaged in hard bargaining and did reject some important recommendations of the IFIs, such as the creation of a specialized bankruptcy court. Indonesia similarly did not create its Commercial Court outside the regular court system as the IFIs wanted. Indonesia was prepared to enact positive sanctions to get debtors to restructure through the Jakarta Initiative, but it successfully resisted enacting negative sanctions.

Refusal to adopt important recommendations may be possible under three conditions. If levels of external leverage are low, as subsequently became the case in Korea, then the country obtains degrees of freedom to go its own way. If a country can show general compliance with IFI demands, and demonstrate a readiness to undertake major initiatives at least on the books, as did Indonesia, then the IFIs tolerate some opposition to specific proposals, even if in the end they would prove troublesome for the general reform programme. If a country can persuade the IFIs that local circumstances will create more problems than the solution, then this also can justify rejection, but this is a reasoned justification rather than a straightforward refusal and thus looks more like (iv) below.

iii Fragmentation of Powerful External Coalitions

Since a co-ordination of foreign lenders and a near-monopoly of supply gives the dominant financial powers a large advantage, the force and focus of pressure can be relieved by either forestalling concerted action or segmenting and dispersing it. In its selective acceptance of assistance from several IFIs and sovereign creditor nations, China essentially controlled the inputs from outside the country. And by spreading those inputs over time and among different reform bodies within China, bodies which may not agree with each other or which compete as centres of power, the Chinese government gave itself maximal degrees of freedom to make its own choices in its own time. Indeed, China so successfully pursued its two-track programme of reform (of bankruptcy law through the NPC, and of state-owned enterprise reform through SETC and now SASAC) that leading officials on one track were not even aware of developments on the other. Moreover, each of the major aid agencies—the German overseas aid agency,[32] the World Bank, and the Asian Development Bank—were given a particular fragment of the overall reforms with limited opportunity to combine forces or develop a concerted approach.[33]

Of course, attempts to fragment the powerful may not be necessary if the IFIs are already divided. In cases, such as Indonesia, where national constituencies know that competing plans were advocated by different IFIs and even different branches of the US government, it may be enough to keep those differences alive when problems arise on the path actually taken. In a sense, an alternative path not taken that had been advocated by a powerful external agency provides some legitimacy for resistance.

The contingencies of dividing exogenous forces therefore arise from outside (ie, global institutions) and inside (ie, from domestic institutions). International institutions not only disagree with each other but often compete with each other for primacy in programme leadership and recognition. If the distance between the local and global is narrow (Carruthers and Halliday 2006), then a nation state will be aware of these differences and can exploit them. To do so will be more possible when diminished pressures for reform, or an absence of crisis, do not require concerted action by IFIs. But if fragmentation of external agents of change can occur without domestic pressure, and if nation states may also on occasion have the capacity to exploit a lack of external policy coherence, it is also the case that fragmentation might occur as a by-product of intra-state rivalries. Fragmentation of the powerful thus occurs less as a result of calculated state tactics and more as a result of state disorganisation. In this sense, the existence of many competing and powerful state agencies provides its own protection from IFI intervention.

iv Invocation of Cultural Exceptionalism

Countries sometimes fend off IFI recommendations by maintaining that implementation would be contrary to cultural mores. This can be a rather

[32] The Deutsche Gesellschaft für Technische Zusammenarbeit (GTZ) GmbH is a private-sector enterprise owned by the Federal Republic of Germany. See <http://www.gtz.de/china/chinese/english/gtzchina.htm>, last accessed 23 October 2004.

[33] Significantly, the World Bank itself operated on two tracks—the report prepared for the SETC on SOEs was primarily driven by economists; the contributions of the Bank to the draft law prepared by the NPC committee came from the World Bank's Legal Department, though they were quite limited by comparison.

powerful shield because the IMF and World Bank, among other international agencies, are often caught in a cleft stick. On the one hand, they usually propagate convergent norms, sometimes in the form of 'best practices', and sometimes as a result of agreements among global norm-making institutions. On the other hand, they are very sensitive to accusations that they force 'one size fits all' solutions on countries regardless of their culture and institutions. Finding a resolution of this tension often proves elusive. For instance, Indonesia seems to have successfully side-stepped negative sanctions on debtors that might have been administered by the Jakarta Initiative by maintaining that they were culturally inappropriate, an approach that echoed an earlier report on commercial law reform drafted before the Crisis (Halliday and Carruthers, 2003a). China frequently invokes its own exceptionalism by championing models of its development that combine a global label (eg, market) with a qualifier (eg, '*socialist* market economy,' 'democracy *with Chinese characteristics*').

The effective use of this weapon increases when global institutions are already under attack for cultural insensitivity from other critics. Since this is a rallying cry of anti-globalisation movements, it strikes IFIs in a sensitive place and may compel them to ease their pressure for adoptions of global norms in all circumstances. On the domestic front, effective playing of the 'culture hand' requires some plausible basis. Domestic authorities must be able to point to well-known cultural practices or rely upon cultural stereotypes (eg, Indonesians avoid conflict) or even construct a cultural practice that has validity for outside observers. It is likely, however, that this strategy will be more effective in minor rather than major elements of structural adjustment and externally-induced reform programmes.

v Symbolic Compliance

Countries, like organisations, can offer signals of compliance to external constituencies, but proceed divergently with internal practices (Hirsch and Rao, 2003; DiMaggio and Powell, 1983; Meyer and Rowan, 1977). This strategy is relatively cheap since promulgation of regulations or enactment of legislation is not capital-intensive but appears to be compliant. Nor does it create the political and administrative problems that might be entailed if implementation were to be taken seriously. There are several variants of symbolic compliance.

A country may enact the principle, but implement partially. Indonesia set up Commercial Courts but it starved them of resources. Korea said it was prepared to create a specialised bankruptcy court but the Budget Office ruled it too costly and instead substituted a division of the Commercial Court in Seoul.

Countries may implement laws perversely in order to maintain control, as was the case in Indonesia where judges were recruited in ways that ensured the Supreme Court would keep control through its recruitment and appellate functions.

Countries will enact legislation, but qualify or subvert it through enabling regulations. Indonesia created a receivers' profession, but ensured its relative ineffectiveness by inserting an Indonesian language requirement which kept most foreign specialists at bay. Korea implemented some taxation measures, but nullified them effectively in some obscure regulations written only in Korean and that were invisible to overseas observers (Interview 2277).

A country will enact legislation, but not enforce it. For instance, new laws gave Indonesian prosecutors authority to bring criminal charges against debtors, but these were not employed.

In practice countries exploit the classic socio-legal gap between law-on-the-books and law-in-action. They send a signal to international organisations with their law on the books but resist in the implementation phase.

This strategy will not work on all circumstances. It requires that external regulators have limited surveillance or enforcement capacities, and internal practices are relatively invisible. It depends upon the attention span and will of the IFIs. If a new crisis, such as September 11, distracts the IFIs then external pressure for compliance is relieved. It can work when nation-states can plausibly plead incapacities of resources, bureaucratic limits, corruption and asymmetries of power between government authorities and those they attempt to regulate.

vi Substitution of a Solution

A country may substitute a home-grown solution to solve an IFI-designated problem. The IFIs wanted Korea to make liquidation a credible threat to firms and to speed up court procedures. Korea responded by adopting the strict economic test which was close enough to IFI intent that the government could maintain it was compliant but flawed in its reduction of judicial discretion. Similarly, Korea passed the Corporate Restructuring Promotion Act (2001), which seemed responsive to IFI pressures for out-of-court work-outs, but it did so in ways which subverted rights, including those of foreign creditors.

Substituting an alternative will be possible when a country has some degrees of freedom from IFIs, when for instance the asymmetry of power diminishes. It requires that national officials are sophisticated enough to craft an alternative and persuasive enough to convince IFIs of its functional equivalence to their proposals. That in turn depends upon the presence of experts within a nation state who can communicate as peers with experts from IFIs. An alternative to a global model may also be more acceptable if the IFIs believe a nation state is generally executing the main terms of the terms attached to the agreement between the nation state and the IFIs.

vii Temporal Delay

Perhaps the least risky and most common tactic is for a country to delay and stall. The government will advise the IFIs that it accepts conditions and recommendations, but then 'drags its feet'—doing as little as possible for as long as possible. Governments, of course, use this strategy with domestic constituencies, by creating commissions and blue-ribbon committees, hoping all the while that the public's interests will wane, or the responsibility will fall to a new government, or other events will have overtaken the problem. The IMF believed this was how Korea had reacted to the IMF's most challenging expectation—the unification of bankruptcy law. The constant extension of completion dates for commitments in the Indonesian Letters of Intent to the IMF reveal a similar pattern. And China suspended the drafting of its bankruptcy reforms for the four years from 1996 to 2000 because domestic concerns were of much greater moment to its leaders than external pressures.

Stalling or slowing implementation is a strong tactic because it avoids direct confrontation and has a surface plausibility as an excuse. It blurs unwillingness and inability to comply. Slow execution of government programmes is also ubiquitous in developed and developing countries. Its effectiveness may increase in two circumstances. One occurs when the IFIs appear reluctant or unable to penalise nation states for non-compliance. Another can be observed paradoxically in those countries where the asymmetry of power between global and local actors is most marked. Weak countries by definition have less administrative and expert capacity to implement programmes.

viii Segmentation of Reforms

A complementary or alternative strategy for stalling can be to break down a larger commitment into innumerable smaller steps. The experience of any one step may then influence the course and pace of later steps. Arguably, this is the strategy adopted by China when it undertook (with SOEs through SETC) a series of progressive experiments in a few and then many cities. This strategy now has the implicit endorsement of the former Chief Economist of the World Bank and Nobel-Prize winner, Joseph Stiglitz (2002), because a gradualist, experimental advance might offer more learning from trial and error, and with less risk. While rational from a government's point of view, this approach gives the government a greater degree of freedom to stall compliance. Korea countered the IFI proposals for reforms to its bankruptcy system by undertaking a series of modest statutory amendments in annual reform cycles. This might be seen as a strategy for complying minimally in the hope that the maximal demand—integration of all its bankruptcy laws in a single unified comprehensive statute—might vanish.

This strategy can work when IFI pressures are not sufficient to obtain a comprehensive solution at the outset. The salience of a crisis for segmentation of reforms is more complicated. On the one hand, a crisis gives IFIs maximal short-term leverage and thus offers a critical moment in which to obtain a major commitment from a government for comprehensive reform. On the other hand, comprehensive reforms cannot readily be designed in a few short weeks. In these circumstances, IFIs might settle for segmented reforms in the short term and a longer-term commitment for comprehensive reform.

ix Construction of Exclusions and Escape Routes

Governments will anticipate that compliance with IFIs may bring risks or threats to current power relations or forms of market regulation. To preserve these, governments build in 'back-doors', exclusions and escape routes. They:

- Carve out exceptions to the law so that politically troublesome or economically risky prospective subjects of the law are removed from its purview. Thus China showed considerable reluctance to include all state-owned enterprises in earlier versions of its draft bankruptcy law and excluded some 2000 SOEs until 2008 in its final version.
- Create escape routes so that unanticipated consequences of law reform may be mitigated on an ad hoc basis. For instance, in earlier versions of the draft bankruptcy law, the State Council in China was given the right to intervene arbitrarily in particular cases. It appears that the Chinese government feared the consequences of handing over reorganisations or liquidations entirely to courts, especially if a particular case might be politically sensitive or cause widespread economic dislocation. Thus the Chinese government sought to retain a right of intervention, a right which would introduce uncertainty into the legal process (Halliday and Carruthers, 2004b). The final Enterprise Bankruptcy Law permits numerous points at which administration interventions can control access to the law.
- Maintain channels of influence that attenuate the force of reforms. When the Korean government enacted the Corporate Restructuring Promotion Act 2001, its officials knew that the government would still have 'back-door' channels, through its equity interest in banks, and so be able to interfere in the very market processes the Act was intended to promote.

C Limitations of the Strong

Given the asymmetries of power, how is it possible for the weak to get away with these tactics? The IFIs are not naïve. They have been in many comparable situations. Their officials have some knowledge of the region or the country. They will have ample access to the best and brightest experts inside the country. They get immediate access to any government officials. And they have their formidable negative sanctions.

In practice, however, it looks rather different. IFIs, and the IMF in particular, operate under severe time constraints in emergency situations. They move from crisis to crisis, their attention span is limited, and their resources are stretched thin, since each lawyer in the IMF Legal Department has responsibilities for many countries on several continents. The World Bank had no lawyer-specialist dedicated to insolvency during the Crisis.

The quality and potential efficacy of 'prescriptions' for ailing economies rely on the accuracy of 'diagnoses'. And those diagnoses depend largely on the abilities of the 'practitioner / diagnostician'. Thus diagnoses may suffer from lack of experienced in-country staff or access to experts in institutions. Indeed, adequate institutional analysis requires skills that IFI experts conventionally do not have (Carruthers and Halliday, 2006). All IFIs are dominated by economists who are neither familiar enough with the political economy of a country nor whose training reflects any sophistication in institutional analysis, including institutional economics. IFI lawyers are trained in substantive law and a mode of reasoning that seldom treats the behavioural and institutional conditions of legal practice. The lawyers do obtain on-the-job training, but the scope of their responsibilities is broad and their targets are constantly moving so that an earnest intent to understand institutional and cultural complexities in a given situation simply cannot be sustained.

Other things can also contribute to a poor outcome. The IFIs draw on precedents from other crises. This seems positive, on the face of it, for it cross-fertilises global learning. But the relevance of the precedent depends on contextual, institutional and cultural conditions that are beyond the usual expertise of IFI professionals to discern. Time pressures also partly account for the failure of IFIs to build support and consensus within countries and political commitment from key constituencies. In bankruptcy law, for instance, the IFIs effectively represent the creditor community, and more accurately the foreign creditor community. Laws based on the preferences of creditor institutions inside and outside a country may run into vigorous opposition from other parties in the market, including debtors and workers, who then act to subvert the agreement.[34]

Additional problems in transplantation stem from the tension-ridden relations between the global exporters and certain national importers of law. The strongest critics of IFIs charge that some IFIs compel countries to accept a 'one-size-fits-all' solution. Countries are not given enough time to make them work or to craft adaptations that fit with the culture (Stiglitz, 2002). In the heat of emergency negotiations, IFIs can appear careless of national sensibilities, of the loss of face of rulers in sovereign nations, and of the limitations in their powers. The exercise of economic muscle from Washington fuels the presumption that the laws represent the imposition of foreign interests. These in turn engender nationalist resentment that can be appropriated by local constituencies for political capital. In Korea, for instance, the Crisis of 1997 has entered popular usage as the 'IMF Crisis'.[35] Such alienation fosters passive opposition and the resort to stratagems of evasion and non-compliance, not necessarily based on the merits or otherwise of reforms. Resentments are intensified when 'rescue' leads to heavier indebtedness and a sense of perpetual dependency, thus vindicating the premises of dependency theory (Tamanaha, 1995). Nevertheless, it must also be remembered that what alienates one section of a debtor nation may be viewed as an opportunity by another national constituency, especially those constituencies oriented towards Western and global norms and actors.

And in the face of this mounting potential resistance, the real powers of enforcement by the IFIs are diminishing. As one veteran of debt crises observed, the real window for opportunity of successful interventions by IFIs lasts for three, or perhaps six, months from the onset of a crisis. Beyond that, governments know that the IMF and World Bank are extremely reluctant to, and in fact, virtually never do, withhold additional tranches of loans because of non-compliance (Interview 2277).

Finally, alongside the asymmetry of financial power in crisis situations there is an asymmetry of expertise. IFIs have access not only to their own expertise but to experts and expert organisations worldwide, who can be mobilised very quickly. Developing nations usually have limited expertise and limited resources to mobilise it from elsewhere. The more extreme that asymmetry, the less local resistance can rely on technical expertise. But in countries, such as Korea, where the asymmetry is much less pronounced, a national technocratic elite can buy itself significant degrees of freedom by countering external experts with national experts, especially when the latter have similar credentials to the former.

[34] This is also true in the United States and Britain (Carruthers and Halliday, 1998).

[35] It should be said that Korean officials are prepared to admit this appellation is grossly unfair, since many of the problems were of Korea's own making.

D Intentional Foiling of IFIs or Institutional Constraints?

The most elusive problem in foiling hegemonic institutions concerns intentionality. To what extent is the frustration of IFI goals a function of deliberate efforts to derail reforms or a result of constraints of inertia that accompanies change anywhere? And how is it possible to tell the difference? The distinction is more than academic. It is theoretically and pragmatically meaningful to differentiate between resistance, which implies a deliberate effort by nationals to forestall exogenous influence (albeit with local allies), and ineffectiveness, which implies a positive intention but an inability to execute. The issue is even more complex because the most sophisticated strategies by governments will be to disguise intentional non-compliance as unanticipated institutional inertia, that is to say, to convince outside powers that limited outcomes are beyond the control of a government.

The excuse, of course, has a surface plausibility. No matter how great the pressure, states may be too over-burdened, politics too contentious, institutions too fragile, costs too high, resistance too entrenched for reforms to be implemented effectively. The issue becomes one less of unwillingness than of inability. And where countries are simultaneously undergoing many transformations simultaneously (for example, economic, political, and legal), the inability exception seems plausible.

Nevertheless, Scott (1987; 1990) would suggest that precisely because the developing countries are weak, they must adopt strategies that limit their culpability and therefore their vulnerability. The 'inability' move offers a strong defence. The most artful of governments will tailor its compliance to an 'inability' defence, predicting that through its design, intervention or neglect compliance will be subverted in practice. This suggests that scholars and practitioners alike might proceed on the premise that all circumstances that forestall IFI compliance are within the control of the government. While this premise is manifestly wrong, it serves as a useful heuristic in order to avoid the mistake too often made about the weak—that they are powerless.

It may also be the case that law reform lends itself to being foiled rather more than economic reforms. The latter are relatively easy to measure and the immediacy of their impact can readily be evaluated. Economic levers, such as interest rates, seem far simpler to manipulate than law reforms. Moreover, long time-lags occur before the effectiveness of law reforms become apparent.

Then, again, transplants of law entail far more than law itself. On the surface, it appears rather simple to enact statutes, issue regulations, or even erect new institutions. But the advocates of law reform, especially in an area such as bankruptcy law, with its enormous distributive implications, may fail to understand how extensively law reform reaches to the fundamental institutional order of a society. It potentially threatens deeply entrenched power elites. It demands extensive changes in market relations (for example, in the prevailing concept of the firm) and political institutions (for example, the operation of political parties). It may demand a recalibration of the balance of power among a society's central institutions (for example, substitution of market for hierarchy).

Thus the imposition of a 'Western' bankruptcy system penetrates far into economic, social and political life. By so doing, it confronts the heavy weight of path dependence, institutional inertia and historical momentum. Successful reform in this putatively technical area of commercial law, therefore, entails not simply debt-restructuring but institutional restructuring (Halliday and Carruthers, 2004a).

The IFIs are not unconscious of this problem and might well respond that it substitutes a maximal for a minimal criterion of success. Of course, as Malaysia demonstrated, countries are not compelled to accept their capital or prescriptions. But even for those countries that do, 'old hands' at the IFI reconstruction game strive for bold changes, but will settle, albeit reluctantly, for something much less. For the most hardened realist, *any* movement whatsoever can be considered a small victory, for without IFI intervention, no movement at all might have occurred. For champions of more comprehensive reform, such as those pursued in Indonesia, a window of opportunity has opened, complete with new indigenous champions, and shells of institutions and laws now exist that might be completed and made effective over time. For these IFI officials, therefore, the Crisis provided an opening. Subsequent IFI leverage kept up a momentum. Over the longer term, lessons will be learnt on all sides about the limits of IFI power and the extent of indigenous resistance. For the IFIs, the bridgehead has been established. For the developing nations, the choice remains whether to repel, resist, co-opt or appropriate the options through IFI interventions. The evidence from corporate bankruptcy law makes plain that developing nations do have choice and, if they so choose, they may significantly foil the financial hegemons, even in the most extreme of circumstances. That foiling of the intentions of the financial hegemons, of course, may be a rearguard action. Whether it can be sustained in the long term remains to be seen.

BIBLIOGRAPHY

ASIAN DEVELOPMENT BANK (1996) 'Final Report, State Enterprise Insolvency Reform, PRC' (Asian Development Bank, Manila, Philippines).

ASIAN DEVELOPMENT BANK (2000) 'Insolvency Law Reforms in the Asian and Pacific Region' [2000] 1 *Law and Policy Reform at the Asian Development Bank* April 2000.

BERKOWITZ, DANIEL; PISTOR, KATHARINA; and RICHARD, JEAN-FRANCOIS (2003) 'Economic Development, Legality, and the Transplant Effect' 47 (1) *European Economic Review.*

BRAITHWAITE, JOHN and DRAHOS, PETER (2000) *Global Business Regulation* (Cambridge University Press, Cambridge).

CARRUTHERS, BRUCE G; BABB, SARAH L; and HALLIDAY, TERENCE C (2001) 'Institutionalizing Markets, or the Market for Institutions? Central Banks, Bankruptcy Law and the Globalization of Financial Markets' in John Campbell and Ove Pedersen (eds) *The Rise of Neoliberalism and Institutional Analysis* (Princeton University Press, Princeton).

CARRUTHERS, BRUCE G and HALLIDAY, TERENCE C (forthcoming) 'Institutionalizing Creative Destruction: Predictable and Transparent Bankruptcy Law in the Wake of the East Asian Financial Crisis' in Meredith Woo-Cumings (ed) *Neoliberalism and Institutional Reform in East Asia* (Cornell University Press, Ithaca).

—— (1998) *Rescuing Business: Making Corporate Bankruptcy Law in the United States and England* (Oxford University Press, Oxford).

—— (2006) 'Negotiating Globalization: Global Templates and the Construction of Insolvency Regimes in East Asia' *Law and Social Inquiry* 31 (3): 521–84.

DEZALAY, YVES and GARTH, BRYANT (2001) 'The Import and Export of Law and Legal Institutions: International Strategies in National Palace Wars' in David Nelken and Johannes Feest (eds) *Adapting Legal Cultures* (Hart Publishing, Oxford) 241–55.

—— (2002) *The Internationalization of Palace Wars: Lawyers, Economists, and the Contest to Transform Latin American States* (University of Chicago Press, Chicago).

DIMAGGIO, PAUL J and POWELL, WALTER W (1983) 'The Iron Cage Revisited: Institutional Isomorphism and Collective Rationality in Organizational Fields' 48(2) *American Sociological Review* 147–60.

FLOOD, JOHN (2001) 'The Vultures Fly East: The Creation and Globalisation of the Distressed Debt Market' in David Nelken and Johannes Feest (eds) *Adapting Legal Cultures* (Hart Publishing, Oxford) 257-78.

G22 (October 1998a) 'Report of the Working Group on International Financial Crises' (G22, Washington, DC).

—— (October 1998b) 'Summary of Reports on the International Financial Architecture' (G22, Washington, DC).

GILPIN, ROBERT (2000) *The Challenge of Global Capitalism: The World Economy in the 21st Century* (Princeton University Press, Princeton).

GOVERNMENT OF INDONESIA, LETTER OF INTENT, 31 OCTOBER 1997, AVAILABLE AT: <http://www.imf.org/external/country/IDN>, last accessed 15 November 2006.

—— Letter of Intent, 29 July 1998, available at: <http://www.imf.org/external/country/IDN>, last accessed 15 November 2006.
—— Letter of Intent, 19 October 1998, available at: <http://www.imf.org/external/country/IDN>, last accessed 15 November 2006.
—— Letter of Intent, 12 November, 1998, available at: <http://www.imf.org/external/country/IDN>, last accessed 15 November 2006.
—— Letter of Intent, 16 March 1999, available at: <http://www.imf.org/external/country/IDN>, last accessed 15 November 2006.
—— Letter of Intent, 16 November 1999, available at: <http://www.imf.org/external/country/IDN>, last accessed 15 November 2006.
—— Letter of Intent, 27 August 2001, available at: <http://www.imf.org/external/country/IDN>, last accessed 15 November 2006.
—— Memorandum to IMF, 24 June 1998, available at: <http://www.imf.org/external/country/IDN>, last accessed 15 November 2006.
GOVERNMENT OF KOREA, LETTER OF INTENT, 31 OCTOBER 1997, AVAILABLE AT: <http://www.imf.org/external/country/KOR>, last accessed 15 November 2006.
—— Letter of Intent, 24 June 1998, available at: <http://www.imf.org/external/country/KOR>, last accessed 15 November 2006.
—— Letter of Intent, 12 July 2000, available at: <http://www.imf.org/external/country/KOR>, last accessed 15 November 2006.
—— Memorandum to IMF, 15 January 1998, available at: <http://www.imf.org/external/country/KOR>, last accessed 15 November 2006.
HALLIDAY, TERENCE C and CARRUTHERS, BRUCE G (2000) *Professionalization from Abroad: International Financial Institutions in the Globalization of Business Rescue* (American Bar Foundation Working Paper 2024, Chicago, Illinois).
—— (2001) 'The Recursivity of Law in the Globalization of Corporate Insolvency Regimes: The Limiting Case of China?' Paper presented at the Joint Conference of the Law and Society Association Annual Meeting and the Research Committee on Sociology of Law, Budapest, 2001.
—— (2003a) *Conformity, Contestation and Culture in the Globalization of Insolvency Regimes: International Institutions and Law-making in Indonesia and China* (American Bar Foundation Working Paper 2214, Chicago, Illinois).
—— (2003b) 'Globalizing Law: Political Influence in the Legal Construction of Markets by the UN' Paper read at the American Sociological Association Annual Meeting, Atlanta, 17-21 August 2003.
—— (2004) 'Epistemological Conflicts and Institutional Impediments: The

Rocky Road to Corporate Bankruptcy Reforms in Korea' in Thomas Ginsburg (ed) *Law Reform in Korea* (Routledgecurzon, New York).

—— (2004a) 'Institutional Lessons from Insolvency Reforms in East Asia' *Forum on Asian Insolvency Law Reform (FAIR), Insolvency and Risk Management in Asia* (World Bank and Asian Development Bank, Delhi).

—— (2004b) 'Legal Certainty, Market Uncertainty, and Social Instability: The Confounding Case of Stalled Bankruptcy Law in China' *Annual Meeting of the Law and Society Association*. Chicago.

—— (2007) 'The Recursivity of Law: Global Normmaking and National Lawmaking in the Globalization of Bankruptcy Regimes' *American Journal of Sociology,*In Press.

HALLIDAY, TERENCE C and KARPIK, LUCIEN (1997) 'Postscript: Lawyers and the Globalization of Liberal Politics' in Terence C Halliday and Lucien Karpik (eds) (1998) *Lawyers and the Rise of Western Political Liberalism: Legal Professions and the Constitution of Modern Politics* (Oxford University Press, Oxford and New York) 349–70.

HALLIDAY, TERENCE C and PAVEL OSINSKY (2006) 'Globalization and Law' *Annual Review of Sociology* 32: 447-470.

HARDING, ANDREW (2002) 'Comparative Law and Legal Transplantation in South East Asia: Making Sense of the "Nomic Din"' in David Nelken and Johannes Feest (eds) *Adapting Legal Cultures* (Hart Publishing, Oxford) 199–222.

HEYDEBRAND, WOLF (2002) 'From Globalisation of Law to Law under Globalisation' in David Nelken and Johannes Feest (eds) *Adapting Legal Cultures* (Hart Publishing, Oxford) 117–37.

HIRSCH, PAUL and RAO, HAYAGREEVA (2003) 'The Schweik Syndrome: The Narrative Power of Resistance by Agreement' in Barbara Czarniawska and Pasquale Gagliardi (eds) *Narratives we Organize By* (John Benjamins Publishing, Amsterdam) 137-48.

INTERNATIONAL MONETARY FUND (1999) *Orderly and Effective Insolvency Procedures: Key Issues* (International Monetary Fund, Washington, DC).

LEV, DANIEL S (2000) 'Judicial Authority and the Quest for an Indonesian Rechtsstaat' in Daniel Lev *Legal Evolution and Political Authority in Indonesia: Selected Essays* (Kluwer Law International, Leiden) 215–44.

—— (1996) 'Between State and Society: Professional Lawyers and Reform in Indonesia' in Daniel S Lev and Ruth McVey (eds) *Making Indonesia* (South East Asia Program, Ithaca, New York)

LUBMAN, STANLEY (1999) *Bird in a Cage: Legal Reform in China after Mao* (Stanford University Press, Stanford).

MEYER, JOHN W and ROWAN, BRIAN (1977) 'Institutionalized Organizations: Formal Structure as Myth and Ceremony' 83(2) *American Journal of Sociology* 340–63.

MEYERMAN, GERALD E (2000) 'The London Approach and Corporate Debt Restructuring in East Asia.' Paper read at a conference on Emerging Markets in the New Financial System: Managing Financial and Corporate Stress, New Jersey, 30 March – 1April 2000.

MOFE (Ministry of Finance and Economy, Republic of Korea) (2001) 'Law for Promotion of Corporate Restructuring' Presentation slides, 9 August 2001.

NAM, IL CHONG and OH, SOOGEUN (2000) *Bankruptcy of Large Firms and Exit Mechanisms in Korea* (Korean Development Institute Seoul).

NELKEN, DAVID (2002) 'Towards a Sociology of Legal Adaption' in Nelken and Feest (eds) *Adapting Legal Cultures* (Hart Publishing, Oxford).

NELKEN, DAVID and FEEST, JOHANNES (2002) (eds) *Adapting Legal Cultures* (Hart Publishing, Oxford).

OBSTFELD, MAURICE (1998) 'The Global Capital Market: Benefactor or Menace?' 12(4) *Journal of Economic Perspectives* 9–30.

OECD (2003) *Investment Policy Review of China – Progress and Reform Challenges* (OECD, Paris).

OECD (2005) *International Investment Perspectives, 2005 Edition* (OECD, Paris).

OH, SOOGEUN (2002a) 'Drafting of New Insolvency Law of Korea' paper read at FAIR Conference, OECD, Bangkok, Thailand, 16-17 December 2002.

—— (2002b) 'Government Intervention in Corporate Exit Mechanisms: The Corporate Restructuring Promotion Act of Korea' Presentation to Hong Kong University Faculty of Law, 18-19 April 2002.

—— (2003) 'Insolvency Law Reform of Korea: A Continuing Learning Process' Paper presented at the Forum on Insolvency Risk Management, The World Bank, Washington, DC, 28 January 2003.

PEERENBOOM, RANDALL (2002) *China's Long March toward Rule of Law* (Cambridge University Press, New York).

PISTOR, KATHARINA (2000) 'Patterns of Legal Change: Shareholder and Creditor Rights in Transition Economies' 1 *European Business Organization Law Review* 59–108.

—— (2002) 'The Standardization of Law and its Effect on Developing Economies' 50 *American Journal of Comparative Law* 97–130.

PISTOR, KATHARINA; KEINAN, YORAM; KLEINHEISTERKAMP, JAN; and WEST, MARK (2002) 'Legal Evolution and the Transplant Effect: Lessons from Corporate Law Development in Six Transplant Countries' unpublished paper.

PISTOR, KATHARINA, RAISER, MARTIN and GELFER, STANISLAW (2000) 'Law and Finance in Transition Economies' 8 *Economics of Transition* 325–68.

PISTOR, KATHARINA and WELLONS, PHILIP A (1999) *The Role of Law and Legal Institutions in Asian Economic Development: 1960-1995* (Oxford University Press, New York).

PISTOR, KATHARINA and XU, CHENGGANG (2002) 'Incomplete Law—A Conceptual and Analytical Framework and its Application to the Evolution of Financial Market Regulation' Working paper, Columbia University.

SHLEIFER, ANDREI and VISHNY ROBERT W (1997) 'A Survey of Corporate Governance' 52 *Journal of Finance* 737–83.

SCOTT, JAMES (1987) *Weapons of the Weak: Everyday Forms of Peasant Resistance* (Yale University Press, New Haven).

—— (1990) *Domination and the Arts of Resistance: Hidden Transcripts* (Yale University Press, New Haven).

STEERS, RICHARD M; SHIN, YOO KEUN; and UNGSON, GERARDO, R (1989) *The Chaebol: Korea's Industrial Might.* (Harper and Row.

STIGLITZ, JOSEPH (2002) *Globalization and its Discontents* (Norton, New York).

SYMPOSIUM OF THE FOREIGN EXPERTS ON THE LAW OF ENTERPRISE BANKRUPTCY and RESTRUCTURE OF THE PEOPLE'S REPUBLIC OF CHINA (Draft June 2000), hosted by GTZ, Changsha, 1–8 July 2000.

TAMANAHA, BRIAN Z (1995) 'The Lessons of Law-and-Development Studies' 89 *The American Journal of International Law* 470–86.

WADE, ROBERT (2000) 'Wheels within Wheels: Rethinking the Asian Crisis and the Asian Model' [2000] 3 *Annual Review of Political Science* 85–115.

WATSON, A (1974) *Legal Transplants: An Approach to Comparative Law* (Scottish Academic Press, Edinburgh).

WORLD BANK (2000) 'Bankruptcy of State Enterprises in China: A Case and Agenda for Reforming the Insolvency System' 20 September 2000 (World Bank, Washington, DC).

—— (2001) 'Key Principles and Features of Effective Insolvency Regimes' (World Bank, Washington, DC).

Index

Please note that page references to non-textual matter such as Tables will appear in *italic* print. References to Footnotes will have the letter 'n' following the page reference.

Ingram Content Group UK Ltd.
Milton Keynes UK
UKHW021324090323
418202UK00002B/27/J

9 781841 136806